Lost Texts in Rhetoric and Composition

Lost Texts in Rhetoric and Composition

Edited by
Deborah H. Holdstein

Modern Language Association of America
New York 2023

© 2023 by The Modern Language Association of America
85 Broad Street, New York, New York 10004
www.mla.org

All rights reserved. MLA and the MODERN LANGUAGE ASSOCIATION are trademarks owned by the Modern Language Association of America. To request permission to reprint material from MLA book publications, please inquire at permissions@mla.org.

To order MLA publications, visit mla.org/books. For wholesale and international orders, see mla.org/Bookstore-Orders.

The MLA office is located on the island known as Mannahatta (Manhattan) in Lenapehoking, the homeland of the Lenape people. The MLA pays respect to the original stewards of this land and to the diverse and vibrant Native communities that continue to thrive in New York City.

Library of Congress Cataloging-in-Publication Data

Names: Holdstein, Deborah H., 1952– editor.
Title: Lost texts in rhetoric and composition / edited by Deborah H. Holdstein.
Description: New York : Modern Language Association of America, 2023.
Identifiers: LCCN 2022046361 (print) | LCCN 2022046362 (ebook) |
 ISBN 9781603296076 (hardcover) | ISBN 9781603296083 (paperback) |
 ISBN 9781603296090 (EPUB)
Subjects: LCSH: English language—Rhetoric. | BISAC: LANGUAGE ARTS &
 DISCIPLINES / Rhetoric | LANGUAGE ARTS & DISCIPLINES / Study &
 Teaching | LCGFT: Essays.
Classification: LCC PE1408 .L696 2023 (print) | LCC PE1408 (ebook) |
 DDC 808/.042—dc23/eng/20230119
LC record available at https://lccn.loc.gov/2022046361
LC ebook record available at https://lccn.loc.gov/2022046362

*To my children, David Gilman, Emily Gilman,
Jonathan Boersma, and Kate Boersma;
to my husband, Jay Boersma;
and to the memory of my parents,
Reinhard Holdstein and Henia Freifeld Holdstein*

Contents

Acknowledgments — xi

Introduction: Reviving the Lost Text — 1
   Deborah H. Holdstein

Part One: The Early Twentieth Century and Before

Isaac Rabinowitz's Translation and Critical Edition of
Judah Messer Leon's *The Book of the Honeycomb's Flow* — 25
   Jim Ridolfo

A Rhetoric of Pen and Brush — 33
   Anne Ruggles Gere

Understanding *English Composition as a Social Problem*: Finding
Sterling Andrus Leonard in Rhetoric and Composition — 43
   Morris Young

Rodolphe Töpffer and the Histories of Rhetoric — 52
   Sergio C. Figueiredo

Talking Teachers into Motion: Rereading William James's
Talks to Teachers — 62
   Kurt Spellmeyer

Part Two: The Mid-Twentieth Century

A Composition Commons: The Stanford Language Arts
Investigation, 1937–1939 — 75
   Jessica Yood

Toward Social Transformation: Renewing the Burkean Theory
of Identification — 88
   Mary C. Carruth

College Composition and Communication, Volume 15, 1964:
Afterglow, Childhood, Obituary?   98
   Douglas Hesse

Part Three: The 1970s

On Recovering Adrienne Rich's "Teaching Language in Open
Admissions"   113
   Howard Tinberg

"A Fresh Progression in Thought and Expression": Remembering
The Plural I, by William E. Coles, Jr.   122
   Peter Wayne Moe and David Bartholomae

Reappraising *Course X*   133
   Rebecca Day Babcock

The Power of Mutable Structures: A Return to Ann E. Berthoff's
Forming/Thinking/Writing   143
   Paige Davis Arrington

Humanizing and Decolonizing Composition: John Mohawk's
"Western Peoples, Natural Peoples"   152
   Rachel B. Griffis

On Reading Roger Sale's *On Writing*   161
   John Schilb

Part Four: 1980–1992

International Linguistics Research and the Legacy of
Frédéric François   173
   Tiane K. Donahue

Before Wireless Networks: Foundational Works in
Computers and Writing   186
   Douglas Eyman

William J. Vande Kopple and Syntactic Subjects   198
   Philip Eubanks

Possibilities Rather Than Certainties: William Irmscher's "Finding a Comfortable Identity"   207
Christine Farris

New Literacies and New Coherencies: The Relevance of Betty Bamberg's "What Makes a Text Coherent?"   219
Larry Beason

Enduring Value: The Case for *Beat Not the Poor Desk*   231
Eric J. Sterling

How the Twenty-First Century Changed Ira Shor's *Critical Teaching and Everyday Life*   243
Michael Bernard-Donals

Lingering Questions from Lynn Quitman Troyka's "Defining Basic Writing in Context"   251
Lynn Reid

"Bound to Sound": Reaffirming Walter J. Ong   261
Clint Bryan

Geneva Smitherman's "Toward a National Public Policy on Language"   272
Staci M. Perryman-Clark

Part Five: After 1992

The Importance of Being Readers Reading in Robert P. Yagelski's *Writing as a Way of Being*   283
Asao B. Inoue

Becoming Which Composition? James Thomas Zebroski's "Toward a Theory of Theory for Composition Studies"   292
Julie Jung

Me, Myself, and All of Us: Revisiting Linda Brodkey's "Writing on the Bias"   301
Jonathan Alexander

Vernacular Scholarship and Craig S. Womack's *Red on Red: Native American Literary Separatism*   310
Stephen Donatelli

CONTENTS

Rediscovering Deborah Cameron's *Verbal Hygiene*   321
   Pegeen Reichert Powell

The Intellectual Work of Composition: James F. Slevin's
Introducing English   330
   Bruce Horner

The Radicalism of Marilyn Sternglass   341
   Joseph Harris

Notes on Contributors   347

Acknowledgments

As usual there are many people to thank: the external reviewers of the manuscript; the members of the MLA Publications Committee; and staff members of the MLA office of scholarly communication, including Susan Doose and Erika Suffern, for their remarkable attention to detail in copyediting the manuscript, and James Hatch, senior acquisitions editor, who has been a sensible, exacting, and helpful touchstone throughout.

Introduction: Reviving the Lost Text

Deborah H. Holdstein

I suspect it will become clear why this volume will and must, of necessity and by implication, be seen as incomplete.

My idea for a collection of essays revealing lost texts likely began with my observations during my editorship of *College Composition and Communication* (2005–09). Always somewhat preoccupied with learning from and reclaiming aspects of the past, I often perused archived issues of the journal. In doing so I was struck by the number of outstanding essays that seemed forgotten, perhaps deliberately neglected, or otherwise invisible to our contemporary conversations in the field. This volume, then, attempts to begin to address these absences, to make the invisible visible, by asking the following: What valuable works of scholarship in composition and rhetoric have been ignored, elided, or forgotten? What might be the value of making present, of restoring to our reading, this type of scholarly absence? How might some of these works enlighten or contribute to current conversations in the field? As I argue, some of the issues that arise from texts being lost, retained, or promoted include and extend different ways of looking at the rhetorical tradition itself.[1]

The myriad ways in which I define the umbrella term *lost texts* can include authors, pedagogical or historical movements, and specific articles or books that merit attention or reconsideration. Indeed, as was the case for audience participants during sessions on the topic at the MLA convention in 2020, the most appropriate response to the work with which readers will become acquainted or reacquainted here might well be "Well, what about . . . ?" or "Why haven't I heard about this before?" or, ideally, "What else is out there?" Accordingly, the works collected here should in no way be taken as the basis for a new canon. Rather, we must reinvigorate the hackneyed phrase that demands we "cast a wide net" and apply this practice to our investigations of scholarly work to support our respective projects. As readers will note, the possibilities for reenvisioning and including authors, texts, or movements may indeed seem endless. Moreover, it is possible that work from fields other than composition and rhetoric—literature, history, comparative literature, transnational studies, and language, for instance—may have been relevant to our scholarship and pedagogy but have been lost or elided as a result of disciplinary firewalls.

The invisibility of strong and compelling scholarship—in this field or any other—can be attributed to any number of factors: the professional or personal politics or prejudices that accompany the selection of articles for publication; the value attributed to the publisher or to the particular journal or book where the piece appeared; the pitfalls of a tenure or review process and perceptions of particular journals or books at one's home institution; whether or where the piece was reviewed; a field's propensity to move on rather than dig deeply into a relevant, scholarly past; the necessary choices made by editors as they shape anthologies, choices that often by default suggest or create a canon; or the common practice of citing only certain scholarship on a particular topic simply because others have cited it before. (Many a graduate student will quote well-meaning faculty members who advise the following: "Don't go past the last ten years" and "Check so-and-so's bibliography to find out what else to read." This prevalent if well-intended advice can clearly be unnecessarily limiting.) Scholarship that has become visible, therefore, seems to remain visible, while other, often equally good work might, however inadvertently, fall by the scholarly wayside. Similarly, there is work that merits our being reminded of it and its ongoing relevance, even in critical counterpoint, to current scholarship and pedagogy. The consequences of a text's being lost suggest that we—perhaps arbitrarily, if sometimes unintentionally—limit our scholarly reach and present a less-than-complete sense of scholarship on a given subject, ennobling some scholars while ignoring others. Certainly the field can distinguish between texts that are simply old and those that are worthy of rediscovery. Indeed, perhaps a previously invisible and otherwise valuable scholarly article, book, or chapter has the power to reopen conversations that had been foreclosed, taking scholarly conversations and our sense of what is or isn't important in different, intellectually challenging and ultimately satisfying directions.[2]

In the fall of 2011 "Rhetorical Silence, Scholarly Absence, and Tradition Rethought: Notes from an Editorship" was published in *Pedagogy* (Holdstein). In it I acknowledge a debt to the historian Steven Hahn, who in 2009 asked similar questions about reclaiming scholarly (and ultimately corrective) history and who wondered what historians haven't written about. Hahn's larger concerns in this regard focused on Marcus Garvey's Universal Negro Improvement Organization. Barely remembered now, it was "[t]he largest political movement of people of African descent in the 20th century—one that commenced in the 1910s, grew spectacularly in the United States during the 1920s . . . and became international in its dimensions" (Hahn). Hahn further stresses that "[a]side from many volumes on Garvey himself, there was little or nothing on [the UNIA's] political geography, social basis, local history or legacies."

Hahn, therefore, reflects on a significant scholarly elision in his field. In addition to inadvertent or designed omissions of some scholarly work from our own conversations and canons, I wondered about a related omission, using Hahn's words as template: "Why are there subjects we so easily avoid or disown, even when they are of genuine significance?" (Holdstein, "Rhetorical Silence" 453). Hahn writes, "Why are there interpretations we are reluctant to embrace, and why do some frameworks of analysis become so deeply entrenched that even when accumulating scholarship calls them into question, they resist being displaced and instead assimilate new findings into more familiar categories?" Just as significant as those areas in composition and rhetoric that have been "left fallow and [are] ripe for scholarly inquiry" is "an examination in composition studies of what 'we don't write about and why'" (Holdstein, "Rhetorical Silence" 453). What previous scholarship or histories of the field must be challenged or rethought or more accountably read and interpreted? What are the theoretical assumptions on which we (still) base thought and action within our field that, on reflection, are centers that cannot truly hold?

History Unwritten, Therefore Rewritten

My first example of a lost text concerns an artifact of popular culture, an early television situation comedy, *The Goldbergs*, and its erasure from a distinctive place in television history as the first television situation comedy, an honor generally and erroneously attributed to *I Love Lucy*. After this, I offer an example of someone whose work is relevant to our conversations in composition and rhetoric and who has all but disappeared from even our most alternative canons: Wallace W. Douglas.

Gertrude Berg and the Lost Television "Text"

In the summer of 2009 a documentary film premiered in Chicago at the now-shuttered Piper's Alley theater, a film venue remarkable for its often out-of-mainstream scheduling. Called *Yoo-Hoo, Mrs. Goldberg*, the film details the career of Gertrude Berg, whose alter ego, Molly Goldberg, became the central character of a hit radio program in the 1930s and 1940s and of an equally popular television program, *The Goldbergs*, in the dawning era of television. A warm, folksy program centering on a highly ethnic, working-class Jewish family, *The Goldbergs* was wildly popular across religious, racial, and ethnic lines. In fact, the documentary relates the tale of a pre-videotape, pre-Internet mother superior who wrote to Berg asking for a copy of the script of the show that would be telecast during Lent—when she and others in her convent would be denying themselves the pleasure of *The Goldbergs*.

As documented in the film, *The Goldbergs*, which debuted in 1949 and ran through 1957, is generally acknowledged as the first television situation comedy,[3] all the more notable because the inexhaustible Gertrude Berg wrote the scripts (more than twelve thousand by the time the show ended), produced them, and acted in them. For good or ill, moreover, Berg was the first to write the show's sponsored commercials, and she delivered them herself, quite successfully, all in the character of Molly Goldberg, a boon to such products as Sanka decaffeinated coffee.

Why was *The Goldbergs* erased from this distinguished and distinctive place in television history?[4] Could it be that an ironic type of honeymoon, a compensatory post-Holocaust period that briefly welcomed open and positive portrayals of Jewish life, had played itself out? Was it the McCarthyism that claimed Philip Loeb, the actor who played Molly's husband on the show, whose blacklisting led to his eventual suicide?

The fate of *The Goldbergs* in popular culture and television history interestingly parallels similar scholarly revisions, absences, and editorial choices about what is published, what is privileged by the authority of the printed (or virtually printed) word. Our ethical obligation is a type of scholarly mindfulness—that is, we must question what does and does not get published and what becomes canonically accepted. I use the example of Berg—and, in the case of Wallace W. Douglas, a scholar and rhetorical tradition all but absent from our visible scholarship—to foreground the elision noted by Hahn.

Certain texts enter a type of canonical pipeline; others, quite simply, do not. And this phenomenon is not merely or always a matter of quality. For instance, how do some editors' visions for their respective journals potentially (and in some instances undesirably) limit rather than expand the scope of scholarly investigation that is ultimately promulgated? What in previous scholarship or research must be challenged or reclaimed or more accountably read and interpreted? What are the philosophical or theoretical assumptions with which we operate that, on brave reexamination, prove to be centers that cannot hold? And to this I reiterate and reframe another question, one that also stems from my editorship: How do we enact a fully accountable scholarship or, more colloquially, the scholarship of an even playing field? How do we create a professional atmosphere that encourages rather than suppresses constructive debate?

Some of these issues might lead one to question the review process for journals, where those with a particular bent who evaluate manuscripts might prefer some types of scholarly perspectives (or citations of certain scholars) over others. But the manuscript review process is allegedly designed—perhaps only in the ideal—to prevent any particular slant. Further, the review process teaches us that the invisibility of certain forms of scholarship or of certain scholars reveals a professoriate that, in some instances, does not do its homework, is not always accountable, and does not always thoroughly review and address what has come before—basic tenets of scholarship. But in addition to the assumptions of and ongoing need for accountable scholarship, the state of the field—or, perhaps more appropriately, the evolution of the field, as *state* implies stasis—demands and deserves a reassessment, one that, among other things, is additionally accountable to missing, wide-ranging aspects of our histories.

Wallace W. Douglas and Scholarly Mindfulness

The following recognizes at least one other significant absence, this time that of a scholar and his noteworthy yet invisible contributions to scholarship in composition and rhetoric. First, some context, which

INTRODUCTION

reveals the extent to which current concerns in our field were equally current during the early days of *College Composition and Communication* (*CCC*). As many readers may be aware, *CCC* is the flagship journal in composition and rhetoric. But many may not be aware that *CCC* began in 1950 as something of a newsletter, primarily serving to memorialize a record of conversations taking place among scholars across the country about the teaching of writing, conversations that took place at what were then new annual meetings of the Conference on College Composition and Communication (CCCC). However, as late as 1969, just as there was a burgeoning sense that there would be a true scholarship of our own (generally marked by Janet Emig's work in the late 1960s and early 1970s, followed closely by Mina Shaughnessy's work in the 1970s), these session conversations, rather than scholarship, were still being summarized and printed in the journal, with different professors serving as recorders or co-recorders for each session. Session topics for the day (several of which are surely flinch-worthy) included "Teaching the Culturally Disadvantaged," "Preparing College Teachers," "Technical Writing in College and Industry," and, interestingly, "The Future of CCCC and NCTE." Given the topics, I am struck by the fact that there really hasn't been anything new since Aristotle, as has long been suspected (although I and others question those august origins as well).

The discussion in "The Future of CCCC" is particularly telling, especially with, if you will, the mellow sharpness of fifty years or more after the fact. "What is the future of CCCC and NCTE," barks the collaboratively written text. "Let us develop the potential power of CCCC and NCTE. The following are some suggestions: preparation for student teachers, which will lead to black studies for black students, working-class studies for working-class students, women's studies, and so forth." Question as we might the suggestions above—isn't the idea of education to get us away from our own levels of comfort, to think outside our own experiences and proverbial boxes?—one might also and appropriately argue that the above recommendation was not meant to be exclusive; rather, it was seen as a crucial acknowledgment that studies targeting diverse backgrounds would welcome greater numbers of students to larger conversations. The following seems particularly significant: "Because as English teachers we constitute the sole market for a certain group of textbooks, it seems reasonable that we should seek to shape the nature of these books. We should study the existing anthologies for implicit racism and discrimination against subordinate groups, including women, in order to issue guidelines for the individual teacher seeking to make choices" ("Future").

The session that day is notable because of its concern with issues that concern us to this day and because of its relevance to the basic question posed by this volume: What scholarly contexts and acknowledgments are missing from our scholarly work? I turn our attention to a particular session. The chairman that day was Wallace W. Douglas of Northwestern University. Not incidentally, the recorder for that day was the legendary scholar-teacher Edward P. J. Corbett, a past editor of *CCC*. At the time, Douglas was the chair of the CCCC, a man with tremendous interest in teaching and in the teaching of writing, an unusual preoccupation, particularly for Douglas's time. While we in composition studies often hear of a "golden age" of composition in the 1980s populated by a "first generation" of composition scholars from literary studies, Douglas predates that generation as a literature-to-composition convert when, in terms of the profession, there was no such thing. Indeed, Douglas's career can serve as a metaphor of sorts for the evolution of composition studies as a full discipline, the recognition of composition studies as a discipline (or at that time, the lack of it), and the evolution of *CCC* to its important position in rhetoric and composition studies.

After transferring to Northwestern as an undergraduate in the early 1970s, I served as a work-study student for Douglas at the Curriculum Center in English, where I received my first lesson in disciplinary marginalization. A literary scholar who had come to Northwestern in the early 1950s expecting to teach Romantic-era poetry (having written a two-volume dissertation at Harvard examining the political views of William Wordsworth), Douglas was apparently told to find something else to do, as the department chair at that time was to be the only expert in that field. Still the literature professor, however, Douglas nonetheless turned his attention—likely based on his progressive politics—to issues related to the teaching of writing, then visible only as a small part of the larger discipline of English education and primarily located in schools of education. Thus began Douglas's long (and, to academe at that time, strangely alternative) association as a member of both the College of Arts and Sciences and the College of Education at Northwestern.

INTRODUCTION

The composition scholar's absence from the pages of *CCC* (or those of *College English*, for that matter) is notable. Douglas's progressive politics and his writing are highly visible in these recorded and mostly summarized conversations, but for various institutional and evolutionary reasons, he is a blip on the compositionist's scholarly radar. For instance, in a 1965 conversation, "Preparing College Teachers," Douglas served as cochair of the group, and it was noted that "Mr. Douglas distinguished between the rhetorical study of the effect of the product (how a writer has succeeded in what he says he set out to do) and the rhetorical study of the fashioning of the product (how a writer explores and develops his subject)" ("Preparing College Teachers" 198). Since the recorder for each session fashioned their own summary—the recorder in this case was Wilma R. Ebbitt of the University of Chicago—one wonders about the ways in which page limits and the attempt to represent each speaker to the same extent (not to mention the interests of the recorder) might not have fully represented the conversation or Douglas's contributions to it.

Listed as "resource," or speaker, at the end of another conversation published in *CCC* in 1958 ("Freshman Anthology" 184), Douglas was already contributing to potential scholarly perspectives on the teaching of writing, and he was prescient, in a way, because of the hybrid mix of in-service (secondary) perspectives as a framework for training graduate students teaching first-year college students. Given the collaborative nature of the published report (Douglas is listed along with no fewer than twenty or so other people), it is impossible to know to what extent he informed this particular publication—a warning, perhaps, to our own gleeful attempts to enter the allegedly egoless world of collaborative, virtual environments. His precise contributions are similarly absent from the texts reporting conversations from 1958 such as "The Freshman Anthology: Its Virtues and Shortcomings" and the extensive report "Articulation of Secondary School and College Work," although he is listed as a consultant in a 1969 report titled "Advanced Composition in the Preparation of Prospective Secondary School English Teachers" (Neville and Papillon). As the recorder for "Experiments in Freshman English," reported and published in 1960, Douglas reported the contributions of Francis Christensen and Richard Beal but masked his own perspectives. He does, however, present the conversation, having obviously written from printed texts (then carbon copies, I presume) of the papers, as he quotes the speakers directly, instead of summarizing them, which served as the modus operandi for other recorders. You get the idea.

As befits the situation of a literature scholar with a more than passing interest in composition studies, a then barely emerging discipline, when Douglas did publish significant work, it was not in the pages of *CCC*. Again, this is notable by its absence—Hahn's words, a "scholarly elision," apply—but the elision might also be attributed to the scholar himself. I surmise that Douglas did not need to preach to the choir of writing teachers who might have already understood and believed in his perspectives, for that was the sole audience in those days for *CCC*, as it was for *College English*, for that matter. I do not underestimate the importance of Douglas's publishing in venues that were at the time considered far more prestigious than the journals identified with teaching, composition studies, or both, although this would not explain several composition-related publications in which his work also appeared. Therefore, he needed to preach instead, and he did, to the people who not only would listen but also might possibly do something about the issues about which he wrote. As we will see, Douglas's scholarship appears elsewhere.

Richard Larson, a longtime editor of *CCC*, regularly published a feature called "Selected Bibliography of Research and Writing about the Teaching of Composition." Douglas makes the list in 1974 for three publications—all published in 1974, and none of them published in *CCC*. The first was an article titled "Barrett Wendell and the Contradictions of Composition," published in the *Arizona English Bulletin*. (Did Douglas assume that the *Arizona English Bulletin* had a wider audience?) The second and third publications, "Notes toward an Ideology of Composition" and "On the Crisis in Composition," appeared in the *ADE Bulletin*, an MLA publication aimed at chairs of English departments.

In "Notes toward an Ideology of Composition," Douglas "[e]xamines the goals of instruction in writing as set forth by Locke in *Some Thoughts on Education*," concluding that "a great deal of the teaching of composition today is for social and vocational sorting," and he "cites the harm done to students' self-esteem and to their ability to communicate by teachers' attitudes toward their language" (Larson 189). In "On the Crisis in Composition," Douglas "examines some recent work on composition, including principally the views of J. Mitchell Morse, and relates this work to old theories of rhetoric, including those of Hugh Blair and Alexander Bain" (189). It is significant that Douglas's work here prefigures more recent writing and critiques of textbooks, commenting negatively on *The Random House Handbook*, for instance, and indicating that much of the teaching going on at that time was for, as he disparagingly puts it, "vocational licensing" (qtd. in Larson 189). Douglas also noted that much more needed to be known about the variety of dialects in America and about the role played by dialect markers with regard to social stratification.

Douglas's most significant publication in composition, or at least the best known, is "Rhetoric for the Meritocracy: Composition at Harvard" (1976). The essay appears in Susan Miller's anthology highlighting a selection of composition scholarship (published by W. W. Norton) and has been cited by James Berlin and Win Horner, among others, but the piece, hardly visible in its day, has disappeared from more current conversations. The article was not originally published in a journal devoted to composition but rather in a book edited by Douglas's friend Richard Ohmann, *English in America: A Radical View of the Profession*. I should also note that Douglas was a presence and highly regarded presenter in the early years of the fabled Dartmouth conference on composition.

Douglas's scholarly career tells us something about composition and the evolution of the discipline as a scholarly field, an evolution whose directions often appear more institutionally political than scholarly, an evolution that merits still further investigation and interpretation. Douglas's work is worthy of our reexamination and merits our scholarly mindfulness—a thoughtful, expansive look at relevant aspects of our scholarly history. Were "Dr. D.," as I called him in my youth, alive today, he would be quite gratified to see the journal that he helped shape, although invisibly, with colleagues such as Edward P. J. Corbett. He would be concerned, as always, about students' rights and about access to education and, I suspect, to technologies (in all sorts of forms), and he would find the increased selectivity of composition journals gratifying but worrisome. His surprising and relative absence from the pages of composition's long-standing journals nonetheless seems inversely proportional to the shaping of these journals by Douglas and other scholars who have brought the field to its current prominence and influence.

Rhetoric Obscured:
There Is More Than One Tradition

As incongruous as the connection between Gertrude Berg, the ethnic comedienne and writer, and Wallace W. Douglas, the Haverford College and Harvard University graduate, might seem, each represents a visible absence; indeed, Douglas is but one example of many historical figures, movements, theories, or assumptions worthy of our renewed or extended inquiry.

When I champion the reconnecting of composition studies with rhetoric, I also want to continue questioning what we mean when we point to a rhetorical tradition, as recent new work on Jewish rhetoric (and recent work foregrounding many other rhetorical traditions) attempts to reconsider. The research for this challenge to our ideological assumptions, a piece I published titled "The Religious Ideology of Composition Studies" (Holdstein), grew out of and borrows from another essay I wrote in response to a 2000 article in *JAC* by Michael Bernard-Donals (Holdstein, "Ironies"), part of further challenges to the Greek tradition (Greenbaum and Holdstein).

In "The Ironies of Ethos," I look at the usually unchallenged term *ethos*—as typically defined, the extent to which an appeal is persuasive, based on the perceived character of a narrator or speaker—and examine its ironies. Bernard-Donals had written about the ethos of testimony, particularly as it relates to the Holocaust. My response raised a question about the term *ethos* itself, the paradox of our describing any form of experience related to the Holocaust through the otherwise rhetorically appropriate yet evocative term *ethos*. Isn't it ironic to have only a Greek term by which to discuss a Hebraic context for ethos? Yet this term, an all-important and productive cornerstone of our work as rhetoricians, a term that bears the connotative weight of morality and personal responsibility, takes on a vexed, charged context and meaning once juxtaposed with Judaic history.[5] It is all the more ironic that ethos itself becomes contested, given the term itself and the firm anti-Semitism of ancient Greece. Clearly, numerous scholarly works in composition and rhetoric have made visible the importance and validity of rhetorical traditions other than the Greek tradition.[6]

INTRODUCTION

Even Anne Frank's diary has become something of a lost (and certainly misused) text in that it has become commodified and transformed, illustrating a need for her legacy to be appropriately reestablished and made visible. In her collection of essays, *Quarrel and Quandary*, Cynthia Ozick condemns what she calls the Anne Frank "industry," one in which her literary achievement and the horror of her Holocaust experience has "been infantilized, Americanized, homogenized, sentimentalized, falsified, kitschified, and, in fact, blatantly and arrogantly denied" (77). The result? Anne Frank has been made "an all-American girl" (93). As Ozick argues, "The diary is taken to be a Holocaust document; that is overridingly what it is not. Nearly every edition—and there have been innumerable editions—is emblazoned with words such as 'a song to life,' 'a poignant delight in the infinite human spirit'" (78). To Ozick, these characterizations mock the events of the Shoah and even mock the end of Frank's own life. She notes, "The diary is incomplete, truncated, broken off; or, rather it is completed by Westerbork (the hellish transit camp in Holland from which Dutch Jews were deported), and by Auschwitz, and by the fatal winds of Bergen-Belsen. . . . A survivor recalled that . . . Anne, heartbroken and skeletal, naked under a bit of rag, died a day or two [after her sister's death]" (78–79). Of course, I suppose that without the strength of Bernard-Donals's argument about the "troubling fact about history and memory" (579), one could examine and wonder about the ethos of the survivor who recalled Anne Frank's death and its transformation by others who ensured that Frank's legacy would be happy rather than tragic.

Reclaiming Lost Texts in Popular Culture

I want to make note of some other, rather surprising (and, to me, delightful) ways in which elisions—scholarly and otherwise—have been ameliorated, lost texts found that might be useful as seasoning for current discussions and scholarly investigations. Eager for a break from class preparation, I read with interest Cathleen Schine's recent novel, *The Grammarians*, and, to my astonishment, found it to some extent an explosion of at least several rare and lost (and some not-so-lost) texts. Schine's characters Laurel and Daphne, mentioned in the following passage, are twin sisters; Larry is Laurel's husband:

> Laurel was . . . preparing her reentry into the world. "By reading *Fowler's Modern English Usage?*" Larry asked. He turned the faded blue volume over in his hands sniffed it, made a face, and gave it back to her. Laurel put it on her bedside table. The 1967 sixth printing, second edition, revised by Sir Ernest Gowers, a high school graduation gift from Daphne. . . . [R]eading *Fowler's*, Laurel was surprised at how newfangled some of his old ideas were. Here was a book that she had always thought of as holding language to the highest possible standards, an Edwardian don with a switch and a sorrowful expression. . . . Daphne was charmed by Fowler's affection—there really seemed to be no other word for it—for made-up words.   (176–77)

More surprising to me, however, was another revelation, a lost text embedded within the narrative, a gift to Laurel (a teacher) from the school principal: of all things, a copy of Charles Carpenter Fries's *American English Grammar*, published in 1940 with the support of the National Council of Teachers of English and the Modern Language Association.[7] Fries was a professor of linguistics at the University of Michigan. In the novel, the principal explains to Laurel that the book can be helpful to her teaching, that "it was revolutionary in its time. It would have been, at any rate, if more people had read it." Laurel asks, "When was its time?" The principal replies, "Nineteen twenty-six." The study began that year, he explains, but the war came along. "One of my professors studied with the author at Michigan. He gave this book to me. And now I give it to you" (199). Six pages are devoted to the characters' discussion of this book (including a debate between the sisters about its merits), the research for which involved Fries's analysis of letters from people of every walk of life from across the country. The idea Laurel takes away from the letters she reads in this lost text "change[s] her life": "[Fries's] point is, informal English is not wrong, and some of it stems from models older than 'standard' English, and he always puts 'standard' in quotes because there is no standard English, language keeps changing. And to understand language and teach it, you have to know what is actually spoken" (209).

Digging through *eBay*, I found and purchased a copy of *American English Grammar* (a library copy decisively and perhaps symbolically, given its negligible impact, stamped "WITHDRAWN" in red on the inside cover), and certainly Fries's ideas are often anything but progressive or appropriate—for instance, his use of the term "Vulgar English." However, he states unequivocally that there can be "no 'correctness' apart from usage and that the *true* forms of 'standard' English are those that are actually used in that particular dialect. Deviations from those usages are 'incorrect' only when used in the dialect to which they do not belong" (209). Fries suggests, moreover, that schools should not denigrate students' own language (as we might now phrase it) but rather educate students on what might now be called code-switching, the ability to use the "standard" English of the United States, "the dialect of the socially acceptable in most of our communities" (14), the nature of which, of course, remains in dispute.

The lessons of Fries's lost text are multilayered: we learn anew that our ideas about language are complex and long-standing and have (or haven't) evolved. Fries's text gives us points to reject and points that resonate with and help clarify current thinking, showing us that some of our most important ideas aren't necessarily recent or new. In terms of the larger profession, we might be surprised to learn that collaboration between two major organizations assumed to be at odds, the National Council of Teachers of English and the Modern Language Association, had been long-standing, productive, and significant.

In larger aspects of popular cultures, one can also witness varieties of making the invisible text visible: for one, the *New York Times*'s recent attempt to compensate for ignoring the deaths of (primarily) important women and minorities at the times of their respective passing by publishing long-overdue obituaries. Similarly, the humorist Mo Rocca has published *MoBituaries: Great Lives Worth Reliving*. His purpose, put simply, is that there are people and situations that he believes we all should know about. Rocca writes:

> A Mobituary is an appreciation for someone who didn't get the love she or he deserved the first time around. This person could be a well-known name. Audrey Hepburn had the misfortune of dying not only way too young but also on the day Bill Clinton was inaugurated. Her own wartime experience—and how it shaped the woman we all fell in love with—is unknown to many.... Distinctions between who is famous now, who used to be famous, and who was never famous are ultimately moot. (3)

Rocca's book exposes "Political Firsts Who Didn't Make Your High School History Book" (72–73) and includes chapters such as "Reputation Assassination: A Story of Three Killings" (176–94) and "Where's Chuck? The Graveyard of Disappeared and Dead Sitcom Characters" (267–71). Susanna Madora Salter (1860–1961), the first woman mayor in the United States, and Romualdo Pacheco (1831–99), the first Hispanic member of the House of Representatives, appear alongside such people as Lawrence Welk and Vaughn Meader. (Look them up. The first, Welk, is fun; the second, Meader, is both fun and tragic.)[8]

Where have I led us from the questions of Berg and Douglas, Schine and Rocca, scholarly elision and absence, *ethos*, testimonies of the Holocaust, and the rhetorical tradition? To the thought, I hope, that everything, even those tenets we hold dear and use as the basis for other thinking, might merit rethinking, expansion, reevaluation. To the hope that we will dig deeply and look for scholarly invigoration beyond the endnotes or bibliography of a recent article by a well-known scholar. To the realization, perhaps, that even our most valorized term to describe the inherent character of the speaker, *ethos*, is not ideologically neutral, that the great minds of the rhetorical tradition brought to it their own problematic ethos or lack of it—with limitations, prejudices, and ideological purposes. At the origins of rhetoric (even in Cicero's work), there is a hatred and a politics in the concept of ethos that is even more troubled and evocative than we think—the "elusiveness of the traumatic experience," in Bernard-Donals's words (580), embracing as well the complex elusiveness of the otherwise brave tradition that we in rhetoric call our own.

In the manuscript of his presentation at the CCCC convention in 2009, Charles Schuster notes that "the great strength of composition derives from its utility." "[B]ut I want to insist," he writes, "that the academic enterprise of composition studies must exceed its utility." Schuster argues for a composition theory that "once again recognizes aesthetics." Schuster acknowledges that the aesthetic has fallen away, possibly from our disavowal of all things MLA, including a love of the literary lie, the metaphor signifier. Many of our graduate students no longer read literature actively, and without such reading, a love of the poetry of language, affirms Schuster, begins to wither. This anti-intellectual turn can be traced from the departmental and stratified politics that became a turning point for Douglas (and likely influenced his decisions about where to be published) and not, of course, from any real intellectual substance. Along with exciting ventures into areas that we have both foreseen and not foreseen in composition—internationalization; the racialization of composition studies; rereading methodologies in composition; classed, gendered, and racialized masculinity in literacy narratives; the licensing of the poetic in nineteenth-century composition rhetoric textbooks; girl zines; and much more—the state of the field demands that we begin to look anew at basic tenets and assumptions that deserve constructive challenge and questioning. Who knows how many Gertrude Bergs—and, more to the point, Wallace Douglases—we can rediscover, reclaim, and spotlight to the enrichment of a deeper, and more accountable, set of traditions to benefit our own learning and that of our students.

Essays in This Volume

The contributors to this volume attempt to do just that—to rediscover, reclaim, and spotlight texts that are useful and, in their respective judgments, to foreground lost texts worthy of being found or found again. The choice of topic for each essay reflects the contributors' own wide-ranging and diverse philosophical and scholarly interests, their longevity (if you will) in the profession, and their personal and scholarly backgrounds. Contributors represent not only a wide range of interests but also their respective professional homes and, at times, perspectives that challenge common assumptions about their respective subjects. Each contributor explicates a work, scholar, or movement and argues for its historical relevance, visibility, or significance to current concerns in the field. Some also suggest that the significance of a particular lost text is that it will be new to most scholars and should therefore be considered part of our current pedagogical or scholarly conversations.

The essays in this volume are comparatively brief, which will allow readers to consider a larger number of pieces than would otherwise be possible. Shorter essays can also give readers a taste of this renewed or first-blush acquaintance with particular lost texts, providing just enough to pique interest but not so much that it would dissuade the reader from further, self-guided exploration.

Essays are organized in chronological groupings. While that choice is somehow imperfect, I'd originally thought to organize the essays in simple chronological order, which seemed equally imperfect: for instance, an author might highlight one scholarly work but compare it with another or others of a different time; the reader will also note that the number of essays increases in part 4, "1980–1992," and part 5, "After 1992," a fact that reflects the particular interest of respective contributors, not a particular or heightened value placed on contemporary scholarship. Similarly, the relative brevity of part 2, "The Mid–Twentieth Century," may suggest that there is much more to be discovered in this time period.

Worthy of note is that there is no particular pattern regarding what this volume and its essays reveal about canon formation—only that some works of scholarship rise to prominence and ready access, while others recede. If anything, the purpose of this volume is to reveal the flaws and limitations of canon formation and to suggest that along with those works determined to be must-reads, there will always be less-known and perhaps equally significant work to uncover and use as the basis for new, more informed and expansive scholarship. In this sense, this volume extends the work of scholars who explored and brought to the fore rhetorical traditions beyond the Greek, similarly contradicting—or at least extending—any attempt at authoritative canon formation in rhetoric and composition. Indeed, through its project of scholarly expansion, this volume could be the start of something big.[9]

I hope that the essays here do, in fact, pique interest in further expanding the field's scholarly reach so that our teaching and writing can benefit from—and honor—a good deal of worthwhile but forgotten or invisible work that has come before us.

Notes

Portions of this introduction first appeared in Holdstein, "Rhetorical Silence," and have been republished with the permission of the publisher.

1. The idea of fashioning a volume on this wide-ranging topic became concrete in the course of several successful sessions on the topic of lost texts in rhetoric and composition that I organized as part of the MLA convention in 2019 and 2020, sessions that were sponsored by the MLA forum RCWS Writing Pedagogies. The lost texts selected by presenters at the MLA sessions included the following: Lillian Robinson's "Dwelling in Decencies" (1971); Ira Shor's *Critical Teaching and Everyday Life* (1987); the work of the linguist

INTRODUCTION

Frédéric François; Roger Sale's *On Writing* (1970); Geneva Smitherman's "Toward a National Public Policy on Language" (1987); William James's *Talks to Teachers* (1899); Gertrude Buck's "The Present Status of Rhetorical Theory" (1899); Wallace W. Douglas's "Rhetoric for the Meritocracy" (1976); less-cited but noteworthy and useful scholarly collections in computers and composition from 1988 to 1992; and others. Some of these appear in this volume in essay form; all are deemed by the eclectic group that proposed them as worthy of scholarly or pedagogical note.

2. Readers will perhaps detect some irony in several of the contributors' (albeit careful and sometimes reluctant) mention of *Google Scholar* as an authoritative measure of an article's or a book's importance in the field. The role of *Google Scholar* in canon formation should, I would suggest, be seen as suspect, since the frequency of a work's citation is an often misguided indication of its merit and possibly the result of many factors unrelated to scholarship.

3. Interestingly, a newer sitcom, also called *The Goldbergs* and purporting to provide nostalgia for the '80s through the eyes of a Jewish family, makes doubly invisible the merits of the original television program. One must dig, even online, to find *The Goldbergs* of 1949.

4. While I emphasize the lost text of *The Goldbergs*, I do not wish to diminish the importance of what is usually assumed to have been the first television situation comedy—*I Love Lucy*—notable not only because it was the first show to present the intermarriage of a Cuban man (Desi Arnaz) and a White American female (Lucille Ball) but also because Arnaz is credited with having demanded three-camera film shoots over kinescope and having invented the rerun to be able to show episodes from an expansive archive (ensuring permanence and residual payments) when production was on hiatus ("How Desi Invented Television"). However, a 2021 book by Jennifer Keishin Armstrong, *When Women Invented Television*, features Gertrude Berg as one of the unsung, early pioneers of television.

5. See Katz, which argues that the ethic of expediency first employed by Aristotle in the *Politics* was embraced by the Nazis along with science and technology. This then formed the convenient "moral basis" of the Holocaust.

6. There exists in composition and rhetoric studies a fairly recent but established tradition of questioning the absence from our work of rhetorical traditions other than the Greek tradition; see, for instance, Bernard-Donals and Fernheimer; Greenbaum and Holdstein; Powell; Gilyard; Smitherman; Gannett and Brereton.

7. The MLA's support of this project contradicts the perception common within the field of rhetoric and composition that historically the MLA has been uninterested in pedagogy.

8. See Gershon for the case of Charles Curtis, President Herbert Hoover's vice president from 1929 to 1933. While Kamala Harris, who took the oath of office in January of 2021, might be the first woman vice president of the United States, she is not the first vice president of color. While the office of vice president is often considered to be somewhat invisible and unmemorable, one might suggest that Curtis is indeed the historically "lost" vice president.

9. I would suggest that the most visible signs of canon formation in rhetoric and composition include Victor Villanueva and Kristin L. Arola's *Cross-Talk in Comp Theory: A Reader* and Susan Miller's *The Norton Book of Composition Studies*. Given that these volumes were each published over a decade ago, studying them might reveal opportunities for expanding the scope of the essays to include lesser-known scholarship. Again, one should not discount the often misguided use of such platforms as *Google Scholar* in determining a work's scholarly significance.

Works Cited

Armstrong, Jennifer Keishin. *When Women Invented Television: The Untold Story of the Female Powerhouses Who Pioneered the Way We Watch Today*. HarperCollins Publishers, 2021.

"Articulation of Secondary School and College Work." *College Composition and Communication*, vol. 9, no. 3, 1958, pp. 192–96.

Bernard-Donals, Michael. "Ethos, Witness, and Holocaust 'Testimony': The Rhetoric of *Fragments*." *JAC*, vol. 20, no. 3, 2000, pp. 565–82.

Bernard-Donals, Michael, and Janice W. Fernheimer. *Jewish Rhetorics: History, Theory, Practice*. Brandeis UP, 2014.

Douglas, Wallace. "Barrett Wendell and the Contradictions of Composition." *Arizona English Bulletin*, vol. 16, no. 2, 1974, pp. 182–90.

———. "Notes toward an Ideology of Composition." *ADE Bulletin*, no. 43, Nov. 1974, pp. 24–33.

———. "On the Crisis in Composition." *ADE Bulletin*, no. 40, Mar. 1974, pp. 3–11.

———. "Rhetoric for the Meritocracy: Composition at Harvard." Ohmann, pp. 93–132.

"Experiments in Freshman English." *College Composition and Communication*, vol. 11, no. 3, 1960, pp. 135–36.

"The Freshman Anthology: Its Virtues and Shortcomings." *College Composition and Communication*, vol. 9, no. 3, 1958, pp. 183–84.

Fries, Charles Carpenter. *American English Grammar: The Grammatical Structure of Present-Day American English with Especial Reference to Social Differences or Class Dialects*. D. Appleton-Century, 1940.

"The Future of CCCC: An Informal Discussion." *College Composition and Communication*, vol. 20, no. 3, 1969, p. 265.

Gannett, Cinthia, and John C. Brereton, editors. *Traditions of Eloquence: The Jesuits and Modern Rhetorical Studies*. Fordham UP, 2016.

Gershon, Livia. "Who Was Charles Curtis, the First Vice President of Color?" *Smithsonian Magazine*, 13 Jan. 2021, www.smithsonianmag.com/history/who-was-charles-curtis-first-non-white-vice-president-180976742/.

Gilyard, Keith. *Let's Flip the Script: An African American Discourse on Language, Literature, and Learning*. Wayne State UP, 1996.

Greenbaum, Andrea, and Deborah H. Holdstein, editors. *Judaic Perspectives in Rhetoric and Composition*. Hampton Press, 2008.

Hahn, Steven. "On History: A Rebellious Take on African-American History." *The Chronicle of Higher Education*, 3 Aug. 2009, chronicle.com/article/On-History—A-Rebellious-Take/47497.

Holdstein, Deborah H. "The Ironies of Ethos." *JAC*, vol. 20, no. 4, 2000, pp. 942–48.

———. "The Religious Ideology of Composition Studies." Greenbaum and Holdstein, pp. 13–21.

———. "Rhetorical Silence, Scholarly Absence, and Tradition Rethought: Notes from an Editorship." *Pedagogy: Critical Approaches to Teaching Literature, Language, Composition, and Culture*, vol. 11, no. 3, fall 2011, pp. 451–64.

"How Desi Invented Television." *NPR*, 22 Jan. 2021, www.npr.org/2021/01/22/959609533/how-desi-invented-television.

Katz, Steven B. "The Ethic of Expediency: Classical Rhetoric, Technology, and the Holocaust." *College English*, vol. 54, no. 3, Mar. 1992, pp. 255–75.

Larson, Richard L. "Selected Bibliography of Research and Writing about the Teaching of Composition, 1973 and 1974." *College Composition and Communication*, vol. 26, no. 2, May 1975, pp. 187–95.

Miller, Susan, editor. *The Norton Book of Composition Studies*. W. W. Norton, 2009.

Neville, Margaret M., and Alfred L. Papillon. "Advanced Composition in the Preparation of Prospective Secondary School English Teachers: Interim Report." U.S. Department of Health, Education, and Welfare, May 1969. *ERIC*, files.eric.ed.gov/fulltext/ED031499.pdf.

Ohmann, Richard M. *English in America: A Radical View of the Profession*. Oxford UP, 1976.

Ozick, Cynthia. *Quarrel and Quandary: Essays*. Alfred A. Knopf, 2000.

Powell, Malea. "Rhetoric on Native Land." *Journal for the History of Rhetoric*, vol. 23, no. 1, 2020, pp. 115–16.

"Preparing College Teachers." *College Composition and Communication*, vol. 16, no. 3, 1965, pp. 198–99.

Rocca, Mo. *MoBituaries: Great Lives Worth Reliving*. Simon and Schuster, 2019.

Schine, Cathleen. *The Grammarians*. Farrar, Straus and Giroux, 2019.

Schuster, Charles. "CCCC 2009: An Argument for Aesthetics." Conference on College Composition and Communication, Apr. 2009, San Francisco.

Smitherman, Geneva. *Talkin and Testifyin: The Language of Black America*. Wayne State UP, 1986.

Villanueva, Victor, and Kristin L. Arola, editors. *Cross-Talk in Comp Theory: A Reader*. 3rd ed., National Council of Teachers of English, 2011.

Yoo-Hoo, Mrs. Goldberg. Directed by Aviva Kempner, Ciesla Foundation, 2009.

Part One

The Early Twentieth Century and Before

Isaac Rabinowitz's Translation and Critical Edition of Judah Messer Leon's *The Book of the Honeycomb's Flow*

Jim Ridolfo

Isaac Rabinowitz (ed. and trans.), *The Book of the Honeycomb's Flow: Sēpher Nōpheth Ṣūphīm*, by Judah Messer Leon (Cornell UP, 1983)

It's been thirty-six years since the Cornell University professor of biblical and Hebrew studies Isaac Rabinowitz published the most significant and comprehensive English translation of Jewish Renaissance rhetoric, Judah Messer Leon's 1475/76 *Sēpher Nōpheth Ṣūphīm*, or *The Book of the Honeycomb's Flow*. Messer Leon's book of rhetoric, the third in a sequence of textbooks that amounted to a Jewish Renaissance argument for the significance of the trivium and scholastic reasoning, was a major curricular reform for the Jews of Renaissance Italy.

The work is equally important today for scholars of rhetoric seeking to understand the intersection and transmission of Greco-Roman and Islamic rhetoric by way of Averroës in fifteenth-century Jewish Italy. As Mark Schaub argues in his article "Rhetorical Studies in America: The Place of Averroës and the Medieval Arab Commentators," while it's not surprising that significant chronological history remains absent from rhetorical seminars largely focused on what I would today call "Mediterranean rhetorics," "[t]he conspicuous lack of attention to important contributions coming from rhetorical traditions outside the Western canon, within standard texts on the history of rhetoric as well as secondary sources, has caused a detrimental narrowing of the scope of the contemporary field of rhetorical studies" (233). Citing Lahcen Ezzaher's 1994 Conference on College Composition and Communication paper, "A Revisionary History of Rhetoric: The Significance of the Medieval Muslim Tradition in the Western Rhetorical Tradition," Schaub notes that there is evidence for "Ezzaher's claim that the work of Averroës, al-Farabi, and Avicenna... is widely ignored" in histories of Mediterranean rhetorical studies (233). To this important thread of historical absence I would add the work of Messer Leon.

This essay, however, is only partly about Messer Leon. I argue that the publication of Rabinowitz's multidecade translation project came too early in the revival of rhetorical studies to be widely received by the field and as a result is only now starting to receive the broader attention within the field that it deserves. While two rhetorical scholars initially reviewed the book, Arthur Lesley in 1984 in *Prooftexts* ("*Sefer Nofet Tsufim*") and James Murphy in 1985 in *Speculum*, the scholarly audience for the text in the decades that followed remained in Jewish Renaissance studies. Additionally, Rabinowitz himself passed away in 1988, less than five years after the publication of his six-hundred-page tome. Drawing on recent scholarship and edited collections in Jewish rhetorics (Greenbaum and Holdstein; Bernard-Donals and Fernheimer), this essay argues that the moment for better understanding and acknowledging the significant contribution of Rabinowitz's translation of the *Sēpher Nōpheth Ṣūphīm* is here, especially in the era of cultural rhetorics approaches to rhetorical traditions and texts. *The Book of the Honeycomb's Flow* provides a rich example from Jewish rhetorical history of a text at the Mediterranean crossroads of Greco-Roman and Averrosian commentary, secularism, Hebraic transmission, and biblical exegesis that is more inclusive of Jewish rhetorical studies and its situated complexities at particular moments history and that deconstructs simple narratives about the transmission, translation, and reception of Greco-Roman rhetorics.[1]

Background

Rabinowitz received his PhD in Semitic languages and literature from Yale University in 1932 but was unable to find a professorship due to the "cultural climate in the United States [that] made it exceedingly difficult for a Jewish scholar of Semitics to find an academic position" (Brann et al.). For the next twenty-three years, Rabinowitz worked in Jewish education and communal service, all the while doing research at night, and eventually his record of excellence as a Dead Sea Scrolls scholar helped him secure an academic appointment as associate professor of Jewish studies at Wayne State University in 1955, and in 1957 he was hired at Cornell University as professor of biblical and Hebrew studies (Brann et al.). According to his *New York Times* obituary, "he retired in 1975, but continued to teach after his retirement" ("Isaac Rabinowitz"). Rabinowitz's connection to rhetorical studies began at Cornell when he met Harry Caplan:

> Upon his arrival at Cornell in 1957, Isaac met Harry Caplan of the classics department, and the two became the closest of friends—true intellectual companions. It was at Caplan's suggestion that Isaac began his translation of the *Sepher Nopheth Suphim* (*Book of the Honeycomb's Flow*) by the Jewish-Italian Renaissance scholar, Judah Messer Leon. The *Nopeth Suphim* was the first attempt to write a classical rhetoric using examples drawn from the Hebrew Bible; it was also the first Hebrew book printed during its author's lifetime. For more than twenty years, Isaac labored over this text, producing a Hebrew edition and annotated translation with a full critical apparatus. Published by the Cornell University Press in 1983, this massive tome has been widely and justly praised by its many reviewers as an exquisite example of meticulous textual scholarship and literary-historical insight. (Brann et al.)

Both Murphy and Lesley note in their reviews of *The Book of the Honeycomb's Flow* that Rabinowitz was colleagues with Harry Caplan (1896–1980), the author of works such as *Of Eloquence: Studies in Ancient and Medieval Rhetoric*. In his review, Murphy begins by noting that "[t]he many friends of the late Harry Caplan will recall his speaking often of the work being done by one of his colleagues on a unique fifteenth-century Jewish rhetoric text. This work is now completed in masterful fashion" (161). Lesley's 1984 review maintains that the project is a "fitting tribute" to Caplan's memory ("*Sefer Nofet Tsufim*" 313).

Murphy, Lesley, and George Kennedy offer three reviews of the book from scholars in rhetorical studies, although to my knowledge no review ever appeared in a field journal aside from Lesley's 1983 review in *Rhetorica* (Review). Murphy writes that there are "two separate values of the book" (163). First, it provides a "lucid glimpse of everyday Jewish life in Italian cities," and, second, the translation justifies, at least in Murphy's view, Rabinowitz's claim that the *Sēpher Nōpheth Ṣūphīm* is "probably the single most original and important work of Jewish scholarship produced in early Renaissance Italy" (Murphy 163; Rabinowitz, *Book* xx). By this reasoning, it is also one of the most important works of Jewish rhetoric completed during the Renaissance.

Lesley writes in his *Prooftexts* review that "what is distinctive about *The Book of the Honeycomb's Flow* is that it combines Latin and Arabic traditions of classical rhetoric, which are also not perfectly uniform, and adapts them to the Hebrew language" ("*Sefer Nofet Tsufim*" 315). This is even more important because the "paucity of rhetorical writings on Hebrew and in Hebrew makes its history more difficult to trace" (313). In his 1984 review in *Renaissance and Reformation*, Kennedy writes that students will be interested in this "curious work" and that he welcomes "the accessibility of this unusual work, edited with such devotion" (Review 154, 155). Kennedy writes that the value of the work is that

> all examples of rhetorical divisions and techniques are illustrated from the Hebrew Bible and the system of classical rhetoric is even used as a critical tool to interpret the scriptures. Classical rhetoric is thus treated, like Aristotelian logic, as universally valid, and the author [Messer Leon] makes no effort to identify those aspects of biblical rhetoric that were distinctive of ancient Israel or of the Hebrew language. Rather, he is at pains to show that the Hebrew Bible, as a source of all wisdom, contains within itself the entire system of classical rhetoric in its finest form. Beyond that he aimed to produce a manual of rhetoric for the training of Jews in the civic life of fifteenth-century Italy. There is some evidence that the work was so used. (155)

Outside of rhetorical studies, the text received attention from scholars at the intersection of Renaissance studies and Jewish studies. In her 1984 review in *Renaissance Quarterly*, Hava Tirosh-Rothschild writes that "Isaac Rabinowitz brought to this difficult task immense erudition in classical and medieval rhetoric, a comprehensive knowledge of biblical, rabbinic, and philosophical literature, and, above all, linguistic sensitivity. All three are put to best use in his critical edition" (235–36). In his 1985 review in *The Sixteenth Century Journal*, David Ruderman writes that "Messer Leon did more than incorporate the Ciceronian ideal of wisdom and eloquence into Judaism. He also tried to portray his new educational image as an intrinsic part of Jewish tradition in the first place. The ideal of the civic orator, so he claimed, was synonymous with the traditional hero of the *zaddik* (the righteous man) and the *hakham kolel* (the *homo universalis*), an image which encapsulated, no doubt, that which Messer Leon conceived of himself" (148).

An Almost Lost Text

Despite these positive reviews in 1984 and 1985 by three scholars of rhetoric and two scholars in Jewish and Renaissance studies, in the late 1980s, 1990s, and 2000s Rabinowitz's work appears to have gone largely unnoticed by rhetorical studies. One exception is Steven Katz's 1995 *Rhetoric Society Quarterly* article "The Epistemology of the Kabbalah: Toward a Jewish Philosophy of Rhetoric," which cites Rabinowitz's work in arguing that the study of Jewish rhetorical tradition

> to a large extent has been ignored by scholars of classical rhetoric except as it has been treated in traditional rhetorical (and literary) studies of the "Old Testament" (e.g., see *The Book of the Honeycomb's Flow*, where a systematic Aristotelian approach to the figures of speech is applied to the Pentateuch), Hellenized in Philo, rationalized in Maimonides, or transmuted in Christian rhetoric. (108)

Referring to the first edition of Kennedy's *Classical Rhetoric and Its Christian and Secular Tradition from Ancient to Modern Times* (1980), Katz further contends that Kennedy "does make passing mention of Jewish rhetoric, but by and large that the Jewish philosophy of language has been generally neglected, misrepresented, or misunderstood" (108). In the second edition of *Classical Rhetoric* (2003), Kennedy mentions *The Book of the Honeycomb's Flow* in a section on Renaissance rhetoric: according to Kennedy, of those works that "apply classical rhetoric to interpretation of the Old Testament," Messer Leon's is "[t]he most important" (230).

Beyond Katz's engagement with Messer Leon's work, however, there are few other examples of an uptake of or engagement with *The Book of the Honeycomb's Flow* in rhetorical studies. Over the last decade I've asked scholars such as Murphy why this is the case, and there's not really a clear answer. I want to hypothesize two reasons. First, Rabinowitz published his tome eight years after he retired, and two years after the book was in print his wife, Alice, died (Brann et al.). Rabinowitz himself died five years after the book was published. To my mind, it seems unlikely that Rabinowitz was at a point in his career where he could promote the manuscript's value to rhetorical studies. However, in 1985 Rabinowitz did publish in *Rhetorica: A Journal of the History of Rhetoric* the first comprehensive bibliography of Jewish rhetorical sources, "Pre-modern Jewish Study of Rhetoric: An Introductory Bibliography," still a valuable resource for scholars today. Rabinowitz reminds the discipline in this work that "[t]he literary history of the Jewish people exhibits remarkably few pre-modern theoretical, perceptual, or analytic treatments of the rhetorical purposes, strategies, methods, and devices that—as modern scholars have begun to make clear—undergird and permeate the texts produced by authors and editors throughout the tri-millennial course of that history" ("Pre-modern Jewish Study" 137). Rabinowitz's publication of this piece in *Rhetorica* leads me to think that if his personal circumstances had been different he would have had more future opportunities to engage with the discipline.

The second possible reason for the lack of scholarly attention to *The Book of the Honeycomb's Flow* is that Rabinowitz's manuscript came too early for rhetorical studies, before the significant growth of doctoral programs in rhetorical studies between the late 1980s and early 2000s and before more extensive work was being done at the intersection of rhetoric and Jewish studies.[2] Were Rabinowitz's translation published today, I think it's likely that the work would be more widely received within the discipline now that there's greater field interest in rhetorical traditions beyond Greek and Roman rhetorics.

As I write this essay, I am heartened to learn that the third edition of *The Rhetorical Tradition*, published in 2020, now includes a short overview of Messer Leon's life and contributions as well as a brief excerpt from *The Book of the Honeycomb's Flow* (Bizzell et al. 661–69). While Rabinowitz's translation is to my mind one of the least appreciated works in rhetorical studies, there is still hope for broader disciplinary engagement moving forward, particularly given the significance of Rabinowitz's work to understanding how differing rhetorical traditions may dialectically intersect at key cultural and historical moments and how these traditions are localized, recomposed, and redistributed by new technologies such as the first Hebrew printing press, changing how entire educational and cultural institutions function. We are, like Messer Leon was, in a moment of significant technological and rhetorical change, and his work is available to us thanks to the scholarship of Isaac Rabinowitz.

Notes

1. See especially Maha Baddar's work, which discusses the translation of Aristotelian rhetoric into Arabic, and John W. Watt's extensive work on Syriac rhetorics, including Anthony of Targit's *The Book of Rhetoric*.

2. For additional context, see especially Greenbaum and Holdstein; Fernheimer; and Ridolfo, which discusses Messer Leon and rhetorical delivery.

Works Cited

Baddar, Maha. "The Arabs Did Not Just 'Translate' Aristotle." *The Responsibilities of Rhetoric*, edited by Michelle Smith and Barbara Warnick, Waveland Press, 2010, pp. 230–42.

Bernard-Donals, Michael, and Janice W. Fernheimer, editors. *Jewish Rhetorics: History, Theory, Practice*. Brandeis UP, 2014.

Bizzell, Patricia, et al., editors. *The Rhetorical Tradition: Readings from Classical Times to the Present*. 3rd ed., Bedford / St. Martin's, 2020.

Brann, Ross, et al. "Isaac Rabinowitz: July 3, 1909–September 11, 1988." *Cornell University Library*, ecommons.cornell.edu/bitstream/handle/1813/19305/Rabinowitz_Isaac_1988.pdf.

Ezzaher, Lahcen E. "A Revisionary History of Rhetoric: The Significance of the Medieval Muslim Tradition in the Western Rhetorical Tradition." Conference on College Composition and Communication, 18 Mar. 1994, Nashville.

Fernheimer, Janice W. "Talmidae Rhetoricae: Drashing Up Models and Methods for Jewish Rhetorical Studies." *Composing Jewish Rhetorics*, special issue of *College English*, vol. 72, no. 6, 2010, pp. 577–89.

Greenbaum, Andrea, and Deborah H. Holdstein, editors. *Judaic Perspectives in Rhetoric and Composition*. Hampton Press, 2008.

"Isaac Rabinowitz, 79, Dead Sea Scroll Expert." *The New York Times*, 20 Sept. 1988, p. 29.

Katz, Steven B. "The Epistemology of the Kabbalah: Toward a Jewish Philosophy of Rhetoric." *Rhetoric Society Quarterly*, vol. 25, 1995, pp. 107–22.

Kennedy, George A. *Classical Rhetoric and Its Christian and Secular Tradition from Ancient to Modern Times*. 2nd ed., U of North Carolina P, 2003.

———. Review of *The Book of the Honeycomb's Flow*, by Judah Messer Leon. *Renaissance and Reformation / Renaissance Et Réforme*, vol. 8, no. 2, 1984, pp. 154–55.

Lesley, Arthur M. Review of *Nofet Zufim, on Hebrew Rhetoric*, by Judah Messer Leon. *Rhetorica*, vol. 1, no. 2, 1983, pp. 101–14.

———. "*Sefer Nofet Tsufim* and the Study of Rhetoric." *Prooftexts*, vol. 4, no. 3, 1984, pp. 312–16.

Murphy, James J. Review of *The Book of the Honeycomb's Flow*, by Judah Messer Leon. *Speculum*, vol. 60, no. 1, 1985, pp. 161–64.

Rabinowitz, Isaac, editor and translator. *The Book of the Honeycomb's Flow: Sēpher Nōpheth Ṣūphīm*. By Judah Messer Leon, Cornell UP, 1983.

———. "Pre-modern Jewish Study of Rhetoric: An Introductory Bibliography." *Rhetorica: A Journal of the History of Rhetoric*, vol. 3, no. 2, 1985, pp. 137–44.

Ridolfo, Jim. "Judah Messer Leon and the *Sefer Nofet Zuphim*." Bernard-Donals and Fernheimer, pp. 46–57.

Ruderman, David B. Review of *The Book of the Honeycomb's Flow*, by Judah Messer Leon. *The Sixteenth Century Journal*, vol. 16, no. 1, 1985, pp. 147–48.

Schaub, Mark. "Rhetorical Studies in America: The Place of Averroës and the Medieval Arab Commentators." *Alif: Journal of Comparative Poetics*, no. 16, 1996, pp. 233–53.

Tirosh-Rothschild, Hava. Review of *The Book of the Honeycomb's Flow*, by Judah Messer Leon. *Renaissance Quarterly*, vol. 37, no. 2, 1984, pp. 234–38.

Watt, John. "Commentary and Translation in Syriac Aristotelian Scholarship: Sergius to Baghdad." *Journal for Late Antique Religion and Culture*, vol. 4, 2010, pp. 28–42.

A Rhetoric of Pen and Brush

Anne Ruggles Gere

> Angel DeCora [*published as* Mrs. William Dietz], "Native Indian Art," *Report of the Twenty-Sixth Annual Meeting of the Lake Mohonk Conference of the Friends of the Indian and Other Dependent Peoples*, edited by Lillian D. Power (Lake Mohonk Conference, 1908)

In 1908 Angel DeCora, a young Winnebago woman, spoke at the Lake Mohonk Conference of the Friends of the Indian and Other Dependent Peoples. Educated at Carlisle Indian School, where the English language supplanted her mother tongue, and at Smith College, Drexel University, and the Boston Art Museum, where she studied with leading artists, DeCora was an accomplished painter and an art instructor at Carlisle. As I demonstrate, she also proved to be an excellent rhetorician who used the strategy of transculturation along with the topoi of definition and justice to persuade her audience that Indigenous aesthetics deserved a place in American art. Given her audience, this move required both courage and skill.

Despite her rhetorical skills, DeCora's work remains largely unknown. This can be explained in part by the fact that she died young, at age forty-eight, and did not have time to become more widely visible. Furthermore, her argument about aesthetics, which eventually became widely accepted, was a new one that turn-of-the-century audiences were not ready to hear, especially not from an Indian woman at a time when Indigenous people were regularly described in deprecating terms. Like other women and men of color, DeCora has remained unknown because rhetoric and composition has been slow to embrace the rhetorics of minoritized populations. Since DeCora's claim was muffled by early death, lack of visibility, and, yes, racism, it was appropriated by others, notably Dorothy Dunn, a white woman, who published at least eighteen articles and a book about Indigenous art that advanced many of DeCora's theories but acknowledged DeCora in a single footnote (Dunn 233n65). Still, however, we can learn from DeCora's work as a rhetorician.

The Lake Mohonk Conference, where DeCora spoke in 1908, was one of several organizations founded in the late nineteenth century to address "the Indian problem," including the Boston Indian Citizenship Association (1879), the Indian Rights Association (1882), and the Women's National Indian Association (1879). Alfred K. Smiley, the owner of the Mohonk resort, convened the conference annually from 1883 until 1916. The "Indian reformers" who attended this conference included mostly white men either in or with close ties to US government agencies responsible for Indian affairs, and, occasionally, an Indian guest. As a group Mohonk conferees embraced principles that, in their view, would enhance the lives of Indigenous people by erasing their traditional identities and assimilating them into European American culture. For example, the resolutions they announced to the public in their 1884 proceedings included the following:

> 1st. Resolved, That the organization of the Indians in tribes is, and has been, one of the most serious hindrances to the advancement of the Indian toward civilization, and that every effort should be made to secure the disintegration of all tribal organizations; that to accomplish this result the Government should . . . cease to recognize the Indians as political bodies or organized tribes. (*Proceedings* 6)

> 4th. Resolved, That all adult male Indians should be admitted to the full privileges of citizenship by a process analogous to naturalization, upon evidence presented before the proper court of record of adequate intellectual and moral qualifications. (6)

> 6th. Resolved, That . . . our conviction has been strengthened as to the importance of taking Indian youth from the reservations to be trained in industrial schools placed among communities of white citizens. (13)

14th. Resolved, That immediate efforts should be made to place the Indian in the same position before the law as that held by the rest of the population. (21)

As these resolutions show, this group of privileged white men sought to strip Indigenous people of the social identities conferred by the languages, customs, and religions of their tribes, just as Indian boarding schools stripped their students of their clothing, cut their hair, and forbade them to speak their mother tongue. In return for erasing their identities and depriving them of their lifeways, these men offered the alternative of so-called industrial schools, where Indigenous people could be transformed into useful members of a lower class ready to serve people like those at Mohonk. Rather than offer full citizenship to any individual with no tribal affiliation, these men wanted to retain authority and impose their own "adequate intellectual and moral qualifications" by means of a "proper court of record" that could grant Indigenous persons full privileges of citizenship. And to ensure that Indigenous people would remain under control of white people, Mohonk conferees wanted them to be ruled by US legal institutions. Although the Mohonk group, like many other reformers, saw itself as an advocate for Indians at a time when US projects of genocide, warfare, and removal had reduced many Indigenous people to extreme poverty and deprivation, the group can be described as an example of what Walter Mignolo calls the "colonial matrix of power" (8). According to Mignolo, beginning in 1500, white, Christian, heteronormative men established control through normalization of their own theology and body politics, and from that time forward such men used coloniality to control the economy, authority, sexuality, and knowledge and subjectivity of Indigenous people (9).

This, then, was the audience that Angel DeCora, a shy woman who dreaded public speaking, was to address. She had spoken once before at the conference, in 1896, when she was still a student, and was being held up as a model for the sort of assimilated Indian whom the conferees hoped to engender. Born in Nebraska to a traditional Winnebago family, DeCora was either abducted or chose to undertake an adventure and arrived at the Hampton Institute in Virginia in 1883 when she was about fourteen. She proved to be an excellent student and received a scholarship to study in the art department at Smith College. On that first occasion at Mohonk, she was introduced as "an art student from Smith College" and began by thanking Smiley and his associates "for the kind resolutions that you have passed here with reference to my people" (qtd. in Waggoner 67). However, when DeCora spoke to the same group in 1908, she was less conciliatory. She explained the importance of reviving and respecting traditional Indian handicrafts and concluded, "The simple dignity of Indian design lends itself well to ways of conventional art, and I think the day has come when the American people must pause and give recognition to another phase of the Indian's nature, which is his art" (DeCora, "Native Indian Art" 18). This declaration, which she refined and repeated in multiple other contexts, eventually took this form: "There is no doubt that the young Indian has a talent for the pictorial art, the Indian's artistic conception is well worth recognition, and the school-trained Indians of Carlisle are developing it into possible use that it may become his contribution to American art" (DeCora, "Angel DeCora" 284). The three claims embedded in this sentence appeared in speeches she gave to the National Education Association, the Society of American Indians, and Quebec's International Congress of Americanists and in a 1911 edition of *The Red Man*, a newspaper published at Carlisle Indian Industrial School (DeCora, "Angel DeCora" 284). In this essay I examine the implications of each of these claims and then demonstrate how DeCora's rhetorical skills as a writer and artist contributed to Indian education and a more inclusive view of American art.

The first of DeCora's claims, that "the young Indian has a talent for the pictorial art," or her assertion of "[t]he simple dignity of Indian design," is a rhetorical deployment of the strategy of transculturation, which Amanda Cobb describes as the process by which "subordinated or marginal groups select and invent from materials transmitted to them by a dominant or metropolitan culture" (120). As one who had moved extensively within white society, DeCora knew that reformers shared a stereotypical view of Indians as natural artists, as people in whom a sense for form and color was inborn. For this reason, she selected a view of Indians that would have been familiar to and uncontroversial for her audience. This claim also addressed the desire of Mohonk conferees to establish Indians as economically self-sufficient. Beginning in 1876, when the Fred Harvey Company began handling tourism in the Southwest for the Santa Fe Railroad, Indian art had become a desired commodity. Harvey hotels sold Indian art in their shops, arranged for Indian artists to perform weaving or jewelry making in train stations, and ran excursions to Indian communities where tourists could purchase artifacts from their makers. As Robert Fay Schrader notes, "[B]etween 1894 and 1904, the Harvey company's sale of Indian art increased 1000 percent" (6–7). Like those who attended the Mohonk conference, officials concerned with Indian education saw Indian art as a means of making Indians more economically independent. Willliam Hailmann, the superintendent of Indian schools from 1894 to 1898, argued for including Indigenous forms of art in the curriculum. His motives were economic rather than aesthetic, however. Students would, he claimed, learn "thrift and relationships between work and wages . . . [and] would want to spend most of their earnings on clothes and would thus save on those supplied free by the school" (Hewes 71). For the Mohonk audience, then, DeCora's first claim would have been viewed in highly favorable terms, and there would likely have been nods of agreement as she uttered these words.

Her second claim, that "the Indian's artistic conception is well worth recognition," used the topos of definition to move beyond seeing Indians as inherently artistic and assert that they, like European Americans, possessed aesthetics or concepts of art that merited attention. Having established an identification with her audience by beginning with a point of common agreement, she moved on to a somewhat more controversial position. For those who saw Indians as "dependent peoples," as suggested in the name of Lake Mohonk Conference, the concept of Indians as individuals with independent critical capacities capable of developing a concept of art different from that of European Americans would have seemed dubious. This seemingly radical view was reinforced by anthropologists at the time. While both amateur and professional anthropologists had collected Indian artifacts for a number of years, the emergence of museums like the Smithsonian (1846) and New York's Museum of Natural History (1869) had increased the rate of collection exponentially. But these collections were not sought by art museums because the projects of Indian artists were seen as having aesthetic value. Rather, they were a means of documenting an exotic culture, one that was presumed (and desired) to be rapidly disappearing as projects of assimilation, like those fostered by the Mohonk conference, gained greater influence and scope.

DeCora was not naive, neither rhetorically nor aesthetically, in making her claim for the aesthetic judgement of Indigenous people. Thanks to her extensive education and her association with other Indian leaders like Charles Eastman, a Sioux physician educated at Dartmouth College who regularly spoke and wrote on behalf of Indigenous people, she understood the rhetorical importance of creating identification with her audience before addressing negative stereotypes attached to her people. By beginning with a claim about the Indian's inherent artistic ability, in effect giving reformers' language back to them, she created a space for inventing a new identity for Indians. Rather than being seen as "dependent peoples," they could, her claim asserted, be seen as operating within an autonomous aesthetic, one not shaped by European American standards and values. DeCora also based her claim on her knowledge of the anthropological work of Franz Boas. In 1897 Boas had published "The Decorative Art of the Indians of the North Pacific Coast," an article that examined the techniques, strategies of representation, and multiple forms used by Indian artists. By focusing on issues like iconography, meaning, and abstraction, Boas demonstrated that these artistic productions were the result of something more than inherent ability. He showed that Indian artists had their own concepts of art that were not subordinate to but simply different from those of Western art. This article and Boas's subsequent publications, which argued for history rather than evolution in considering the meaning of art, provided a substantive scholarly basis for DeCora's claims about the value of recognizing Indians' concepts of art. She not only knew Boas's work but also shared it with her students at Carlisle, so she stood on firm rhetorical and intellectual ground in asserting conceptual independence for Indian artists.

DeCora's third claim, that "school-trained Indians . . . are developing it [Indian concepts of art] into possible use that it may become his contribution to American art," employed the topos of justice to assert that Indigenous artists should be recognized as American artists. Here she challenged the cultural enterprise of American art—its artists, its collectors, its critics, its museums—to incorporate the aesthetic views and artistic products of Indigenous people into a more inclusive whole. DeCora had been invited to speak as a product of the Lake Mohonk Conference's assimilationist policies, but she spoke to a larger goal of American art more broadly: to develop an art that declared its independence from European models. Given her long and broad study of American art, DeCora would have been aware of this goal, so she was strategic in suggesting that Indian conceptions could contribute to the larger tradition of American art. Furthermore, DeCora spoke knowingly to another American anxiety: worries about growing commercialization and the increasing presence of technology in the United States. One manifestation of this anxiety was the US appropriation of the craft revival that emerged in England during the middle of the nineteenth century. Termed the arts and crafts movement in the United States, the prizing of handcrafted objects, simplicity in design, and a less complicated lifestyle all suggested an opening for rethinking the status of Indian art. Another manifestation of the anxiety about technology and commercialization appeared in the very positive response to the display of art produced by Indigenous women in the Women's Building of the 1883 World's Columbian Exposition in Chicago. The simplicity of design brought praise because it fit well into the aesthetic of the arts and crafts movement. This exhibit was held just two years after the massacre at Wounded Knee, where nearly three hundred Lakota men, women, and children were slaughtered by US Army soldiers, a horrific reminder of the extended warfare between Indigenous people and European Americans. In addition to challenging her audience to think more inclusively, DeCora offered Indian art as a means of creating a uniquely American art, and she portrayed art as a less lethal form of interaction between Indigenous people and the Europeans who had taken up residence on their continent.

DeCora took the position at Carlisle in 1905 with the explicit intention of fostering the development of Indian artists who could contribute to American art, as she had already begun to do. When she left her studies with Howard Pyle, an instructor at the Drexel Institute of Art, she explained that students copy their teachers, and "I am an Indian and don't want to draw just like a white man" (qtd. in Curtis, "American Indian Artist" 64). When Francis Leupp, Commissioner of Indian Affairs, proposed that she join the Carlisle faculty to foster the native talents of Indian students at Carlisle, she declared, "I shall not be expected to teach in the white man's way, but shall be given complete liberty to develop the art of my own race and to apply this, as far as possible, to various forms of art industries and crafts" (qtd. in Curtis, "American Indian Artist" 65). And DeCora did exactly that, changing a curriculum based on "designs of borders and surface patterns; light and shade; objects in natural science; illustrations; space divisions" (*Catalog* [1902]) into one that asserted the following: "One of the aims in teaching drawing to Indians is to standardize, perpetuate, and give to the world at large the priceless decorative designs peculiar to the race" (*Catalog* [1915]). She supplemented her art education with summer visits to Indian tribes, where she studied the designs women produced; with careful examination of reports from the Bureau of American Ethnology that included descriptions of designs created by various tribal groups; and with artifacts she borrowed from the Bureau of Indian Affairs. Many of DeCora's students went on to further training in art and then on to careers that extended her ideas about Indian art into exhibits, publications, and an expanded market for Indian art.

From her earliest productions, DeCora's brush enhanced and illustrated her speeches and writing about Indian art. In 1899 four of her illustrations appeared along with two of her short stories in *Harper's Monthly*. These stories, both of which take place in traditional domestic Indian settings, were accompanied by images that displayed Indian art and life experiences. "The Sick Child," a daughter's first-person account of the illness and death of her baby sister, features an abstract image of the narrator and an image of a medicine man framed by the sky. The third image includes five female figures and an array of weaving, baskets, pottery, jewelry, leather work, and a decorative cradle board, all positioned at or near the center of the image, illustrating the many forms Indian art takes. "Gray Wolf's Daughter," a story about a daughter's last day at home before going to a distant boarding school, includes an image of a ceremonial dance and the daughter examining her many beads. In both, ceremonial regalia is displayed as art and as objects of reflection.

Only a small portion of DeCora's presumably many paintings and illustrations have been found, but the body of work available demonstrates her rhetorical skill with brush as well as pen. As an illustrator of books on the Indian experience, she drew on traditional resources. For example, in her illustrations for Zitkala-Sa's *Old Indian Legends*, she created characters making various gestures, raising an arm, folding their hands, or bowing. These gestures mirror traditional Indian pictographs, a form that DeCora described as "symbolic records" that Indians developed "into a system of designing, drawing [their] inspiration from the whole breadth of [their] native land" (*Report* 84). She saw the pictograph as a vital and malleable form that could retain its traditional validity and still be legible to European Americans. In addition to illustrations, DeCora produced book covers for books dealing with Indian topics, including those by Francis La Flesche, Zitkala-Sa, Mary Catherine Judd, Elaine Goodale Eastman, and Natalie Curtis. Nearly all her book covers employed geometric designs, each one featuring a slightly more intricate design than the previous. In commenting on her work in design, DeCora noted that while she had done some design work as a student, "I had never taken any special interest in that branch of art. Perhaps it was well that I had not over studied the prescribed methods of European decoration, for then my aboriginal qualities could never have asserted themselves" ("Angel DeCora" 285).

DeCora's most significant design contribution appeared in Curtis's *The Indians' Book*, where she developed unique lettering that employed shapes and motifs used by artists of specific tribes along with visual images that provided insight into the lifestyle and values of that tribe in order to create introductions to the twenty tribes included in the book. In so doing she engaged with but resisted the alphabet of the dominant culture by transforming it to portray Native American culture, thereby proving that Indians have artistic talent that is worthy of recognition and that they can contribute to American art. Her untimely death in the pandemic of 1918 silenced her voice and stilled her brush, but the lost text of DeCora's speech demonstrates how marginalized people can employ rhetoric to insist on their own value.

Works Cited

Boas, Franz. "The Decorative Art of the Indians of the North Pacific Coast." *Bulletin of the American Museum of Natural History*, vol. 9, no. 10, 1897, pp. 123–76.

Catalog. Carlisle Indian Industrial School, 1902.

Catalog. Carlisle Indian Industrial School, 1915.

Cobb, Amanda. *Listening to Our Grandmothers' Stories: The Bloomfield Academy for Chickasaw Females, 1852–1949*. U of Nebraska P, 2000.

Curtis, Natalie. "An American Indian Artist." *Outlook*, 14 Jan. 1920, pp. 64–65.

———, editor. *The Indians' Book: Authentic Native American Legends, Lore and Music*. 1907. Reprint ed., Crown, 1987.

DeCora, Angel. "Angel DeCora—An Autobiography." *The Red Man by Red Men*, Mar. 1911, pp. 279–85.

DeCora, Angel [*published as* Henook-Makhewe-Kelenaka]. "Gray Wolf's Daughter." *Harper's New Monthly Magazine*, vol. 101, no. 606, Nov. 1899, pp. 860–62.

———. "The Sick Child." *Harper's New Monthly Magazine*, vol. 98, no. 464, Feb. 1899, pp. 446–48.

DeCora, Angel [*published as* Mrs. William Dietz]. "Native Indian Art." *Report of the Twenty-Sixth Annual Meeting of the Lake Mohonk Conference of the Friends of the Indian and Other Dependent Peoples*, edited by Lillian D. Power, Lake Mohonk Conference, 1908, pp. 16–18.

Dunn, Dorothy. *American Indian Painting of the Southwest and Plains Areas*. U of New Mexico P, 1968.

Hewes, Dorothy W. "Those First Good Years of Indian Education: 1894–1898." *American Indian Culture and Research Journal*, vol. 5, no. 2, 1981, pp. 63–82.

Mignolo, Walter. *The Darker Side of Western Modernity: Global Futures, Decolonial Options*. Duke UP, 2011.

Proceedings of the Second Annual Meeting of the Lake Mohonk Conference of the Friends of the Indian and Other Dependent Peoples. Lake Mohonk Conference, 1884.

Report of the Executive on the Proceedings of the First Annual Conference of the Society of American Indians Held at the University of Ohio, Columbus, Ohio. Society of American Indians, 12–17 Oct. 1911.

Schrader, Robert Fay. *The Indian Arts and Crafts Board: An Aspect of New Deal Indian Policy*. U of New Mexico P, 1983.

Waggoner, Linda M. *Fire Light: The Life of Angel DeCora, Winnebago Artist*. Oklahoma UP, 2008.

Zitkala-Sa. *Old Indian Legends*. Ginn, 1901.

Understanding *English Composition as a Social Problem*: Finding Sterling Andrus Leonard in Rhetoric and Composition

Morris Young

> Sterling Andrus Leonard, *English Composition as a Social Problem* (Houghton Mifflin, 1917)

Published in 1917, *English Composition as a Social Problem*, by Sterling Andrus Leonard, provides a compelling and provocative framework for understanding writing as a social practice in ways that anticipate the social turn that we see in modern composition studies (Trimbur; Rhodes and Alexander). Informed by John Dewey's work to democratize education, Leonard explores the teaching of composition in primary education during a period of increased immigration and growing American nativism. Here composition is not posed as a "social problem" in the sense of a "literacy crisis" (Fleming 33) but is situated as a practice that connects students more directly to their learning, promotes students' understanding of their social world, and functions as a means for action. Thus, English composition engages the "social problem" to explore what students are seeing in their daily lives rather than pursuing theme writing organized around abstractions or ideals that may be too distant or disconnected to produce meaningful texts. Leonard anticipates and theorizes a range of practices that are part of everyday teaching in modern composition studies, among them the use of real-life experiences as the sources for composition projects, the theorization of groups as part of the composition process, the "prevision of ideas" as the opportunity for invention and organization (68), and a consideration of "expressional standards" in the context of language use rather than simply as an application of rules (114).

Who was Sterling Andrus Leonard, someone seemingly ahead of his time and positioned to be among the leading composition and rhetoric scholars of the time? And why has *English Composition as a Social Problem* been forgotten? I first encountered Leonard when I reviewed *Traditions of Inquiry*, edited by John Brereton, for my Research in Composition Studies seminar, which I took as a student with Anne Ruggles Gere at the University of Michigan. Initially, I was intrigued by the essay on Fred Newton Scott, professor of rhetoric at the University of Michigan in the early twentieth century, because I wanted to learn more about the University of Michigan's place in the history of the discipline, but the essay on Leonard stayed with me because of the tragic and sensational circumstances of his death, drowning at just forty-three in 1931 while boating with I. A. Richards on Lake Mendota on the University of Wisconsin campus (Brereton, "Sterling Andrus Leonard"). Later, as a new faculty member at the University of Wisconsin, Madison, I wanted to learn more about the University of Wisconsin's place in the discipline.

What I learned about the University of Wisconsin revealed to me contributions to composition and rhetoric in the early part of the twentieth century that were elided as English studies more broadly and the Department of English at the University of Wisconsin specifically turned toward literary studies for much of the rest of the century until scholars like Deborah Brandt, Brad Hughes, and Martin Nystrand began in the 1980s and 1990s to bring attention back to writing at the university. David Fleming's institutional history about the university's composition requirement, *From Form to Meaning: Freshman Composition and the Long Sixties, 1957–1974*, not only provides a deeply nuanced story about institutional politics and the teaching of composition in the long sixties but also describes the university's innovations in the early twentieth century, among them eight composition books written between 1907 and 1915 by seven different faculty members, including Frances Campbell Berkeley, Edwin Woolley, Frederick A. Manchester, Karl Young, and Warner Taylor (Fleming 35–36; Brereton, *Origins* 133). However, Leonard is not to be found in Fleming's history, and the essay by Brereton ("Sterling Andrus Leonard"), a *College English* article by Greg Myers, and brief mentions of Leonard in relation to Fred Newton Scott are about the extent of the attention he receives in any scholarly work.

What we do know about Leonard is evident in his scholarly biography and his own research. Leonard completed a BA (1908) and MA (1909) at the University of Michigan, where he worked with Fred Newton Scott

(Stewart 541). He subsequently held teaching appointments at the University of Michigan, Milwaukee Normal School, and the Horace Mann School before being appointed as assistant professor of English at the University of Wisconsin in 1920 and then promoted to associate professor in the teaching of English in 1925. He received his doctorate from Columbia University in 1927 and served as NCTE president in 1926 (Brereton, "Sterling Andrus Leonard" 81–82). Despite his training, publications, and academic positions, Leonard has been largely forgotten in composition and rhetoric (Myers 154; Brereton, "Sterling Andrus Leonard" 81). This may be due in part to his untimely death, but his contributions to the field may have been overlooked because his theories of composition emerged primarily in the context of elementary and secondary education. This was not unusual for educational reformers of the time, including those trained under Fred Newton Scott (Gere 27). According to Brereton, Leonard's career consisted of two distinct phases, the first from 1915 to 1926, when he published often in NCTE's *The English Journal* on a range of pedagogical issues, including the teaching of writing ("Sterling Andrus Leonard" 81). This was followed by work informed by his doctoral dissertation that focused primarily on English language and resulted in the influential studies *The Doctrine of Correctness in English Usage* (1929) and *Current English Usage* (1932), completed by an NCTE committee and published by NCTE after his death (82). Despite these achievements, Leonard's scholarly contributions to composition and rhetoric have not been explored deeply beyond Brereton and Meyers.

In 2007, as I planned my first graduate seminar at the University of Wisconsin, I recalled the story about Leonard and tracked down a copy of *English Composition as a Social Problem* in the university's Memorial Library. Typical of the handbooks and textbooks of the time in its 4½" x 7" format, it had a provocative modern title that reminded me of *English Composition as a Happening*, by Geoffrey Sirc (though Sirc does not reference Leonard). As I began to leaf through its pages, I was unsure what to make of it, primarily because it focused on elementary-level students but also because of the time when it was written, when books like Leonard's might easily have been dismissed as "current-traditional rhetoric" (Carr et al. 208). Initially, the contents did not seem to deliver on the promise of the title, but as I read and became accustomed to the language, I saw the concepts and practices that we take for granted today—student-centered instruction, writing groups, project-based curricula—as thoroughly situated within the social turn. At the time, however, these were seen as a radical reimagining of teaching and learning in traditional classrooms. As David Gold argues, we are "wary of agonistic or prescriptivist language instruction" that might lead us to ignore "the potential value of such instruction for empowering students as rhetors and inspiring civic participation" (2). I had to look past language for practice and theory.

Published when Leonard was a teacher at the Horace Mann School, *English Composition as a Social Problem* is a study that "attempts a review of current practice in the teaching of English Composition in the light of present theories of education" (xi). Acknowledging a great debt to Professor John Dewey, "who has stated with most helpful cogency the ideals of education as a social problem," and to "Professors [George R.] Carpenter, [Franklin] Baker, and [Fred Newton] Scott" for their "basic study of the Teaching of English" (xii), Leonard believed the social provided the grounding for his pedagogical theories and practice, identifying three main points as the principal suggestions of his text:

> The first is the ideal of social teaching of composition; the English class is here presented as a group of good-spirited cooperators and critics working upon real projects. The second is the attempted handling of organization problems as we may suppose that children's minds will work best in mastering them. The third is the apparently fundamental distinction between matters essential for fixation in *unconscious* habit, on the one hand, and equally essential expressional powers, on the other, to be developed through *conscious* application of composition principles. (xi–xii)

The editor's introduction, by Henry Suzzalo, recognizes the novelty of Leonard's approach and reinforces the idea and value of composition as a social practice (ix), and reviews were quick to point out the pedagogical innovation. W. Wilbur Hatfield praises Leonard in particular for his concept of "prevision," which he develops through repeated illustrations to show that this is "not mere outlining but genuine planning beforehand—real preparation for writing or speaking" (432). A review in *The Journal of Education* concluded, "If there is any well-defined purpose for all composition writing it is that the writer should have something that he wants to write about, and ability to write about it so that others will care to know what he writes because of the way he writes about it. This is merely saying in our own way what is admirably and elaborately said in 'English Composition as a Social Problem'" (Review).

English Composition as a Social Problem provides a foundational concept about composing in each of its four chapters, offering genealogical glimpses of modern composition theories and practices. In chapter 1, "The Sources of Composition Projects in Child Activities" (1–34), Leonard begins with an exposition on the need for children to not merely engage in the "repetition of phrases" or to work with ideas that "we have determined . . . [they] should have and have assigned [them]," maintaining that "our composition materials have again and again been hopelessly abstract and futile" (2–3). Instead, Leonard argues, "good subjects" must come from "vital realized experiences of the child's own and naturally call for verbal expression" (6). To do this, children learn to understand the subject matter and its relationship to personal lived experience, credit their ideas to source materials and analyze these ideas critically, and, finally, adapt the expression of these ideas to a new audience to secure the reality of those expressions for that audience (9–15). What we see here is an emerging rhetorical approach to composing that also engages students in practices of modern composition pedagogy such as analysis, information literacy, and rhetorical appeals as determined by purposes and audience.

Leonard also identifies three types of "motives"—the "story-teller," the "teacher," and the "community worker" (16)—that serve as rhetorical exigencies and ethical positions for the student. The "story-teller motive" holds "tremendous potentiality in the composition class" because it not only "stirs up an eager desire to transfer [the student's] experiences and . . . fancies into just as real ideas for [their] classmates" (17) but also provides "the direction to socially useful ends of the ideas thus aroused" (21). While the "teacher motive" may seem to reduce composition to simple explanation, for Leonard this provides opportunities for students to "do their own interpreting and perform the functions of critic and teacher for one another, a healthy stimulation of the spirit of research is induced that should carry young people deep enough into any difficulty" (25). Finally, the "community-worker" motive is informed by "observation, discussions, and activities that center around *group* or *neighborhood needs*" (26). English composition becomes a tool for the community worker—

the student who assumes this ethos—to transform the "thinking of the children and their powers of expression to meet actual social problems" (28). What Leonard theorizes in 1917 anticipates what Michelle Eodice, Ann Ellen Geller, and Neal Lerner confirm nearly a hundred years later in their empirical study, *The Meaningful Writing Project*, where they describe "meaningful writing projects" as "opportunities for agency; for engagement with instructors, peers, and materials; and for learning that connects to previous experiences and passions and to future aspirations and identities" (4).

Perhaps Leonard's most obvious contribution to composition and rhetoric is his theorization of peer workshops, a common practice in today's college composition course that Anne Ruggles Gere has traced to literary societies and college courses in the late nineteenth and early twentieth century (10–17). In chapter 2, "The Social Group as an Agent of Expressional Development" (35–67), Leonard offers a detailed theorization of group work, identifying three processes: thorough preliminary group discussion; class criticism; and criticism of written work. Building on the idea of conversation—the "freedom of expression and interchange of experience"—and anticipating Kenneth Bruffee's concept of collaborative learning, Leonard's first step is to use the group for "organized theme work, class discussion of the project and of serviceable ways and means" (44) where students engage in conversations "guided by their enthusiastic suggestions of what they each will talk about" (45). Next, students present their compositions to the class, and peers not only provide feedback about description, detail, and organization but also commend "whatever is well expressed,—of fineness or clearness or vigor of presentation, and pleasing form and manner,—just as in discussing ideas and their organization" (54). Leonard discourages the "random, fowl-like pecking at small verbal infelicities" and centers the feedback of students who will learn to "think out reasons for their own judgments by [being asked] to tell always why they commend one way or suggest another, and to answer and discuss such opinions freely" (50). The final step is "organized study to raise the class standards of thought and expression" (64). Interestingly, Leonard does not give much description of this stage, and in part it seems to serve as the final revision process for student compositions, perhaps an acknowledgment that the substantive work has occurred in earlier conversations and group interactions. One final point to make about Leonard's description of group work is his decentering of the teacher in the classroom, the teacher being someone who is "at best one of the group and a good-spirited helper" and can make themself "less prominent and schoolmasterish by sitting at the back of the room, perhaps having one of the class as chairman to call the speakers and keep order" (48). Leonard's goal was to promote the democratic space of the class and to allow students to be "free to make evaluation of one another's work themselves" and without the judgment of adults who would be biased by their own expectations and "mature standards" (48).

In chapter 3, "The Organization of Ideas" (68–113), Leonard conceptualizes "previsioning," a process that functions similarly to prewriting or freewriting in helping students generate and sort through ideas and begin the work of narrowing and focusing topics in planning a draft. Leonard walks the reader through several initial steps to previsioning, beginning with a listing activity to be "worked out on the blackboard by the whole class" (71), followed by a sorting process to select the ideas that will become the subjects of students' compositions (72), and then to some preliminary organization or planning of the composition where students identify important details or actions, describe complex activities or ideas, and put forward interpretations about their topics. Proposing "arrangement and connection of material" as another step in the organization of ideas, Leonard takes a decidedly rhetorical approach, suggesting that "real composition is a matter of always adapting materials of one's own experience to the comprehension of someone else" (90). Thus, he recommends that related ideas be kept together and then arranged using one of four principles: time order; emphasis of key ideas, actions, or details; putting basics first; and sense impressions or the outline of a scene (91). While these steps may sound prescriptive, Leonard cautions the reader against the imposition of strict guidelines or forms and again emphasizes experimentation, criticism, and discussion, arguing that "organization power is here presented as a matter of increasing skill in dealing with every sort of problem in real expression" (113).

Leonard saves his instruction on usage and language conventions for chapter 4, "Evolution and Attainment of Expressional Standards" (114–93). In this sense, he has reversed what might be expected for the era, especially in language arts education at the elementary level, by focusing first on the social contexts for expressions and composition and ending with what some might consider the basics of language learning in grammar, punctuation, and spelling and pronunciation (116–17). Leonard touches on style and taste but takes a progressive view on the way language standards are used to mark social value: "Certainly we desire that children's talk and writing should always be couched in reasonably acceptable forms; it should be decent in tone and be socially pleasing; but it should not be judged by a standard that is ideal in so many respects that it is unattainable in any" (132–33). This somewhat agnostic and pragmatic view of language should not be a surprise given Leonard's focus on the social group as a site of cooperation and commendation. In this view language and its use in composition are living processes of the social group of students, to be invented, negotiated, and shared. His goal of "expressional standards" is not meant to serve as a form of gatekeeping but rather as an aspiration to achieve "expressional power" (193).

So, what have I found in Sterling Andrus Leonard and *English Composition as a Social Problem*? In part, I have come to appreciate the early influences of University of Wisconsin, Madison, faculty members and their contributions to the history of composition and rhetoric, but Leonard continues to be an absent presence (and a mystery) in this history. We have evidence of his contributions to English education and to English language studies and have begun to draw this connection to composition and rhetoric, but the person himself seems to be lost. However, in *English Composition as a Social Problem* I have found a text that reminds us of the pedagogical kinship between composition and English education and that reconnects the field of composition to Dewey's theories of democratic education. *English Composition as a Social Problem* is a unique and pivotal text in which we see a capacious understanding of writing as a social practice that offered students at the earliest levels the opportunity to connect the formal curriculum of schooling to their extracurricular lives. At the same time, it documents the provocative and forward-looking ideas of a teacher and scholar who in the early 1900s began to articulate many of the theories and practices that have since become commonplace in the teaching of writing and serves as an origin point for a field that continues to understand English composition as a social problem.

Works Cited

Brereton, John C., editor. *The Origins of Composition Studies in the American College, 1875–1925: A Documentary History*. U of Pittsburgh P, 1995.

———. "Sterling Andrus Leonard." *Traditions of Inquiry*, edited by John Brereton, Oxford UP, 1985, pp. 81–104.

Bruffee, Kenneth A. "Collaborative Learning and the 'Conversation of Mankind.'" *College English*, vol. 46, no. 7, Nov. 1984, pp. 635–52.

Carr, Jean Ferguson, et al. *Archives of Instruction: Nineteenth-Century Rhetorics, Readers, and Composition Books in the United States*. Southern Illinois UP, 2005.

Eodice, Michelle, et al. *The Meaningful Writing Project: Learning, Teaching, and Writing in Higher Education*. Utah State UP, 2016.

Fleming, David. *From Form to Meaning: Freshman Composition and the Long Sixties, 1957–1974*. U of Pittsburgh P, 2011.

Gere, Anne Ruggles. *Writing Groups: History, Theory, and Implications*. Southern Illinois UP, 1987.

Gold, David. *Rhetoric at the Margins: Revising the History of Writing Instruction in American Colleges, 1873–1947*. Southern Illinois UP, 2008.

Hatfield, W. Wilbur. "The Point of View." *The English Journal*, vol. 6, no. 6, June 1917, pp. 431–32.

Leonard, Sterling Andrus. *English Composition as a Social Problem*. Houghton Mifflin, 1917.

Myers, Greg. "Reality, Consensus, and Reform in the Rhetoric of Composition Teaching." *College English*, vol. 48, no. 2, Feb. 1986, pp. 154–74.

Review of *English Composition as a Social Problem*, by Sterling Andrus Leonard. *The Journal of Education*, vol. 85, no. 9, Mar. 1917, p. 246.

Rhodes, Jacqueline, and Jonathan Alexander. "Reimagining the Social Turn: New Work from the Field." *College English*, vol. 76, no. 6, 2014, pp. 481–87.

Sirc, Geoffrey M. *English Composition as a Happening*. Utah State UP, 2002.

Stewart, Donald C. "Rediscovering Fred Newton Scott." *College English*, vol. 40, no. 5, Jan. 1979, pp. 539–47.

Trimbur, John. "Taking the Social Turn: Teaching Writing Post-Process." *College Composition and Communication*, vol. 45, no. 1, 1994, pp. 108–18.

Rodolphe Töpffer and the Histories of Rhetoric

Sergio C. Figueiredo

> Rodolphe Töpffer, *Réflexions et menus propos d'un peintre genevois; ou, Essai sur le beau dans les arts* (J. J. Dubochet, Lechevalier et Cie, 1848, 2 vols.)

I first came across Rodolphe Töpffer in 2006, when I read Scott McCloud's *Understanding Comics* in preparation for my MA comprehensive exams at Marshall University, and then again in 2008 when rereading the book for a cultural research methods course in Clemson University's PhD program in rhetorics, communication, and information. These first two references yielded little more than a passing recognition of Töpffer's iconic status as the "father of the modern comic strip . . . whose light satiric picture stories, starting in the mid-1800s, employed cartooning and panel borders, and featured the first interdependent combination of words and pictures seen in Europe" (McCloud 17). Even while working on my dissertation, which examined the potential of comics to support composition students in learning the role of visual and media rhetorics in the era of electracy,[1] I paid little attention to Töpffer.

My interest in Töpffer began in 2013 as I explored the possibility of revising my 2011 dissertation into a monograph and came across David Kunzle's biography of Töpffer, *Father of the Comic Strip: Rodolphe Töpffer*, and Kunzle's compendium of Töpffer's published and unpublished graphic works, *Rodolphe Töpffer: The Complete Comic Strips*. In a brief chronology at the beginning of *Rodolphe Töpffer*, Kunzle notes that Töpffer served as a lecturer of French literature at the Academy of Geneva (xiv); similarly, the French literary scholar Philippe Willems notes that Töpffer was offered an appointment equivalent to an assistant professor position in the academy's Department of Rhétorique et Belles-Lettres (227), a department he would chair from 1842 until his death in 1846.

As I considered his role as a scholar, I wanted to know if Töpffer had published works other than graphic novels and quickly discovered that Töpffer's publication record included scripts for stage plays, novels, short stories, travel journals, critical essays, and correspondences. However, other than Ellen Wiese's out-of-print translation of Töpffer's *Essai de physiognomonie* (*Essay on Physiognomy*), none of Töpffer's works had been made available in English. While translating two of Töpffer's essays for a book project I thought would be a starting point for a monograph, I was able to find open access copies of two dozen or so of Töpffer's publications. Perhaps the most important text I discovered was Töpffer's posthumously published monograph, *Réflexions et menus propos d'un peintre genevois; ou, Essai sur le beau dans les arts* (*Reflections and Short Remarks of a Geneva Painter; or, Essay on the Beautiful in the Arts*; 1858), in which he self-identifies as a "professor of rhetoric" ("professeur de rhétorique"; 283) and theorizes how the fine and liberal arts can best perform their function of promoting new ethical values for a society experiencing massive social transformation due to European industrialization.

Among scholars and artists working with comic books and with graphic storytelling more generally, Töpffer is a central figure in visual storytelling. However, scholars of rhetoric seem to have paid little attention to Töpffer throughout the twentieth and twenty-first centuries, perhaps because of a sense that nineteenth-century rhetorical theory and pedagogy remained focused on the literacy needs of an emerging commercial and industrial European society. However, recovering Töpffer's work has significant implications for contemporary work in visual rhetoric and for how scholars in the field think about the historical role of new and emerging media in the development of nineteenth-century rhetoric. For instance, rather than situating the development of the subfield of visual rhetoric in the last quarter of the twentieth century, recognizing Töpffer's work as an early foray into rhetorics of visual and other sensory media offers opportunities for exploring a more robust understanding of nineteenth-century rhetorics beyond the verbal and linguistic as well as the role of invention during that century.

While there is still much to learn about Töpffer's role in the histories of rhetorics,[2] this essay focuses on the value and significance of recognizing Töpffer as a key figure in the Western, Greco-Roman rhetorical tradition. In fact, it is this tradition that Töpffer aimed to engage with in order to transform rhetorical theory, practice, and pedagogy for the world he saw developing in the nineteenth century. Building on his predecessors in these histories of rhetorics, Töpffer's work on graphic novels aimed to adapt Cicero's work for an increasingly urban, industrial, and democratic Europe, using the popular media of the age to promote social and cultural values to communities with relatively low literacy rates and to teach students enrolled in his school how to use graphic storytelling to engage in public discourse.

Littérature en Estampes as an Act of Rhetorical Invention

Töpffer's primary and longest-lasting contribution to rhetorical studies is what many consider his invention of graphic novels. However, even Töpffer acknowledged that his work on graphic novels—*littérature en estampes* (literally, "literature in prints"), the term Töpffer uses to refer to graphic novels—was nothing new. In his 1845 book, *Essai de physiognomonie*, Töpffer identifies William Hogarth's eighteenth-century painterly triptychs as exemplars for his own graphic novels, the key difference being that Hogarth's works were intended for exhibition halls frequented by aristocrats, whereas Töpffer's graphic novels were meant to be read by a public without the means to attend art exhibitions. Still, Töpffer shared Hogarth's philosophy that art was a force for promoting social and cultural values. For Töpffer, the rhetorical value of graphic novels was in their potential to instruct a general public with little access to literacy while serving as an antidote to "morally vicious and deleterious" books by writers like George Sand, Honoré de Balzac, and Eugène Sue (Figueiredo 17).

Töpffer acknowledges that his contribution to the development of graphic novels resulted from two interrelated experiences. To understand the connection between these two experiences, it is worth noting that during his youth Töpffer had not intended to pursue a career as a teacher or scholar. His ambition had been to follow in his father's footsteps and become a professional artist in portraiture and caricature. Having lived among the aristocratic classes of his time, he apprenticed with his father and progressed in his artistic skill and technique, eventually earning an opportunity to continue his apprenticeship in Paris in 1819. He stayed in Paris through 1820, studying the fine arts, rhetoric, philosophy, theology, and other liberal arts while also participating in the social life of a city undergoing almost constant revolutions. After a mere nine months, he was diagnosed with a degenerative eye disease and decided to return home to Geneva. The two experiences that set Töpffer on the path to inventing graphic literature happened within three to five years of his return.

During the first two years, Töpffer pursued a career as a portraitist. In his 1830 essay, *Réflexions et menus propos d'un peintre genevois (Reflections and Short Remarks of a Geneva Painter)*, he details his experience working on commission for local aristocrats and his decision to abandon a career as a professional artist. Specifically, Töpffer offers a critique of the state of the arts in Europe, taking to task patrons who care only for purely representational art rather than an artistic practice grounded in producing works that reflect the aura an artist perceives in their subject. In addition, Töpffer critiques patrons for no longer paying artists a living wage. The first part of the essay ends with Töpffer's acknowledgment that pursuing a career as an artist will mostly likely lead him to an early grave and that his best option is to become a schoolteacher. The second half of the essay addresses his early experience as a teacher in a boarding school with a traditional curriculum focused on Greek and Latin. Töpffer describes his students as the children of families from the lower classes, mostly first-generation students pursuing a formal education in order to participate in the new industrial society that was reshaping life in Europe, students with little interest in a traditional curriculum designed for children of the upper classes. He recognizes, moreover, that students in his classes are bored with the learning experience created by traditional pedagogical methods and strategies, preferring instead to draw caricatures of Romans slaying Carthaginians or that mock a bourgeois professor (Figueiredo 167–71).

With the support of his father-in-law, Töpffer established his own boarding school after only two years in his first teaching position. His boarding school included a curriculum based on Ciceronian rhetoric and adapted to the needs of nineteenth-century European societies. In an 1836 essay, "Réflexions a propos d'un programme" ("Reflections on a Program"), Töpffer offers a clear picture of his modern pedagogical program, channeling book 3 of Cicero's *De Oratore* (*On the Orator*) and book 4 of Quintilian's *Institutio Oratoria* (*Institutes of Oratory*): "Hogarth . . . published various series of prints forming coherent narratives, still more remarkable for the thought he developed through them with such striking ability than for their material execution" ("Hogarth . . . publia diverses suites de gravures formant des drames complets, plus remarquables encore par la pensée qui s'y développe avec une frappante énergie, que par l'exécution matérielle des planches dont ils se composent"; qtd. in Wiese xv; "Réflexions" 1: 52). For "simple people,"[3] Töpffer continues,

> every statement misses its mark if it is not converted into some image, activity, and movement; if it does not appeal simultaneously to the senses, the imagination, and the heart. In the sermon of an impassioned missionary, it is not so much the meaning of his words that sways the watchful crowd, but rather the gestures, the emphasis, the expressive face of the orator: whatever can be seen, rather than what must be understood; what takes by shock, more than what works by persuasion or argument. Now then, the function of prints is precisely to synthesize these various features: to translate every statement into an image from life, all reasoning into a form that is animated, definite, clear. (qtd. in Wiese xv–xvi)

> toute proposition manque son but si elle ne se transforme en image, en action, en mouvement, si elle n'agit à la fois sur les sens, sur l'imagination et sur le cœur. Dans le discours d'un fougueux missionnaire, ce n'est pas tant le sens des paroles qui agit sur la foule attentive, ce sont bien plutôt les gestes, l'accent, la physionomie du harangueur: ce qui se voit plus que ce qui se comprend; ce qui frappe, plus que ce qui persuade ou éclaire. Or, c'est le propre des estampes, que de réunir à un haut degré ces diverses conditions d'action; que de réduire toute proposition en image vive; que de transformer tout raisonnement en spectacle animé, distinct, lumineux.
> ("Réflexions" 2: 315)

In many ways, Töpffer may be one of the earliest rhetorical scholars to seriously consider the role of the image in the public and deliberative discursive practices of industrial and postindustrial society. As

Wiese puts it, at first Töpffer intended for graphic novels to serve as "a record, fixed on paper, of the live act of oratory," having "taken to heart the classical authorities on rhetoric"; however, after more than a decade of working with and in the genre, he "assessed his graphic work soberly," finding it valuable for the "ability to give heightened impact to the force of a verbal message" (xvi). Over the course of the next and final decade of his life, Töpffer would continue to refine his theory of an image-based rhetorical practice influenced by the entirety of the fine and liberal arts, resulting in a posthumously published monograph, *Réflexions et menus propos d'un peintre genevois; ou, Essai sur le beau dans les arts* (*Reflections and Short Remarks of a Geneva Painter; or, Essay on the Beautiful in the Arts*).

Réflexions et menus propos d'un peintre genevois

Réflexions, as Töpffer describes it, addresses "the particular means which my art offers me" ("par les moyens particuliers que m'offre mon art"; *Réflexions* 5), a means designed to work on the senses, imagination, and affections of the reader and viewer. The "art" Töpffer refers to is the comic strip and the graphic novel, an art that he understood as having been made possible by advances in industrial production and scientific discovery and informed principally by the histories of rhetoric and subsequently by the other liberal and fine arts. A quick skim of the 1858 edition of the French manuscript reveals Töpffer working in an interdisciplinary manner, building connections among concepts and methods in major historical and contemporary works from fields as wide-ranging as rhetoric, poetry, literature, music, theater, philosophy, drawing, painting, sculpture, and architecture. The manuscript develops the rhetorical foundations for the art of graphic storytelling, building on Cicero's theoretical and practical approach to deliberative rhetoric and to creatively address the senses and evoke affective responses in audiences—usually by means of laughter and joy.

To understand the scope and significance of Töpffer's monograph, however, it is important to understand the scholarly and public conversations that ground his theoretical views about the value and significance of graphic storytelling. In "Réflexions a propos d'un programme," Töpffer claims that the arts are the expression of society and that "it is apparently because of this that they currently have no expression" ("c'est apparemmentà cause de cela qu'ils n'ont pour l'heure aucune expression"), since, as he claims, contemporary art relies on "skepticism [and criticism] as a principle of art, undermining the foundations of public morality" ("leur ouvre, et leur succès même n'est pas la moindre atteinte portée à cette morale publique"; 1: 44). Töpffer's critique is likely a result of an affiliation he claims in a letter to a colleague, in which he refers to himself as a "comrade" of the "avant-garde" ("nos camarades de l'avant-garde"; Pitteloud 220; see also Töpffer, *Correspondance complète* 323n55). While there is little evidence about precisely when Töpffer came across the term *avant-garde*, it is likely that he began associating with the avant-garde as a young man in Paris, where he travelled in circles with social theorists and revolutionaries associated with Henri de Saint-Simon's work on designing a new model of social organization for an industrialized Europe.

In Saint-Simon's model, all of European society would be reorganized to support the transition from an agrarian economy to an industrial economy.[4] The model itself consists of three primary social institutions—industry, the sciences, and the arts—each of which has equal responsibility for promoting, supporting, and maintaining a productive and just society. Although each institution shared equal responsibility in Saint-Simon's proposed social structure, each would have its own area of responsibility. The arts would serve as the front lines—the avant-garde—of this society, taking responsibility for promoting new social and cultural values[5] that would increase individual and collective equity by using the popular arts to influence public opinion; the sciences consisted of the savants (scholars), people adept in the systematic (scholarly) study of natural and cultural phenomena, responsible for inventing new methods and technologies that supported the social and cultural values promoted by the arts; finally, industry would be responsible for the production and sale of the products developed by the sciences and supported by the arts. The arts, in this model, would fulfill their institutional mission by popularizing "new ideas among the people" ("idées neuves parmi les hommes") through the popular media of the era—sculpture, painting, poetry, music, literature, theater, architecture, and so on (Saint-Simon, "L'artiste" 341–42). Perhaps the most interesting part of Saint-Simon's social model has to do with the art that would build, organize, and lead the avant-garde (social institution): eloquence (rhetoric), what Saint-

Simon calls "the first of the arts" ("New Christianity" 103). Why rhetoric? Because its function is to establish the "common impulse and general idea" ("une impulsion commune et une idée générale") that Saint-Simon believed would be essential to organizing and exercising the power of the arts and their ability to fulfill their institutional mission as the avant-garde of industrial societies ("L'artiste" 342).

When compared with Saint-Simon's avant-garde, *Réflexions* clearly has the same goal: to articulate a comprehensive and cohesive theory of the arts as a social institution dedicated to supporting and promoting an increasingly just and equitable society across Europe. As Töpffer puts it, the work of *Réflexions* is to explain that "the beauty of art proceeds absolutely and solely from human thought freed from any other servitude than that of manifesting itself through the representation of natural objects" ("Le beau de l'art procède absolument et uniquement de la pensée humaine affranchie de toute autre servitude que celle de se manifester par la représentation des objets naturels"), with the understanding that representations will "vary perpetually with the times, with nations, with schools, with individuals" ("ils varient au con traire perpétuellement avec les époques, avec les nations, avec les écoles, avec les individus"; *Réflexions* 283), and to rehabilitate the contemporary view of the arts as tools used to "justify or excuse wrongdoings or moral scandals" ("pour faire sa pâture et son profit des sophismes qui justifient ou excusent les écarts de conduite ou le scandale des mœurs"; "Réflexions" 1: 45). Indeed, even Töpffer's *Essai de physiognomonie*, a handbook on the rhetorical and practical elements of composing *littérature en estampes*, challenged the popular view that phrenology could determine the intellectual capacities of an individual or group.[6]

Today, Töpffer is considered a central figure in the history of graphic storytelling and comics studies, often going unacknowledged for his work as a scholar and professor of rhetoric despite following in and building on the traditions of Western, Greco-Roman rhetoric. However, Töpffer saw his graphic novels as an outgrowth of his interest in rhetorical theory and the value and significance of the arts in promoting social equity. In addition, Töpffer's graphic novels represent an attempt to develop a modern rhetorical theory and practice derived from and supplementing traditional oral and literate rhetorics that prefigure twentieth-century theories of visual, digital, and multimodal rhetorics. Töpffer's work in the nineteenth century most clearly resonates with Gregory Ulmer's theory of electracy, "an image metaphysics within which the politics, ethics, and aesthetics of an Internet public sphere might thrive," devised as "a practice that does for new media what narrative did for orality and argument for literacy." That Töpffer's work also focused on countering repressive, exploitative, and unjust rhetorical speech acts is a testament to his affiliation with historical figures like Cicero and Quintilian and with contemporaries who sought to offer marginalized and disenfranchised peoples more opportunity in emerging industrial societies. The relevance, value, and significance of Töpffer's work for rhetorical scholars today should be apparent to anyone working in the field.

Notes

Unless otherwise noted, quotations from the original French texts cited in this essay have been translated by the author.

1. *Electracy* is a term coined by Gregory Ulmer to describe the rhetorical, cultural, institutional, ideological (individual and collective), ethical, political, and pedagogical implications of the transition from a primarily literate culture to a primarily digital culture, similar to the transition faced by oral cultures when transitioning to a literate culture.

2. In using "histories of rhetorics," I refer to Victor Vitanza's *Negation, Subjectivity, and the History of Rhetoric*, specifically to Vitanza's call for thinking about "the history of rhetoric" as multiple histories of multiple rhetorics and rhetorical traditions.

3. Wiese's term.

4. Saint-Simon is often credited with proposing that all European nations form a union, a proposal possibly influenced by the formation of the United States, as Saint-Simon fought against the British in the Revolutionary War.

5. The primary ethical value Saint-Simon envisioned for this new society was based on the principle of "primitive Christianity" as defined by St. Paul: "Thou shalt love they neighbor as thyself" (Saint-Simon, "New Christianity" 81–82). Beyond this principle, Saint-Simon proposed doing away with the rest of Christian dogma. One of his primary critiques of previous models of social organization—that is, monarchies—was the undue influence of the Pope and the Vatican on monarchs. Saint-Simon's model also de-emphasized the role of "governors" ("gouvernants") in organizing and maintaining society—because all they knew was "the regulatory form" ("la forme réglementaire"; "L'artiste" 334).

6. Specifically, Töpffer refers to the institutional use of phrenology to claim that people of African descent were intellectually inferior to people of European descent (Figueiredo 61, 63).

Works Cited

Figueiredo, Sergio C., editor and translator. *Inventing Comics: A New Translation of Rodolphe Töpffer's Reflections on Graphic Storytelling, Media Rhetorics, and Aesthetic Practice*. Parlor Press, 2017.

Kunzle, David. *Father of the Comic Strip: Rodolphe Töpffer*. UP of Mississippi, 2007.

———. *Rodolphe Töpffer: The Complete Comic Strips*. UP of Mississippi, 2007.

McCloud, Scott. *Understanding Comics: The Invisible Art*. William Morrow, 1994.

Pitteloud, Antoine. *Rodolphe Töpffer en Valais: Textes extraits des "Voyages en Zigzag" et de "Nouvelles genevoises."* L'Age d'Homme, 2006.

Saint-Simon, Henri de. "L'artiste, le savant, et l'industriel." *Opinions littéraires, philosophiques, et industriels*, by Saint-Simon, Paris, 1825, pp. 331–92.

———. "New Christianity." *Social Organization, the Science of Man, and Other Writings*, by Saint-Simon, edited and translated by Felix Markham, Harper Torchbooks, 1952, pp. 81–116.

Töpffer, Rodolphe. *Correspondance complète*. Vol. 3, Droz, 2007.

———. *Essai de physiognomonie*. Schmidt, 1845.

———. "Réflexions a propos d'un programme." *Bibliothèque Universelle de Genève*, vol. 1, B. Glaser, 1836, pp. 42–61.

———. "Réflexions a propos d'un programme." *Bibliothèque Universelle de Genève*, vol. 2, B. Glaser, 1836, pp. 314–41.

———. *Réflexions et menus propos d'un peintre genevois*. P. A. Bonnant, 1830.

———. *Réflexions et menus propos d'un peintre genevois; ou, Essai sur le beau dans les arts*. L. Hachette, 1858.

Ulmer, Gregory L. "The Chora Collaborations." *Rhizomes: Cultural Studies in Emerging Knowledge*, no. 18, winter 2008, www.rhizomes.net/issue18/ulmer/index.html.

Vitanza, Victor. *Negation, Subjectivity, and the History of Rhetoric*. State U of New York P, 1996.

Wiese, Ellen. *Enter the Comics: Rodolphe Töpffer's Essay on Physiognomy and The True Story of Monsieur Crépin*. U of Nebraska P, 1965.

Willems, Philippe. "Rodolphe Töpffer and Romanticism." *Nineteenth-Century French Studies*, vol. 37, nos. 3–4, 2009, pp. 227–46.

Talking Teachers into Motion: Rereading William James's *Talks to Teachers*

Kurt Spellmeyer

> William James, *Talks to Teachers on Psychology: And to Students on Some of Life's Ideals* (Henry Holt, 1899)

William James's influence on the fields of composition and rhetoric, and on English studies as well, would be difficult to overestimate even though we seldom acknowledge it. In composition, any roster of his heirs would include the names of Theodore Baird, Ann E. Berthoff, William E. Coles, Jr., and David Bartholomae. In literary studies, we might have a harder time tracing out one unbroken lineage, but on any list we would see the names of Richard Poirier and Reuben Brower. Some of us may recognize Baird and Brower as the instigators of a pragmatist revival in the mid–twentieth century at the University of Massachusetts, Amherst, where Baird oversaw Composition I and II, and at Harvard University, where Brower directed the famous Hum 6, a course taught by Poirier and Paul de Man, who helped formulate what became the deconstructionism championed by his friend and ally Jacques Derrida. But to these lists we should also add another, expressivist lineage often understood as ideologically opposed to the first. Here we would find Ken Macrorie, Walker Gibson, Donald Murray, and, of course, Peter Elbow. Still another line of influence, starting with John Dewey, James's brilliant protégé, might include Kate Ronald and Hephzibah Roskelly, Brian Jackson and Gregory Clark, Nathan Crick and, through Cornel West, Keith Gilyard. Then, of course, there's the lineage that descends from Kenneth Burke, branching so widely and wildly that even a word like *network* is inadequate. Here we would find rhetoricians like Cheryl Glenn and Jessica Enoch; critics like Giles Gunn, Frank Lentricchia, and Stanley Fish; the historians

John Patrick Diggins and Robert Westbrook, Jr.; the philosopher Stanley Cavell; and even a few anthropologists, not least of all Clifford Geertz.

Yet hardly anyone in writing studies today would expect to see William James among the ranks of our early thinkers, for reasons that have less to do with James himself than with defects in the legacy he has come to represent. Quite simply, pragmatism has often set aside history in the sense Marx had in mind when he pointedly observed, "Men make their own history, but they do not make it as they please; they do not make it under self-selected circumstances, but under circumstances existing already, given and transmitted from the past" (5).

As individuals and as a society, we can play with skill and even virtuosity the cards that life has dealt us, just as pragmatists have always emphasized. But history decides the cards we get, and in this light pragmatism looks naive when it comes to matters of concern to those of us who study writing: discourses, disciplines, genres, styles, and institutions on the scene long before we arrived. Worse yet, pragmatism seems willfully obtuse when we turn to matters of a graver kind: breathtaking economic inequality, the overt corruption of our political class, the growth of an authoritarian Right, and our incipient collision with climate catastrophe. To be sure, pragmatism had its moment in our field when the generation after World War II imagined a future full of possibility, a prospect far from where we find ourselves now. But precisely because we feel boxed in and blocked, pragmatism may deserve a second look. A renewed sense of possibility could be exactly what we need.

James must have thought so as he brought to press his *Talks to Teachers on Psychology: And to Students on Some of Life's Ideals*, which began in 1892 as lectures addressed to educators in the Cambridge area. In those lecturers, James invokes the promise of psychology, the nascent field that he helped launch. And the major contribution he believes the field can make is to refocus teachers' attention on the cognitive processes that learning involves rather than on the course content, an unheard-of proposition at the time. Beyond that, James wants his audience to embrace a radically different understanding of the mind, not as a theater of rationality or a storehouse of information but as a "stream of consciousness," always changing dynamically in its interaction with the environment.[1]

Indeed, he even argues that interacting with the environment is the mind's primary task, and it does so, he says, by continuously transforming itself—how it sees and how it understands what it sees. And once the mind has transformed itself, it can act on its environment in turn. The basics of education prior to this time—names and dates to be memorized, abstract ideas, unchanging moral principles, and the cultivation of taste—have a "cash value," James insists, only when they align with the task of worldly engagement (*Pragmatism* 53). But James takes this reasoning one further step by implying that the same principle holds true for the achievements of great thinkers in the past—Plato, Aquinas, Dante, Shakespeare, Goethe, and the rest. Their ideas, too, began as creative responses that had the effect of channeling streams of consciousness in immediately useful ways. Only gradually did their ideas get detached from the business of living, and then they ossified into obstacles to future action, or, sometimes, into raw material for creative repurposing later on.

This distinctly Jamesian subversion—putting culture into motion again after its impoundment by authorities with a vested interest in keeping things unchanged—remains a stock-in-trade of writing studies, though often mediated by figures now more visible—Gilles Deleuze and Félix Guattari, for example, and Bruno Latour, who once revealingly described himself as "the only French pragmatist."[2] But contemporary work by figures as diverse as Jenny Rice and Derek Mueller, though they might not call themselves pragmatists, shares with James the conviction, I would say, that culture, knowledge, languages, tropes, genres, and words are better understood processually—that is, as parts of systems constantly in flux—than as discrete objects or entities.

If we set *Talks to Teachers* alongside a work like Matthew Arnold's *Culture and Anarchy*, published about thirty years earlier, we can see just how radically James transformed the common thinking on education in the United States. "Culture," Arnold wrote, "is the study of perfection" (Super 91). Educators here, as in Great Britain, thought of learning as the internalization of "the best that has been thought and known in the world," in Arnold's memorable phrasing (113). But *Talks to Teachers* asks instead, and quite radically, what thinking actually involves. James assumes that attention to the content of thought, even when that content qualifies as "the best," is a kind of misdirection, since what really matters is thinking, and thinking he conceived as an activity that couldn't be learned by memorizing ideas but only by engaging in the practices that produced them. The younger Dewey translated James imperfectly into the "instrumentalist" credo that we learn by doing, but Dewey—while starting his odyssey as a Hegelian idealist—never shared his older colleague's fascination with the phenomenon of consciousness.[3] Instead, his functionalist psychology was primarily concerned with the way that organisms adapt to their material and social environments.[4]

But Dewey shared James's conviction that the models of the mind offered to us by Plato, Aristotle, Thomas Aquinas, and so on all conflate thought with reason. And reason is conceived of as a faculty—indeed, the highest of all faculties, one with which we are naturally endowed but from which we become estranged by our passions, our fantasies, and the moral failures arising from our conceptual confusion. Even a thinker like David Hume, who opposed this privileging of reason, still relied half-heartedly on a faculty psychology to challenge it, but it was exactly the faculties model that pioneering psychologists like James, Dewey, and Wilhelm Wundt rejected as begging the question of how the mind actually works. When we reason, the faculties model holds, our activity must be the product of a reasoning faculty. When we feel emotions, there must be a faculty for those—the passions. When we visualize something that doesn't exist, the imagination or fancy has come into play. In this manner, however, our mental processes are not explained but simply explained away. James recognized, by contrast, that the mind has a mind of its own, so to speak—with processes that we cannot understand simply by observing our behavior or the artifacts that we have produced. Instead, James argued for the value of an introspective and empirical attention to mental events that paralleled the physical sciences' attention to events in the material world. And this approach led him to give particular weight to what he called "interest," the arousal of attention that often precedes conscious awareness (*Talks* 91–97). In James's account, the subconscious stirring of interest possessed an affective and somatic dimension as well, completely overturning the division of labor that the faculties model presupposed.

We can begin to appreciate, then, how the paradigm shift to consciousness, as in "stream of consciousness," made it possible for a field like composition to arise at all—a field that also overturned long-held assumptions about the mind.[5] Rhetoricians a century before James—like George Campbell and Richard Whately—could see the world around them changing rapidly, with resources pouring in from across the British Empire while the coal-fired factories darkened the skies. Both Campbell and Whately recognized the urgent need for a more robust theory of invention, but they simply couldn't let go of reason as the master key to consciousness, and that meant that they couldn't jettison the faculties model.[6] Although it has become commonplace to say that they wedded rhetoric to psychology, their understanding of the mind roughly corresponded to the account of evolution that we find in William Paley's theory of intelligent design in his book *Natural Theology*. But James's psychology replaced the intelligent design theory of the mind with a truly Darwinian account that made it possible to account for consciousness as what we today would describe as a complex, self-organizing system guided by trial, error, and adaptation. Complexity and self-organization were ideas unfamiliar to James, of course, but as a reader of Darwin's work, he began to develop an account of how the "booming, buzzing" chaotic stream of consciousness could organize itself spontaneously into recurrent patterns that would become regularities over time through habit (*Principles* 488). Especially in the later version of his thought, which he called "radical empiricism," James could see that faculties weren't needed to explain how mental worlds become orderly.[7] Interest and habit, all by themselves, could account for everything.

We might say that the field of composition arose in the space opened up by the retreat of faculty psychology and the rise of a distinctly psychological approach to the mind, a turn that begins with James. And the approach to writing as a process that requires moment-by-moment observation in an empirical spirit—a form of research inaugurated by figures like Janet Emig and refined with extraordinary virtuosity in Linda Flower's brilliant work—can be traced directly back to him. But this approach required compositionists at the time to separate themselves from rhetorical tradition, first because of that tradition's reliance on the superannuated faculties model, and second because of its persistent concern with quasi-permanent tropes or *topoi* (literally, "places"), which rhetoricians often understood as standardized components that speakers could draw on as they assembled their arguments. James might say that rhetoricians concerned one-sidedly with topoi had reified thinking in the same way as had teachers who were obsessed with coverage of the material; they were like the intellectual historians who represented the past as a procession of invariant great ideas rather than a series of crises, predicaments, and contractions plunging everyone involved into radical uncertainty and demanding new, jerry-rigged responses. Of course, language itself is a system of regularities perpetuated by social convention—a point not lost on Aristotle—but by focusing too much on the regularities, rhetoricians in the past arguably overlooked the processes operating behind or before the emergence of those regularities. Even structures need to be structured, after all, and to the degree that those structures respond innovatively to a changing world beyond themselves, they follow not rules but the kind of Darwinian mechanisms that James came to appreciate later in his life (Skrupskelis). By analogy, one could say that individual animals of the same kind—rabbits, wolves, chimps—appear to be more or less uniform and unchanging, but when we look at species over geological time, we realize that they have never ceased to reinvent themselves in ways nobody could have foreseen. An Aristotelean rhetoric of biological species, supposing that such a thing existed, would look at features that seem to persist—the morphology, ethology, ecology, and so on—whereas a Jamesian compositionist would attend to the process of revision that allowed, say, a pig-like, littoral omnivore to return to the ocean after a long digression on land to become the dolphin we know today.

Yet, in spite of its promise, the study of writing as a process suffered much the same fate as the Jamesian project, eclipsed in the 1980s by the arrival in the United States of continental philosophy—not only structuralism and post-structuralism but also Marxism and the critical theory of the Frankfurt school, Jürgen Habermas, and other German thinkers. Anybody looking at the pages of *College English* or *College Composition and Communication* from the mid-1980s on can see the revision or, perhaps, evolution of the field in the gradual displacement of Linda Flower's elegant, complicated diagrams by densely argued articles referencing Michel Foucault, Jacques Lacan, Hélène Cixous, and a dozen other Europeans. And one way to explain this paradigm shift is to say that the continentals recognized what James himself ignored—the actual environment to which thinking responds. In Europe, James's legacy has always remained rather marginal, and one explanation may lie with thinkers like Pierre Bourdieu, who approaches experience quite differently from the way compositionists often have—and from the way that James himself did. James wants to stress the mind's fluidity and its constant reinvention of itself, whereas Bourdieu, who worked briefly as a lycée teacher in France, presupposes the inescapability of the "habitus," which he defines as our enduring internalization of the social order, starting in the first moments of our lives.[8] And Bourdieu certainly has a point: culture and history matter. They get into our minds and under our skin. James's unwillingness to recognize the social and cultural constraints on thought and action runs like a thread throughout his entire legacy, and that legacy includes *Talks to Teachers*, which never pauses to consider the concrete history that allowed some students to go to school while excluding others—while, indeed, excluding most children in James's day. It's worth remembering, after all, that until World War II, the average American had a ninth-grade education. And educators in the 1890s generally thought of the public school, an institution James himself never attended, as preparation for factory work, with all its rigidity and repetition.

Unlike James, Bourdieu focused on the role that schooling plays in the reproduction of inequality. In particular, he approached culture as one form of capital—like money—distributed unevenly up and down the social pyramid, and he acknowledged that the task of the public school is to withhold that capital from some students while lavishing it on their "betters." Regrettably, here in the United States, the commitment to broad access to social goods has so diminished that most people in other parts of the developed world—in western Europe, for example—enjoy far greater upward mobility. Indeed, we come in at twenty-seventh worldwide by most measures. At the same time, higher education has had to compensate for the retreat of state support by operating entrepreneurially, renting undergraduates luxury dorms and purveying other amenities signifying a middle-class status that is slipping out of reach for millions of Americans. While a BA or BS still provides many aspirants an entrée into the middle class, millions of degreed Americans now belong to the ranks of indentured workers who may never manage to pay off their college loans before they retire. James's pragmatism cannot even start to explain how or why any of these hugely consequential changes have occurred, and although researchers on the writing process in the 1980s typically shared a commitment to various forms of equality, any study of discourse focused narrowly on that process today would arrive at an impoverished account of how language works. When we treat the writer as an individual engaged in a cognitive routine unfolding outside history or social life, we have returned to a reification not so different from the ones that James objected to at the start of his career. The writer, as imagined by the cognitive approach, is a fiction, a useful one but a fiction all the same. I don't mean to suggest that we have no mental life of our own but that the writing self is a persona achieved on the page by working with and working through the often contradictory subject positions offered to us by our society at any historical moment. And it goes without saying that "working with and working through" is a struggle for most writers, not only because they lack the acquired cognitive skills, as James would have recognized, but also because our society has contrived to keep those skills broadly out of reach. And this is the problem James overlooked.

Perhaps because James belonged to the generation that came of age within living memory of the Civil War—he was twenty-three when it ended, and two of his brothers fought for the Union—he tried to develop throughout his life a way of describing human relations that would prevent conflicts like the Civil War from ever happening again. And like his work on philosophy and religion, his psychology took the form, mostly implicit and unrecognized, of a search for a common ground prior to all our differences—cultural, political, social, historical, and so on. We see this same search for a shared "substance" in Kenneth Burke, and because we ourselves inhabit the habitus James helped create, we have often embraced his pragmatism as generous and deeply humane but not, in parallel, as an evasion of differences that dialogue and understanding by themselves will never resolve (Burke 20–23). But hard truths emerging from Bourdieu's very different personal history prepared the French social theorist to address them head on. Bourdieu, too, witnessed a civil war—the struggle of Algerians, then technically French citizens after a century of occupation, to secede from the Fourth Republic. Once the French were driven out of Algeria, Bourdieu remained behind to help with the country's reconstruction, eventually assuming a teaching post at the national university. And then, when he later returned to France, he could readily appreciate the parallels between the hierarchies of wealth, status, and agency that he saw in colonial Algeria and those operating more subtly back at home in France, the former colonizer.

In the debate I have staged here between the pragmatist philosopher and the French sociologist, Bourdieu appears to get the last word, and it's certainly a word worth hearing in the United States, where the myth of endless opportunity masks the very opposite. But it's also possible that Bourdieu might learn from the American something overlooked and undervalued by the latter's sociology. Later in Bourdieu's long career, he observed with growing alarm the global rise of neoliberalism, and he saw how effectively it dissolves all the structures that define the habitus, leaving everyone increasingly exposed to the shifting tides of finance.[9] Precisely because those structures fail, even though they are among the most enduring, we need James to remind us that the persistence of anything attests to the constant human ingenuity required to keep it going. The more things seem to stay the same, in other words, the more they have actually had to change. We're always inventing the world from scratch, and now, as that world fails more and more rapidly, we still have the power to construct something from the fragments. If Bourdieu and others force us to recognize the rhetoric that governs lives, the time may have come, I would suggest, for the return of composition—now understood in a new way, as the constant remaking of the world both on and off the page.

Notes

1. As James writes in *Principles of Psychology*, "Consciousness, then, does not appear to itself chopped up in bits. Such words as a 'chain' or a 'train' do not describe it fitly as it presents itself in the first instance. It is nothing jointed; it flows. A 'river' or a 'stream' are the metaphors by which it is most naturally described. *In talking of it hereafter, let us call it the stream of thought, of consciousness, or of subjective life*" (243).

2. See, for instance, Duvernoy; Sheehey.

3. As Dewey observes in *The Quest for Certainty*, "[A]ll reflective knowledge as such is instrumental. The beginning and the end is the things of gross everyday experience" (218).

4. In Dewey's words, "All life operates through a mechanism, and the higher the form of life the more complex, sure and flexible the mechanism. This fact alone should save us from opposing life and mechanism, thereby reducing the latter to unintelligent automatism and the former to an aimless splurge" (*Human Nature* 71–72).

5. One excellent resource on this subject is Portanova et al. See in particular Carillo; Dryer and Russell.

6. See, for example, book 1, chapter 7, of Campbell's *Philosophy of Rhetoric* (93–117) and parts 1 and 2 of Whately's *Elements of Rhetoric* (33–178).

7. In James's words, "To be radical, an empiricism must neither admit into its constructions any element that is not directly experienced, nor exclude from them any element that is directly experienced. For such a philosophy, the relations that connect experiences must themselves be experienced relations, and any kind of relation experienced must be accounted as 'real' as anything else in the system. Elements may indeed be redistributed, the original placing of things getting corrected, but a real place must be found for every kind of thing experienced, whether term or relation, in the final philosophic arrangement" (*Essays* 42).

8. As Bourdieu defines it, the "habitus, a product of history, produces individual and collective practices—more history—in accordance with the schemes generated by history. It ensures the active presence of past experiences, which, deposited in each organism in the form of schemes of perception, thought and action, tend to guarantee the 'correctness' of practices and their constancy over time, more reliably than all formal rules and explicit norms" (*Logic* 54).

9. See Bourdieu, "Utopia," *Acts*, and *Firing Back*.

Works Cited

Bourdieu, Pierre. *Acts of Resistance: Against the Tyranny of the Market*. Translated by Richard Nice, New Press, 1999.

——. *Firing Back: Against the Tyranny of the Market 2*. Translated by Loïc Wacquant, New Press, 2003.

——. *The Logic of Practice*. Translated by Richard Nice, Stanford UP, 1990.

——. "Utopia of Endless Exploitation: The Essence of Neoliberalism." *Le Monde Diplomatique*, Dec. 1998, mondediplo.com/1998/12/08bourdieu.

Burke, Kenneth. *A Rhetoric of Motives*. U of California P, 1969.

Campbell, George. *The Philosophy of Rhetoric*. 1776. Harper and Brothers, 1860.

Carillo, Ellen C. "The Evolving Relationship between Composition and Cognitive Studies: Gaining Some Historical Perspective on Our Contemporary Moment." Portanova et al., pp. 39–55.

Dewey, John. *Human Nature and Conduct: An Introduction to Social Psychology*. Henry Holt, 1922.

———. *The Quest for Certainty*. Minton, Balch, 1929.

Dryer, Dylan B., and David R. Russell. "Attending to Phenomenology: Rethinking Cognition and Reflection in North American Writing Studies." Portanova et al., pp. 57–76.

Duvernoy, Russell J. "'Pure Experience' and 'Planes of Immanence': From James to Deleuze." *Journal of Speculative Philosophy*, vol. 30, no. 4, 2016, pp. 227–51.

James, William. *Essays in Radical Empiricism*. Longmans, Green, 1912.

———. *Pragmatism: A New Name for Some Old Ways of Thinking*. Longmans, Green, 1907.

———. *Principles of Psychology*. Vol. 1, Henry Holt, 1890.

———. *Talks to Teachers on Psychology: And to Students on Some of Life's Ideals*. 1899. Henry Holt, 1925.

Marx, Karl. *The Eighteenth Brumaire of Louis Bonaparte*. Marxists Internet Archive, www.marxists.org/archive/marx/works/download/pdf/18th-Brumaire.pdf.

Portanova, Patricia J., et al., editors. *Contemporary Perspectives on Cognition and Writing*. UP of Colorado, 2017.

Sheehey, Bonnie. "Methodologies of Travel: William James and the Ambulatory Pragmatism of Bruno Latour." *Journal of Speculative Philosophy*, vol. 33, no. 4, 2020, pp. 571–89.

Skrupskelis, Ignas K. "Evolution and Pragmatism: An Unpublished Letter of William James." *Transactions of the Charles S. Peirce Society*, vol. 43, no. 4, fall 2007, pp. 745–52.

Super, Robert H., editor. *Culture and Anarchy*, with *Friendship's Garland and Some Literary Essays*. By Matthew Arnold, U of Michigan P, 1965. Vol. 5 of *The Complete Works of Matthew Arnold*.

Whately, Richard. *Elements of Rhetoric*. 1828. Harper and Brothers, 1877.

Part Two

The Mid–Twentieth Century

A Composition Commons: The Stanford Language Arts Investigation, 1937–1939

Jessica Yood

> *Stanford Language Arts Investigation* (1937–39, archived at Stanford University Libraries)
> Walter V. Kaulfers and Holland D. Roberts (eds.), *A Cultural Basis for the Language Arts* (Stanford UP, 1937)
> Walter V. Kaulfers, Grayson N. Kefauver, and Holland D. Roberts (eds.), *Foreign Languages and Cultures in American Education* (McGraw-Hill, 1942)
> Walter V. Kaulfers, *Modern Languages for Modern Schools* (McGraw-Hill, 1942)
> Holland D. Roberts, Walter V. Kaulfers, and Grayson N. Kefauver (eds.), *English for Social Living* (McGraw-Hill, 1943)

In 1936 three faculty members at Stanford University sought funding for a general education experiment that would become known as the Stanford Language Arts Investigation (SLAI). They proposed a pilot class for high school and college students that integrated elements from the foreign languages, English, and social studies and included ideas from progressivism and humanism, the two dominant intellectual and educational reform movements of the time. Their project promised what the philosopher John Dewey called an "experience education" (341), grounded in teaching skills for a prosperous future, and what the literary critic I. A. Richards called a "unifying" curriculum, rooted in great works of the past. They got the grant.[1]

And then they created a writing program. From 1937 to 1939 Holland D. Roberts, a compositionist and labor activist; Walter V. Kaulfers, a scholar of foreign languages; and Grayson N. Kefauver, dean of education, recruited two hundred educators to teach and document these courses in recently built public high schools and colleges around the country. By 1942 the SLAI had published four monographs and amassed an archive of classroom artifacts, case studies, scholarly essays, and writing produced by ten thousand students.[2] Defying disciplinary orthodoxies and resisting reformist agendas, the SLAI called this student writing the "socially significant content" of a new kind of education (Kaulfers and Roberts 18), one where "common learnings" could be engendered in composition practices.[3] The SLAI named their theory "creative Americanism": shared knowledge built by students of public education and their "potential power to write" (Kaulfers et al. 281).

Prominent scholars took note. One scholar dismissed the project as "without design" (Smith 232). Another declared it politics, not pedagogy, a "radical" agenda obsessed with those who "have-not" (Pendleton 125, 126). At one point the SLAI was a serious topic in scholarly circles. By 1945 it was debunked, then forgotten.[4] The short life of the SLAI speaks to its countercultural claim, made at a critical moment in the history of higher education. As World War II was coming to a close, the nation looked to higher education to bind together a changed global order. How the academy responded would have ramifications for decades to come.

We are at another transformative time in our history, and it's a good time to recover these classroom archives and revisit their central questions. As of this writing, when we try to recover from a global pandemic, reckon with systemic racial injustice, and reconsider what students need, educators are once again asking what matters in higher learning. Is a shared core possible or desirable? What role might composition play in contributing to such a core?

This 1930s experiment provides an opportunity for writing studies to wrestle with these questions and to consider the SLAI's proposal for inventing a commons in composition. The SLAI didn't call its writing program a *commons*. I take on the term as a replacement for *creative Americanism*. Though *creative Americanism* was the term Cold War curriculum reformers deemed too radical, the phrase has roots in nativist, white supremacist ideologies. By telling the story of this project, I run the risk of overlooking that racist history. To avoid this, one of my colleagues suggested I focus on the content of the archives and dump *creative Americanism* and its cringey connotations.

The SLAI leaders thought that would be a mistake. They knew the phrase was a problem but urged educators to reclaim creative Americanism, to rip it from its "chauvinistically suppressive" handlers and realize its potential in the hands of a new public (Kaulfers et al. 16). They wanted scholars to be "accountable" to the messy and "vital energies" of literacy as they emerged in classrooms, and they urged researchers to dig into their artifacts, to embrace the creativity of students before committing to ideological "mastery" (269).

I am taken with the SLAI's faith in scholars to take up the project's mission but have chosen to adopt *commons* instead of *creative Americanism* to conjure the essence of this experiment. *Commons* is also a complex term. Historically, the term referred to shared land or resources managed or owned by ordinary people. Yet the term can be traced back to settler colonialism and enclosure laws. However, a *commons* can also refer to collective, social justice, ground-up projects, like the work of the Latinx Student Alliance, a student group that inspired a recent curricular overhaul at my college.[5] Adopting this term speaks to the paradoxes and possibilities of the SLAI and, I hope, makes my project accountable to the present needs of our discipline.

Counterstories, Continued Legacies, Creative Americanism

The SLAI seems to be the origin of *creative Americanism* as the term was used in print. *Americanism*, however, traces back to the eighteenth century, with its political connotations widely known by the 1920s. Historians and writing scholars link the Americanization movement to literacy policies that excluded or marginalized immigrants and Black citizens.[6] Jonathan Hansen details how the term *Americanism* became attached to racist ideologies and to pragmatist philosophers of the 1930s, who attempted to dislodge the Anglo and white supremacist roots of the term. John Dewey's letters to the philosopher Horace Kallen offer evidence of the progressive turn to Americanism.[7] Dewey pushed against an assimilationist view of Americanism and argued that a "genuine assimilation *to one another*—not to Anglo-Saxondom—seems to be essential to an America" (qtd. in Hansen 82).[8]

Though Dewey sought to move away from a melting-pot idea of America, philosophers who theorized equality but maintained the authority of the white patriarchy often used assimilation to justify accommodationist racism, classism, and sexism.[9] The SLAI leaders would discover the limits of a progressivism accommodated in theory but not in practice. Roberts, for example, was a fierce advocate for public schools and an activist in the labor movement. He had been a prolific scholar and a president of the NCTE. Yet he was forced to resign from Stanford after refusing to sign a loyalty oath to the US government.[10] Reclaiming the work of scholars like Roberts reminds us of our field's roots in K–12 education and connects language arts experiments of the last century to literacy advocacy today.[11]

Yet it's a kinship with the student writing that propelled me to these archives. Though much of the project took place in the western United States in the late 1930s, I recognize these classrooms. They remind me of the dynamic work of writing that happens where I teach, at the City University of New York. The SLAI rooted its idea of education in the classrooms in what were then new kinds of institutions: the public high school and the public college. Most of the students who attended these institutions were working, taking care of family, and commuting. Many were multilingual students of color and the first in their family to go to college. Today this population represents the undergraduate majority in the United States.[12]

In the early twentieth century, these students were the minority. And still the SLAI saw the potential in their cultures and literacies. The SLAI reflected on the history of the US academy and the irony of its so-called common core curricula, which had, for nearly a century, been crafted for and by the elite. In 1939 the project asked a question we still ponder: Isn't it time to find a new source for common learnings in the United States?

Background Knowledge from the Beginning

For the SLAI teacher-educators, educating for the commons meant investing in composition. For the leaders of the general education movement, it meant crafting a national curriculum. In 1945 a Harvard University committee published a curricular manifesto, *General Education in a Free Society*, that would serve as a model for hundreds of colleges and universities for decades to follow (Harvard Committee). Harvard's report declared the discipline of English to be the central humanistic discipline, critical to general education, which would provide "background for citizens of a free nation" (Conant viii). Great books became the content of general education, and close reading, or "close study of well-written paragraphs," the methodology for obtaining "cultural literacy." A cultural literacy curriculum would yield the "binding experience" necessary to hold democracy together (Harvard Committee 112, 135, 102).

The SLAI directors sought background knowledge and "binding experience" elsewhere: in literacies present *"from the beginning"* and produced in classroom writing practices (Kaulfers et al. 7). The SLAI's *"from the beginning"* is not the same as our first-year composition courses. The differences are instructive. This was a pilot project with no institutional ties, and the teacher-researchers wanted to keep it this way. Everyone involved took responsibility for collecting, coding, aggregating, and writing about student writing. Though some scholars think of classroom-based research as a conservative, even anti-intellectual enterprise, the SLAI argued for the rigor in recognizing ideas in gestation. Throughout the archives teachers highlight the "power" of "unfinished" composition that emerges in the present and is embedded in the "stuff" of the everyday world (Kaulfers et al. 287). This was the stuff that oriented students to what we might call today a "vital neomaterialism" concentrated on "the value of embodied ways of knowing" (Braidotti 34; Rìos 60).

The SLAI borrowed phrases from natural and civic life to conjure the diversity and interdependence of literacy interactions, declaring that the language arts could seed "a new world culture of variety and fertility" (Kaulfers et al. 281). "Fertility" is another cringey word, but these researchers discovered that their practice-oriented courses had particularly rich "soil" to create new content about culture and literacy in the United States (271). The SLAI understood that the composition class is not the only place where we write. It acknowledged that "language is, of course, used in all subjects" and "power in communication" can develop outside of school (7). Yet the program believed in the language arts classroom as a uniquely productive space of the American academy and in writing practices as necessary for a democratic academy, because writers can collect knowledge emerging in real time and in community with others.

Implementing this vision across hundreds of classes led to uneven results. And not all the instructors in every pilot course made the distinction between creative Americanism in practice and Americanism in theory. The project tried to pilot classes that made these paradoxes evident, all the while documenting its practices as evidence of a nation's new cultural resource.

Case Studies in Content Creation

One of the more interesting illustrations of the project comes in a chapter called "A Reconstructed Language-Arts Curriculum in Action" (Kaulfers et al. 239–68). Written by the principal investigators, the chapter offers an amalgamation of several pilot courses taught in the program. We learn that students write for the school paper, read a play and research its context, create a radio script, send letters to the editor of a national magazine, and map out the school's electricity system. The researchers acknowledged that some educators seemed overwhelmed by all the activity. "How do you manage to keep so many different things going at the same time?" they report one observer asking (244). "In these Manila folders," answers a student, where classroom compositions are stored and studied (245). The SLAI researchers insisted that the variety of student work is necessary and is a resource for scholars, "as vital a concern ... as any other" (244).

Though the folders themselves are lost to history, the archives saved a few student papers and allow us to trace the vitality of these classrooms. One is a midterm essay about the relationship between technology and learning. The student's argument begins with a "meditation on composition" and moves to a discussion of updated approaches to communication: "short-hand" instead of "handwriting," for example ("Visit" 6). The student concludes by asking readers to consider how writing courses study and enact important shifts in communication and gather a wide "community of interest" around "constructive work in public service" (14).

Like so many of the student artifacts, this essay resurfaces throughout the project, most notably as a resource for current and future SLAI classrooms ("Guide" 1–2). The essay is part of a detailed reading list put together by Max Schiferl, a linguist interested in connecting writing to research in semantics and anthropology.[13] That bibliography includes the *Anthology of World Poetry* and the *Anthology of World Prose*, edited by Mark Van Doren and Carl Van Doren. Both were established writers, and one was an architect of Columbia University's humanities curriculum. These famous authors are listed as "contributors," just as the student authors are. In the SLAI, esteemed writers and great books matter, but only if they are related to the content of those manila folders and the "constructive and creative" work developed by students (Kaulfers et al. 216).

Principles, Practices, and a Reconstructed Idea of the University

These SLAI materials emphasize representation of marginalized student voices; moreover, they realize the rich intellectual content that emerges from these voices. The monographs and archives are full of private reflection and political rants, researched reports, and chatty letters. Drafts of engineering analyses written in several languages sit next to piles of index cards with lesson plans, budget requests, and literary criticism. All this content is not easy to wade through and does not, as the SLAI researchers explained, fit a "formula" (Kaulfers et al. 393). To trace the development of one course, it's necessary to sift through the lesson plans of another; to track the development of one rhetorical theory, one must locate its origins in a student essay or syllabus.

That was how the SLAI liked it. The work of discovering connections required scholars to approach these archives as cultural texts, using what they named a "reconstructive" methodology that cultivates "world civilizations" (Kaulfers et al. 17). A "reconstructive" language arts resonates with what critical race theorists like Aja Y. Martinez call "counterstories," stories "by people whose experiences are not often told" (34). I consider the SLAI a counterstory of general education and also a continuation story for composition. The students in my classes at the City University of New York and all over this country carry on a little-known legacy in higher education: using the power of student writing to remake the world.

Writing Studies at the Threshold

As World War II was ending and the window for common learnings experimentation was closing, some scholars suggested the SLAI tone down its talk of power and diversity, clean up its classroom artifacts, and incorporate its project into the reform agenda of cultural literacy (Tharp).

The SLAI recognized the allure of outcomes and paradigms but decided to leave everything as it was: a collection of student artifacts and teacher reflections bound to particular persons and places but pointing to a future of students writing their world. They refused, in our professional parlance, to name what they knew.

In the end, this program's recalcitrance proved fatal, and its project was erased from history. But its rebellion suggests another way to think about writing studies, challenging two directions our discipline has taken in the last decade. The first is the "postcomposition" theory of writing, which "disrupts" the field's focus on classroom practice (Dobrin 188). The second is the discipline's turn to threshold concepts or to best practices and core principles (Adler-Kassner and Wardle 2). Threshold concepts, to some, can help embed our field in aspects of academic life. They may provide a way to understand paradigms—a disciplinary past—and secure a path to professional future—what's "critical for epistemological participation" (Cover copy). But the SLAI posited something other, something more, than epistemology: an ontology and ethics of participation. In this program, practice can never be disrupted; it is the ongoing work of a more free, diverse world society.

That world society comes into view when our scholarship takes a reconstructed view of the academy. We've begun to do that in refuting liberal humanist orthodoxies and by taking an anti-racist approach to pedagogy. In reorienting rhetoric toward an object-oriented, posthumanist frame, Casey Boyle considers the ecology of practice and how to attune to its *"ways of becoming"* (543). And in researching and promoting an anti-racist, socially just theory of writing, Asao B. Inoue argues for an ecological approach to practices and structures that dominate educational systems (25). We cannot claim our way out of racist ideologies, nor can composing pedagogies liberate us from structural constraints. But we can pursue practices that make visible and intercede in these structures. When we attend to practice embedded in time and over time, we activate attention and form resonances with human and natural systems. This is a focus on "the repetitive production of difference even if that difference looks, to our conscious awareness, the same" (Boyle 547). An ecological orientation toward classrooms engages all of us in the endeavor of noticing the "locally diverse" networks unfolding in these 1930s language arts courses (Inoue 177).

The pilot program dreamed up by the SLAI can't be replicated today. But I think it's worth imagining how we might pilot a creative, constructed core composition course for our world society. As I see it, this course would not be a permanent fixture of the curriculum. Instead, it could be a provisional space to take stock of where we are now. And it would be compulsory in the best sense, because every student and their cultures and literacies would be needed to create an inventory that matters in rethinking the academy. There would be no prerequisite or exit exam because its purpose would be to cultivate and question shared knowledge as it emerges. What counts as shared knowledge would be defined by the local context of a particular community and in light of the students in that community.

I realize this is a vague definition. But that is what a commons does: it forms connections and challenges the status quo, allowing for nuance and complexity. The SLAI didn't settle for a cultural literacy curriculum defined outside the local diversities of classrooms. The group promoted knowledge capacities rather than competencies, content emergent rather than concepts enshrined, and an archive of differences rather than an anthology of core principles. I have returned to their experiment because I think it speaks to an urgent need of the present: to revive an idea of the university as a composition commons.

Notes

1. "Unifying" is a term used to describe general education in the influential postwar manifesto *General Education in a Free Society: Report of the Harvard Committee* (Harvard Committee). Richards is credited with writing the section on English (107–24). For more on Dewey and general education, see G. Miller. Geoffrey Galt Harpham's *What Do You Think, Mr. Ramirez?: The American Revolution in Education* details Richards's role on the Harvard committee that produced the manifesto. The grant for the Stanford Language Arts Investigation came from the General Education Board, a philanthropy chartered by the United States Congress in 1903. For a thorough description of the General Education Board, see Watkins 118–35.

2. The four monographs are cited at the outset of the essay. The Stanford Language Arts Investigation is archived as bulletins 1 through 80 in the Stanford University Special Collections.

3. The term "common learnings" is used in some of the first federal reports about general education and defined in the United States Bureau of Education's 1913 report *Economy of Time in Education*.

4. No writing scholar addresses "creative Americanism," and only a few histories acknowledge the SLAI. Arthur N. Applebee writes a paragraph about the SLAI in a chapter about progressive education (139–84). He is right to criticize some researchers for evading elements of Dewey's civic project in favor of attention to individualistic "life adjustment" concerns (146). But because he looks only at one monograph, *English for Social Living*, his conclusion that "progressive" experiments, like the SLAI, were "lacking any external principles" is unfounded (150). Dorothy E. Moulton categorizes the project as one of the "problems" of progressivism, also relying on *English for Social Living* (63). Thomas P. Miller's *The Evolution of College English* offers a thoughtful take on progressive-era experiments. However, Miller, too, only addresses *English for Social Living* and overlooks the project's attention to public education and its relationship to general education (169).

5. For a discussion of the commons in the context of education and knowledge formation, see Hess and Ostrom. For an account of commons work happening at Lehman College and specifically through the college's Latinx Student Alliance, see "Lehman College's Latinx Student Alliance."

6. See especially Wan.

7. The Seattle Civil Rights and Labor History Project chronicles the history of the Ku Klux Klan and offers archival history of its use of the term "Americanism" in the 1923 publication *Watcher on the Tower* (Cook).

8. The term gained in popularity when the journalist and cultural critic H. L. Mencken published *The American Language* in 1921. For a discussion of Americanism in the works of Dewey, Kallen, David Walker, and Frederick Douglass, among other writers, see Hansen.

9. Carmen Kynard discusses accommodationist racism in *Vernacular Insurrections*. Kynard addresses progressive education's intersection with quotas at elite colleges and universities (29–40). Zoe Burkholder's discussion of race in the progressive "intercultural" curricula of the era is covered in *Color in the Classroom: How American Schools Taught Race, 1900–1954* (96–135).

10. Russell K. Durst describes Roberts's radical labor politics in "Practical Progressivism: W. Wilbur Hatfield, Deweyan Pedagogy, and the Future of English Teaching" (233).

11. What Jacqueline Jones Royster and Jean C. Williams call our "naturalized" grand narratives of composition inspired important recovery projects in writing studies, including this one (565). I had my own "naturalized" perspec-

tives and needed to recalibrate my understanding of the relationship between elite, historically white institutions like Stanford and writing experimentation in public, working-class-serving institutions with a majority-non-white population, where the SLAI research took place.

12. For a discussion of the demographics of secondary and college students in this period, see Thelin 153. For a discussion of student demographics throughout the case studies recorded in the monographs of the SLAI, see especially Kaulfers et al. 394–95. The National Center for Education Statistics tracks undergraduate trends through the early 2000s. What were then considered new students are the academic majority now. Almost half the undergraduate population in the United States attend two-year or community colleges, and three-quarters of undergraduates attend a public college or university ("Definitions").

13. Schiferl praises the work of Alfred Korzybski, noted for bringing semantics to American universities; see Korzybski 889. Sharon Crowley dismisses the dubious research and conservative politics of the general semantics movement, as did Roberts and Kaulfers; see Kaulfers, "Observations"; Crowley 274.

Works Cited

Adler-Kassner, Linda, and Elizabeth Wardle. *Naming What We Know: Threshold Concepts of Writing Studies*. UP of Colorado / Utah State UP, 2015.

Applebee, Arthur N. *Tradition and Reform in the Teaching of English*. National Council of Teachers of English, 1974.

Boyle, Casey. "Writing and Rhetoric and/as Posthuman Practice." *College English*, vol. 78, no. 6, July 2016, pp. 532–54.

Braidotti, Rosi. "A Theoretical Framework for the Critical Posthumanities." *Theory, Culture and Society*, vol. 36, no. 6, May 2018, pp. 31–61.

Burkholder, Zoe. *Color in the Classroom: How American Schools Taught Race, 1900–1954*. Oxford UP, 2011.

Conant, James Bryant. Introduction. *General Education in a Free Society: Report of the Harvard Committee*, Harvard UP, 1945, pp. v–x.

Cook, Brianne. "*Watcher on the Tower* and the Washington State Ku Klux Klan." *Seattle Civil Rights and Labor History Project*, depts.washington.edu/civilr/kkk_wot.htm.

Cover copy. *Naming What We Know: Threshold Concepts of Writing Studies*, edited by Linda Adler-Kassner and Elizabeth Wardle, UP of Colorado / Utah State UP, 2015.

Crowley, Sharon. *Composition in the University*. Pittsburgh UP, 2008.

"Definitions and Data." *National Center for Education Statistics*, nces.ed.gov/pubs/web/97578e.asp.

Dewey, John. *The Child and the Curriculum*. U of Chicago P, 1902.

Dobrin, Sidney I. *Postcomposition*. Southern Illinois UP, 2011.

Durst, Russell K. "Practical Progressivism: W. Wilbur Hatfield, Deweyan Pedagogy, and the Future of English Teaching." *English Language Arts Research and Teaching: Revisiting and Extending Arthur Applebee's Contributions*, edited by Durst et al., Routledge, 2017, pp. 227–41.

"A Guide to Bibliographies and Aids in Selecting Books for Teachers of the Language Arts Preliminary Edition." Stanford Language Arts Investigation, Stanford University Libraries, Special Collections and University Archives, bulletin 53, vol. 2.

Hansen, Jonathan. "True Americanism: Progressive Era Intellectuals and the Problem of Liberal Nationalism." *Americanism: New Perspectives on the History of an Ideal*, edited by Michael Kazin and Joseph A. McCartin, U of North Carolina P, 2006, pp. 73–89.

Harpham, Geoffrey Galt. *What Do You Think, Mr. Ramirez?: The American Revolution in Education*. U of Chicago P, 2017.

Harvard Committee on the Objectives of a General Education in a Free Society. *General Education in a Free Society: Report of the Harvard Committee*. Harvard UP, 1945.

Hess, Charlotte, and Elinor Ostrom, editors. *Understanding Knowledge as a Commons*. MIT Press, 2006.

Inoue, Asao B. *Antiracist Writing Assessment Ecologies*. Parlor Press, 2015.

Kaulfers, Walter V. *Modern Languages for Modern Schools*. McGraw-Hill, 1942.

———. "Observations on the Question of General Language." *School Review*, vol. 36, no. 4, 1928, pp. 280–81.

Kaulfers, Walter V., and Holland D. Roberts, editors. *A Cultural Basis for the Language Arts*. Stanford UP, 1937.

Kaulfers, Walter V., et al., editors. *Foreign Languages and Cultures in American Education*. McGraw-Hill, 1942.

Korzybski, Alfred. *Collected Writings, 1920–1950*. Collected and arranged by M. Kendig, Institute for General Semantics, 1990.

Kynard, Carmen. *Vernacular Insurrections: Race, Black Protest, and the New Century in Composition-Literacies Studies*. State U of New York P, 2013.

"Lehman College's Latinx Student Alliance Pens Letter Demanding Diversity in English Department Curriculum." *Latino Rebels*, 21 Nov. 2019, www.latinorebels.com/2019/11/21/lehmancollegestudentletter/.

Martinez, Aja Y. *Counterstory*. National Council of Teachers of English, 2020.

Miller, Gary E. *The Meaning of General Education*. Teachers College Press, 1988.

Miller, Thomas P. *The Evolution of College English*. Pittsburgh UP, 2010.

Moulton, Dorothy E. "Years of Controversy in the Teaching of English." *The English Journal*, vol. 68, no. 4, Apr. 1979, pp. 60–66.

Pendleton, Charles S. "Frontier Adventure." *The English Journal*, vol. 33, no. 3, Mar. 1944, pp. 125–26.

Rìos, Gabriela. "Cultivating Land-Based Literacies and Rhetorics." *Literacy in Composition Studies*, Mar. 2015, pp. 60–70.

Roberts, Holland D., et al., editors. *English for Social Living*. McGraw-Hill, 1943.

Royster, Jacqueline Jones, and Jean C. Williams. "History in the Spaces Left: African American Presence and Narratives of Composition Studies." *College Composition and Communication*, vol. 50, no. 4, 1999, pp. 563–84.

Smith, Dora V. "Creative but without Design." *The English Journal*, vol. 33, no. 5, May 1944, pp. 232–36.

Tharp, James B. "Reviewed Works." *Educational Research Bulletin*, vol. 25, no. 1, Jan. 1946, pp. 23–24.

Thelin, John. *A History of Higher Education*. Johns Hopkins UP, 2011.

United States Bureau of Education, Committee of the National Council of Education. *Economy of Time in Education*. No. 38, Government Printing Office, 1913.

"A Visit with Frontier Workers in the Language Arts." Stanford Language Arts Investigation, Stanford University Libraries, Special Collections and University Archives, bulletin 43, vol. 1.

Wan, Amy. *Producing Good Citizens: Literacy in Anxious Times*. Pittsburgh UP, 2014.

Watkins, William H. *The White Architects of Black Education*. Teachers College Press, 2001.

Toward Social Transformation: Renewing the Burkean Theory of Identification

Mary C. Carruth

Kenneth Burke, A *Rhetoric of Motives* (Prentice Hall, 1950)

I first encountered Kenneth Burke's rhetorical theories in a pedagogical article by Dale M. Bauer, "The Other 'F' Word: The Feminist in the Classroom," published in *College English* in 1990. Bauer applies Burke's notion of identification to a method of inquiry she developed to foster students' critical thinking in the literature classroom, a dialectic of resistance and identification, which springs from what she, as a feminist, believes is students' unacknowledged ambivalence about the "system" (387) and dominant ideology (390).

At the time, I was enrolled in a graduate course on composition theory. Uninspired by trenching through such required texts as James Kinneavy's *A Theory of Discourse* and more enthusiastic about feminist and literary studies, I decided to write my seminar paper on one of my long-term interests—teaching critical thinking and writing. I was already passionate about the works of bell hooks, especially *Talking Back: Thinking Feminist, Thinking Black*, though her *Teaching to Transgress: Education as a Practice of Freedom*, inspired by radical texts like Paulo Freire's *Pedagogy of the Oppressed*, had not yet been published. My research on critical thinking led me into fuller explorations of critical and political pedagogies, which in turn introduced me to Burke's theory of identification, first proposed in detail in his *A Rhetoric of Motives*. As I discovered, Burke's dialectical method of writing, complicated by his impressive but diffuse cross-disciplinary references, is a painstaking read. The philosopher Sidney Hook observed in a review of one of Burke's earlier books, "The greatest difficulty that confronts Burke is finding out what he means" (qtd. in McKenzie). While Burke's work is not exactly "lost," in that he is recognized as a central figure in twentieth-century American rhetoric, I would speculate that his texts in the early twenty-first century are more often read about in secondary sources than read by current students of rhetoric. Confounding the challenge of Burke's readability is some current scholars' perceptions, as John M. McKenzie indicates, that although significant in the history of rhetoric, Burke "was but a man of his own era" whose system of thought is outdated, "inadequate to the challenges rhetorical theory and criticism face today."

Acknowledging these challenges to understanding and judging Burke's work, I would like to suggest that, rather than outright avoid his primary texts, contemporary readers should anchor their focus on a particular theory of his or on particular chapters in his books. I have chosen to focus here on part 1 of *A Rhetoric of Motives* because his theories of identity and identification are foundational to Western rhetoric. Since they are on the cusp of postmodern theory, they are, in fact, conducive to considering the challenges of today's rhetorical criticism, open to ongoing interrogation and revision. As Sonja K. Foss and colleagues recognize in *Contemporary Perspectives on Rhetoric*, "[Burke's] methods, more than many others, allow for expansion and freedom rather than reduction and confinement" (215). Because of my commitment to feminism and anti-racism, I focus in this short essay on the uses and revisions of Burkean theory by feminist theorists. It is true that, as Bernard L. Brock writes, "[Burke] never spoke to the oppression resulting from the gender framing/roles in society" (Introduction 11). Nevertheless, rethinking and readapting Burke's theories may help those of us committed to social justice conceptualize tools of communications that lead to critical thinking about differences in the classroom, to activism, and ultimately to cultural transformation.

As a contributor to the "new rhetoric" of his postwar era, Burke reversed the assumption of the old rhetoricians that identification is "a means for persuasion" and proposed the opposite—that "persuasion is but one means for identification within rhetorical discourse" (Hansen 51). His concept of rhetoric as a method of identification expanded theories of the social use of language and illuminates "the ways in which people establish and negotiate their identity within a social context" (54). In fact, stressing sociality, Burke defines rhetoric as "a symbolic means of inducing cooperation in beings that by nature respond to symbols" (*Rhetoric* 43). In *A Rhetoric of Motives,* Burke introduces his theory of identification in simple logic: "A is not identical with his colleague, B. But insofar as their interests are joined, A is *identified* with B, or he may *identify himself* with B even when their interests are not joined, if he assumes that they are, or is persuaded to believe so" (20). A synonym Burke uses for *identification* is "consubstantiality." He explains that "to identify A with B is to make A 'consubstantial' with B" (21). He continues: "In being identified with B, A is 'substantially one' with a person other than himself. Yet at the same time he remains unique, an individual locus of motives. Thus he is both joined and separate, at once a distinct substance and consubstantial with another" (21). One entity becomes "consubstantial" with another by sharing—or believing or being convinced that it shares—a common "property" (21, 23), all the while maintaining its separateness. "In the realm of Rhetoric," Burke explains, "identification is frequently by [means of] property in the most materialistic sense of the term, economic property" but also, more generally, by "properties in goods, in services, in position or status, in citizenship, in reputation, in acquaintanceship and love" (24). It is through properties that people's identities are formed and their "moral growth" is organized (24). Unfortunately, it is from these simultaneous processes of multiple people's "forming their identi[ties] in terms of property" that "turmoil and discord" can result (24). Consequently, Burke concludes, identification is "compensatory to division": "If men were not apart from one another, there would be no need for the rhetorician to proclaim their unity. If men were wholly and truly of one substance, absolute communication would be of man's essence" (22).

Burke's emphasis on identification as a means of pursuing cooperation makes historical sense in that he was writing in the aftermaths of World War II, the ascendancy of Fascism, and the Holocaust. Having witnessed human beings collectively identifying with destructive ideologies and forces, he calls war a "perversion of communion" (*Rhetoric* 22). These global disasters seem to haunt him as he reasons that rhetoric "considers the ways in which individuals are at odds with one another, or become identified with groups more or less at odds with one another" (22). He poses the rhetorical question, "Why 'at odds' . . . when the titular term is 'identification'?" His answer: "Because, to begin with 'identification' is, by the same token, though roundabout, to confront the implications of *division*" (22). Burke makes identification so central to rhetoric that in *A Rhetoric of Motives* he claims, placing "identification and division ambiguously together . . . is the characteristic invitation to rhetoric" (25). Implied in the very concept of identification is its counterpart, division, for without division, as Burke points out, the persuader's motive to communicate and to bring about cooperation or even community does not exist (23). As Burke further develops his theory, he shows how identifications can become tools for exposing undetected ideological assumptions in persuasive discourse and, more generally, "equipment for living" (*Philosophy* 293–304), useful strategies, too, for the practice of critical and feminist pedagogies.

Using examples from religion, science, education, and postwar politics, Burke complicates what at first seems to be a simple notion of identification. He clarifies that "often we must think of rhetoric not in terms of some one particular address, but as a general *body of identifications* that owe their convincingness much more to trivial repetition and dull daily reinforcement than to exceptional rhetorical skill" (*Rhetoric* 26). This "*body of identifications*" may encompass, for example, adulating God—"and in terms that happen also to sanction one system of material property rather than another"—or adulating science—"when that same science is at the service of imperialist-militarist expansion" (26). What Burke calls "the impurities of identification" incites "a typical Rhetorical wrangle . . . that can never be settled . . . but belongs in the field of moral controversy" (26).

Fueling these rhetorical wrangles that call for moral consideration are two phenomena Burke recognizes: identification as an "undetected presence" (*Rhetoric* 26)—a hidden assumption—or as an unconscious process. As a relativist, Burke critiques the positivism so prominent during the 1930s and 1940s, recognizing rhetoric as epistemic and paving the way for the ideas of other twentieth-century thinkers like Michel Foucault and for feminist and Marxist pedagogues. The fundamental difference, as the Marxist teacher and thinker Charles Paine indicates, between positivism, which depends on an objectivist approach, and relativism is that the former assumes absolute truth to be permanent and transmittable while relativism assumes truth to be contingent and ever-changing (569). Revealing a Foucauldian distrust of the neutrality of language for conveying knowledge, Burke insightfully points out that identification sometimes operates as an "undetected presence"—for example, in the objectivist speech of advocates of science who fail to explicitly disidentify themselves from the fact that after World War II in the United States "so much scientific research had fallen under the direction of the military" (*Rhetoric* 26). He suggests that by identifying their standpoints with the undetected presence of these "reactionary implications," some educators implicate their philosophies in military dominance (26–27). At this juncture where the rhetorician may recognize the undetected presence of an identification, Burke acknowledges, "the rhetorician and the moralist become one" (26).

To explain the operation of the undetected presence, Burke proceeds to analyze the relationship between a presumably autonomous activity and identification. He looks forward to Foucault's notion that discourse, by creating knowledge, controls social practices and consolidates institutional power. In turn, these insights into the constructed nature of knowledge corroborate feminist understandings of gender socialization and the reproduction of gendered power relations. His hypothetical educators, then, may trust that their fundraising for the science department is "autonomous," but as Burke proceeds to argue, "[a]ny specialized activity participates in a larger unit of action. 'Identification' is a word for the autonomous activity's place in this wider context, a place with which the agent may be unconcerned" (*Rhetoric* 27). On a different note, a person's engagement in a specialized activity may bring about an identification, for example, in that it "makes one a participant in some social or economic class" (28).

Burke's concept that identification refers to an "autonomous activity's place in this wider context, a place with which the agent may be unconcerned" (*Rhetoric* 27), reflects his interest in social systems theories, which are so conducive to feminist analysis, helping earn him the label "sociological rhetorician." Ann Branaman credits Burke with contributing to sociological thought "his conception of identity as a rhetorical tool of criticism" (448). Like contemporary sociologists, he defines identity in relation to social categories, but he also recognizes it as "the key *instrument* of social criticism" (444). Branaman praises Burke for explaining "how patterns of identification can be critical and transformative rather than merely reproductive despite the fact that experience is always already socially patterned" (445).

It is the use of Burke's theory of identification, in particular, as a means for transformation of both identity and the social order that interests me and other feminist scholars like Bauer and, most recently, Krista Ratcliffe. In "The Other 'F' Word: The Feminist in the Classroom," Bauer applies Burke's idea of identification to her political pedagogy to inspire students to engage in feminist activism. Fifteen years later, Ratcliffe supplements Burke's theory as she foregrounds the act of rhetorical listening for the purposes of cross-cultural communication and the eradication of racism. Interestingly, in her much later 2007 essay "Another F Word: Failure in the Classroom," Bauer presents a disclaimer to her 1990 article, admitting that her younger self "was inadvertently advancing a version of the surface/depth model (whereby we fill unenlightened students with enlightened political content)," which she considers "inadequate to teaching in the present context" (157). Bauer's disclaimer does not address her use of Burke's theory of identification, but it does bring to light the importance of adapting critical pedagogy to particular generations and historical contexts, something with which Burke would agree.

I offer Bauer's example of her assignment of an identificatory reading in the literature classroom in order to concretize Burke's theory and also indirectly raise some questions about it. It is not surprising that Bauer would incorporate Burke's notion of identification into her teaching since he frequently uses literature, which he considers a form of rhetoric, as a vehicle for explicating his theories. However, unlike Burke, who in *A Rhetoric of Motives* examines authors' identifications with the figures they choose as their subjects, Bauer, influenced by later reader-response criticism, focuses on readers' identifications with characters or other literary elements. Bauer bases her method of fostering a dialectic between identification and resistance on Burke's distinction in *A Rhetoric of Motives* between two kinds of identification, realistic and idealistic; in "realistic identification, persuasion compels social action," while in idealistic identification "the powerful identify with someone less powerful" (Bauer, "Other 'F' Word" 390). She suggests that feminist teachers can promote critical thinking, ethical choices, and ultimately, social action by using in the classroom "identificatory readings rather than (or only) resisting ones" (391). She hopes that as a result of the identificatory reading, her students will work through their resistances to feminism.

In "The Other 'F' Word: The Feminist in the Classroom," Bauer explains her assignment of an identificatory reading, Pat Barker's *Blow Your House Down*, an ostensible murder mystery about British working-class women, many of whom have turned to prostitution because of the 1974 coal strike and the suffering economy. First, Bauer foregrounds her feminist subject position, telling her students that they will use feminism as a frame of reference for their discussion of the assignment. Bauer believes that Barker's novel calls into question "middle-class notions" about sexual violence against women—that is, that "[sexual violence] happens only to women who provoke men, women who work on the streets" ("Other 'F' Word" 394). The way this "rupture of ... moral expectations" occurs is through the rape of the "respectable" character, Maggie—a wife, mother, and factory worker, not a prostitute—who functions as an "identificatory model" for middle-class readers (394). (Bauer's students are apparently primarily female and middle-class.) Because the novel itself is interested in stereotypes of gender and class, Bauer focuses mostly on these social categories, not on other identity markers like race, ethnicity, sexual orientation, and gender identity. Maggie's assault and her revictimization by the police and neighbors compel readers, Bauer suggests, to examine their uncritical assumptions about class and gender—similar to Burke's "undetected presence"—that have been naturalized in the dominant culture (394).

Bauer's article raises some interesting questions about her implementation of identification in her pedagogy and, in turn, about Burke's theory. Many of these more general questions have been explored in scholarship by practitioners of critical pedagogies. Here I focus on the questions I consider central to feminist theory and practice: According to Burke, why is it that identification—a sense of sameness in a property—is necessary for closing, though ambiguously, a division? Are human beings so narcissistic that only a sense of shared sameness in a particular property can motivate them toward unity? Clearly, Bauer sees Burke's notion of identification as usable and effectual for feminist consciousness-raising and activism. In particular, she seems to understand his juxtaposition of identification and division as a concept that embodies contradictions. As she explains, "Burke implies that identification allows for another voice to be in sync but not to erase difference ("Other 'F' Word" 391). She trusts that a dialectic of identification and resistance, stimulated by dialogue, will bring out her students' different voices and points of view.

In her admirably ambitious study, *Rhetorical Listening: Identification, Gender, Whiteness*, Ratcliffe addresses the following question: Is it possible to enlist identification—and ultimately, cross-cultural communication—by means of not only sameness but also difference? Ratcliffe does so, though not by means of Burke's theory but Diana Fuss's postmodern notion of identification, explored in her *Identification Papers*. Ratcliffe interprets Burke's idea of the coexistence of identification and division differently than Bauer does. Ratcliffe observes, "Burke's identification does provide a place of personal agency and a place of commonality, yet it often does so at the expense of differences" (53). It seems that Bauer's and Ratcliffe's interpretations differ, in part, because of their different reasons for using Burke's theory. Bauer wants to galvanize students' commitment to feminism through a dialectic of identification and resistance. As a white feminist committed to making white privilege visible to its bearers, Ratcliffe wants to understand "how rhetorical listening [a stance of openness] may help listeners negotiate troubled identifications with gender and whiteness" not only in the classroom but also in public debates and scholarly research (xiii). I also attribute the different interpretations offered by these scholars to their divergent understandings of Burke's use of the word *division*. In part 1 of *A Rhetoric of Motives*, Burke does not substitute the word *difference* for the term *division*. By suggesting that division is put in abeyance by the rhetor's establishing a common identification with the other person or group, he is not necessarily equating division with difference. Nor is he constructing the elicitation of identification as a metaphorical bridge across division. (This is why, for lack of a better term, I used the phrase *put in abeyance* in the previous sentence.) In fact, he stresses the ambiguity of the juxtaposition of identification and division in the following statement: "But put identification and division ambiguously together, so that you cannot know for certain just where one ends and the other begins" (*Rhetoric* 25). Thus, it seems that Bauer might perceive Burke's concept as more postmodern than Ratcliffe does, for Burke's philosophy is located "near the center of [the] postmodern-modern debate" (Brock, Introduction 9). Ultimately, Ratcliffe favors Diana Fuss's postmodern definition of *identification* as "the play of difference and similitude in self-other relations" (Ratcliffe 60). To Ratcliffe, this idea "does not stand against identity but structurally aids and abets it" (64). Believing that Burke's concept of identification erases difference, Ratcliffe hopes to acknowledge and give voice to differences in order to build cross-cultural understanding in the classroom, in antiracism movements, and in the larger community.

That many feminist rhetorical scholars continue to address the totality of Burke's theories attests to their foundational value and their capacity for ongoing revision. Karen A. Foss and Cindy L. White critique Burke's notion of human symbol use for not developing "the midpoint of the action-motion continuum," the foundation of his theory (99). Therefore, they formulate a theory that supplies the "in-between realm," which they call "being" (101). Their concept of the act of being is applicable in classrooms and social justice settings. They argue that "being" invites transformation that comes not from persuasion or coercion but from "a person being fully centered, connected, and present, and in that capacity of aliveness and awareness, facilitating the creation of an environment in which others can also change" (108). Phyllis M. Japp cautions against any assumption that "inherent feminist tendencies [are] hidden within the Burkean perspective," but she acknowledges that "the full potential of Burke's critical system has not been realized, embedded as it has been in traditions that have constrained it" (117). She brilliantly offers an alternative interpretive approach to Burke's work—the feminist reclamation of texts—especially in the critical strategies of the feminist theologian Elizabeth Schussler Fiorenza, which proceed from "suspicion" and "proclamation" to "remembrance" and "creative actualization" (Japp 118–21). To demonstrate the compatibility of Burke's system with the effort of feminist revision, she aligns each one of Burke's tropes with Fiorenza's, thus completing the task of reclamation (122–24). Japp enacts the process of producing counterhegemonic knowledge for educators who may engage their students in similar feminist reclamations of androcentric or canonical texts. While I have emphasized here how Burke's notions are adaptable to feminist projects, his idea of identity as an instrument of social criticism is applicable to diverse disciplines and critical schools. His theory of identification is always renewing, as rhetorical scholars return to, revise, and adapt it for the purpose of political pedagogy, activism, and social transformation.

Works Cited

Barker, Pat. *Two Novels:* Union Street *and* Blow Your House Down. Picador USA, 1999.

Bauer, Dale M. "Another F Word: Failure in the Classroom." *Pedagogy*, vol. 7, no. 2, Apr. 2007, pp. 157–70.

———. "The Other 'F' Word: The Feminist in the Classroom." *College English*, vol. 52, no. 4, 1990, pp. 385–96.

Branaman, Ann. "Reconsidering Kenneth Burke: His Contributions to the Identity Controversy." *The Sociological Quarterly*, vol. 5, no. 3, Aug. 1994, pp. 443–55.

Brock, Bernard L. Introduction. Brock, *Kenneth Burke*, pp. 1–15.

———, editor. *Kenneth Burke and the Twenty-First Century*. State U of New York P, 1999.

Burke, Kenneth. *The Philosophy of Literary Form*. 3rd ed., U of California P, 1990.

———. *A Rhetoric of Motives*. U of California P, 1969.

Foss, Karen A., and Cindy L. White. "'Being' and the Promise of Trinity: A Feminist Addition to Burke's Theory of Dramatism." Brock, *Kenneth Burke*, pp. 99–111.

Foss, Sonja K., et al. *Contemporary Perspectives on Rhetoric*. 30th anniversary ed., Waveland Press, 2014.

Hansen, Gregory. "Kenneth Burke's Rhetorical Theory within the Construction of the Ethnography of Speaking." *Folklore Forum*, vol. 27, no. 1, 1996, pp. 50–59.

Japp, Phyllis M. "'Can This Marriage Be Saved?' Reclaiming Burke for Feminist Scholarship." Brock, *Kenneth Burke*, pp. 113–30.

McKenzie, John M. "Reading Resistance to Kenneth Burke: 'Burke the Usurper' and Other Themes." *KB Journal*, vol. 7, no. 1, fall 2010, p. 7, www.kbjournal.org/mckenzie.

Paine, Charles. "Relativism, Radical Pedagogy, and the Ideology of Paralysis." *College English*, vol. 51, no. 6, 1989, pp. 557–70. *JSTOR*, www.jstor.org/stable/377940.

Ratcliffe, Krista. *Rhetorical Listening: Identification, Gender, Whiteness*. Southern Illinois UP, 2005.

College Composition and Communication, Volume 15, 1964: Afterglow, Childhood, Obituary?

Douglas Hesse

> *College Composition and Communication*, volume 15 (1964)

The year 1963 is regularly cited as the watershed year in composition studies, the year things got serious. Two landmark events draw the most attention: the publication of Richard Braddock, Richard Lloyd-Jones, and Lowell Schoer's *Research in Written Composition* and the annual Conference on College Composition and Communication (CCCC) in Los Angeles. That meeting yielded a host of influential articles in *College Composition and Communication* (*CCC*), among them Wayne Booth's "The Rhetorical Stance," Francis Christensen's "A Generative Rhetoric of the Sentence," Edward Corbett's "The Usefulness of Classical Rhetoric," and Albert Kitzhaber's "4C, Freshman English, and the Future." Regularly invoked and cited, the 1963 publications and events are far from lost.

Far less famous nearly sixty years later are the CCCC events and publications of 1964, especially a series of articles that alternatively embrace and abjure the role of research and rhetoric celebrated the year before. Among the crosscurrents that swirled within *CCC* volume 15 was a vision of composition and composition studies as a creative art of all writing, a vision that ultimately lost out—occasionally revived but regularly vilified.

Given the spirit of this book, the choice of a journal volume as a lost text may seem odd, so let me offer three reasons. First, the journal article represented the dominant form of sharing ideas during the first couple of decades of modern composition, pre-discipline decades when composition studies was constituted almost solely as a teaching field and scholarly books were almost wholly absent. Books carrying the field's knowledge were mostly certain textbooks, which Bob Connors (69–111) and others have noted performed something of a scholarly role. Second, positions on contested issues were directly performed in the juxtapositions of dozens of short articles and also, importantly, in the broader text of book reviews, conference reports, and editorial matter. *CCC* volume 15 is rather a catalog of the times. Third, the nature of the articles themselves reveal a more humanistic approach to writing than one common in recent years. The pieces are short (a fifth the size of contemporary articles), conversational, personal, and essayistic—evocative of the earlier field. Reading *CCC* volume 15 provides an understanding not only of the contested content and focus of the proto-disciplinary composition studies but also of the form of the contestations: the discourse conventions that authors should follow in a field still making itself. I'll come back to that point.

First, however, an overview. Volume 15 was the last volume edited by Ken Macrorie, the author of *Telling Writing*, *Uptaught*, and *The I-Search Paper* and a proponent of student interest and voice against "Engfish," the term he coined to dismiss inauthentic academic writing. The volume contains five issues, each announcing a theme on its cover. February is "Composition as Art," May "Generative Grammars," and October "Tagmemics." November is a special issue, "Directory of Assistantships and Fellowships for Graduate Study in English and the Teaching of English," some 140 pages of names, addresses, stipends, and conditions in 246 graduate programs. December's theme is "The Graduate Experience in English," and the issue features ten "case studies," each a dystopic narrative (few things change) written by a graduate student whom Macrorie had asked "to write anonymously, both to protect them in their careers and to insure that readers will not recognize the university being reported upon" (Macrorie 211). Four of the issues contain poems, some by students, including "Mouse," by eight-year-old David Bergsten of Topsfield, Massachusetts. There is no advertising.

Issue 1, "Composition as Art," enacts Macrorie's belief that rhetoricians and linguists "have gained such power that they will probably dominate the restructuring of the freshman course for decades to come," with the result that "the teaching of writing may become too mechanical or analytical." Macrorie's blurb on the back cover of the issue concludes, "How does a writer write? Through conscious manipulation of grammar and rhetoric? Sometimes yes, more often no." Key, of course, is how the practices of experienced writers should be taken up by students learning to write. The issue includes essays by poets Marvin Bell ("Poetry and Freshman Composition," written just as Bell was drafted for Vietnam) and William Stafford; Janet Emig's "The Uses of the Unconscious in Composing;" "The Essay as Art," by Harold Simonson, whose argument prefigures by thirty years claims made for literary nonfiction; and twelve other essays, for a total of sixteen in fifty-nine pages. That prolific compression illustrates how much this journal differs from today's, where an issue of *CCC* might have five or six articles. There are several book reviews, only one of them about disciplinary scholarship: Albert Kitzhaber's *Themes, Theories, and Therapy: The Teaching of Writing in College*. The others are of Frank O'Connor's *The Lonely Voice*, five textbooks, and, oddly, Adolf Hitler's *Mein Kampf*.

Stafford's essay "Writing the Australian Crawl" might surprise some contemporary readers who call for the profession to embrace narrative and personal elements of academic writing, as if such things were new and unprecedented. We've been there. Here's Stafford's opening paragraph: "Our daughter Kit, six years old, stands by the lighted dashboard talking to Daddy as he drives home from a family trip to the beach. The others have gone to sleep, and Kit is helping—she talks to keep me awake. The road winds ahead, and she bubbles along, composing with easy strokes, imagining a way of life for the two of us" (12). Stafford continues in this voice and style, alternatively narrative and exploratory, in an extended analogy between writing and swimming, explaining the limits of conscious technique and the virtues of trusting experience, noting, "Just as the swimmer does not have a succession of handholds hidden in the water, . . . so the writer passes his attention through what is at hand, and is propelled by a medium too thin and all-pervasive for the perceptions of nonbelievers" (14). This is "shaping at the point of utterance" before James Britton, Peter Elbow before Peter Elbow, the kind of romantic expressivism that Jim Berlin teed up to smack out of composition studies. But notice two things: first, the genres that Stafford implies—not academic or civic but belletristic and liberal—and second, the style of the piece itself. Given more room I'd demonstrate how common this approach was (it runs through Walker Gibson and Ann Berthoff, for example) before the drive took over to establish disciplinarity through performing method. That method derived largely from the social sciences, as Steve North would explain over twenty years later in *The Making of Knowledge in Composition*. In 1964 the field's flagship journal could publish with great seriousness, "When you write, simply tell me something. Maybe you can tell me how we should live" (Stafford 15).

The May issue, "Generative Grammars," begins with John Viertel's article summarizing Noam Chomsky, replete with graphic illustrations of transformational grammar at work. Then follows a curious article by Kenneth Pike, "A Linguistic Contribution to Composition," which begins with a disclaimer that Pike's experience "includes little direct connection with the teaching of composition" (82) but nonetheless proceeds to offer assignments based on axioms about language. Some are familiar stylistic exercises ("Write a brief essay in which only complex sentences are used.... Rewrite, utilizing exclusively short, simple sentences" [87]), but others are the kind that likely drove Macrorie to advocate "Composition as Art": "Build some verse in which you use choices in phonological slots, leading to rhyme. Then a few lines exploiting phonologically-controlled sequence, leading to alliteration. Then build some verse in which the smaller bits are integrated with a larger pattern of recurrent stresses" (86). Pike, of course, is famous for his work with Richard Young and Alton Becker on tagmemics, the subject of his lead article, "Beyond the Sentence," in the October issue.

Three other elements of the May issue are interesting. First is the "Staffroom Interchange" section. Emphasizing practical advice, often anecdotal, "Staffroom Interchange" was a regular part of the journal until Richard Gebhardt's editorship in the late 1980s. One piece presciently outlines a planned PhD curriculum at Rensselaer Polytechnic Institute, with two tracks (Spencer). One track has fewer than half its requirements in literary study, the rest in theory, rhetoric, and composition. The other, focusing on technical communication, requires no literature. This is 1964, decades earlier than many might usually think of writing studies leaving literature-heavy English departments. The second noteworthy element is an annotated bibliography of over 150 sourcebooks: textbooks compiling articles, documents, illustrations, and so on designed to support source-based writing on a single topic (Kogan). Book topics are more or less evenly divided between issues and ideas (*School Desegregation: Documents and Commentaries*; *The Chicago Strike of 1894*; *Extrasensory Perception*), on the one hand, and literary works and authors (*A Scarlet Letter Handbook*; *Young Coleridge*; *A Casebook on Ezra Pound*), on the other. The bibliography outlines teachers' topical interests sixty years ago, when there were still seventeen textbook publishers; implies pedagogies supported by sourcebooks decades before the Internet obviated the approach; and illustrates the imperative of *CCC* to provide practical resources to first-year instructors. The pedagogy was sufficiently well-established that workshop 12 at the 1964 convention (its proceedings reported in issue 3) focused on "Using Controlled Research Materials" ("Workshop 12" 187).

A third notable aspect of the May issue is a fascinating article about a program to teach spelling, written by Devra Rowland, College English Editor at D. C. Heath, who describes learning some techniques while working as an assistant to B. F. Skinner at Harvard for $1.25 an hour. More interesting than Rowland's early explanation of using computers to teach an aspect of writing is the piece's style. Ostensibly a report of an experimental study, the piece has none of the research article's IMRAD (Introduction, Methods, Results, Analysis, Discussion) trappings; for example, there's no literature review (in fact, there are no sources) or statistical analysis. While its aspirations could hardly be more different, Rowland's essay is similar in approach to Stafford's "Australian Crawl": both are narrative, conversational, written in the first person, and occasionally self-deprecatory. Rowland's story of creating and testing her program begins, "Suddenly in the spring 1956, I had the feeling that if I learned one more thing without being able to go out and teach anyone anything, I'd burst" (90). She reports that a dean at the University of Kentucky "allotted me $35 for my dehumanizing scheme and sent me on my way" (91) and characterizes results from her first experiment: "The girls who had come to the university to get married hated the program. The Korean veterans who regretted having wasted their time in high school loved it" (92). Try to imagine a current reviewer for *Written Communication* or *Research in the Teaching of English* or *CCC* responding to Rowland's manuscript.

Most probably, Rowland's article wouldn't have passed muster for Braddock, Lloyd-Jones, and Schoer's *Research in Written Composition*, which is positively reviewed twice in the October issue. The direction of the field is signaled in J. Stephen Sherwin's assessment that "[i]nspiration and intuition will always have a place, but they must be the start of inquiry and not its end. To those who deny that the teaching of the English language lends itself to controlled, experimental research, it is necessary to reply that the challenge to teaching has not been met by other means" (171).

Issue 3 continues the practice since *CCC*'s inception (discontinued in 1974) of including reports from the various workshops that made up the annual spring convention. Those workshops were imagined in 1950 as "the most extensive and concerted frontal attack ever made on the problems of teaching college freshman English" (C. W. R.). The short reports sketch the profession's interests. The report for workshop 1, "Rhetoric and Composition," finds, for example, that all participants "wanted rhetoric to govern the freshman English course" ("Workshop 1"). Not surprisingly, members of workshop 2 ("Language and Composition"), workshop 3 ("Literature and Composition"), workshop 4 ("The New Grammar and Composition"), and workshop 5 ("Logic, Semantics, and Composition" [chaired by Neil Postman, by the way, a few years before *Teaching as a Subversive Activity* and decades before *Amusing Ourselves to Death*]) tend to think otherwise. It might surprise relatively new English professors and teachers to learn that sixty years ago the federal government funded Project English to support research in English and over a dozen national centers for curriculum study. The report for workshop 8, "Project English and the English Department," asked, "What will the future English department look like if literature moves out of its central place? What contributions will research make to the teaching of reading and writing?" (183). Posing the question was John Fisher, then executive director of the MLA. But rather than a spirited debate about the nature of English, the report mainly explores issues in empirical and statistical methodology. The profession conjured in workshop 8 differs substantially from the belletristic world of Macrorie's "Composition as Art."

With more room, I'd describe more than twenty percent of *CCC* volume 15, but I hope this is enough to see what's at stake in it. There's the scientific versus the humanistic study of writing; the production of practical versus literary texts; the relationships between composition, creative writing, and literature; the relationship between rhetoric and linguistics; and the relationship between formal analysis and reading.

By 1964 CCCC had existed for fourteen years, and the institution of freshman composition had existed about a century, sustained more by tradition and lore (in North's sense) than by a disciplinary canon. By 1964 there was at least recognition that teaching writing ought to require knowledge and credentials, but workshop 19, "Preparing College Composition Teachers," was mostly silent on the nature of the knowledge, parenthetically mentioning linguistics and rhetorical theory ("Workshop 19"). Over a decade later, Carl Klaus, himself a scholar of prose style and the literary essay, still worried that writing teachers (himself included) were "at best dedicated amateurs, who for all our dedication may well be doing our students more harm than good" (338). To linguistics and rhetoric, Klaus added the philosophy and psychology of language. (Later scholars would add to what Janice Lauer called a "dappled discipline," including political theory and economy, sociology, anthropology, critical race theory, and many others.) My point is that while teaching required writing had been a long-established practice by the early sixties, there was practically no explicit, codified base informing that enterprise.

For professional teachers of writing—and by professional I'm imagining a low threshold: those teachers who were willing to join CCCC—the credential was less what you knew and more how you participated with other teachers, less about logos than about ethos. The personal essayistic style of articles in *CCC* volume 15 is actually, then, a constitutive feature of a field that was far from a discipline. A discipline would be defined by a body of knowledge, a methodology for producing it, and a cumulative literature. In contrast, composition studies in 1964 had ongoing conversations about some common topics and interests. Writers contributed to that conversation by saying things that others might find interesting or useful, in a compelling voice as a member—and keep this in mind—of an English department. It's telling that the only formal citations included in the "Composition as Art" issue, which sprinkles references to writers and texts throughout its articles, come in the form of six footnotes in the article by Emig, who was a graduate student at the time. When composition studies—or is it writing studies or something else?—accrued disciplinary status, or even whether it has, is a matter of long debate. Members of the field generally agree that it has, with the only serious discussions concerning the nature (rather than the existence) of the discipline, as reflected in books like *Composition, Rhetoric, and Disciplinarity* (Malenczyk et al.). Kathleen Yancey's thoughtful analysis in that volume suggests that disciplinary status really started to congeal only in the past twenty years, its four markers being a research agenda, the consolidation of knowledge in the field, the development of majors in rhetoric and composition, and the occasional relocation of writing studies within institutions.

In the half century since *CCC* volume 15, a coherent research agenda for the field has failed to emerge, at least as reflected in *CCC*, still our flagship journal. I did a quick review of *CCC* volume 71 (2019–20), the most recently published volume as of the time of this writing. Its twenty-one articles trace a wide range of issues and questions, with an almost equally wide range of approaches, variously historical, quantitative, qualitative, interpretive, critical, and polemic. Only six of those pieces directly address pedagogical issues or approaches, a significant change from *CCC* volume 15. Even these six articles differ vastly from their counterparts fifty-five years earlier by locating ethos in the performing of reading rather than in the narrative of experience or thought. Like most recent *CCC* articles, they heavily employ citation, an average of forty-nine citations per article (Hesse, "Journals" 372–75), demonstrating Yancey's criterion of knowledge consolidation. Articles are necessarily much longer as a result, twenty-five to thirty pages versus four to five in volume 15. The stylistic and epistemological contrasts are profound. Earlier pieces were essayistic, in the long tradition from Montaigne through Emerson, Virginia Woolf, James Baldwin, and Rebecca Solnit, following the associative narrative logic of the essay as tracing the shape of thinking. Current pieces participate in the tradition of the formal article, something one is obliged to read to claim membership in a knowledge community. They're marked, for example, by extensive metadiscourse ("In this article I will first . . . I will next . . . Finally, I will . . .") to provide signposting to negotiate complex evidence for claims. They're up to serious business, with professional standing at stake for authors. The style and brevity of their mid-sixties forebears often more closely resembles work that might be found in a magazine or trade journal, the kind of publication that has poems and in which an editor like Macrorie may print correspondence with a young girl as a freestanding piece:

> Dear Susan,
> I wish we had stayed out in the rain longer. I wish we had gotten a cold. It would have bin fun.

> I love you Susan. Don't forget to call me. My foghn number is DA 7 9987. Today Thersday I cannot play with you. Mom is at collig.
> Love,
> Janet (Bowman)
>
> Dear Janet:
> May I have permission to reprint your letter to Susan in *CCC*, the magazine I edit?
> Sincerely,
> Ken Macrorie
>
> Dear Mr. Macrorie,
> You may use my letter. I don't think it is very good. I am writing because I feel like it.
> Yours truly,
> Janet ("Three Letters")

Please note that I'm not denigrating current formal practices of discipline-building, which manifests how the profession has heeded Braddock, Lloyd-Jones, and Schoer's call to get serious. However, I would remind folks who ahistorically call for scholarship that's more personal or narrative that they invoke an occluded tradition, as illustrated by many pieces in *CCC* volume 15.

I'm similarly bemused by the field's purported discovery of creative nonfiction, which ignores belletristic and narrative genres that once were central to composition studies (Hesse, "Who Owns Creative Nonfiction?") but which got replaced over the years by three primary foci: academic discourse, leading to a new practice of current-traditional rhetoric that has students write toward disciplinary forms; argument that privileges logos over other forms of persuasion; and textual or cultural analyses, often with direct or indirect political aims of representation or critique such as righting wrongs or illuminating occluded lives and practices. Occasionally, composition remembers genres beyond classrooms and scholarly journals, reasons for writing beyond judicial and forensic rhetoric, beyond presenting information to obliged readers. There's a whole nonfiction galaxy that composition has abjured or forfeited: journalism, features, profiles, travel writing, memoir, and essay—variously personal, lyric, and exploratory—spaces of the expressive and aesthetic, produced to win attention from self-sponsored readers who may choose other options. In 1964 Harold Simonson called attention to some of this parallel tradition, explaining, "My case is for the essay as art. It is not for the essay as rhetorical mechanics or as erudition. It is not for the essay as instruction except insofar as instruction becomes delight" (36). Composition could have embraced a larger textual territory for study and teaching, even without the creative writing, manifested as poetry, short stories, and film, in *CCC* volume 15.

Only in convenient retrospect do 1963's twin peaks of rhetorical theory and formal research appear as pivotal and dramatic bases for composition/writing studies in the decades that followed. (Curiously, a third peak that year, linguistic approaches, had eroded by the 1980s.) Reading *CCC* volume 15 illustrates how the contours of composition studies were hardly inevitable, let alone entirely desirable, in the aftermath of the landmark year 1963. The exceptionally detailed minutes of the CCCC executive committee meeting on 27 November 1963 trace an energetic debate that ultimately rejected a common content for first-year writing and instead privileged "hunches" and "experience" alongside research (Clifton 203). At present, when some current compositionists champion interests beyond academic discourse or argument, for both study and teaching, and as some also resist the scholarly article as the default genre for circulating ideas, we'd do well to recall earlier practices in our field. It's possible, certainly, to see 1964 as a disciplinary adolescence out of which we thankfully matured. But it's also possible to see that maturation as happening at the cost of stunted identities and limited borders for composition studies, some of which are now being rearticulated and rediscovered.

Works Cited

Bell, Marvin. "Poetry and Freshman Composition." *College Composition and Communication*, vol. 15, no. 1, Feb. 1964, pp. 1–5.

Bergsten, David. "Mouse." *College Composition and Communication*, vol. 15, no. 4, Dec. 1964, p. 256.

Berlin, James A. *Rhetorics, Poetics, and Cultures: Refiguring English Studies*. National Council of Teachers of English, 1996.

Booth, Wayne. "The Rhetorical Stance." *College Composition and Communication*, vol. 14, no. 3, Oct. 1963, pp. 139–45.

Braddock, Richard, et al. *Research in Written Composition*. National Council of Teachers of English, 1963.

Britton, James. "Shaping at the Point of Utterance." *Prospect and Retrospect: Selected Essays of James Britton*, edited by Gordon Pradl, Boynton/Cook, 1982, pp. 139–45.

Christensen, Francis. "A Generative Rhetoric of the Sentence." *College Composition and Communication*, vol. 14, no. 3, Oct. 1963, pp. 155–61.

Clifton, Lucille. "Secretary's Report No. 45." *College Composition and Communication*, vol. 15, no. 3, Oct. 1964, pp. 200–03.

Connors, Robert J. *Composition-Rhetoric: Backgrounds, Theory, and Pedagogy*. U of Pittsburgh P, 1997.

Corbett, Edward P. J. "The Usefulness of Classical Rhetoric." *College Composition and Communication*, vol. 14, no. 3, Oct. 1963, pp. 162–64.

C. W. R. "Foreword: Workshop Reports of the 1950 Conference on College Composition and Communication." *College Composition and Communication*, vol. 1, no. 2, May 1950, p. 3.

Emig, Janet. "The Uses of the Unconscious in Composing." *College Composition and Communication*, vol. 15, no. 1, Feb. 1964, pp. 6–11.

Hesse, Doug. "Journals in Composition Studies, Thirty-Five Years After." *College English*, vol. 81, no. 4, Mar. 2019, pp. 367–96.

———. "Who Owns Creative Nonfiction?" *Beyond Postprocess and Postmodernism: Essays on the Spaciousness of Rhetoric*, edited by Theresa Enos and Keith D. Miller, Erlbaum, 2003, pp. 251–66.

Kitzhaber, Albert. "4C, Freshman English, and the Future." *College Composition and Communication*, vol. 14, no. 3, Oct. 1963, pp. 129–38.

Klaus, Carl. "Public Opinion and Professional Belief." *College Composition and Communication*, vol. 27, no. 4, Dec. 1976, pp. 335–40.

Kogan, Bernard. "Current Sourcebooks: 3." *College Composition and Communication*, vol. 15, no. 2, May 1964, pp. 102–09.

Lauer, Janice. "Composition Studies: Dappled Discipline." *Rhetoric Review*, vol. 3, no. 1, Sept. 1984, pp. 20–29.

Macrorie, Ken. "The Graduate Experience in English: An Introduction to Ten Case-Histories." *College Composition and Communication*, vol. 15, no. 4, Dec. 1964, pp. 209–52.

Malenczyk, Rita, et al., editors. *Composition, Rhetoric, and Disciplinarity*. Utah State UP, 2018.

North, Stephen. *The Making of Knowledge in Composition: Portrait of an Emerging Field*. Boynton/Cook, 1987.

Pike, Kenneth. "Beyond the Sentence." *College Composition and Communication*, vol. 15, no. 3, Oct. 1964, pp. 129–35.

———. "A Linguistic Contribution to Composition." *College Composition and Communication*, vol. 15, no. 2, May 1964, pp. 82–88.

Rowland, Devra. "A Decade in the Life of a Programmer." *College Composition and Communication*, vol. 15, no. 2, May 1964, pp. 90–96.

Sherwin, J. Stephen. "Research—Ugh, Braddock—Aye." *College Composition and Communication*, vol. 15, no. 3, Oct. 1964, pp. 170–71.

Simonson, Harold. "The Essay as Art." *College Composition and Communication*, vol. 15, no. 1, Feb. 1964, pp. 34–37.

Spencer, Robert A. "A Ph.D. Communication Curriculum for Teachers of English." *College Composition and Communication*, vol. 15, no. 2, May 1964, pp. 121–24.

Stafford, William. "Writing the Australian Crawl." *College Composition and Communication*, vol. 15, no. 1, Feb. 1964, pp. 12–15.

"Three Letters." *College Composition and Communication*, vol. 15, no. 3, Oct. 1964, p. 199.

Viertel, John. "Generative Grammars." *College Composition and Communication*, vol. 15, no. 2, May 1964, pp. 65–81.

"Workshop 1: Rhetoric and Composition." *College Composition and Communication*, vol. 15, no. 3, Oct. 1964, p. 175.

"Workshop 8: Project English and the English Department." *College Composition and Communication*, vol. 15, no. 3, Oct. 1964, pp. 182–83.

"Workshop 12: Using Controlled Research Materials." *College Composition and Communication*, vol. 15, no. 3, Oct. 1964, pp. 187–88.

"Workshop 19: Preparing College Composition Teachers." *College Composition and Communication*, vol. 15, no. 3, Oct. 1964, pp. 192–93.

Yancey, Kathleen Blake. "Mapping the Turn to Disciplinarity: A Historical Analysis of Composition's Trajectory and Its Current Moment." Malenczyk et al., pp. 15–35.

Part Three

The 1970s

On Recovering Adrienne Rich's "Teaching Language in Open Admissions"

Howard Tinberg

> Adrienne Rich, "Teaching Language in Open Admissions: A Look at the Context," *The Uses of Literature*, edited by Monroe Engel (Harvard UP, 1973)

I admit openly that my knowledge of the City University of New York (CUNY) open admissions experiment (and in particular the SEEK program—Search for Education, Elevation, and Knowledge) came from various secondhand sources rather than Adrienne Rich's firsthand account in "Teaching Language in Open Admissions." I recall reading academic accounts like David Bartholomae's "The Study of Error," Min-Zhan Lu's "Redefining the Legacy of Mina Shaughnessy," and of course Mina Shaughnessy's own writings about the program, most notably *Errors and Expectations* and "Diving In: An Introduction to Basic Writing." Jane Maher's biography of Shaughnessy's life has also proved influential, as has the somewhat critical version given by the writer and journalist James Traub. In many of these accounts I had come to see Rich's name prominently featured. She was a prominent poet, who at the time and by her own admission had led the kind of privileged life that would make her role in this experiment in democracy somewhat unexpected. I had been intrigued by the dissonance: What would a Harvard- and Radcliffe-educated white poet (whose father was Jewish) be able to teach inner-city kids about writing and reading? I happen also to have taught both writing and literature these past three decades in an urban, open access community college and am thoroughly committed to the mission of providing access and paths for success to all who desire them. When asked to contribute to this collection, I wanted to know more about this noble experiment at CUNY, which has inspired me over the years. In particular

I wanted the perspective of a teacher in the SEEK program. For that, I went to Adrienne Rich.

It could be argued that in revisiting the open admissions experiment that took place at CUNY from roughly 1970 to 1975 I am embarking on either a nostalgic, liberal fantasy or a fool's errand. What value could there be in revisiting another account of that long-ago, faraway event, of returning to a purportedly idyllic past in which all citizens of New York City, regardless of race or ethnicity, were allowed admittance to college, tuition-free, so many of these students being the first in their family to go to college?

After all, in today's world, even public higher education is becoming out of reach for many families. Open admissions community colleges, due to diminished public support, have for some time found themselves relying increasingly on tuition. And because of the COVID-19 global pandemic, an event that has unfairly afflicted Americans along racial and class lines, many underserved students find attending college even further beyond their grasp.

And why spend time recounting Rich's efforts to attend to the needs of underprepared writers or, as they came to be known thenceforward, basic writers? After all, stand-alone basic writing instruction at the college level is fast becoming a relic of the past. It is now a foregone conclusion that the more time students spend in a developmental course the less likely they are to pass the required first-year writing course, a key predictor for retention (Adams et al. 51–52). Corequisite courses in which students take both basic writing and the universally required first-year composition course have quickly become the norm at community colleges, to which four-year colleges and universities have long since ceded remedial instruction in math and English.

And why invoke the name of Mina Shaughnessy, Rich's mentor and to whom Rich pays tribute in her essay? True, Shaughnessy has been seen as a progressive teacher and an enlightened administrator, doing battle against a system that persisted for generations in, as Shaughnessy herself put it, "GUARDING THE TOWER," or, once the gates were opened, "CONVERTING THE NATIVES" ("Diving In" 234, 235). Yet as decades have passed, reevaluations of Shaughnessy's tenure and writing have brought less worshipful attention and severe critiques. The inconsistencies between her stated goals for these first-generation college students and her pedagogy have been well noted (Lu). Even as she argued that the errors of basic writers have a logic and are worthy of careful study and research, Shaughnessy's teaching essentially focused on grammar and correctness: how to get these inexperienced writers to compose in ways acceptable to academe.

More recently, the grand narrative that our field has promoted—which suggests that heroic and selfless figures such as Shaughnessy, Rich, and Toni Cade Bambara were prime movers in establishing open admissions at CUNY—has been shown to exclude the vital social justice work of Black and Puerto Rican students at the time, who demanded proportional representation among CUNY's student body as part of a larger effort to gain community control over the schools (Kynard 17; Steinberg).

In light of all these reservations, it's not surprising that this essay by Rich, who was a poet and not a composition specialist or even an academic, has been set aside (more so than Shaughnessy's work, which was groundbreaking in establishing basic writing as a subject of serious academic concern and thus has special historical significance). Why resurrect the essay? Why now?

I'd like to defer answering that question for now. Instead, I'd like to draw attention to aspects of the essay that I have found worthy of recovery. It is my hope that in doing so I will slowly assemble an answer to the question posed. You can be sure that as I conclude I will return to the current moment and point out explicitly why we would do well to draw insight from Rich.

The Call to Teach

In her brief preface—written some six years after the publication of "Teaching Language" and just after CUNY's board of trustees voted to cut back open admissions and the SEEK program and charge tuition for the first time—Rich admits to the program's "profound if often naively optimistic experiment in education" (51). She confesses to underestimating the power of the city's "political machinery" that would use the city's racial divides to amass power—pitting Black people against Puerto Ricans, the poor against various ethnic groups—with the effect of retrenching the program (51). And yet despite retrenchment, despite the city's swift and certain withdrawal from the idealism a few shorts years before, Rich clearly sees use in reprinting her essay. What might that use be? Indeed, what is the use of recovering this "lost" essay now?

I write this essay at a time of intense polarization—defined tragically along lines of race, class, and gender—a polarization that is all too reminiscent of the time described by Rich. Certainly, the cost of such polarization is evident, particularly in the era of COVID-19 and Black Lives Matter. And while I credit Rich for acknowledging her own early and flawed romanticism about teaching (grounded in her reading of Emlyn Williams's *The Corn Is Green* when she was young) and her own privileged position—educated as an undergraduate at Harvard and Radcliffe and employed to teach at Columbia—I discovered in Rich's account something else more noteworthy than the realization of privilege. Here I need to tread warily. Rich was not trained to be a teacher when propelled by "white liberal guilt" to interview to teach in the SEEK program (Rich 53). She was hired as a "poet-teacher" but had little training in the teaching of writing (55). In fact, at first, her students would be taught grammar by a specialist (that would subsequently change under budget stress, and Rich would need to take up grammar instruction as well). As a teacher and scholar of writing—someone who has worked hard to understand my teaching subject—I resist the notion that the practice of writing, even by a poet as accomplished as Rich, is equivalent to the teaching of writing. To her credit, Rich admits to her lack of teaching knowledge, spending hours with colleagues "trying to teach ourselves how to teach and asking ourselves what we ought to be teaching" (56). Should she have entered the classroom better prepared?

Of course, I am asking the wrong question. Instead I should be asking this question: What was Rich bringing to her SEEK classroom that would assist her students? I believe the answer can be found in this stirring passage from her essay:

> Many of our students wrote in the vernacular with force and wit; others were unable to say what they wanted on paper in or out of the vernacular. We were dealing not simply with dialect and syntax but with the imagery of lives, the anger and flare of urban youth—how could this be *used*, strengthened, without the lies of artificial polish? ... Some students who could barely sweat out a paragraph delivered (and sometimes conned us with) dazzling raps in the classroom: How could we help this oral gift transfer itself onto paper? (56)

This is not the language of a naive, dewy-eyed white liberal who refuses to see what is right in front of her and charges forward to impose her idealism on a rough and incongruous reality. Instead, Rich sees clearly what her students are bringing (and not bringing) to her class. She sees the flaws, and she sees force in students' work. She is no fool—she cannot be easily "conned," as she puts it, by bursts of language. She knows that this group of mostly first-generation college students will need more than "artificial polish" to succeed in college and beyond. They will need to work so very hard. And yet she can see the gifts that many bring with them. The goal here is not to paper over those gifts but to transfer their power onto paper. What is not directly stated in this passage but is in fact alluded to earlier in the essay is Rich's motive for assisting these students in the first place. It is, simply, love—love for her city and for all its residents in all their glorious and breathtaking possibility.

Who Are These Students?

As is obvious by now, I read Rich's essay through the lens of my own, decades-long experience at an open access, urban, public community college. I see my students in her students: "Some were indeed chronologically older than the average college student; many, though eighteen or twenty years old, had had responsibility for themselves and their families for years. . . . They had held dirty jobs, borne children, negotiated for Spanish-speaking parents with an English-speaking world . . ." (Rich 58). But I see differences as well. Where Rich sees her students occupying "dirty" jobs, I see my students working as aides at care facilities and schools, as clerks at the local supermarket, or as packers at Amazon. I see among my students professionals who have returned to college for new or upgraded skills. In this time of the pandemic, we call many of these students "essential" or "frontline" workers, yet we often don't reward them with appropriate compensation or protection from the virus. Are these the "dirty jobs" that Rich sees her students doing? Perhaps. Yet I think it important not to essentialize or identify students solely by their employment. They are so much more than that.

I wonder whether in her desire to avoid romanticizing her SEEK students, Rich succumbs to another limitation: to reduce them mostly to victims—victims of tracking at an early age, victims of "the intellectual poverty and human waste of the public school system," victims of drugs and despair (Rich 59).

But here, I believe, I am straying from the original context of Rich's essay. New York City in the 1960s and 1970s: a march of eight thousand mostly African Americans to protest the police shooting of a young Black man (Steinberg); the riots in the city and across the nation in the wake of the assassination of Martin Luther King, Jr.; and the ongoing struggle for social justice, equality, and, yes, genuine and meaningful integration of the city's schools (Kynard 17). Yet as I write this, I again hear the echoes of this previous time in our own: legal segregation of our public schools, police shootings of Black men and women, inequities in health care, and, of course, in criminal justice. You can see how Rich's essay, while very much part of its time, speaks to our moment as well.

Reading in a Writing Class

From the vantage point of this moment—a moment defined in K–12 and higher education by accountability and standardized assessment—the instructions given to Rich at her hiring seem the stuff of a bygone era: "My job, that first year, was to 'turn the students on' to writing by whatever means I wanted—poetry, free association, music, politics, drama, fiction—to acclimate them to the act of writing" (55). This freedom may simply have been the result of a recognition of Rich's status as a noted poet. ("She is a celebrated writer—let her do what she thinks is appropriate.") And it likely was seen as quite a coup to have Rich work in the program. Lest her open-ended charge be seen as a signal not to challenge her students, however, Rich makes it clear that the reading will occupy a significant space in her class and that the reading—George Orwell, Richard Wright, Leroi Jones, D. H. Lawrence, James Baldwin, and Plato—will be a challenge to her students (55). The work of Black male authors will be highlighted. (Rich apologizes in her preface for not assigning more work by non-white women authors—these authors had not yet received their proper attention, Rich asserts.)

Rich and her colleagues were making an effort to include works by Black authors, works that they themselves had not read: "In this discovery of a previously submerged culture we were learning from and with our students as rarely happens in the university" (Rich 57). In having students read works by Black authors, Rich's motives were twofold: to enable students of color to engage concepts and vernacular language of meaning to them; and to use such readings to provoke and motivate students' writing. While not probing deeply the relationship between reading and writing, Rich asserts the importance of immersing basic writers in language, both familiar and new. This portion resonates for many of us who teach reading in our writing classrooms. The field of composition has seen a renewed interest in reading pedagogy—especially deep reading—as a college-level subject (Sullivan et al.). While Rich sees reading primarily as a way to provoke student writing and to achieve engagement with the work, many of us see writing as a way to deepen students' understanding of what they read—a writing-to-read approach as opposed to reading as a provocation to write. Still, Rich and her SEEK colleagues are to be commended for putting reading in such a prominent place—especially in a classroom full of inexperienced and tentative writers. Fundamentally, for Rich and for many of us, the teaching of reading and of writing—and perhaps teaching more generally—requires the building of trust between teacher and student, between writer and reader.

"Released into" Language

In her essay Rich refers to herself as a "teacher of language" (63). She uses this term as a poet might, for "whom language has implied freedom" (63). When she began to teach in the program, Rich assumed that some students would be so entranced by the magic inherent in language that they would be "released into" that language (67). Presumably that meant that their lives would suddenly be enriched by the encounter with language. All she had to do was expose students to great literature—canonical works (written mostly by white men) and the thrilling works of emerging Black authors (mostly men)—and those same tentative students would become confident writers themselves. Teaching the SEEK students brought a different realization for Rich, however: "But my daily life as a teacher confronts me with young men and women who have had language and literature used *against* them, to keep them in their place, to mystify, to bully, to make them feel powerless" (63).

Precisely. As I look out among my own students, I see evidence of language's power to disrupt, to distance, and, yes, to bully (especially in this age of social media). So many of these students have essentially been told that they do not belong in this classroom or any classroom, that they are not worthy. How reassuring is it, then, that Rich, despite her privilege, sees that there is work to be done to lift these students up—not by the magical incantation of great literature but by an abiding belief in students' possibilities. There is no simple key to success—no learning of academic language that will inevitably ensure better lives for Rich's or my own students. Instead, we teachers need to believe our students capable of imagining and creating a better world and of coming to view language "as a means of changing reality" (Rich 67).

At this moment we need to take Rich's lessons as our own. I realize that so many of us are driven by good intentions when we argue for a speedier path to success for our students—in particular, when we quickly mainstream basic writers so that they do not lose heart languishing in remedial courses—at a financial and psychological cost. Yet I worry that some writers will not be able to benefit from our good intentions. If we are truly committed both to access and success for our students we must leave no writer behind—not one. We must believe in the ability of all our students to succeed and we must afford them the confidence to do so.

Works Cited

Adams, Peter, et al. "The Accelerated Learning Program: Throwing Open the Gates." *Journal of Basic Writing*, vol. 28, no. 2, fall 2009, pp. 50–69.

Bartholomae, David. "The Study of Error." *College Composition and Communication*, vol. 31, no. 3, Oct. 1980, pp. 253–69.

Kynard, Carmen. *Vernacular Insurrections: Race, Black Protest, and the New Century in Composition-Literacies Studies*. State U of New York P, 2013.

Lu, Min-Zhan. "Redefining the Legacy of Mina Shaughnessy: A Critique of the Politics of Linguistic Innocence." *Journal of Basic Writing*, vol. 10, no. 1, spring 1991, pp. 26–40.

Maher, Jane. *Mina P. Shaughnessy: Her Life and Work*. National Council of Teachers of English, 1997.

Rich, Adrienne. "Teaching Language in Open Admissions." *On Lies, Secrets, and Silence: Selected Prose, 1966–1978*, by Rich, W. W. Norton, 1995, pp. 51–68.

Shaughnessy, Mina P. "Diving In: An Introduction to Basic Writing." *College Composition and Communication*, vol. 27, no. 3, Oct. 1976, pp. 234–39.

———. *Errors and Expectations: A Guide for the Teacher of Basic Writing*. Oxford UP, 1979.

Steinberg, Stephen. "Revisiting Open Admissions at CUNY." *Clarion*, Feb. 2018, psc-cuny.org/clarion/february-2018/revisiting-open-admissions-cuny.

Sullivan, Patrick, et al., editors. *Deep Reading: Teaching Reading in the Writing Classroom*. National Council of Teachers of English, 2017.

Traub, James. *City on a Hill: Testing the American Dream at City College*. Da Capo Press, 1994.

"A Fresh Progression in Thought and Expression": Remembering *The Plural I*, by William E. Coles, Jr.

Peter Wayne Moe and David Bartholomae

> William E. Coles, Jr., *The Plural I: The Teaching of Writing* (Holt, Rinehart and Winston, 1978)

"None of the students with this first writing assignment behaved any differently from what I expected," writes William E. Coles, Jr., in *The Plural I: The Teaching of Writing* (17–18). Writing from within his classroom, he has just finished looking over the first stack of student papers he's received in Humanities 1, a required first-year composition course he taught in the fall of 1965 at what was then Case Institute of Technology.

The Plural I tells the story of that course. Each chapter opens with an assignment before moving to two to three papers written in response, followed by Coles's dramatization of the ensuing classroom discussion. For the first assignment of the term, Coles asked students to define the terms *amateur* and *professional*, and here's what he makes of their work:

> Triumphs of self-obliteration the papers were, put-up jobs every one of them, and as much of a bore to read as they must have been to write. I found myself being talked to as though I were a rube ("Now it may, perhaps, be thought by my reader . . ."), unoffendable ("It has probably never been a matter of concern to the reader . . .") or a confederate, someone in on the joke of why none of it mattered ("of course, we, in a college classroom, can hardly hope to settle the question of . . ."). No observation was too trivial to escape oratorical pronouncement ("It is unfair to call the amateur a 'clumsy bastard!'"); no moral stance too obvious to assume ("After all, professionals are not necessarily good people"). So far as the proposition was concerned,

> the students handled it in the way that a Themewriter traditionally handles the Themetopic, as a moral issue (on about the level needed to condemn the man-eating shark), which is to say inside a moral vacuum from which all living concerns are carefully excluded. . . . There wasn't one student who convinced me that he had a modicum of interest in anything he was saying. (*Plural I* 18)

This paragraph captures not only what is most remarkable about Coles's teaching but also what makes it, in compelling ways, so problematic. In Coles's assessment of his students' writing, we see a pedagogy that invites readers to consider how a teacher might read, engage with, and teach with student writing and, most important, what it might mean to make student writing the centerpiece of a course in practical criticism. Coles demonstrates this for us, his readers, and then awaits our response.

Coles was well aware of the difficulties his book would present for readers. Its method was (and remains) unconventional, his way of talking about student writing difficult to swallow. The first press Coles sent *The Plural I* rejected it, calling the book "arrogant" and "self-aggrandizing." "Neither term," Coles says, "was in a subordinate clause." These criticisms helped Coles see that, despite his commitments to student writing, early drafts of *The Plural I* failed to present students as more than "just sticks." "I had to create something to play against the all-consuming voice of my narrator," Coles writes. "My students, in other words, had to get a hearing." Fleshing out the students, though, wasn't enough: "And then I found I had to create my teacher as someone who could listen to them." The final revision builds itself around more fully characterized students. The dialogic drama between his narrator-teacher and these revised students, Coles says, "is what I think saved the book, or rather turned it into one" ("—and After" 275).[1]

That drama is carried out through Coles's assignment sequence— "a fresh progression in thought and expression" (*Plural I* 12)—where a "nominal subject" (6), in this case the difference between an amateur and a professional, is investigated from one angle and then another, but always through close readings of a student paper, and often in reference to some excerpt of published writing. The sequence is both "repetitive and incremental" (16). The true subject of the course, however, is language,

language in use. And so *The Plural I* collects ninety-four pieces of student writing. Of all the scholarship in composition studies, few (if any) provide such a close and extended reading of such a substantial corpus of student writing.[2]

The course calls attention to the problem of meaning—meanings don't reside in words, words are put into play by writers trying to say something. Writers struggle to communicate, to make the words meaningful to themselves and to others. The better the writer, the more self-conscious the struggle. The opening assignment begins, then, with the problem of definition. Coles gives students something said on the topic (words already in play) and then asks, as always, "[W]here and how do you locate yourself with this way of speaking," "To what extent and in what ways is that self definable in language?" And, crucially, "What has this self to do with you?" (*Plural I* 12).

Student writing is the cornerstone of this course and this pedagogy. Papers are reproduced for each class, and students learn to give close, critical reading to the language on the page. At first it is quite simple. *Who is speaking here? Who do you have to be to take this form of address seriously? Who do you think you're kidding?* The discussion characterizes students as "the Jolly Green Giant" (*Plural I* 21, 81) or "three hundred feet high or a hundred and fifty years old" (22). Their papers are called "mayonnaise," "cocoa-marsh," "sky writing," "bulletproof" ("Teaching of Writing" 112). Flat characters become "Steve" (*Plural I* 70–71), and Coles gives papers where "Steve" appears in mock titles: "Steve for Coach of the Year" or "Steve Saves Lab Partner from Electrocution" or "Steve as Miss Lonelyhearts" (78).[3]

The primary challenge of the course is for students to understand that these are writing lessons, not personal confrontations, not ad hominem attacks. In the opening class, Coles begins a difficult discussion, one that continues week by week, leading (we know) to varying levels of sophistication and success at the end of a semester. "I wish to make it clear that the self I am speaking of here," he writes in a handout for his students, "is a literary self, not a mock or false self, but a stylistic self, the self construable from the way words fall on a page. The other self, the identity of a student, is something with which I as a teacher can have nothing to do, not if I intend to remain a teacher" (*Plural I* 12). The course Coles teaches, which he learned to teach at Amherst, was informed by Cambridge English and by the work of I. A. Richards, F. R.

Leavis, and Ludwig Wittgenstein, among others—that is, philosophical investigations into language, meaning, and the application of a practical criticism, a critical investigation into ordinary language and its uses, with student writing as the necessary point of reference.[4]

The overriding critical concern is consistently focused on what Richards calls "stock responses," writing that is routine or empty, submissive (228). Coles calls this "Themewriting," with a capital *T*. Early class discussions often turn to cliché, but as the semester continues, students move beyond the simple policing of commonplaces to surprisingly complicated and nuanced discussions of what Richards calls "tone" (a critical relationship to language, reader, and the world) and "sense" (having something to say, but also "catching up to words," to "distinctions toward which we are still groping" [208]). One late assignment has Coles's students explaining a concept in physics to someone who is not a physicist. Coles uses their writing to consider the difficulty, even the impossibility of translation, of using someone else's words as though they were yours—Wittgenstein's problem of agreement.

The first paper presented for discussion opens as follows, and a single sentence is enough to recognize the paper and its version of knowledge; it is the standard opening of a student writer in a first-year writing class: "The question of the amateur's place in a society of professionals is one that has greatly been changed by the scientific and cultural revolutions of the nineteenth and twentieth centuries" (*Plural I* 19). The discussion of this (and every) paper in class is represented through dialogue. Coles says:

> I began, as I generally do, with the question of voice, not as a way of suggesting that writing is speech, but to get students used to the idea that sensitivity to words on a page is analogous to one's response to the tonal variations of the spoken word—a response that for all of us, whatever difficulty we may have in describing how we hear what we do, is immediate and full. The concept of voice, then, involving as it does the *feel* of words, can, after a time, become an appropriate metaphor for the life of writing—or the lack of it.
>
> What sort of voice speaks in this first paper? I asked after reading it aloud with the students. How do you characterize it? What's your response to what you hear? (*Plural I* 21)

Composition was fully invested in voice in the late 1970s, and *voice* is a key term for Coles; he offers a rather nuanced understanding of it quite different from that of his colleagues—even so, it took him ten years to find a publisher for *The Plural I*. Perhaps his trouble stems from his method. The book is unlike anything in composition before, at the time, or since.

At the time of its publication, when composition was beginning to develop a set of methods, a literature, a constellation of stars, *The Plural I* proved largely unreadable. Those who reviewed it, wrote about it, or spoke about it at meetings missed the point.[5] For one thing, the book requires a sophisticated ear. And it assumes that a reader will give time and attention to the student writing. A reader can't skip over the student papers. They are not just illustration; they are where the action is, and so one has to read closely and with particular attention to tone and voice—that is, one has to read the same way Coles was trying to teach his students to read.

Another difficulty is that *The Plural I* blurs genres. It's the "earliest example" of long-form narrative nonfiction in composition (Coles, "Failure" 19). Though creative nonfiction is now part of the stock-in-trade of every MFA program, in the 1970s, when composition was turning to ethnography, looking for positive, empirical access to student learning using descriptive accounts of scenes of instruction, the book's audience was poorly prepared for narrative nonfiction and predisposed to place it outside the categories of scholarship. *The Plural I* was misread, and the book was characterized, perhaps inevitably, as either touchy-feely or as a narcissist's memoir. Its subtle and challenging account of language use was reduced to a single term: *expressivism*.

Peter Elbow was also labeled an expressivist, but as Coles's classroom shows, his pedagogy is far from Elbow's. And it turns out that the very thing Coles is so insistent about in his teaching—voice—is what sets readers against him. Since its publication, readers have been offended by the figure of the teacher in *The Plural I*—brash, arrogant, macho, aggressive, a tough guy in the mold of Humphrey Bogart. We've both taught this book recently (in graduate and undergraduate classes), and it has been almost impossible for students to move beyond their antipathy toward the central character.

The teacher in this narrative is, of course, a figure, a character in a book, like Captain Ahab or the Thoreau of *Walden*, and the Bill Coles of

The Plural I is part of a particular historical moment and university setting. It can also be argued that criticism requires an aggressive stance against the hegemony of common sense and standard practice. A course in criticism must, by its nature, be agonistic. In that sense, the figure at the center of *The Plural I* resonates with key figures in criticism in the 1980s—from Paul de Man, Richard Ohmann, and Richard Poirier (all of whom taught at Amherst) to Stanley Fish, Jacques Derrida (think of the exchange between Derrida and John Searle), Gayatri Spivak, and Eve Sedgwick.

The figure we hear in this text, however, is F. R. Leavis, speaking from within the project of Cambridge English in the 1940s. Leavis is important to our reading of Coles not only because of the genealogy here but also and even more so because he troubles the too-easy divide between literature and composition, reminding us that reading a student paper as a piece of writing, and with attention to what the language does, not just what it says, requires disciplined close reading and practiced literary judgment. Leavis called this kind of skeptical, close attention "discrimination" (a difficult term in our day and time), and he believed that its exercise in the classroom could have positive (Leavis would have said "redemptive") bearing not just on the work of literature but also on ways of understanding and participating in the work of everyday language and everyday life.

Leavis's *Education and the University: A Sketch for an "English School"* was meant to prepare teachers for a new curriculum of an "English school," one that centered on "practical criticism"—that is, a criticism meant to inform all uses of language, including the most ordinary. In his book, Leavis provides a reading of Matthew Arnold's sonnet "Shakespeare" to demonstrate how a teacher might confront and challenge fundamental problems of reading and writing. He begins with this line in Arnold's poem: "Planting his steadfast footsteps in the sea." Leavis says the trope of the hill (representing Shakespeare) planting its feet in the sea is "static," easy to pass over, but

> "Footsteps" (arrived at through "apt alliteration") introduces a ludicrous suggestion of gigantic, ponderously wading strides. Or rather, it would do so if the line were anything but a matter of words of no very particular effect. For clearly, it could only have been offered by

> an unrealizing mind, handling words from the outside. And if we ask how it is that any reader (as clearly many have done) lets it pass, the answer is that the sonnet imposes the kind of attention, or inattention, that it needs. It imposes an unrealizing attention, if "attention" is the word. The reader (the right one) yields himself deferentially, and responds with unction, to the familiar signals. (73–74)

And, he concludes,

> The whole sonnet turns out to be an orotund exercise in thuriferous phrases and generalities, without one touch of particularity or distinction. Arnold is not using a conventional Grand Style for the expression of a personally felt theme; he is using it, in the absence of anything to say, as a substitute; the vague prestige-value inhering the phrases because of the work of other poets has to serve instead of meaning. (75)

Arnold is what many would consider one of the greats, yet here he is revealed as "handling words from the outside," as a Themewriter, to use Coles's term, failing in the same manner as the students in Humanities 1. This is one of the things we admire about *The Plural I*, where a number of recognized, published writers (like J. D. Salinger or Charles Darwin) are read with the same close scrutiny as student writers, where criticism recognizes that the problems of writing belong to all writers, where student writing demands (and repays) the same close reading we would give to one of the so-called greats. The achievement of *The Plural I*, and of the work of the group teaching English 1–2 at Amherst, was the well-tested application of critical close reading to the work of student writers.

The Plural I focuses attention on the pedagogy of critical theory. It argues that it is one thing to persuade students to adopt new positions or points of view but another to prepare them to radically revise their sentences. A teacher can (maybe) change students' minds about gun control, but that doesn't mean students won't continue to approach sentences routinely, trading one set of slogans for another or, as Leavis says, "handling words from the outside." Coles's book foregrounds something that remains largely hidden or unacknowledged in most critical texts of that period and of the present, asking, What does criticism look like if practiced by students and practiced on the page?

Even so, the aggression acted out between a teacher and his students is difficult to reconcile. A case in point is the tone of Coles's contention that students' papers were "[t]riumphs of self-obliteration" (*Plural I* 17). That's what makes this book so challenging. The readings of the students' papers remain, we believe, brilliant and compelling, and the argument of the course, in our consideration, is exemplary. And yet it is almost impossible now to identify with the teacher.

And maybe that's the point. "When it comes to the teaching of art," Coles writes, "what teaches finally is style. Learning, the other end of the activity, would seem to be connected with a stylistic response to style" (*Plural I* 1). How do we—as both writers and teachers—respond stylistically to Coles's voice, to Coles's style? This is the problem *The Plural I* presents to the profession at this moment in time. How do we teach criticism, practical criticism, as a shared enterprise? Serious writing is difficult, demanding. How might we engage students in this struggle, in a contest with words, without patronizing them, one the one hand, or silencing them, on the other? These are some of the pressing questions Coles's book makes possible—and, uniquely, makes possible within the scene of a first-year writing class.

Notes

1. Given Coles's extensive revisions of *The Plural I*, it's surprising the course he teaches leaves no room for revision. Granted, his sequence does invite continual revision of one kind as students revisit the same intellectual problems again and again with each new assignment; even so, students aren't given real time (as represented through space within the sequence) to revise. They are never asked, for example, to rewrite in assignment 8 what they wrote for assignment 7. This is a missed opportunity, we believe, because revision turns practical criticism into a place of pedagogical possibility.

2. Coles's *Seeing through Writing* uses a similar method, gathering assignments and student papers written in response. So, too, does Coles and James Vopat's *What Makes Writing Good*. Coles laments the "failure" of this way of writing about the classroom to "catch on" ("Failure" 19). Coles eventually gave up scholarship for young adult fiction, though even his fiction echoes his earlier

books: *Another Kind of Monday* is built around a scavenger hunt in Pittsburgh, the scavenger hunt itself a kind of assignment sequence. For more of Coles's fiction, see *Compass in the Blood* and *Funnybone*. For a full list of Coles's publications, see the appendix.

    3. These critical terms serve an epideictic function, convening a community around them while also providing the tools for a rhetoric of praise and blame. See Moe.

    4. The line of thought and practice from Cambridge English to *The Plural I* and beyond is rarely present in our accounts of the history of composition in the United States. For more, see Bartholomae. For particulars on the Amherst course forming the foundation for Coles's teaching, see Varnum. For Coles's own account of teaching under and with Theodore Baird, see "Teaching Writing."

    5. For reviews of *The Plural I* and its reissue ten years later, see Flachmann; Higgins; Keith; Keroes; and Walker. For nuanced and careful readings of Coles's work, see Horner; Harris.

Works Cited

Arnold, Matthew. "Shakespeare." *Poetry Foundation*, poetryfoundation.org/poems/43603/shakespeare-56d2225fc8ead.

Bartholomae, David. "Teacher Teacher: Poirier and Coles on Writing." *Raritan*, vol. 36, no. 2, winter 2017, pp. 25–53.

Coles, William E., Jr. "—and After: Looking Back on *The Plural I*." *The Plural I—and After*, by Coles, Boynton/Cook, 1988, pp. 271–77.

———. *Another Kind of Monday*. Avon Books, 1996.

———. *Compass in the Blood*. Atheneum, 2001.

———. "'Failure Is the Way We Learn': An Interview with William E. Coles, Jr." Conducted by John Boe and Eric Schroeder. *Writing on the Edge*, vol. 13, no. 1, fall 2002, pp. 6–22.

———. *Funnybone*. Atheneum, 1992.

———. *The Plural I: The Teaching of Writing*. Holt, Rinehart and Winston, 1978.

———. *Seeing through Writing*. Harper and Row, 1988.

———. "The Teaching of Writing as Writing." *College English*, vol. 29, no. 2, Nov. 1967, pp. 111–16.

———. "Teaching Writing, Teaching Literature: The Plague on Both Houses." *Freshman English News*, vol. 9, no. 3, winter 1981, pp. 3+.

Coles, William E., Jr., and James Vopat. *What Makes Writing Good: A Multiperspective*. D. C. Heath, 1985.

Flachmann, Kim. Review of *The Plural I—and After* and *Seeing through Writing*, by William E. Coles, Jr. *College Composition and Communication*, vol. 40, no. 3, Oct. 1989, pp. 357–60.

Harris, Joseph. "The Plural Text / The Plural Self: Roland Barthes and William Coles." *College English*, vol. 49, no. 2, Feb. 1987, pp. 158–70.

Higgins, David M. Review of *The Plural I: The Teaching of Writing*, by William E. Coles, Jr. *College Composition and Communication*, vol. 30, no. 1, Feb. 1979, pp. 105–06.

Horner, Bruce. *Terms of Work for Composition: A Materialist Critique*. State U of New York P, 2000.

Keith, Philip M. Review of *The Plural I: The Teaching of Writing*, by William E. Coles, Jr. *Rhetoric Society Quarterly*, vol. 8, no. 1, winter 1978, pp. 16–19.

Keroes, Jo. Review of *The Plural I—and After*, by William E. Coles, Jr. *The Quarterly*, vol. 10, no. 4, Oct. 1988.

Leavis, Frank Raymond. *Education and the University: A Sketch for an "English School."* Chatto and Windus, 1943.

Moe, Peter Wayne. "Reading Coles Reading Themes: Epideictic Rhetoric and the Teaching of Writing." *College Composition and Communication*, vol. 69, no. 3, Feb. 2018, pp. 431–55.

Richards, I. A. *Practical Criticism: A Study of Literary Judgment*. Transaction Publishers, 2004.

Varnum, Robin. *Fencing with Words: A History of Writing Instruction at Amherst College during the Era of Theodore Baird, 1938–1966*. National Council of Teachers of English, 1996.

Walker, Laurence. Review of *The Plural I—and After*, by William E. Coles, Jr. *Curriculum Inquiry*, vol. 21, no. 2, summer 1991, pp. 253–60.

Appendix: A William E. Coles, Jr., Reading List

"—and After: Looking Back on *The Plural I*." *The Plural I—and After*, by Coles, Boynton/Cook, 1988, pp. 271–77.

Another Kind of Monday. Avon Books, 1996.

"A Comment on 'The Rhetoric of Masculinity: Origins, Institutions, and the Myth of the Self-Made Man.'" *College English*, vol. 52, no. 8, Dec. 1990, pp. 930–31.

Compass in the Blood. Atheneum, 2001.

Composing: Writing as a Self-Creating Process. Boynton/Cook, 1974.

Composing II: Writing as a Self-Creating Process. Hayden, 1981.

"English 285 Teaching Composition: Evolving a Style." *Freshman English News*, vol. 5, no. 1, spring 1976, pp. 1–2.

English Is a Foreign Language: A Report on an Experimental Freshman English Course Taught Fall Semester, 1965–66, at Case Institute of Technology. Case Institute of Technology, 1966.

"Freshman Composition: The Circle of Unbelief." *College English*, vol. 31, no. 2, Nov. 1969, pp. 134–42.

Funnybone. Atheneum, 1992.

"New Presbyters as Old Priests: A Forewarning." *CEA Critic*, vol. 41, no. 1, Nov. 1978, pp. 3–9.

The Plural I—and After. Boynton/Cook, 1988.

The Plural I: The Teaching of Writing. Holt, Rinehart and Winston, 1978.

"Reply." *College English*, vol. 29, no. 5, Feb. 1968, pp. 404–06.

"Response to William E. Coles, Jr., 'Teaching the Teaching of Composition: Evolving a Style.'" *College Composition and Communication*, vol. 29, no. 2, May 1978, pp. 206–09.

Seeing through Writing. Harper and Row, 1988.

"The Sense of Nonsense as a Design for Sequential Writing Assignments." *College Composition and Communication*, vol. 21, no. 1, Feb. 1970, pp. 27–34.

Teaching Composing: A Guide to Teaching Writing as a Self-Creating Process. Hayden, 1974.

"The Teaching of Writing as Writing." *College English*, vol. 29, no. 2, Nov. 1967, pp. 111–16.

"Teaching the Teaching of Composition: Evolving a Style." *College Composition and Communication*, vol. 28, no. 3, Oct. 1977, pp. 268–70.

"Teaching Writing, Teaching Literature: The Plague on Both Houses." *Freshman English News*, vol. 9, no. 3, winter 1981, pp. 3+.

"An Unpetty Pace." *College Composition and Communication*, vol. 23, no. 5, Dec. 1972, pp. 378–82.

"The Unteachables." *Journal of Higher Education*, vol. 35, no. 2, Feb. 1964, pp. 76–78.

"The Way Johnny Can't Read." *AAUP Bulletin*, vol. 49, no. 3, Sept. 1963, pp. 240–42.

What Makes Writing Good: A Multiperspective. D. C. Heath, 1985.*

"Writing across the Curriculum: Why Bother?" *Rhetoric Society Quarterly*, vol. 21, no. 4, autumn 1991, pp. 17–25.

---

*Coauthored by Coles and James Vopat.

Reappraising *Course X*

Rebecca Day Babcock

> Leonard A. Greenbaum and Rudolf B. Schmerl, *Course X: A Left Field Guide to Freshman English* (J. B. Lippincott, 1970)

The publisher's foreword to Leonard Greenbaum and Rudolf Schmerl's *Course X* states that the book is perhaps the first "critical study" of freshman English to be "addressed to the student by experienced and concerned teachers." *Course X* is not a textbook but rather a user's guide for the student. In it Greenbaum and Schmerl propose something akin to Peter Elbow's teacherless classroom in *Writing without Teachers*: "We propose a way of learning how to write outside of any imposed system. We propose a way of learning . . . by creating your own classroom" (xxi). Alongside a critique of the university system and composition program, they put forth the idea of a student-centered, socially constructed, process-oriented classroom able to be produced by the students themselves, whether the teacher is involved or not. The authors highlight the problems with freshman composition—many of which are the same today—such as its amorphous curriculum and the luck of the draw in terms of what kind of course any student will find themselves in. Given that the book prefigures important movements in composition studies, it seems truly to be a lost text deserving of some recognition.

The strength of this 1970 book—and perhaps its downfall—is its brutal honesty. The tone is chatty and conspiratorial, very much a product of its rebellious time. Greenbaum and Schmerl seem to be airing the English department's dirty laundry as well as that of the university system as a whole. The book echoes the criticisms of the educational system set out by the educator and civil rights activist Jerry Farber, who critiqued the university system as one of master/slave exploitation of the student by the teacher. (He later amended this to put the administration in the master role.) Perhaps this radical tone of honesty (and the suggestion to abolish composition) is part of the reason that writing studies scholars have not embraced *Course X*. Perhaps the fact that it is addressed to students themselves has caused professionals to tune out since they are not its intended audience. Perhaps they just didn't know the book existed. Despite this, and besides being a darn entertaining read, the book's criticisms and solutions still speak to composition studies today.

The book starts out with an overview of the workings of the university system. Things have not changed much in fifty years, as most of what the authors have to say rings true today. Perhaps the sarcasm, irreverence, and tongue-in-cheek delivery hits too close to home for some. For instance, Greenbaum and Schmerl categorize the concerns of professors as follows, allowing for the default male pronoun of the day: "What he knows about the (not *his*) university is that it's incredibly inefficient, wastes vast sums on ridiculous pursuits, has neither understanding of nor respect for the significance of his work (not teaching—*his* work!), and can't provide adequate parking" (*Course X* 17). At the same time, some of what Greenbaum and Schmerl discuss no longer resonates today. They note, for instance, that receiving training as a writing teacher was impossible in 1970: "Not one ever had any special training as a teacher of writing.... Of course not: such training isn't to be had" (27). (Actually, it was, but only at a few schools.)

In their description of the freshman English course in chapter 3, the authors explain the workings of the textbook racket, prefiguring more recent scholarship about textbooks and composition.[1] Do we expose our students to this information? (Should we?) The authors deconstruct everything from the book exhibits at the Conference on College Composition and Communication to free exam copies and publishers offering "Scotch, bourbon, teenie-weenies in hot ketchup, rock and roll bands, potato chips, gin, pretzels and business cards" (Greenbaum and Schmerl, *Course X* 47). They expose some of the darker secrets of the practices surrounding complimentary textbook copies—for instance, instructors selling their exam copies and even giving them as gifts: "[D]ictionaries make fine gifts, as do the individual editions of novels and plays. The one book that makes a lousy gift is the Freshman Reader" (54). The description of the attitude of graduate student instructors toward required texts (disdain? rebellion?) is also insightful. The authors advise students to discern the teacher's attitude toward the textbook and its role in the course. For instance, they explain that a teaching assistant required to use a certain book may think it "a monstrous error, dull, tedious, a drag to go through class after class" and that if the instructor is "intellectually alienated" from the textbook they may "change direction every other week" and "the student, as usual, is the one who pays the price" (67).

The ideas behind *Course X* are closest in content to the writing-about-writing (WAW) approach, in which teachers expose students to theories and research about writing studies. Certainly, when *Course X* was written, theory and research about writing studies was scant, and *writing studies* as a name for the field was years away. Instead, what the authors offer is a glimpse of the lived experiences of teachers and students of composition at the time, much of which prevails. Greenbaum and Schmerl write about most freshman English teachers wanting to be somewhere else—before composition defined itself as a field and when teaching literature was seen as most desirable—and it's still mostly true that "[n]o professor of any standing has anything to do with the course, unless he supervises it somehow and therefore has to teach one section" (*Course X* 30). The authors go on to explain the exploitation of graduate student instructors (remember the audience is freshmen themselves!) and how well-meaning teacher-mentors suggest that instructors spend only five minutes per paper on grading. And then of course there is the reckoning for graduate student instructors that they need to spend less time grading to bring them up to minimum wage. (On my campus graduate students are paid double what adjuncts are paid, but I digress.) Greenbaum and Schmerl then go on to explain their view of the demeaning hiring process at the MLA convention. Though fifty-odd years have passed since the book was published, one might argue that certain things still hold true—for instance, the class-based discrimination that Greenbaum and Schmerl describe (43). Despite the current proliferation of rhetoric and composition programs and scholars, many instructors who teach first-year writing may "regard it as the price [they have] to pay to get to teach Literature—if not now, then eventually" (44). Further, current scholars of rhetoric and composition quickly become writing program administrators, which takes them away from the composition classroom; senior scholars replace first-year composition in their schedules with what they believe to be necessary, upper-level theory and pedagogy courses.

Greenbaum and Schmerl clearly state that the point of the book is for students to form their own student-centered groups to get through the class. If the class is not student-centered, students can make it so. This is the heart of the book, where the authors present their team-learning approach to composition (see also Greenbaum and Schmerl, "Team Learning Approach"). It's almost like a pop-up writing center: that is, if there is no writing center, make your own, in the hallways, at dinner, in the library, in one another's rooms and apartments. The authors write that these efforts must be "submerged" unless "your instructor is using some kind of team-learning approach to composition" (*Course X* 154). The writing-center-like approach is explained thusly: "The way to learn [to write] is to practice talking to other people about the paper you are going to write" (181). The team, in essence, has become a writing group. Greenbaum and Schmerl also detail workshop procedures that have become standard in courses that use that approach: "Discussing class papers with other students is one of the most effective ways to improve your own writing, provided that the discussion is structured appropriately" (173). The idea here is to reflect on the papers after they are written and after everyone has had a chance to read the papers outside of class.

Although much of the book is laced with the authors' (often justified) cynicism, the team approach is useful, but it, too, is laced with suspicion: the team approach encourages students to make sure teachers do their jobs. Student teams—again, prefiguring practices related to assessment and teaching—must force instructors to make connections between assignments and make explicit the purpose or goals of an assignment. Greenbaum and Schmerl suggest that students make the following demands en masse: "1.) a request for a specific statement of goals for Course X; 2.) a request for a specific statement of criteria for grading papers in Course X; 3.) a request that the purpose of each assignment be written and circulated to the class when the assignment is given, with an example of what would get a good grade; 4.) a request that papers graded by the teacher be distributed to demonstrate his consistency in using the specified criteria" (*Course X* 146). Decades on, the first and second requests are likely to be granted (and even anticipated) by the instructor, the third less so, and the fourth unlikely. Again, in a later chapter, the authors encourage students to exert pressure on the teacher to articulate goals and procedures for assignments through "strong-arm tactics" such as confronting the teacher in class and during office hours (176–77). Other advice includes pressing the instructor for specifics regarding writing style and the qualities of a successful paper while in teacher-student conferences.

As for the book's physical appearance, the cover strikes one as different. Published at the very beginning of the 1970s, it features bright yellow, pink, and red words on a black background. A gray spoon is poised over a bowl of cereal (or ice cream?). The white material (milk?) is bursting over the top of the bowl, and the cereal or ice-cream toppings are words like *theme* and *essay*, sprinkled with punctuation marks and a star, presumably the gold star that the student would get on their essay by following the book's advice.

One of the book's lasting and pertinent critiques is similar to that of scholars who focus on the WAW approach, such as Doug Downs and Elizabeth Wardle (Downs and Wardle; Wardle and Downs)—namely, that the stuff of English papers is traditionally literary because professors have been trained as literary critics and that is what they are familiar and comfortable with. Greenbaum and Schmerl argue that assigning literary and personal experience papers does not assist the student in learning about writing. The authors imply that the goal of the course should be, rather, to learn "how to go about writing something, especially if that something isn't literary" (*Course X* 83). The approach that uses prose models, they argue, as others would years after, does little to teach students to write. The argument still current, and that Greenbaum and Schmerl refute, is that students' prose will improve as a result of their being inoculated with these classic texts. Many of the same texts and authors that Greenbaum and Schmerl mention, such as essays by E. B. White, George Orwell, Henry David Thoreau, and Plato, are still staples of textbooks and readers. What I am calling the "inoculation" or "osmosis" approach is the apparent theory that students need only read or spend time with these classic texts for the writing style of these texts to rub off on students' prose. Greenbaum and Schmerl explain it like this: "[I]f a student reads and is exposed to well-written prose, he will, as when exposed to the flu virus, catch a little of it" (58). They maintain, however, that there is "no evidence" to support this claim (58). Greenberg and Schmerl liken this approach to learning about the qualities of good writing without actually studying the skill (or process) of writing itself.

Greenbaum and Schmerl also devote an entire chapter to rehearsing the history of the movement to abolish freshman composition, starting in 1911 with the formation of the NCTE and the report of the Committee on Composition. The frankness that Greenbaum and Schmerl provide to their freshman audience is astounding. Certainly they are not there to propose or persuade freshmen to abolish the course—the students have neither the authority nor the means to do so. (Although Jerry Farber would argue that the boycott would be an effective method.) So, since the students can't abolish the course, *Course X* will provide a structure for them to be able to get through it—and even excel or heaven forbid—learn something. The critique of the vacuousness of the composition course aligns with the work of Downs and Wardle and others from the WAW movement (Downs and Wardle; Wardle and Downs). But rather than abolish the course, as Greenbaum and Schmerl would clearly like to do, WAW proponents want to make the content of the course the material of composition studies, a field that didn't really exist back in 1970. Studies such as those by Linda Flower and John Hayes and Janet Emig were just being conducted. For instance, Emig published some definitions of and a call for research on composition in 1967 ("On Teaching Composition"), and her landmark study *Composing Processes of Twelfth Graders* was published in 1971. Her first paper, "We Are Trying Conferences," was published in 1960. Perhaps Greenbaum and Schmerl would have been part of the WAW movement had it existed at the time. They also show disdain for members of the Conference on College Composition and Communication, characterizing them as self-absorbed and self-indulgent (*Course X* 108).

Despite its cynicism, the importance of *Course X* lies in its contention that students must take charge of their own education. The book can be looked at alongside Peter Elbow's teacherless classroom, a concept introduced only three years later in *Writing without Teachers*. Greenbaum died in 1973 but did not teach freshman composition when *Course X* came out. Greenbaum also worked with the Michigan Memorial Phoenix Project (dedicated to the peaceful use of nuclear technology) and was editing its publication as early as 1961. He was assistant professor in the College of Engineering at the University of Michigan (Tobin). Schmerl continued his academic career at the University of Michigan, where he was a teacher in the College of Engineering's writing program, and later worked as an administrator at the University of Hawai'i. Schmerl passed away in the spring of 2020.

Perhaps a large part of the reason why the book was lost was that Greenbaum died shortly after its publication. Greenbaum published a revised version of his dissertation as *The* Hound and Horn: *The History of a Literary Quarterly* (1966). He also wrote an academic mystery novel called *Out of Shape*, published in 1969. This novel echoes several of Greenbaum's concerns, such as a scene where the protagonist examines issues of the *Hound and Horn* in the library (*Out of Shape* 30), and mentions a faculty member who is "opening brochures from publishers advertising the latest *New Rhetoric, The Contemporary Universal Freshman Reader, The Do-It-Yourself Composition Handbook*" (244). Finally, in the novel, a group of students are found to be cheating: "They had systems. The more serious students formed groups and divided the reading list between the members, each of whom would write a master appraisal that the others would vary slightly to make it appear their own work" (7). This system is very much like the one described in *Course X*.

Schmerl did not continue to publish widely in composition. As Holocaust survivors, he and his immediate family had escaped Germany in the 1930s, and several extended family members were killed in concentration camps, which likely influenced his desire to seek justice and truth in all its forms. According to his friends and colleagues, Schmerl was a remarkable man. He showed insight into the nature of the university (Schmerl, "Strange Places"), and the issues apparent in 1970 have not changed much in ensuing decades. Schmerl suggests that "a university's essential function" is "to question accepted dogma, to encourage unconventional thought, to hold nothing so sacred as to be beyond examination" ("Strange Places"). Some pithy advice from *Course X*: "[I]t's faster to go out and get information than to spend hours agonizing over a blank sheet of paper" (191).

Another point to consider is that the authors were, as noted earlier, seeking to abolish freshman composition. They apparently don't much like the course they describe and that they train students to game. The book is rather cruel and sardonic toward instructors and encourages students to be combative—even insubordinate. Greenbaum and Schmerl write that "[t]he teacher of freshman English ha[s] little to say about writing [and] lack[s] a discipline of his own" (*Course X* 223). That may have been true in 1970, but clearly it is no longer true. However, the authors do propose a solution to their vexed sense of first-year writing in "A Team Learning Approach to Freshman English," published in 1967. There they describe a program in which students prepare reports based on original research, in one case a report about a local election and in another about the freshman class of the Tuskegee Institute. They conclude, "In order for freshman composition to improve, it has got to be taken seriously as a learning experience, and that means innovation, experimentation, change" ("Team Learning Approach" 152).

The invisibility of *Course X* is somewhat of a detriment to writing studies. The book prefigures other, more visible scholarship, offering an often constructive critique of composition courses as well as advice that is still relevant today—its critique of textbooks remains especially relevant, as most of our student-facing texts continue to be readers, rhetorics, handbooks, and the like, whether in print or online. Now, students who want to game the system can resort to the Internet and cheat sites such as *Chegg, Course Hero,* and *SparkNotes,* but unlike the aims of Greenbaum and Schmerl, the goals of these sites, of course, are not student learning but rather ways to get around it. The field—and certainly its students—could benefit from reading with and against a work like *Course X* that exposes the (admittedly, sometimes outdated) workings of freshman composition with the end goal of improving student learning, collaboration, and outcomes, no matter or despite the preparation and pedagogy of the teacher.

Notes

Thanks to Jack Fishstrom and Dwight Stevenson for providing crucial information about Rudolf Schmerl.

1. Greenbaum and Schmerl's writing also prefigures important scholarship connected to the movement to abolish first-year composition; see, for instance, Crowley. Claude Hurlbert has been especially vocal in speaking out against the textbook market. In an interview, he critiques "the textbooking of composition and the corporate influences on composition" ("Where" 370), maintaining that "when we adopt textbooks, we also adopt an educational agenda set by transnational corporations" (374) and, finally, that "textbooks aren't simply teach-

ers' aides. They are merchandise produced by corporations to make money, and they surely do. . . . We need to consider the extent we participate in the commodification of the imagination and the exportation of oppressive literacy policies" (384). See also Holdstein; Miles; Gale and Gale; and similar arguments in Hurlbert (*National Healing* 156–63).

Works Cited

Crowley, Sharon. *Composition in the University: Historical and Polemical Essays*. U of Pittsburgh P, 1998. Composition, Literacy, and Culture.

Downs, Doug, and Elizabeth Wardle. "Teaching about Writing, Righting Misconceptions: (Re)Envisioning 'First-Year Composition' as 'Introduction to Writing Studies.'" *College Composition and Communication*, vol. 58, no. 4, 2007, pp. 552–85.

Elbow, Peter. *Writing without Teachers*. Oxford UP, 1973.

Emig, Janet. *The Composing Processes of Twelfth Graders*. National Council of Teachers of English, 1971.

———. "On Teaching Composition: Some Hypotheses as Definitions." *Research in the Teaching of English*, vol. 1, no. 2, 1967, pp. 127–35.

———. "We Are Trying Conferences." *English Journal*, vol. 49, no. 4, Apr. 1960, pp. 223–28.

Farber, Jerry. *The Student as N—: Essays and Stories*. Contact Books, 1969.

Gale, Xin Liu, and Fredric G. Gale. *(Re)Visioning Composition Textbooks: Conflicts of Culture, Ideology, and Pedagogy*. State U of New York P, 1999.

Greenbaum, Leonard. *The Hound and Horn: The History of a Literary Quarterly*. Mouton, 1966.

———. *Out of Shape*. Harper and Row, 1969.

Greenbaum, Leonard A., and Rudolf B. Schmerl. *Course X: A Left Field Guide to Freshman English*. J. B. Lippincott, 1970.

———. "A Team Learning Approach to Freshman English." *College English*, vol. 29, no. 2, 1967, pp. 135+. *JSTOR*, www.jstor.org/stable/374052.

Holdstein, Deborah H. "Corporate Textbook Production: Electronic Resources and the Responsible Curriculum." *Beyond English Inc.*, edited by David B. Downing et al., Boynton/Cook, 2002, pp. 52–61.

Hurlbert, Claude. *National Healing: Race, State, and the Teaching of Composition*. Utah State UP, 2012.

———. "Where Meaning and Being Gathers." Interview by Krystia Nora et al. *Teachers on the Edge: The WOE Interviews, 1989–2017*, edited by John Boe et al., Routledge, 2017, pp. 368–86.

Miles, Libby. "Constructing Composition: Reproduction and WPA Agency in Textbook Reproduction." *WPA: Writing Program Administration*, vol. 24, nos. 1–2, 2000, pp. 29–54.

Schmerl, Rudolf B. "Strange Places, Familiar Ways." *The University of Michigan Faculty Memoir Project*, apps.lib.umich.edu/faculty-memoir/apps.lib.umich.edu/faculty-memoir/faculty/rudolf-b-schmerl.html.

Tobin, James. "Mysteries at Michigan." *University of Michigan Heritage Project*, heritage.umich.edu/stories/mysteries-at-michigan/.

Wardle, Elizabeth, and Doug Downs. *Writing about Writing*. 3rd ed., Bedford / St. Martin's, 2017.

The Power of Mutable Structures: A Return to Ann E. Berthoff's *Forming/Thinking/Writing*

Paige Davis Arrington

> Ann E. Berthoff, *Forming/Thinking/Writing: The Composing Imagination* (Boynton/Cook, 1978)

Considered one of the founders of the field of rhetoric and composition, Ann E. Berthoff haunts its scholarship. Haunts. Like a waiting, unpeaceful spirit. Berthoff appears in contemporary discussions of composition history: two paragraphs in Joseph Harris's introduction to *A Teaching Subject* (3) and a mention in Byron Hawk's *A Counter-history of Composition* (16–18, 36–37). Bruce McComiskey considers Berthoff's notion of "dialectic" in half a chapter (44–53). Kevin Rutherford and Jason Palmeri's essay, "The Things They Left Behind," is devoted to a contemplation of Berthoff and materiality. Other scholars quote Berthoff or draw on her powerful terms and phrases—"gangster theories" and "killer dichotomies" (Berthoff, "Problem-Dissolving"). Berthoff's presence today is easy to find and often acknowledged. But the nature of that presence has Berthoff, at age ninety-three, claiming that what she was trying to do—to move the purpose of teaching writing away from teaching students how to express themselves or to communicate—never got across. Berthoff meant to move the field toward "a new way of understanding why we're teaching in the first place.... To teach *with* things, not *the* things. To teach them [students] to produce *things to think with*" (Arrington 219).

My own effort to understand Berthoff has had me wondering why her work seems simultaneously celebrated and ignored. Berthoff was honored as an exemplar of the field in 1997, but as far as I can tell, very few composition programs or instructors have ever practiced her pedagogy. Berthoff's 1978 textbook, *Forming/Thinking/Writing: The Composing*

Imagination (*FTW*), was lauded by James Berlin in 1982 as emblematic of "the new rhetoric" (774–77). The book reviewers, however, deemed *FTW* too philosophical for undergraduate students and their teachers. Art Young claimed that the textbook is "a demanding and worthwhile text for students of composition. Its level of sophistication may make it inappropriate for Mina Shaughnessy's basic-writing students" (64). Yet Berthoff wrote the book for precisely this kind of student: "I wrote the book for teaching basic writers, students, you know, who had failed the placement exams or whatever" (qtd. in Arrington 198). Other reviewers deemed the textbook "richly provocative" but condemned it as "much too challenging," arguing that "a comp class that could read, understand, and assimilate what Berthoff says about writing would be a heavy group of people indeed" (Reising and Liner 70).

How to account for composition's disparate responses to Berthoff? The field awards her and yet has also dismissed her work as too philosophical or, as Berlin would have it in 1990, "retrograde" (qtd. in Enos 28). My experience tells me that the implications of Berthoff's pedagogy have rarely been understood, but the problem isn't college freshmen. Rather, I wonder if the culture of composition just hasn't yet been ready to centralize the idea that the greatest resource for teaching and learning writing is the humanity of our students. I'm not sloganizing here; there is nothing especially romantic about the claim that Berthoff's pedagogy understands shared humanity as the source of good writing. We often talk a big game of social justice, and our scholarship is littered like a post-parade main street with ticker-tape strategies born of critical theory. And yet Berthoff's challenge to composition—and to English studies more broadly—remains largely ignored. It's a challenge set forth by *FTW*, a textbook as relevant as ever, perhaps even more so today, given recent surges of power within and around the Black Lives Matter movement.

I am suggesting that Berthoff's philosophy and pedagogy offers a unique dimension to culturally sensitive writing instruction. Although it is beyond the scope of this essay to explain how Berthoff's philosophy achieves this dimension, I hope to encourage scholars to consider this possibility in future research. In the 1970s, Paulo Freire apprehended the social justice dimension of the pedagogy grounding Berthoff's *FTW*

(Arrington 160–66). I refer to it in this essay as "the pedagogy of forming," and I'm certain it's as useful and revolutionary today as it was in 1978. But simply reading *FTW* won't do; you have to *do FTW*.

Triadic Semiosis and a Philosophy of Writing

Berthoff's pedagogy, demonstrated in *FTW*, is rooted in C. S. Peirce's notion of triadic semiosis—the idea that all meaning is mediated by meaning. Every human is present with their past: memories, sense experience, media experience, dreams, feelings, interactions and relationships, and so on. When we experience the word *sunlight*, for instance, many of us associate positive concepts with the word—warmth, heat, brightness, summer, and so on. But people never completely share the same experience or emotion, as we make sense of the new through meanings already comprising us. For people living in desert landscapes, *sunlight* might evoke a sense of oppression. Many of our meanings tap shared experiences, like sunlight. Some meanings register through unique experiences: one person has eaten *beshbarmak*; another has never heard of it, let alone tasted it. The meanings we compose come through our prior experiences—shared and unique—simultaneously, constantly. It's our nature. Perhaps it's nature itself.

What does this have to do with teaching and learning writing? Everything. To talk of aesthetics or author intention or grammar, to talk of semantics and style, charts and design, formatting and genre is always also to be talking about writing as forming, as making meaning. And yet, except for Berthoff's *FTW*, it's nearly impossible to find a textbook centralizing the notion that writing is a form of meaning-making. It's as if all these other things we teach when we teach writing—thesis statements, textual analysis, business writing, digital media, cultural rhetorics, and so on—are lush continents, and we invite our students to experience and consider them. But we never invite our students to talk about the planet itself, its layers and operations. Our programs treat such discussion as if it were too deep for undergraduate students (and perhaps their instructors), as if it were better to keep them frolicking over surfaces. If we ever get more than superficial writing from students, we should be shocked, look for plagiarism, or chalk it up to the natural, ineffable, unteachable soulfulness or talent that a few young people seem to possess.

Berthoff's *FTW* offers composition a method for teaching writing as what it is first, foremost, and always: forming, making meaning. Making meaning is something all students do naturally and expertly all the time. *FTW* operationalizes this tendency to make meaning by having students do it consciously in their writing. This approach tends to challenge core values and perceptions of the field and of the academy. I'm thinking especially of the notion of plurality—the idea that composition is better off embracing a wide range of approaches to writing and philosophies of writing (or of culture, cognition, aesthetics, etc.) than seeking some kind of theory of everything (TOE). In Berthoff's view, triadicity, while perhaps not a TOE, was able to account for more aspects of the relationship between writing and thinking than any other theory of writing. The problem is that triadicity is incommensurate with conceptions of the meaning-writing connection that do not account for the mediating nature of meaning. Sadly for Berthoff, most of the thinking that informs the intersection of writing and pedagogy does not account for this, and so her philosophy gets short shrift, even when her terms figure into new scholarship. Linda Adler-Kassner and Elizabeth Wardle's collection of "threshold concepts," for instance, features essays that centralize meaning as "mediating" (Russell) and as material for future meanings (Bazerman; Lunsford). Yet there is no mention of method or pragmatic practice, concepts that, according to Berthoff, are essential in the consideration of writing as meaning-making (*Sense* 127–49).

Berthoff's philosophy of writing as meaning-making is rendered inaccessible when her teaching practice is separated from her philosophy. And it matters; with the passing of time, Berthoff's philosophy continues to wane, despite, or perhaps because of, citations of her books and articles that never discuss her theory of language.

The only way to apprehend the enormous potential of Berthoff's philosophy of forming—a philosophy with the capacity to address a fundamental phenomenon, the forming imagination, foundational to all concerns and interests at the intersection of teaching, literacy, and the language arts—is to do it.

Mutable Structures: *Forming/Thinking/Writing* in Practice

I teach first-year writing at Georgia State University. I have 103 students, many of them dual enrollment high school students from the Atlanta area. As of fall 2020, due to COVID-19, I teach strictly online. Berthoff's pedagogy of forming, the teaching philosophy underlying *FTW*, enables me to do this. In accordance with *FTW*, students consider given rubrics as they interpret the quality of their own work and assign that work grades. Students write and think about what they desire—there is no theme. And the primary text of the course is always students' own writing and their own thinking.

At the beginning of the course I always tell students that I've designed an English 101 that can't be faked; every student must write something they really think and feel and care about in order to succeed. Usually at least one student will consider that a challenge, but in the end, they realize that trying to produce meaningless writing is still producing writing, and meaninglessness is actually quite hard to compose. All writing counts. What we do during the semester is think about writing as a way of making meaning. The only way to fail the course is to disengage, to refuse to write, refuse to think, refuse to participate in dialogue about writing as a way of making meaning.

I offer here a description of how I employ Berthoff's pedagogy of forming. *FTW* teaches writing, but it does so on a level that makes composition instruction barely recognizable from traditional perspectives. The book invites students to write grocery lists, to group unlikely objects, to create classifications, to make chaos, recognizing that all writing counts. The goal is to observe the mind in action through writing, and then to shove potentiality in the face of insignificance. It's writing as a way of making meaning, as opposed to using writing merely as a way to do what we're told, to remake—as best one can—the meanings of others, and then to communicate them correctly. Writing makes meaning; it doesn't just communicate meanings. Turning our attention to how we make meaning through writing is the pedagogy of forming established by *FTW*.

One of the foundational practices suggested in *FTW* is an observation notebook. Students are invited to observe texts—broadly conceived as organic objects, short philosophical passages, maps, dictionaries, and so on—and write what comes to mind in the observation process. The true object of observation in this exercise is the mind, observable by means of a "dialectical notebook" (Berthoff, *Forming* 28). The idea is that before students can begin to control their meanings in writing, they must develop an awareness of the relationship between their meanings, their writings, and the world. Thus, the first practice inherent in *FTW* and the pedagogy of forming is to develop an awareness of form and forming.

One of the exercises I currently use in my classes, an adaptation of Berthoff's practice, asks students to create and maintain a notebook in which they write only on the left-hand pages, leaving the right-hand pages blank for a few weeks. On the left-hand pages they record thoughts, notes, homework activities, musings, sketches, and so on throughout the semester. Early on I ask students to record what comes to their minds when encountering the figure shown here. We discuss what they write, noting words and ideas common in their responses (for instance, "incomplete" or "unfinished"). We muse on what it is about us that produces so much shared anxiety over a sense of incompleteness. What surfaces during these conversations is inevitably that so much of our perception comes from shared experience. We notice that the more detailed our responses are, the more individualized and unique the writing tends to be. We observe that the more detailed the image of observation, the more we name and describe it. This is the phenomenon of forming; a constant dialectic between conception and perception resourced by writing, among other meaning-making modes.

Importantly, constitutive of the pedagogy of forming is pragmatism. It's not enough to observe the forms constituting your thoughts, perceptions, and writing; you've got to grow the sense that your forms could be otherwise. All forms, all meaning-making structures, are mutable. What happens if you put it this way or that? The entire experience of *FTW*, cast as a series of invitations, is a way of encouraging students to produce options, perceptions, conceptions for making meaning, and the awareness necessary to be able to think through and choose which meanings they wish most to embody and produce. An in-class activity allows me to demonstrate how students should use the right-hand pages of their dialectical notebooks. The right-hand side of the following example shows reformulations (not "corrections") of the writing on the left-hand side:

It is an unfinished circle.	It looks like an unfinished circle.
	It's an incomplete circle.
	The shape looks like a warped, almost closed loop.

What difference does it make when we write "It looks like an unfinished circle" as opposed to "It is an unfinished circle"? The potential meaning effect of "is" versus "looks like" results in deep conversations among college freshmen and their instructors. Try to teach someone the meaning value of *is* as a verb without such practice. Certainly, such deep conversations beat the convenient lies we tell our students—for instance, that the passive voice is bad and should be avoided—lies that only set them up for failure in their attempts to achieve a sense of satisfaction from their writing.

From Reading Berthoff's Textbook to Doing the Exercises

Crucially, the pedagogy of forming is not merely a matter of invention. It addresses the foundations of writing practice at all levels. Students cultivate an attention to the way their minds craft associations and to the role of written forms—commas, words, paragraphs, titles, images, essays, podcasts, business letters, slide presentations, and so on—in that crafting. Students learn how to question where the forms of their writing come from and to imagine how they might write—and thus mean—differently. Instead of talk of correctness we talk of usefulness, of situation, and of purpose. As a teacher well versed in the grammar and punctuation of Standard American English, I am able to offer what I call "textbook suggestions." If a student tends to omit articles consistently, I might focus on one sentence, offering a technically correct version and asking how the meaning changes when using or omitting articles. Students tend to notice patterns of forming as a result of this dialogue, and they can choose to leave out articles, as long as they have a reason for doing so. This technique replaces correctness with authorial choice and honors the vital role of rhetorical situations in determining correctness in the first place.

The practice laid out in *FTW* is revolutionary. *Do* the book, all the exercises included in it. Adapt and change them. Craft a curriculum based on its philosophy, even if doing so requires a major shift in thinking about what you're teaching when you teach writing. As a student of Berthoff's philosophy and pedagogy, and as a teacher embedded in underserved communities I care very deeply about, I see more value in Berthoff's work now than ever; the pedagogy of forming is a pedagogy of humanity and a potential resource for social justice. I worry that if we don't revisit Berthoff's ideas in the terms of her philosophy, we risk never achieving our full potential as a field to engender in students the practiced awareness and imagination they need to write their meanings into the world. Some will do it anyway, in spite of us. But isn't it our duty to nourish the humanity in all our students if we can? *Forming/Thinking/Writing: The Composing Imagination* is a testament to the fact that writing instruction can be this kind of experience for students.

Works Cited

Adler-Kassner, Linda, and Elizabeth A. Wardle, editors. *Naming What We Know: Threshold Concepts of Writing Studies*. Utah State UP, 2015.

Arrington, Paige Davis. *Ann Berthoff from the Margins: An Infusion of All-At-Once-Ness for Contemporary Writing Pedagogy*. 2019. Georgia State U, PhD dissertation. *Scholar Works @ Georgia State University*, scholarworks.gsu.edu/cgi/viewcontent.cgi?article=1238&context=english_diss.

Bazerman, Charles. "Writing Expresses and Shares Meaning to Be Reconstructed by the Reader." Adler-Kassner and Wardle, pp. 21–23.

Berlin, James A. "Contemporary Composition: The Major Pedagogical Theories." *College English*, vol. 44, no. 8, 1982, pp. 765–77.

Berthoff, Ann E. *Forming/Thinking/Writing: The Composing Imagination*. Boynton/Cook, 1978.

———. "Problem-Dissolving by Triadic Means." *College English*, vol. 58, no. 1, 1996, pp. 9–21. *JSTOR*, https://doi.org/10.2307/378531.

———. *The Sense of Learning*. Boynton/Cook, 1990.

Enos, Theresa. "Professing the New Rhetorics." *Rhetoric Review*, vol. 9, no. 1, autumn 1990, pp. 5–35.

Harris, Joseph D. *A Teaching Subject: Composition since 1966*. Utah State UP, 2012.

Hawk, Byron. *A Counter-history of Composition: Toward Methodologies of Complexity*. U of Pittsburgh P, 2007.

Lunsford, Andrea A. "Writing Is Informed by Prior Experience." Adler-Kassner and Wardle, pp. 54–55.

McComiskey, Bruce. *Dialectical Rhetoric*. Utah State UP, 2015.

Reising, Robert W., and Tom Liner. "Two Views." *The English Journal*, vol. 67, no. 9, 1978, pp. 69–70. *JSTOR*, https://doi.org/10.2307/815136.

Russell, David R. "Writing Mediates Activity." Adler-Kassner and Wardle, pp. 26–27.

Rutherford, Kevin, and Jason Palmeri. "The Things They Left Behind: Toward an Object-Oriented History of Composition." *Rhetoric, through Everyday Things*, edited by Scot Barnett and Casey Boyle, U of Alabama P, 2016, pp. 96–107.

Young, Art. Review of *Forming, Thinking, Writing: The Composing Imagination*, by Ann E. Berthoff. *College Composition and Communication*, vol. 30, no. 1, 1979, pp. 63–64. *JSTOR*, https://doi.org/10.2307/356753.

Humanizing and Decolonizing Composition: John Mohawk's "Western Peoples, Natural Peoples"

Rachel B. Griffis

> John Mohawk, "Western Peoples, Natural Peoples: Roots of Anxiety,"
> *Akwesasne Notes* (1976)

Originally published in 1976, "Western Peoples, Natural Peoples: Roots of Anxiety" was included in a 2010 collection of essays that memorialized the historian and activist John Mohawk (1945–2006). In this essay Mohawk confronts Western educational institutions that teach young people how to succeed in a culture that rewards the exploitation and domination of people, communities, and places. He argues that young people "live in a culture that creates behavior patterns that have been destructive to the Natural World and Natural Peoples" (264–65). He contends, moreover, that destructive behaviors and lifestyles are connected to the misuse and abuse of language. As Mohawk observes, "Native people discover quickly that Westernized peoples often do not mean what they say, and they do not say what they mean. Duplicity is found in every culture; in the West, it is expected. In short, they lie a lot" (261). The concerns Mohawk expresses in relation to the link between human and ecological flourishing and responsible language align with other thinkers often cited in placed-based composition studies. For example, Wendell Berry contends in *Standing by Words* that "the disintegration of communities and the disintegration of persons" is related to "the unreliability of language" (24).

Mohawk's and Berry's ideas have much in common, yet Mohawk's essay deserves additional visibility due to its emphasis on the deleterious effects of Euro-American colonization of Native people and lands. As Eve Tuck and K. Wayne Yang point out, educators' discussions about decolonizing classroom instruction often "make no mention of Indigenous peoples, our/their struggles for the recognition of our/their sovereignty, or the contributions of Indigenous intellectuals and activists to theories and frameworks of decolonization" (2–3). These omissions are due to what Austin Channing Brown refers to as the "default setting" of white culture in the academy (53). In particular, Mohawk's work has likely been overlooked due to his moral, rather than pragmatic, vocabulary of "human standards" (Mohawk 265), which contrasts starkly with the default, results-oriented perspective of Western educators. In the field of rhetoric and composition, more scholars have begun to draw on Native American traditions as they contribute to social justice work—for instance, Damián Baca and Victor Villanueva, the editors of *Rhetorics of the Americas*. Nevertheless, there is a need for more scholarship on theoretical approaches to writing instruction and the study of language that draws significantly on Native intellectuals, especially given the moral, humanistic perspective these figures provide regarding the link between the care of place and language. Berry, in the opening of *The Unsettling of America: Culture and Agriculture*, acknowledges the devasting and unethical practices of settler colonialism when he comments on Europeans' abuses of land, a contrast to Native Americans' "relation to place [which] was based upon old usage and association, upon inherited memory, tradition, veneration" (6). However, Berry suggests only briefly that Native practices represent more sustainable and ethical approaches to life-giving resources, such as land and language, and neither does he substantially reflect on contributions from the Native community for correcting the problems he outlines in his work.

This essay consequently explores how Native American writing about language, particularly Mohawk's "Western Peoples, Natural Peoples: Roots of Anxiety," provides further guidance for the task of humanizing and decolonizing composition instruction. Given the long tradition in Euro-American culture of using language to dominate, control, and manipulate people and places, I argue that extricating composition curriculum in the West from such unethical uses of language requires intentional effort, awareness, and resistance to consumeristic ideologies. Mohawk's work speaks to the need for a shared understanding of language in composition classrooms, specifically one that views language as vital to the cultivation of community and preservation of culture and places. Rhetoricians and composition instructors seeking to decolonize curricula and classrooms consequently have much to learn from Mohawk, who draws attention to problematic ideologies in Western culture that influence writing instruction while also demonstrating uses of language that actively care for people and places.

Mohawk's interpretation of Western culture highlights specific abuses of language to which twenty-first-century students have likely become accustomed. When he asserts that "[d]uplicity is found in every culture; in the West, it is expected," he alludes to ways Euro-American people and policies have historically co-opted the English language to colonize and oppress non-white people and communities (261). His essay resonates with past accounts of disingenuous language, such as the statement by William Apess, a Pequot minister and political leader, from an 1836 speech: "Although in words they deny it, yet in the works they approve of the iniquities of their fathers" (287). Similarly, in a remarkable letter written in 1774 by the prodigy and slave Phillis Wheatley to the Mohegan minister Samson Occom, Wheatley draws attention to "the strange Absurdity" of Americans fighting for independence from the British because their "Words and Actions are so diametrically opposite" (153). In the same vein as Apess and Wheatley, Mohawk recasts, with more recent examples, the dishonesty and hypocrisy that is prevalent in Euro-American communication. He writes that Westerners "understand that television commercials regularly misrepresent their products, that politicians make promises they do not intend to keep, that most movies and magazine articles are either fiction or gross exaggerations," which creates the situation wherein "[p]eople who believe everything are said to be naïve" (261). The label of "naïve" for a person who simply believes what others say, Mohawk suggests, is a particularly damning feature of Euro-American culture, one which reveals the great damage done to individuals, communities, and places by corrupt language.

While attributing the prevalence of duplicity in Western culture to what Sitting Bull calls "the love of possessions" (qtd. in Mohawk 260), Mohawk argues that educational institutions participate in teaching young people the cultural vices that result in such dishonest uses of language (260). He states, "People in the West become obsessed in their quest for wealth and power to a degree that defies rational explanation," an obsession he implies is reinforced in Western education (263). As he explains, "Schools teach people how to more successfully compete for affection.

They teach how to reach careers with increased amounts of money and/or control," and he names "the schools" as among the forces that "draw us deeper and deeper into this false way of being" (264, 269). As he indicts education for its complicity in exacerbating the culture of consumerism, Mohawk aligns himself not only with the work of the environmentalist Berry, who argues that education has wrongly become "a commodity" and "a kind of weapon," but also with the scientist Wes Jackson, a friend of Berry's, who famously quips, "The universities now offer only one serious major: upward mobility" (Berry, *Home Economics* 52; Jackson 3). Mohawk consequently lambasts the norm of Western life wherein "everyone's capability of stretching the truth is trained and honed," and contrasts this phenomenon with Native traditions of language, which hold that "lying destroys language and the destruction of language means the destruction of culture, the nation" (261).

Mohawk's contention that schools are complicit in the cultural vices that lead to people becoming "trained and honed" in "stretching the truth" is an argument that has appeared in scholarship not only on rhetoric and composition but also on education more broadly. James Berlin's well-known article, "Rhetoric and Ideology in the Writing Class," argues that "a way of teaching is never innocent" and that "[e]very pedagogy is imbricated in ideology," which includes particular perspectives on "how power ought to be distributed" (492). More recently, in the 2019 Conference on College Composition and Communication chair's address, Asao B. Inoue asks a question with moral underpinnings and political overtones: "How do we language so people stop killing each other?" Inoue answers the question through metaphors of imprisonment that describe the state of language in American culture and with the argument that composition instructors need to use multiple, diverse modes of judgment regarding student writing rather than reinforcing white, privileged modes of communication (357). Whereas Mohawk's critique of education is indeed sympathetic to Berlin's, Inoue's, and others' perspectives, Mohawk is not primarily concerned with teaching that distributes power more evenly but with cultural values that encourage young people to desire power and to use learning as a vehicle to achieve it. He helps readers consider the ordinary ways students are formed through education to become liars, opportunists, and consumers and the ways these roles negatively affect communal life and the natural world.

In the situation Mohawk describes, composition instruction often entails showing students how to use language to compete, dominate, and gain control, which are skills and ends he represents as fundamentally inappropriate and unethical. His work consequently provides standards for composition instruction that illuminate the pernicious ways colonialism influences American education, even in materials that are self-consciously pluralistic and politically progressive. Many of the commonly assigned textbooks in first-year writing classes have become more inclusive and diverse in recent years, yet the assumption that language is a tool for competition and accomplishment undergirds the logic of these textbooks. For example, *Everyone's an Author*, by Andrea Lunsford and colleagues, includes a chapter encouraging students to major in rhetoric, which begins with the hook, "employers rank the ability to communicate well at the top of their list of the qualities they look for in those they hire," and contains a section titled "What Jobs Will Studying Rhetoric Prepare You For?" (53, 56). Although the authors include mitigating statements that admittedly decenter Euro-American language traditions, such as "the U.S. way of writing academically is not the only way" and "Nor is it a better way," the textbook nevertheless assumes students are seeking to hone their written communication skills for social and financial success and thus encourages them in such motivations (52).

The popular handbook *"They Say / I Say": The Moves That Matter in Academic Writing*, by Gerald Graff and Cathy Birkenstein, contains a perspective on written language similar to that of Lunsford and her coauthors. Graff and Birkenstein provide a nonpolarizing perspective on argumentation by recommending that writers present their ideas "not as uncontestable givens but as entries in a conversation or a debate" (x), which, like *Everyone's an Author*, creates welcoming conditions for students to share and explore various, perhaps conflicting, ideas. However, *"They Say / I Say"* is stringently focused on teaching students to use others' language to maximize the effectiveness of their own. Graff and Birkenstein explain that "to argue well you need to do more than assert your own position. You need to enter a conversation, using what others say (or might say) as a launching pad or sounding board for your own views" (3). While the authors indeed instruct students to represent others' views accurately and ethically, their work still points to an assumption in Euro-American thinking that often remains unquestioned in composition instruction: the paramount purpose of studying communication—written and oral—is for the individual's effectiveness, advancement, and achievement. For Mohawk, people who are educated and formed to prize and pursue such ends are doomed to perpetuate the denigration of life itself on individual, communal, and ecological levels.

Mohawk accounts for the difficulty educators may face when they are challenged to teach counter to Western norms, especially according to purposes that affront what Sitting Bull calls "the love of possessions" (qtd. in Mohawk 260). Accordingly, Mohawk writes, "The culture, the system, the way of life are presented as unchangeable, mandated by God, history, and charts of progress" (264). As a result, instructors who present the study of writing divorced from its economic power need to be prepared to disavow, both in words and practice, the ubiquitous messages about language that appear in textbooks, in course descriptions, on college websites, and in popular media. For example, Toni Morrison describes the arduous work of "learn[ing] how to maneuver ways to free up the language from its sometimes sinister, frequently lazy, almost always predictable employment of racially informed and determined chains" (xi). Furthermore, in an anecdote about his own experience with manipulative language, Ibram X. Kendi states that "[t]he racist ideas sounded so good, so right, as racist ideas normally do" (105). What Mohawk, Morrison, and Kendi make evident is that language that facilitates control and domination has become so embedded in Western thinking that it often feels and sounds as if it is "mandated by God" and cannot be used another way (Mohawk 264). Writing instructors are therefore likely to struggle with disentangling their teaching from such perspectives on language, possibly more so in mundane interactions with students than in formal explanations of the course objectives.

In spite of his censure of Western culture, Mohawk nevertheless exudes hope when he outlines "treatment" for the cultural vices he connects to language (267). This "treatment," he argues, "must involve a release from needs to dominate or be dominated, to possess or to have power over" (267). The application of Mohawk's treatment in the composition classroom will entail teaching students how to write about people and places without attempting to dominate, possess, or have power over their audience or subject. Mohawk argues that the opposite of "human standards of behavior" manifests as "ambitions for power and possessions," which "produces destructive, cold-blooded people hostile to everything and everyone failing to serve their needs" (265). In contrast, he posits that "living in a loving, sharing community is the norm for humans," and he articulates a plan for "reestablish[ing] community, where human standards of conduct are once again normal standards, where truthfulness and constancy and trust are possible" (267). As the popular composition textbooks cited earlier reveal, standards that assume that "ambitions for power and possessions" are normal and worthy pursuits often undergird writing instruction in Western education (265). These standards are implicit in statements that motivate students to master writing for employment opportunities or that instruct students to use others' words to maximize their own rhetorical success. Mohawk's writing, alternatively, provides "human standards" as both a linguistic and conceptual resource that can guide students away from domineering and consumeristic modes of writing and toward more humane ones (265).

Although, broadly speaking, nonsectarian education in the United States is committed to pluralistic definitions of the meaning of life and other existential questions, standards and values associated with "the love of possessions" nevertheless underlie the daily operations of the academy (qtd. in Mohawk 260). These standards inform curriculum, marketing strategies, student life, retention efforts, and more. Whereas reformation is indeed necessary in all realms of the academy, the composition classroom is a fundamental place for Mohawk's concept of "human standards" to take hold and radiate outward (265). It is a place where students can begin to detect their expectations about others whose "capability of stretching the truth is trained and honed" as well as their own assumptions about how they use language to aid themselves in their own pursuits and ambitions (261). Composition instructors have the opportunity not only to help students locate perfidious language but also to structure writing assignments and activities in ways that promote truthful communication and the care of community and place. Additionally, Mohawk's warning, specifically that "lying destroys language and the destruction of language means the destruction of culture, the nation" (261), speaks to the significance of what happens in writing courses as students are essentially coached to damage themselves and others, undermine communal life, and abuse the natural world.

Ancillary to Mohawk's warning is his compelling faith in language itself as a powerful resource that will strengthen communal bonds and facilitate the communication of truth. "Western Peoples, Natural Peoples: Roots of Anxiety" connects language to culture, evincing a compelling vision for how language might be discussed, treated, and used in ways that are humane and contrary to Western norms. Layli Long Soldier, an Oglala Lakota poet, writes in *Whereas*, a book that grapples with the perpetually manipulative nature of Euro-American writing and speech, "[E]ach People has been given their own language to reach with" (75). By delineating the purpose of language as a resource "to reach with," Long Soldier defines it as a tool beyond monetary function that facilitates neighborliness, care, and truth. In its treatment of community and neighborliness as indispensable aspects of life that language is meant to support and nourish, Long Soldier's work resonates with Mohawk's use of the phrase "human standards," which he believes does not need justification as he implores his audience to free themselves from the dishonest speech and false ways of living he associates with Western culture (265). Both of their appeals, specifically to the communal nature of language, repudiate composition curricula governed by beliefs in the monetary and materialist potential of language and offer a counterperspective: that students will profit, in a human and moral sense, by learning to write in order to connect with and care for their audience and subject. By studying Mohawk's work, and other Native American writers who bear witness to the ongoing colonization of people and land through Euro-American abuses of language, composition instructors and rhetoricians will not only understand more deeply the malicious uses of language that pervade Western education but also find guidance to humanize their teaching.

Works Cited

Apess, William. *On Our Own Ground: The Complete Writings of William Apess, a Pequot*. Edited by Barry O'Connell, U of Massachusetts P, 1992.

Baca, Damián, and Victor Villanueva, editors. *Rhetorics of the Americas: 3114 BCE to 2012 CE*. Palgrave Macmillan, 2010.

Berlin, James. "Rhetoric and Ideology in the Writing Class." *College English*, vol. 50, no. 5, 1988, pp. 477–94.

Berry, Wendell. *Home Economics*. Counterpoint, 1987.

———. *Standing by Words*. 1979. Counterpoint, 1983.

———. *The Unsettling of America: Culture and Agriculture*. Counterpoint, 1977.

Brown, Austin Channing. *I'm Still Here: Black Dignity in a World Made for Whiteness*. Convergent, 2018.

Graff, Gerald, and Cathy Birkenstein. *"They Say / I Say": The Moves That Matter in Academic Writing*. 4th ed., W. W. Norton, 2018.

Inoue, Asao B. "How Do We Language So People Stop Killing Each Other; or, What Do We Do about White Language Supremacy?" *College Composition and Communication*, vol. 71, no. 2, 2019, pp. 352–69.

Jackson, Wes. *Becoming Native to This Place*. Counterpoint, 1994.

Kendi, Ibram X. *How to Be an Antiracist*. Penguin Random House, 2019.

Long Soldier, Layli. *Whereas*. Greywolf Press, 2017.

Lunsford, Andrea, et al. *Everyone's an Author*. 2nd ed., W. W. Norton, 2017.

Mohawk, John. "Western Peoples, Natural Peoples: Roots of Anxiety." 1976. *Thinking in Indian: A John Mohawk Reader*, edited by José Barreiro, Fulcrum Publishing, 2010, pp. 259–70.

Morrison, Toni. *Playing in the Dark: Whiteness and the Literary Imagination*. Vintage Books, 1993.

Tuck, Eve, and K. Wayne Yang. "Decolonization Is Not a Metaphor." *Decolonization: Indigeneity, Education and Society*, vol. 1, no. 1, 2012, pp. 1–40.

Wheatley, Phillis. *Complete Writings*. Edited by Vincent Carretta, Penguin Books, 2001.

On Reading Roger Sale's *On Writing*

John Schilb

Roger Sale, *On Writing* (Random House, 1970)

Near the start of "Unknown Novels," an essay published in the winter 1973–74 issue of *The American Scholar*, Roger Sale makes the following mournful observation: "If the author is at all serious about the book, it must be very disheartening to struggle to get it right, get it into print, only to have it spottily noticed, and then disappear" (86). After this lament, Sale gets more specific. He says, "I want to write about a few books and writers who are, for all intents and purposes, unknown, and who deserve better" (88). He then discusses certain novels that, to his regret, have slipped from view. Sale's piece focuses solely on fiction. But countless works in other genres have suffered the same neglect. I think of Sale's own *On Writing*, published three years before. It's definitely a book that, in the last few decades, has been "spottily noticed." It did get some extended treatment in Robin Varnum's *Fencing with Words*, her 1996 history of Amherst's English 1–2 sequence. Because Sale had taught in the Amherst program, and because it shaped his thinking, Varnum included *On Writing* in her institutional account (237–39). But since the early 1980s, few scholars have cited it. The audience for it has ebbed. Heck, it's no longer in print.

When *On Writing* debuted, it gained more attention. Sale probably wasn't "disheartened" by the notice it first received. Wilma Ebbitt reviewed it—favorably, for the most part—in *College Composition and Communication* (63–64). And, for a while, the book did have its fans. A number of writing instructors read it and recommended it, especially to those who had recently joined their ranks. I was one such neophyte. At the time, I was desperately looking for how-to books like Sale's. When I began teaching composition in the 1970s, I did so with little background in the field. Like many English graduate programs, mine focused on literature; it didn't include what's now called writing studies. I was glad to hear that a book entitled *On Writing* even existed. I bought it and devoured it in one night. I loved the intellectual heft—and the practical advice—it brought to topics that I labored to teach. It made me aware of something else I hadn't known: that what I was teaching could be a fulfilling career. Though I never met him in person, Sale was one of the people who led me to specialize in composition.

In fact, *On Writing* remains on my shelves to this day. I have the same copy I originally bought. Sadly, though, it's on the verge of collapse. Sections of it are now unbound; it's literally coming apart. I can pick it up when I want to consult it, but thank goodness for rubber bands! I do all I can to save the book from oblivion.

Our whole field should undertake the same rescue mission. *On Writing* "deserve[s] better" than our current disregard. To explain why, I take my cue from Sale's study of unknown novels. Not only does he identify their forgotten merits. He also considers the forces that led them to "disappear."

On Writing remains relevant because it sheds light on a genre. Despite its title, it doesn't cover every sort of writing. Sale states right out that he'll focus on what he waggishly calls "the English paper" (*On Writing* 4). The kind of essay he's thinking of is what I'd call an analytical argument. It's not a proposal for a policy or action. Rather, it's a commentary on a text. Students develop a claim that builds on a piece they've read. They grapple with the author's vocabulary and ideas; they weigh the text's implications. They have to interpret, define, evaluate, and synthesize. The goal is to make thoughtful points of their own. The prompt that they're reacting to may be a brief quotation. Then again, it may be an entire book. For instance, a text that Sale himself is fond of is James Baldwin's *The Fire Next Time*, and *On Writing* includes a fourteen-page excerpt from it (95–109). More important to Sale, however, is how students respond to Baldwin. Throughout *On Writing*, he's chiefly concerned with the texts *they* compose. So he follows the Baldwin excerpt with four student papers about it. Then he examines the language and structure of these analyses.

Sale focused on the analytical argument because this type of writing assignment was common back then. It was standard, he notes at the start, in courses "all over America" (*On Writing* 3). And this remains the case. True, our field has come to pursue a broader range of interests. Numerous writing classes nowadays pose other composing tasks. The analytical argument, though, has stayed a curricular staple. In many a college, it's still at the core of the first-year writing course. There it survives for an understandable reason: In their time at college, students will have to write in this genre repeatedly. Besides, being able to argue thoughtfully is a civic virtue—especially now, when public debate is so often bursts of rage.

But there's a risk with this kind of writing. When students attempt it, they may succumb to "the fallacy of the arguable proposition" (*On Writing* 39). This is one of Sale's key terms, and he explains it at length. The "fallacy" he has in mind isn't an error in logic. It's an unproductive belief. The writer assumes that simply because a certain idea is reasonable, it will serve adequately as a claim. We can all probably spot the problems with this premise. Many rhetoricians would say you must also think about exigence. What are your argument's stakes? Why should these particular readers entertain your specific idea? Sale deserves credit for stating an often-hidden truth: "[A]nything is arguable, and most broad assertions are demonstrable as well" (49). Given this fact, students may feel they don't have to be ultraselective; they can pick any claim that gets the paper done. In such cases, Sale observes, the prose is often predictable, clichéd, trite, and—worst of all—boring. The supposedly good student churns it out with a fair amount of competence; the student perceived to be bad goes awry. But neither writes with genuine conviction. Therefore, Sale thinks writing classes should tackle two basic questions: What can students actually gain from the act of writing? Why perform this act at all?

On Writing is essentially Sale's answer. Every chapter suggests that writing is most worthwhile when you wind up forging links you didn't expect. You shouldn't try to argue for a view you already cling to. At its best, writing helps you explore. Through it, you discover relations between your subject and your experience. At the same time, you're considering how to connect your sentences too. From one to the next, ideally, those sentences will help evolve your argument. They won't just repeat your starting point. In sum:

> To develop an argument is to essay one's mind, to try something out, to push as far as one can. It is to recognize that one can know what one knows and with great security and yet, in relation to what the subject offers, not know very much. So the mind moves out, constantly examining the relation of one thing to another, constantly asking "If this, then what?" The task is never to "cover" the subject, for that task can safely be left to others. It is, rather, to find out what one thinks. (*On Writing* 126)

Sale doesn't deride all other kinds of writing. I doubt, for instance, that he'd snort at courses in technical communication, a popular college offering today. He might even welcome the curricular breadth that our field has achieved. In any case, his vision of writing seems vital. The type of argument he esteems is intellectually daring. It seeks out nuance and complexity. It's anything but the monotonous touting of preconceived opinion. It's writing through which students stretch themselves.

Because he wants students to write in a spirit of inquiry, he recommends they begin without an outline. Leave your text's itinerary open, he advises. Ponder your possible steps as you move along. You'll be more probing and interesting if you don't plan each stage in advance. I realize his suggestion may sound anarchic; in fact, what results may be a mess. I confess: I've often prodded my classes to work from outlines, and I've made use of them myself. But whenever I read Sale, I reconsider. No matter what, he's surely right to warn against fixed schemes. Writers committed to inquiry are flexible. As they compose, they're attuned to emerging issues. They're willing to go with new-sprung ideas. As Sale points out, writing isn't for them "a quarter-mile track." It's not a standard course they have to run. Instead, they see it as "a path [to be] cut through a forest" (*On Writing* 93). And they are the ones intrepidly wielding the axe.

Rest assured, Sale isn't content with stream-of-consciousness freewriting. For him, a draft is just stage one; the writer has more to do. Through his feedback and through class discussions, he nudges students to revise. His book includes several sample papers, which he dissects in detail. He identifies structural turns taken by the authors. He also points out moves they might have made. He'd like students to note especially their moments of repetition: spots where their argument spins in place. He prods them to think of ways they can get it moving forward. What, for example, are the further implications of this idea? What can be added that would complicate it? Sale also attends to elements of coherence. He lingers over words that writers use to bridge ideas. He contends that "[t]he life of any writer is expressed in his sense of small moment-to-moment relationships." These include "the relation of clause to clause and sentence to sentence" (*On Writing* 73). He's even concerned with seemingly minor choices. For him, they aren't trivial at all. He goes so far as to recommend that every writer "ask himself if his sentences, each one of them, should begin with an 'and' or a 'but,' implied or real" (75). Many teachers of writing, no matter how experienced, still wonder how to comment on students' texts. Even today, we can all learn from Sale. He demonstrates what it means to read these texts closely—and what it means to take them seriously at all.

Sale is interested in a draft's unfolding dynamics. He reveals this interest early, with his Zen-like title for chapter 2, "Writing Can Be Learned but It Can't Be Taught" (*On Writing* 15). Out of context this slogan may seem merely enigmatic. But it distills the philosophy he expresses throughout his book. When he declares that writing "can't be taught," he has in mind didactic modes of instruction. Sale doubts that such forms of teaching inspire. To bombard students with maxims, drills, and grammar manuals is to ensure they'll write like mere machines.

To be fair, many writing instructors today aren't this overbearing. Yet Sale's caution against didacticism is, I think, still apt. Consider the current commercial success of one composition textbook, Gerald Graff and Cathy Birkenstein's *They Say / I Say*. It's filled with argument templates that students can use in their papers. Here's an example: "Of course some might object that _____. Although I concede that _____, I still maintain that _____" (xviii). To be fair, the authors sincerely want to be helpful, and other methods of writing instruction might be combined with theirs. Still, the book's wide adoption is telling. Quite a few teachers, apparently, have absolute faith in its fill-in-the-blanks approach. By contrast, Sale emphasizes writing as discovery. For him, it's a process of *figuring out* how to expand ideas.

His view of writing deserves attention in light of another trend. Increasingly people in composition want first-year writing courses to focus on our discipline's threshold concepts (e.g., Adler-Kassner and Wardle). Classes like these discuss at length current rhetorical theory; students are obliged to learn its key tenets and terms. In major ways, this curriculum differs from one centered on templates. Above all, it's more attuned to recent scholarship. In both cases, though, there's a lot of time spent on imbibing information. Students supposedly need it if they're ever to write well. Sale proposes what I think is a more productive priority. He stresses the insights students can achieve *as* they draft and revise.

Given *On Writing*'s perpetual pertinence, why did it "disappear"? How did it become a "lost text"? Not because conspirators plotted its removal. The main problem, rather, is the way we've viewed our discipline's history. The lenses we've used can't capture Sale's pedagogical slant. I'm thinking of our eagerness to classify—the habit I've elsewhere referred to as "taxonomania" (Schilb 129). We like to partition the writing studies landscape into a few schools of thought. In doing so, we risk overlooking scholarship that doesn't fit into them. This is what happened to *On Writing*. Because it proved hard to categorize, it vanished from the map.

In particular, the book failed to fit a typology popular in the late 1980s. This was the system of classification promoted by James Berlin. He divided the field into three kinds of rhetoric. In a much-read 1988 *College English* article, he gave them names that stuck: "cognitive," "expressionist," and "social-epistemic." Over the last two decades or so, an increasing number of scholars have questioned Berlin's set of terms (e.g., Gold 19). For these scholars, Berlin's labels leave too much out. Prior to this increasing skepticism, though, Berlin's framework ruled. If it didn't cover books like Sale's—well, that was Sale's bad luck.

We can see how *On Writing* eludes Berlin's categories if we compare it with another book from 1970, namely Ken Macrorie's *Uptaught*. Berlin has no trouble at all classifying Macrorie. He's an expressionist: the kind of writing teacher who values "authenticity," "genuine self-discovery," "self-revelation" (Berlin 485). Macrorie does, in fact, clearly prize such qualities. He fondly recalls a class of his where "the students were speaking in their own voices about things that counted for them" (Macrorie 21). At times, Sale's ideals seem the same. He wants students "to say exactly what they believe is true" (*On Writing* 51). He hopes that each of them will learn that "writing is a form of being himself" (52). The two authors also have a common target. "The great fault of the style of most students," Sale declares, is "stiffness, solemnity, and pompousness" (127). Similarly, throughout his book, Macrorie attacks "Engfish":

the "bloated, pretentious language" students often use (18). Ultimately, though, Sale is no Macrorie. His emphasis is different. He's more concerned with the art of building and connecting ideas. Macrorie would have students "spend a weekend recording *fabulous realities*" (Macrorie 112). Sale would have students brood about whether to use *and* or *but*. When Ebbitt reviewed their books together in *College Composition and Communication*, she recognized where the two "part company" (63). She observed that "[t]hough they deplore the same kind of writing and though the main concern of both is the writer's response to his own experience, the kind of response Sale is talking about is much more complex, much more intellectual. And the process of writing is much more disciplined" (63). The "much mores" that Ebbitt registers here are significant contrasts. They're signs that Sale's book wouldn't suit Berlin's taxonomy. And, therefore, its virtues would be ignored. The lesson to draw: Even today, our discipline should be mindful of outliers. They shouldn't have to represent some "ism" we've established. Great ideas may lurk in liminal works like Sale's.

Sale's book might have lingered in our memory had Sale clearly remained affiliated with our field. But this wasn't the case. After leaving Amherst in 1966, he spent the rest of his career at the University of Washington. There he wrote about subjects other than those we typically associate with our discipline. One of his most popular books was a local history, *Seattle, Past to Present*. For *On Not Being Good Enough*, he gathered criticism he wrote for *The New York Review of Books*, where he regularly reviewed new fiction and nonfiction. Most of his books were literary histories, covering various periods (*Modern Heroism, Fairy Tales and After, Literary Inheritance, Closer to Home*).

To be sure, Sale didn't turn his back on writing studies. At various times, he still taught writing courses. He ran summer classes for high school writing instructors (Sale, "'Alternative Teacher'" 11). At his death in 2017, the book in progress he left behind included writing pedagogy (14). Even so, Sale never published a sequel to *On Writing*. No wonder he didn't make it into Stephen North's *The Making of Knowledge in Composition: Portrait of an Emerging Field*. Indeed, the bulk of Sale's output suggests that literature was more his thing. So, even today, I can easily imagine people in composition saying, "Why should we read *On Writing*, let alone rescue it? Its author wasn't really one of us."

Dismissive views like this are now rife in writing studies. Many of us assume that specialists in literature don't ever share our concerns. Rarely at composition conferences is literature even mentioned. Meanwhile, there's a surge in independent writing programs, many of which proudly keep their distance from English departments. Moreover, hundreds of graduate programs now focus on rhetoric and composition alone. But whatever the merits of these trends, they risk becoming myopic. They deter us from exploring how literary critics—and the texts they study—shed light on issues of rhetoric, language, discourse, and style. In any case, Sale's book is wise about our field's main subject. Whatever Sale's interest in other disciplines, *On Writing* is a resource for ours.

At the end of "Unknown Novels," Sale gets wistful. Wouldn't it be nice, he suggests, if "the books we should read, the books that could be memorable, could always be announced to us" (104)? This collection, in its own way, gratifies his wish. And yet: To say that I'm "announcing" a book in this essay feels odd. *On Writing* isn't hot off the press; it wasn't published last week. It's been around for over fifty years. So, what I've been doing here is more akin to reminding. Sale's book still lives, if barely. Let's give it new attention. And the biases that buried it? They warrant study too.

Works Cited

Adler-Kassner, Linda, and Elizabeth Wardle, editors. *Naming What We Know: Threshold Concepts of Writing Studies.* Utah State UP, 2015.

Berlin, James A. "Rhetoric and Ideology in the Writing Class." *College English*, vol. 50, no. 5, Sept. 1988, pp. 477–94.

Ebbitt, Wilma R. Review of *Uptaught*, by Ken Macrorie; *On Writing*, by Roger Sale; and *Course X: A Left Field Guide to Freshman English*, by Leonard A. Greenbaum and Rudolf B. Schmerl. *College Composition and Communication*, vol. 22, no. 1, Feb. 1971, pp. 62–65.

Gold, David. "Remapping Revisionist Historiography." *College Composition and Communication*, vol. 64, no. 1, Sept. 2012, pp. 15–34.

Graff, Gerald, and Cathy Birkenstein. *They Say / I Say: The Moves That Matter in Academic Writing.* 4th ed., W. W. Norton, 2018.

Macrorie, Ken. *Uptaught.* Hayden, 1970.

North, Stephen. *The Making of Knowledge in Composition: Portrait of an Emerging Field.* Boynton/Cook, 1987.

Sale, Roger. "'The Alternative Teacher': An Interview with Roger Sale." Conducted by John Boe. *Writing on the Edge*, vol. 16, no. 1, fall 2005, pp. 6–21.

———. *Closer to Home: Writers and Places in England, 1780–1830*. Harvard UP, 1986.

———. *Fairy Tales and After: From Snow White to E. B. White*. Harvard UP, 1978.

———. *Literary Inheritance*. U of Massachusetts P, 1984.

———. *Modern Heroism: Essays on D. H. Lawrence, William Empson, and J. R. R. Tolkien*. U of California P, 1973.

———. *On Not Being Good Enough: Writings of a Working Critic*. Oxford UP, 1979.

———. *On Writing*. Random House, 1970.

———. *Seattle, Past to Present*. U of Washington P, 1976.

———. "Unknown Novels." *The American Scholar*, vol. 43, no. 1, winter 1973–74, pp. 86–104.

Schilb, John. "Future Historiographies of Rhetoric and the Present Age of Anxiety." *Writing Histories of Rhetoric*, edited by Victor J. Vitanza, Southern Illinois UP, 1994, pp. 128–38.

Varnum, Robin. *Fencing with Words: A History of Writing Instruction at Amherst College during the Era of Theodore Baird, 1938–1966*. National Council of Teachers of English, 1996.

Part Four

1980–1992

International Linguistics Research and the Legacy of Frédéric François

Tiane K. Donahue

> Frédéric François, "De la variation et de ses variétés dans différents discours d'enfants: Diversité, mélanges, métaphores, irruptions, et leurs familles," *Repères* (1988)
> Frédéric François, "Langage et pensée: Dialogue et mouvement discursif chez Vygotski et Bakhtine," *Enfance* (1989)
> Frédéric François, *Morale et mise en mots* (L'Harmattan, 1994)[1]

In Memoriam J. Frédéric François

This essay offers a somewhat loose interpretation of a "lost text." Here I focus on lost disciplinary questions grounded in the study of language, understanding "text" in two ways: the text of a body of knowledge, French functional linguistics specifically but also linguistics generally, and the lost text of the linguist Frédéric François's body of work, lost before it was ever found. Two disciplinary phenomena led to this work's being lost: first, writing studies has generally marginalized linguistics until very recently, as has been thoroughly documented over time; and second, we have missed the breadth and depth of writing scholarship outside US anglophone contexts (and so this scholarship has been lost in part because it is not available in English, but it isn't just about language).[2] These two phenomena are inextricably intertwined, but I tease them out separately.

We see the missed opportunity of non-US-anglophone scholarship directly addressed in the work of Bruce Horner and colleagues,[3] but the indirect reality is that research on writing, while globally widespread and published in many languages, is just as often grounded in disciplines other than composition (for example, in linguistics, didactics, education sciences, psychology, and so on), which leads anglophone composition scholars to misrecognize it or glide past it. Much of this work has been lost to writing studies because it is most often not written in English or it does not appear in US journals.

European research on writing in higher education fills many gaps in research conducted in the United States, focusing, for example, on the writing of master's and PhD students (Castelló et al.; Jahic and Pavlovic; and many others), on cognitive processes the United States had set aside (using, for example, eye tracking and eye-and-pen analyses [Leijten and Van Waes]), on corpus analyses of academic or scientific writing (Schlitz; Boch and Rinck; Grossmann), or on working and long-term memory processes in writing (Galbraith et al.). Australian work in writing across the curriculum has explored multidisciplinary students and their writing experiences, writing development transitions from secondary education to tertiary education, and differences between the arts and the humanities, on the one hand, and the sciences, on the other (Vardi; Skillen; Chanock).

Research on writing can also be dismissed because of the decades-long rejection of linguistics (Crowley; Nystrand et al.; Parker and Campbell; Matsuda; Silva and Leki; Leki). That rejection is founded partly on lack of generalized knowledge of linguistics beyond the subfields of linguistics in play in the 1960s and 1970s. Kim Parker and Frank Campbell note that rejections of linguistics have often been based on structuralist assumptions—which linguistics had moved past by the 1980s—and partly on the resulting inattention to fields of linguistics that developed these past forty years.

The field of writing studies in its earlier history included linguistic text analysis; speech, foreign language, and writing instruction interactions; and "second" language writing work grounded in applied linguistics. Early investments are detailed by Paul Matsuda, Tony Cimasko and Melinda Reichelt, Tony Silva and Ilona Leki, and others. The scholarship of the 1970s and 1980s shows a broad investment in approaches such as text analysis in the discipline of composition. Writing studies moved away from these in later years for complicated reasons (Silva et al.; Nystrand et al.) that have left us much less equipped to take on the challenges of new areas of research grounded in an understanding of language, including translingualism, multimodality, big data analyses, and the discussion of "knowledge transfer." In this sense, the text of linguistic research is indeed lost—once visible, then invisible in mainstream writing studies.

For sure, linguistic approaches in composition needed to move away from the approaches mentioned above, as composition scholarship took its social turn and further evolved into multiple strands of inquiry. Unfortunately, changes in linguistics itself were not followed when the field as a whole was set aside—and linguistics has indeed developed new strands of inquiry. A simple current example is the robust field of computational linguistics, which could be a deep resource for evolving big data research in writing studies. Translingual work in linguistics is another example. While writing studies has taken up questions of translingual writing, code-switching, code-meshing, translanguaging, polylingualism, cosmopolitanism, and so on, it has done so largely without referencing the linguists who have worked in these areas, sometimes since the 1980s. Writing knowledge transfer, while not technically a question of language, would also benefit in significant ways from understanding both analysis of linguistic transfer and European analyses of the transfer question more broadly (Donahue, "Writing"). We have lost ground, creating potentially unnecessary divisions—for example, between applied linguistics and composition or between corpus linguistics and digital humanities—in terms of some pertinent methods and shared questions.[4]

In contexts outside the United States, scholars have continued to work with linguistic theory and analytic methods in order to understand how writing works. For instance, recent studies of higher education writing research in Latin America seeking to identify theoretical configurations and epistemologies suggest that linguistics, broadly speaking, is a key disciplinary frame. Natalia Avila-Reyes notes:

> Members of this group are Teun Van Dijk, Michael Halliday, John Swales, Ken Hyland, Jim Martin, and Vijay Bhatia. While only Halliday and Martin come from a recognizable school—Systemic Functional Linguistics (SFL)—Swales, Hyland, and Bhatia might be placed together in a group of applied linguistics with an English for Specific Purposes (ESP) orientation. Most cited documents from SFL are linguistic tools, such as grammar . . . and appraisal theory. . . . Swales and Bhatia are mainly credited for their work on genre analysis of

academic and professional texts . . . , whereas Hyland is drawn on for his work on academic writing. . . . This divides international linguists into at least two groups: one providing mostly linguistics *tools*, and another providing mostly linguistic *analyses* of writing. (28–29)

Another study, by Mónica Tapia-Ladino and colleagues, identifies the top four disciplinary frames in Latin American work as literacy, linguistics, rhetoric, and education, with linguists such as Halliday, Van Djik, Martin, and Mikhail Bakhtin in dominant positions. While some writing studies scholars have worked closely with Bakhtinian thinking (Schuster; Halasek; Ewald; Bazerman), that is the exception. Entering into exchanges with Latin American scholars of higher education writing demands the ability to enter fully into linguistics theory and method.

Expanding our horizons as we consider texts we have lost thus includes expanding our thinking beyond our usual institutional, disciplinary, and national borders. We have foundational thinkers beyond these borders, in the sense that they are developing knowledge we need, and we don't always know it. There is of course a rich tradition of recognizing a few—and always the same few—foundational voices from beyond the United States, such as Michel Foucault or James Britton, for interesting historical and contextual reasons I cannot develop here. But the much broader body of available work is largely neglected.

I would like to offer the specific example of work by the French linguist Frédéric François to explore facets of the lost text of linguistics research. François, whose work has provided powerful ways to operationalize Bakhtinian thinking into an effective analytic tool, offers writing studies ways to think about language and writing that are essential to key disciplinary topics, including the study of students' knowledge transfer, intertextuality and work with sources, and translingual practices. I learned of François's work while I was a graduate student. I spent part of a semester at Université de Paris V before contracting scarlet fever and returning home early. But I had already attended a few of François's classes and was intrigued by his unique approach to language and linguistics. As I continued to work from home, I read one of his seminal works, *J'cause français, non?* (*I Talk French, Don't I?*), about the language development of children living in urban areas, and was fundamentally reoriented by his grounded analysis of language-in-practice, "la mise en mots," the moments at which we create utterances, as seen in written and spoken texts (François, *Morale* and *Enfants*). This was to me a new way of thinking about student writing as a dynamic text, full of possibilities for studying it and for considering what it's made of, how it does its work. Years later I decided to pursue a PhD in France and reconnected with François as I embarked on a cross-cultural study of university students' writing, looking at student work from France and the United States.

Why Frédéric François? He is the single most important scholar of French linguistics for compositionists to come to know. He is important in his own right, a unique thinker who transformed the French landscape of discourse analysis and attention to the construction of meaning in everyday discourses. But he is also important as a representative of the "text" that is French writing work grounded in linguistics and of linguistics as a disciplinary force. François developed a way to operationalize Bahktinian thinking as we analyze texts.[5]

His approach brings linguistic analysis, often considered reductive because limited to the text, into the highly contextualized domain of language in use, discursive and textual "mouvements," or movements always understood in dialogic context (François, *Le discours* 29). His field is French functional linguistics—not at all the same as UK- and Australian-based systemic functional linguistics. Rather, French functional linguistics is entirely focused on exploring how texts do what they do in context, how they function, how readers enter into relationships with texts (or listeners with speech), and how analyzing textual movements is a way to understand that relationship, which is at the heart of meaning-making. As I argued, presenting François's thinking, in *Écrire à l'université* (*Writing at University*):

> These movements construct the progressive development of a text, following the key idea or the point of view in several different ways, each one linked to the others without entirely repeating them. A given utterance is thus a realization of different discursive ways of functioning in a contact zone. It is never completely "regulated" by the zone's norms nor completely "original": we can say with Bakhtin that "the problem of what, in language, is grounded in current usage and what is grounded in the individual is the very question of the utterance." (my trans.)

> Ces mouvements construisent le développement progressif du texte en poursuivant l'idée principale ou le point de vue de plusieurs façons, chacune liée aux autres sans les répéter entièrement. L'énoncé particulier est ainsi une réalisation de diverses façons discursives de fonctionner d'une zone de contact. Il n'est ni complètement "réglé" par les normes de la zone, ni complètement "original": on peut dire avec M. Bakhtine que "le problème de ce qui, dans la langue, revient respectivement à l'usage courant et à l'individu est le problème même de l'énoncé."
> (Donahue, *Écrire* 108)

François's work on genre also emphasizes this relationship, conceptualizing genre as a fluid relation-based way to understand how a text is working rather than as a category used to classify texts. François emphasized the ways in which any text can be any genre depending on its use and function, rejecting genres as static, fixed categories before genre was thought of in that way in composition (see, for instance, François, "De la variation"). As I have noted elswhere when describing his framing:

> Even as we accept that the term "genre" is a way to identify a text in relation to its similarities-differences with other texts, as well as a way to understand a text in relation to its situation (a social practice and the activities that nourish it), we can, with F. François, adopt the idea that identifying a text's genre is not an objective in and of itself, and that sketching its features does not give us its identity.
> (my trans.)

> Tout en acceptant que le mot "genre" est une façon d'identifier un texte en fonction de ses ressemblances-différences avec d'autres textes, ainsi qu'une façon de comprendre un texte en fonction de sa situation (une activité sociale et les activités qui l'animent), on peut avec F. François s'accrocher à l'idée que fixer un genre n'est pas un objectif en soi, et que dessiner ses caractéristiques ne nous donne pas son identité.
> (Donahue, *Écrire* 112)

This fluid conception of genre as a way to understand a text in its contexts brings new layers of meaning to North American genre theory and puts genre analysis in the service of understanding how genres work on the boundaries of similarity-difference among texts as received by readers.

François gives us the most wonderful terms for analysis of phenomena that matter to us. For example, one of the terms he worked with later in his career is *orientation* (François, *Essais*). We can use this concept to gain insight into what writers do as they take on new tasks and as they engage in meaning-making. *Orientation* is both a physical term and a metaphorical one. François depicts successful speakers and writers who engage with new communicative exchanges as "orienting"—reading contextual cues, assessing the landscape, being aware, drawing on prior knowledge to navigate the new context—and also as knowing orientation is necessary. The beauty of its physical sense is what makes the metaphor work. I think, for example, about how people who travel become adept at orienting to new spaces. We can analyze what those abilities are and how that translates to writers or readers adept at orienting to new tasks, contexts, and audiences. This set of considerations is directly relevant to the exploration of knowledge transfer in writing, an apt model for explaining what a writer does as they engage a new discursive space and "orient."

Similarly, François develops the notion of "reprise-modification" (*Le discours* and *Morale*)—literally, "re-taking-up-modifying"—as the textual movement in which the take-up of language and its modification in that taking-up are always intertwined. This is Bakhtin operationalized. Any utterance, from a single word to an entire text, can be analyzed for the many ways it reprises-modifies, from linguistically local (particular words, sounds, indexes, morphemes, etc.) to contextually local (the texts read, the class discussion, dinnertime family discussions, etc.) to global (echoes of genres, of cultural commonplaces, of rhetorical traditions, *l'air du temps*...). The simplicity of the utterance enables broad application. We can, for example, analyze the multiple facets of intertextuality that are essential to the field's understanding of students' source use—for instance, students' drawing on linguistic resources, students' ability to cognitively manage new tasks, and so on. This core analytic notion of "reprise-modification" is a powerful way to operationalize what happens when knowledge does transfer—the way it is both reused and, at the same time, necessarily transformed. We can study features that are simultaneously specific to an utterance and interrelated with all utterances in complex ways.

"Reprise-modification" shows the heteroglossic complexity of work any writer does when working, explicitly or implicitly, with the ideas and voices of others:

> There are of course reprises that make a language work (syntactic reprises, lexical reprises, everything that comes from a language's structure and is thus more or less obligatory or at least strongly coded). But we are interested equally here with the reprises-modifications that we find in everything that is more weakly coded: particular ways to word things, to take back up notions, style, abstract choices or ways to organize a thought, an expression, or the re-elaborations of a shared background. In the text itself, that which is shared is more likely to be coded (normed), but each individual takes back up, reorganizes, reaccentuates this generic commonality based on their own experiences, discursive objects, perceptions, etc. (my trans.)
>
> Il y a, bien sûr, les reprises qui font fonctionner la langue (reprises syntaxiques, reprises lexicales, tout ce qui provient de la structure de la langue et qui est ainsi plus ou moins obligatoire ou au moins fortement codé). Mais on s'intéresse également ici aux reprises-modifications qu'on trouve dans tout ce qui est plus faiblement codé : les façons particulières de mettre en mots, de reprendre les notions, le style, les choix abstraits ou les façons d'organiser une pensée, une expression, ou bien les ré-élaborations d'un fond commun. Dans le texte même, ce qui est commun a plus tendance à être codé, mais chacun reprend, réorganise, et réaccentue ce générique en fonction de ses propres expériences, objectifs discursifs, perceptions, etc.
> (Donahue, *Écrire* 104)

Reprises-modifications are also textual movements that displace. Existing utterances (spoken or written) are always displaced—not removed, but displaced (moved over, if you will)—by the newly uttered. While we often hear talk of student writers "taking their place" in the conversation, dialogic understandings of academic discourse really demand displacement.

The dynamic identification of layers of reprise-modification also invites new, finer-grained ways to study translanguaging. Li Wei has pointed out that it is not terribly useful to try to tease apart the shifts between languages that constitute much translingual activity, the way linguists studying code-switching have done (14). But reprises-modifications are an entirely different way of teasing apart how translanguaging does its meaning-making work using a network of micro-, meso-, and macro-reprises that use and modify language.

François emphasizes everyday texts, including college students' writing, as worthy of such analysis. He spent many years studying children's writing in and out of school, their stories, their accounts of dreams, their school essays, with the same deep care, respect, and focus as a literary specialist would study a famous poem (François, *Le discours*). He looked for the ways these texts work, what we learn of language, of surprise, of craft and creativity. He loved to ask, "What does this text do that we [adults] could never do?" This attention is always accompanied by careful analysis of multiple examples to make concrete the kinds of reprises-modifications in play.

François's work underscores why we should in fact see linguistics itself as a lost text. Linguistics is often marginalized in our approach to composition, is often seen as alien to our field, as technical, as reductive, and so on. But it's not. It offers a systematic, rich perspective on the way language in use does its work. International scholarship also represents a body of lost texts. That this scholarship has been lost is partly due to the belief that there is no work outside the borders of the United States aside from the brilliant, abstract, inspiring but obtuse thoughts of the few select international literary scholars we've adopted that could possibly interest us. International scholarship also offers ways to understand work with big data research in writing studies that might address some of the concerns writing scholars have about these corpus-based approaches. Let me conclude, then, by calling on us to recover those lost texts that exist outside US borders—because we should, and because, in the globalized future in which we are already living, we must.

Notes

1. While this work falls slightly outside the period of time considered in this part of the volume, it is at the heart of François's thinking and represents a culmination of his earlier publications of that period.

2. These statements assume that second language writing is an independent field. I'm providing a brief sketch of a highly complex question, not trying to take a stand about the relationship between second language writing and writing studies; I could rephrase the framing here to say "writing studies, if we do not focus on the subfield of second language writing," but it is quite possible to argue that the same marginalizations I am treating here have contributed to the tensions frequently noted between composition scholarship and second language scholarship, for instance.

3. See also Donahue, "Bakhtin's 'Responsive Understanding'" and "Writing"; and Donahue and Delcambre.

4. Recent softening of these divisions has included linguistic attention to style, grammar, corpus linguistics (Aull), digital humanities, and advanced discourse analysis.

5. And yes, I say "Bakhtinian," although there is much controversy there. François himself published a book titled *Bahktine tout nu* (*Bakhtin All Naked*) in which he responds to recent scholarship that exposes Bakhtin's work as not Bakhtin's (Bronckart and Bota) by suggesting that we might focus more on the theory and approach and less on the sensationalist politics of who or why in Bakhtin's work (though of course crediting the thinking effectively remains important).

Works Cited

Aull, Laura. *First-Year University Writing: A Corpus-Based Study with Implications for Pedagogy*. Springer, 2015.

Avila-Reyes, Natalia. "Postsecondary Writing Studies in Hispanic Latin America: Intertextual Dynamics and Intellectual Influence." *London Review of Education*, vol. 15, no. 1, Mar. 2017, pp. 21–37.

Bazerman, Charles. "Intertextualities: Volosinov, Bakhtin, Literary Theory, and Literacy Studies." *Bakhtinian Perspectives on Language, Literacy, and Learning*, edited by Arnetha F. Ball and Sarah Warshauer Freedman, Cambridge UP, 2004, pp. 53–65.

Boch, Françoise, and Fanny Rinck. "Enunciative Strategies and Expertise Levels in Academic Writing: How Do Writers Manage Point of View and Sources?" *University Writing: Selves and Texts in Academic Societies*, edited by Montserrat Castelló and Christiane Donahue, Brill, 2012, pp. 111–27.

Bronckart, Jean-Paul, and Cristian Bota. *Bakhtine démasqué: Histoire d'un menteur, d'une escroquerie et d'un délire collectif*. Droz, 2011.

Castelló, Montserrat, et al. "Learning to Write a Research Article: Ph.D. Students' Transitions toward Disciplinary Writing Regulation." *Research in the Teaching of English*, vol. 47, no. 4, May 2013, pp. 442–77.

Chanock, Kate. "Academic Writing Instruction in Australian Tertiary Education." *International Advances in Writing Research: Cultures, Places, Measures*, edited by Charles Bazerman et al., Parlor Press, 2012.

Cimasko, Tony, and Melinda Reichelt. *Foreign Language Writing Instruction: Principles and Practices*. Parlor Press, 2011.

Crowley, Sharon. "Linguistics and Composition Instruction: 1950–1980." *Written Communication*, vol. 6, no. 4, 1989, pp. 480–505.

Donahue, Christiane. "Bakhtin's 'Responsive Understanding' and Receptivity to Global Writing Research." *Writing for Engagement: Responsive Practice for Social Action*, edited by Mary P. Sheridan et al., Lexington Books, 2018, pp. 251–66.

———. *Écrire à l'université: Analyse comparée en France et aux États-Unis*. PU du Septentrion, 2008.

———. "Writing and Global Transfer Narratives: Situating the Knowledge Transformation Conversation." *Critical Transitions: Writing and the Question of Transfer*, edited by Chris M. Anson and Jessie L. Moore, UP of Colorado, 2016. Perspectives on Writing.

Donahue, Christiane, and Isabelle Delcambre. "What's at Stake in Different Traditions? Les Litteracies Universitaires and Academic Literacies." *Working with Academic Literacies: Case Studies towards Transformative Practice*, edited by Theresa Lillis et al., WAC Clearinghouse / Parlor Press, 2015, pp. 227–36.

Ewald, Helen. "Waiting for Answerability: Bakhtin and Composition Studies." *College Composition and Communication*, vol. 44, no. 3, Oct. 1993, pp. 331–48.

François, Frédéric. *Bakhtine tout nu ou une lecture de Bakhtine en dialogue avec Vološinov, Medvedev et Vygotski ou encore dialogisme, les malheurs d'un concept quand il devient trop gros, mais dialogisme quand même*. Lambert-Lucas, 2012.

———. "De la variation et de ses variétés dans différents discours d'enfants: Diversité, mélanges, métaphores, irruptions, et leurs familles." *Repères*, vol. 76, 1988, pp. 13–32.

———. *Le discours et ses entours*. L'Harmattan, 1998.

———. *Enfants et récits*. PU du Septentrion, 2004.

———. *Essais sur quelques figures de l'orientation: Hétérogénéités, mouvements et styles*. Lambert-Lucas, 2009.

———. *Morale et mise en mots*. L'Harmattan, 1994.

Galbraith, David, et al. "The Contribution of Different Components of Working Memory to Knowledge Transformation during Writing." *L1: Educational Studies in Language and Literature*, vol. 15, 2005, pp. 113–45.

Grossmann, Francis. "L'auteur scientifique." *Revue d'anthropologie des connaissances*, vol. 4, no. 3, 2010, p. 410.

Halasek, Kay. *A Pedagogy of Possibility: Bakhtinian Perspectives on Composition Studies*. Southern Illinois UP, 1999.

Horner, Bruce, et al. "Toward a Multilingual Composition Scholarship: From English Only to a Translingual Norm." *College Composition and Communication*, vol. 63, no. 2, 2011, pp. 269–300.

Jahic, Alma, and Tanja Pavlovic. "Writing a Master's Thesis: Challenges and Coping Strategies." *Students' Bachelor's and Master's Dissertation Writing Journeys: A Transnational European Perspective*, edited by Montserrat Castelló et al., Multilingual Matters, forthcoming.

Leijten, Mariëlle, and Luuk Van Waes. "Keystroke Logging in Writing Research: Using Inputlog to Analyze and Visualize Writing Processes." *Written Communication*, vol. 30, no. 3, 2013, pp. 358–92.

Leki, Ilona. "The Legacy of First-Year Composition." *The Politics of Second Language Writing: In Search of the Promised Land*, edited by Paul Kei Matsuda et al., Parlor Press, 2006, pp. 59–74.

Matsuda, Paul. "Composition Studies and ESL Writing: A Disciplinary Division of Labor." *College Composition and Communication*, vol. 50, no. 4, 1999, pp. 699–721.

Nystrand, Martin, et al. "Where Did Composition Studies Come From?" *Written Communication*, vol. 10, no. 3, 1993, pp. 267–333.

Parker, Kim, and Frank Campbell. "Linguistics and Writing: A Reassessment." *College Composition and Communication*, vol. 44, no. 3, 1993, pp. 295–314.

Schlitz, S. A. "Exploring Corpus-Informed Approaches to Writing Research." *Journal of Writing Research*, vol. 2, no. 2, 2010, pp. 91–98.

Schuster, Chuck. "Mikhail Bakhtin as Rhetorical Theorist." *College English*, vol. 47, no. 6, 1985, pp. 594–607.

Silva, Tony, and Ilona Leki. "Family Matters: The Influence of Applied Linguistics and Composition Studies on Second Language Writing Studies: Past, Present, and Future." *The Modern Language Journal*, vol. 88, no. 1, 2004, pp. 1–13.

Silva, Tony, et al. "Broadening the Perspective of Mainstream Composition Studies." *Written Communication*, vol. 14, no. 3, 1997, pp. 399–428.

Skillen, Jan. "Teaching Academic Writing from the 'Centre' in Australian Universities." *Teaching Academic Writing in UK Higher Education: Theories, Practices and Models*, edited by Lisa Ganobcsik-Williams, Palgrave-Macmillan, 2006, pp. 140–53.

Tapia-Ladino, Mónica, et al. "Milestones, Disciplines and the Future of Initiatives of Reading and Writing in Higher Education: An Analysis from Key Scholars in the Field in Latin America." *Ilha do Desterro*, vol. 69, no. 3, 2016, pp. 189–208.

Vardi, Iris. "Writing Experiences in Multidisciplinary First Years: A Basis for Confusion or Development?" *Refereed Proceedings of the Third Biennial Communication Skills in University Education (CSUE) Conference: "Making the Critical Connection,"* edited by Colin Beasley, Murdoch U, 2009.

Wei, Li. "Translanguaging as a Practical Theory of Language." *Applied Linguistics*, vol. 39, no. 2, 2017, pp. 9–30.

Before Wireless Networks: Foundational Works in Computers and Writing

Douglas Eyman

> Gail E. Hawisher and Cynthia L. Selfe (eds.), *Critical Perspectives on Computers and Composition Instruction* (Teacher's College Press, 1989)
>
> Carolyn Handa (ed.), *Computers and Community: Teaching Composition in the Twenty-First Century* (Boynton/Cook, 1990)
>
> Deborah H. Holdstein and Cynthia L. Selfe (eds.), *Computers and Writing: Theory, Research, Practice* (Modern Language Association of America, 1990)
>
> Gail E. Hawisher and Cynthia L. Selfe (eds.), *Evolving Perspectives on Computers and Composition Studies: Questions for the 1990s* (National Council of Teachers of English, 1991)
>
> Gail E. Hawisher and Paul LeBlanc (eds.), *Re-imagining Computers and Composition: Teaching and Research in the Virtual Age* (Boynton/Cook, 1992)

In this essay I examine influential edited collections in the field of computers and writing that were published between 1989 and 1992—that is, scholarship about practices of digital rhetoric that predate the advent of the World Wide Web and the mainstream adoption of cell phones.[1] The five collections I draw on constituted my own introduction to the field, and my work accounts for some of their more recent citations. I think this demonstrates both that scholars tend to go back to their starting points and—particularly in the case of fields that focus on technology and technological change—that that starting point is continuously moving forward as new scholars enter our PhD programs and begin their own research.

Within the larger discipline of writing studies, the subfield of computers and writing, focused as it is on the application of new technologies to the teaching of writing (composition) and the study of written communication (digital rhetoric), always seems to be looking forward, seeking the cutting edge of advances in communication technologies. But I want to start by looking back and tracing a bit of the history of the field, as I believe the impulse to always look forward can encourage teachers and scholars to overlook work that is assumed to be obsolete because it engaged technologies that are no longer widely used. I also want to briefly review this history as it is central to my argument that losing sight of important works of scholarship simply because they are not current leads to an impoverished understanding of how technology works (on a foundational level) and to a continual stream of claims of new discoveries that have already been documented in the literature.

In 1969 the United States experienced three major cultural touchstones that each had an impact on our discipline: in July the first humans landed on the moon, in October the first message was sent between two networked computers on the Arpanet, and in November the first episode of *Sesame Street* debuted on PBS. The moon landing jump-started many of the industries that would produce the technologies that support modern communication networks, the Arpanet would eventually become the Internet, and *Sesame Street*, with its emphasis on parody and multimedia, set the tone for educational programming and demonstrated that literacy instruction could be effectively delivered on the television screen. Just ten years later, Hugh Burns wrote the first dissertation explicitly demonstrating how computers can be used to teach composition (*Stimulating Rhetorical Invention*). Although computer classrooms wouldn't become commonplace for quite some time, a small number of faculty members and graduate students in writing studies took up the question of how advances in technology might affect composition, beginning with the effect of word processors on composing. The 1980s saw the establishment of the field of computers and writing as the first computers and writing conference took place in 1982; the following year, Cindy Selfe and Kate Kiefer circulated the first *Computers and Composition* newsletter, which would eventually become the field's flagship journal. A number of books and journal articles did circulate in the 1980s; because they are too numerous to list here, I would direct interested readers to the archives of the *Research in Word Processing Newsletter* (1983–89), which regularly published bibliographies of research and scholarship related to computers and writing.[2]

One of the reasons I've delved into this history of the field is that it predates my participation[3]—and I believe that understanding the trajectory of a field's epistemological development is critical to claiming full-fledged membership in the field. Another reason is that we each approach scholarship from within the framework of our own experiences and histories, which may lead us to dismiss past work without fully understanding its provenance or import. My own history joins the field's in the early 1990s, just as personal computers and computer classrooms for writing instruction were beginning to appear in colleges and universities. As Gail Hawisher and colleagues note, "The microcomputer had come to be known as the personal computer in the 1980s, but the period 1989 to 1991 saw the evolution of the personal computer in the interpersonal computer, connected to other computers through networks and/or modems" (Hawisher et al. 180), and it is from this time period that I've selected the works I want to draw attention to in this essay.

As a newcomer to the field, I remember collecting as many books on the subject of computers and writing as I could find, and many of these were edited collections. It strikes me that the field has invested in the edited collection more than in monographs and, at least until fairly recently, more than in journal articles (partly due to having only one peer-reviewed journal fully devoted to the research of the field from 1979 to 1996). Aside from the natural inclination of new scholars to look forward rather than back (seeking what they see as gaps in the literature that need to be filled), I believe another contributing factor to the loss of recognition for older works may be the publication venue: traditionally, edited volumes were not as often cataloged in bibliographic resources (such as the *MLA International Bibliography*), and they were almost never included in the citation databases in the social sciences and STEM fields, even once humanities and arts journals began to be included.

Rather than selecting an individual text for this essay, I have instead elected to highlight the edited collections that I found particularly important to my own understanding when I joined the field. I selected five collections that were published between 1989 and 1992; rather than discuss each volume in detail, I provide a general overview and then focus on one representative chapter from each. While some of the chapters in these early collections do focus on technologies that have either significantly evolved or ceased to exist, there are also many chapters in each volume that take up questions of theory, method, or politics that are still germane to present concerns. That these works are not as visible as they should be is perhaps not surprising: these collections mark a moment when the field matured from an interest group to a full-fledged disciplinary subfield with its own publication venues and annual conference, but the community of scholars who identified as being part of the field of computers and writing was fairly small. Within the first decade of publication, these collections garnered a good number of citations, but in the past decade citations have fallen sharply; after 2009 each collection received on average only one citation per year. Additionally, because of the common words in their titles, they are not as easily discovered in general searches of the literature.

When I entered the field in the early 1990s, computer classrooms were slowly starting to appear, usually a single instance for any given English department.[4] At the time, many English faculty members—both in writing studies and in literature—resisted the shift to using computers for teaching writing.[5] In an interview, Cindy Selfe recalled the experience of pushing for computer-based composition in the face of such opposition, noting that colleagues in the humanities "were skeptical about computers. . . . [P]eople were highly suspicious whether those machines would distract teachers from paying attention to students in the composition classroom" (Hawisher and Selfe, "Reflecting" 350).

It seems to me that there is a tension in the field of computers and writing, as it simultaneously understands technology (computers and networks and devices, in addition to writing itself) as a primary object of study while also remembering that it had to fight for its place in the larger discipline of writing studies, which had actively rejected technology as a legitimate pursuit in the teaching and scholarship of composition.[6] And this history is reflected in these collections—both *Critical Perspectives* (Hawisher and Selfe) and *Computers and Writing* (Holdstein and Selfe) specifically invoke the need to shift from promotion of computer use in writing studies to a critical unpacking of both the affordances and potential pitfalls of bringing computational resources into the sphere of the humanities. In *Critical Perspectives*, Hawisher and Selfe note that "[w]e are now aware that both effective and ineffective uses of computer technology coexist within our profession and that there is a need to clarify the emerging role of technology in our work. . . . [W]e have passed the initial stage of uncritical acceptance and now see the necessity of constructing a more mature and balanced vision of technology's role in our teaching" (ix). Just a year later, Holdstein and Selfe claim that *Computers and Writing* "takes a 'second generation' view of issues surrounding computer use in departments of English," giving shape to "a healthy skepticism about computers that marks our more developed understanding of the technology—a position contrasting dramatically with our profession's initial flurry of bland enthusiasm" (1).

Critical Perspectives

Critical Perspectives aims to "challenge the profession to use computers in ways that build upon sound composition pedagogy while simultaneously extending the current knowledge base in computers and writing" (Hawisher and Selfe, *Critical Perspectives* xi); while that knowledge base might seem quite limited from a current perspective, the authors and editors did have a decade's worth of research to draw on. At the same time, they acknowledge the limitations of research that couldn't yet take into account broad access to personal computers or the affordances of the networked writing platforms that were just becoming available to nonspecialist users. As Hawisher and Selfe note in their introduction, "Until we define how computers alter our traditional notions of composition, we lack the means to develop a pedagogy specifically suited to the particular advantages afforded by computers" (1). Each chapter in this collection includes concerns that resonate with current challenges posed by computer-mediated communication, albeit in the context of different systems and platforms.

In the first essay in this collection, Selfe addresses a key issue we are still wrestling with today as new technologies require new functional and critical literacies. In "Redefining Literacy: The Multilayered Grammars of Computers," Selfe explores the implications of multilayered literacies—that is, literacies that build on each other, from reading in print to composing on-screen. She argues that "computers add several new grammars to the lists of things that individuals must learn before they become successfully literate in a computer-supported communication environment.... [C]omputers change the way we 'see' text and construct meaning from written texts" (6). This shift in literacy practices continues as the tools for image composing and editing and, more recently, video and audio composing have become widely available and relatively easy to use without specialized training. We can trace the research trajectory in computer-based literacies, if not to this particular work, then at least to this moment, spread out across these collections.

Computers and Community

Carolyn Handa's *Computers and Community* is the first collection to focus not only on the affordances of composing and editing on-screen but also more specifically on the connections that can be made through a networked interface. Handa's claim that "the computer offers immense possibility for restructuring relations in both our classes and society" was both prescient and correct (xvii), although this collection limited its purview to using computers to foster and enact community in writing classes. As with the other collections from this era, this work pushes back against prior technology enthusiasm: "Some of us feel that we must also bring to the computer some suspicion of the cultural biases and blindnesses inherent in its creation if only to become less susceptible to them" (Handa xvii); I would suggest that if we replaced "computer" with "social network" in that statement, it would be eminently applicable to our current challenges.

And in an essay that addresses issues we are still wrestling with in the present, Mary J. Flores pushes back against algorithmically derived writing tools (which to this day are not particularly effective at providing useful feedback to writers) and instead argues for instructor-led response using computer conferencing. In "Computer Conferencing: Composing a Feminist Community of Writers," Flores argues against a suggestion by Hugh Burns that computers can provide "'smart' algorithms for representing writing expertise, for capturing writing performance, and intelligently providing the appropriate feedback" (Burns, "Computers and Composition" 400), positing that such approaches "threaten to further divorce language from experience, and in so doing, to further alienate our students (especially our women students) from their writing, their peers, and their teachers" (Flores 109). As I write this, many students and teachers are engaged in online writing instruction, and it's helpful to see that we have a precedent for understanding both the value of online conferencing and for standing firm against forces of automation that threaten to disempower teachers in favor of instructional software.

Computers and Writing

In *Computers and Writing: Theory, Research, Practice*, Holdstein and Selfe offer a collection that not only privileges the development of composition theory specific to computer-facilitated writing pedagogies but also considers larger issues of power (both inside and outside the classroom) and the ethics of teaching with technology. As the editors note in their introduction, "[A]lthough the new technology in and of itself may seem value-free, its application entails implicit ethical choices, including those involving class, race, and gender" (3)—a sentiment that is at the heart of important current work like Safiya Umoja Noble's *Algorithms of Oppression*. Lisa Gerrard's essay in *Computers and Writing*, "Who Profits from Courseware?," also takes up questions of ownership and intellectual property that continue to vex writers and writing teachers.

I want to highlight Helen Schwartz's essay, "Ethical Considerations of Educational Computer Use," as an essay that seems practically contemporary in terms of its focus: Schwartz discusses "three different areas that raise ethical considerations: the design and classroom use of software, the funding and distribution of software, and access to computers" (18). The access issue in particular is still pressing—as recently as August 2020, a report by the State Council of Higher Education for Virginia indicated that "one in five Virginia students (K–12 and college) lack either high-speed internet or a computer in the home" and that "Black and Latinx students are twice as likely as white students not to have a computer in the home" (Allison).

Evolving Perspectives

This edited collection was the first book I purchased for my own use as a scholar in the field, so it was particularly influential to me. The essays in this collection were assembled from a competition held in the spring of 1989, with the goal of setting the research agenda for the field of computers and writing for the following decade. As the editors explain, "The chapters do not describe a specific localized study, lab, classroom, or program" (Hawisher and Selfe, *Evolving Perspectives* 1). The collection is arranged around four main topics: research, classrooms, hypertext, and politics. While the section on hypertext has not aged as gracefully as the other sections, John McDaid's "Toward an Ecology of Hypermedia" nonetheless provides a series of useful rubrics for framing our discussions of digital media and digital culture.

But it is Nancy Kaplan's "Ideology, Technology, and the Future of Writing Instruction" that continues the theme of understanding the ways technology works on us as much as it works for us. Kaplan argues that, "[a]s the material instantiations of discursive practices, tools or technologies necessarily embody ideologies and ideological conflict" (14), which is as true of *Twitter* or *Facebook* as it is of the first personal computers. While the example technologies referenced in Kaplan's essay are generally obsolete, the call to understand computers, and in particular networks, as both existing in and contributing to ideological systems is still a useful reminder. As Kaplan notes, the "limitations of . . . networks do not derive from insurmountable problems of current technological know-how any more than inequitable access to technology does. Both problems are grounded in the political and economic arrangements within which systems are designed, developed, and disseminated" (26). The same issues arise, for instance, in Siva Vaidhyanathan's *Antisocial Media: How Facebook Disconnects Us and Undermines Democracy*. Indeed, many of the ideas in all of these collections are echoed in and resonate with contemporary work that critiques the effects and affects of networked technologies on individuals who may not have received adequate training in digital literacies.

Re-imagining Computers and Composition

Gail Hawisher and Paul LeBlanc's *Re-imagining Computers and Composition: Teaching and Research in the Virtual Age*, published in 1992, is the most recent of the collections I consider here. I've included this volume as its aim is to imagine the future, and it's quite interesting to see how well the authors forecast the future, now our present. They were able to see some of the possibilities of and imagine some of the barriers to the most effective uses of technology. Some of the essays, such as Charles

Moran's "Computers and the Writing Classroom: A Look to the Future," foresee a radical revision of the writing class that takes the student out of the classroom—a vision that looks quite like current approaches to online writing instruction. Teacher training and preparation is seen as both a barrier and an opportunity in several essays, and the best writing programs right now are investing heavily in scaffolding professional development for online teaching.

One essay from this collection demonstrates the power of synthesis that animates some of the most innovative work in writing studies, as scholars gain expertise in other realms and then appropriate and adapt theories and methods to work in their own research and teaching contexts. Much of my own work focuses on such synthesis (see in particular Eyman, *Digital Rhetoric*), and that impulse may well have begun with Paul Taylor's "Social Epistemic Rhetoric and Chaotic Discourse," which I remember fondly as a powerful example of computers and writing scholarship. Taylor uses chaos theory as a framework for examining and understanding student-student interactions in a computer-based writing class. Describing the results of a Hallidayan analysis of functional grammar in classroom discussion logs, Taylor notes that "cohesive ties are much stronger for the text taken as a whole than they are for any individual's comments. The text thus displays a coherence that is not the result of hierarchical planning or explicit collaborative decisions" (140)—a finding of critical importance to the study of online social media interactions.

The work represented across these collections resonates with current issues, if not directly, then at least in a profound connective way. I certainly believe this work still has value. One of the challenges I've had in teaching graduate students in the field is their sense that information and communication technologies change so rapidly that a continuous obsolescence is built in, hence there is no sense in studying older technologies and platforms (like Usenet, text-based multiuser chat systems, or precursors of the web) if they aren't currently available to actually use. But it's not the application per se that is often at issue; rather, it's how we theorize its use, find methods to understand what it does to and for us, and examine the underlying ideologies and politics of the technology. As Selfe points out, "[W]hat persists in our field is what resonates between and among people as we experience periodic explosions of technology.

Technology is not really as important as the people" (Hawisher and Selfe, "Reflecting" 351).

As I was working on this essay, it occurred to me that one of the challenges that leads to work being lost is declining visibility, exacerbated by the economics of print production. These books are hard to find, and there aren't many that have been scanned or made available by legal means or otherwise; they are effectively out of print. And that leads to a question I've been wrestling with as I write this: Can lost texts be found? I'm hoping that some enterprising institutions might find value in digitizing and making available an open access online archive of early works so that they can garner more visibility—and this could be a project that benefits all the texts referenced and recovered in this volume, not just those in the field of computers and writing. Doing so would help ensure that important works don't get lost again.

Notes

1. While the first mobile phone dates to 1973, cell phones didn't start to become widely available until 1989, and it would be several more years before mobile phones would include texting capabilities.

2. The archives are available online at wac.colostate.edu/comppile/archives/rwpn/. It's worth noting that the MLA published some of the earliest book-length scholarship on computers and writing, including Alan McKenzie's edited volume *A Grin on the Interface: Word Processing for the Academic Humanist* (1984) and Deborah H. Holdstein's monograph, *On Composition and Computers* (1987).

3. At least in terms of membership in the field; as I was born not long before the mission to the moon, the changes in technology were lived experiences for me as I learned to write using crayon, pencil, pen, typewriter, word processor, and finally computer. Unlike many of my students, however, I still cannot compose on a cell phone.

4. The slow adoption of computer classrooms was almost solely the province of colleges and universities; community colleges across the nation were much quicker to employ computer classrooms for writing instruction, most likely due to the need for computer-based skills in industry and government jobs.

5. However, these same faculty members had no objections to using computers for their own writing and research, a fact that tended to undermine their position on the issue.

6. More recent members of the field may have only experienced writing instruction as digital writing instruction; those from my generation have plenty of firsthand experience being told that computers had no place in the writing classroom. We don't need to revisit those tensions, but it is important to understand that they still exist beneath the surface.

Works Cited

Allison, Tom. "A Closer Look at Virginia's Digital Divide in Education." *State Council of Higher Education for Virginia*, 10 Sept. 2020, www.schev.edu/index/reports/insights/insights/2020/09/10/a-closer-look-at-virginia-s-digital-divide-in-education.

Burns, Hugh. "Computers and Composition." *Teaching Composition: Twelve Bibliographic Essays*, edited by Gary Tate, Texas Christian U, 1987, pp. 378–400.

———. *Stimulating Rhetorical Invention in English Composition through Computer-Assisted Instruction*. 1979. Air Force Institute, PhD dissertation.

Eyman, Douglas. *Digital Rhetoric: Theory, Method, Practice*. U of Michigan P, 2015.

Flores, Mary J. "Computer Conferencing: Composing a Feminist Community of Writers." Handa, pp. 106–17.

Gerrard, Lisa. "Who Profits from Courseware?" Holdstein and Selfe, pp. 104–23.

Handa, Carolyn, editor. *Computers and Community: Teaching Composition in the Twenty-First Century*. Boynton/Cook, 1990.

Hawisher, Gail E., and Paul LeBlanc, editors. *Re-imagining Computers and Composition: Teaching and Research in the Virtual Age*. Boynton/Cook, 1992.

Hawisher, Gail E., and Cynthia L. Selfe, editors. *Critical Perspectives on Computers and Composition Instruction*. Teacher's College Press, 1989.

———, editors. *Evolving Perspectives on Computers and Composition Studies: Questions for the 1990s*. National Council of Teachers of English, 1991.

———. "Reflecting upon the Past, Sitting with the Present, and Charting Our Future: Gail Hawisher and Cynthia Selfe Discussing the Community of Computers and Composition." Interview by Estee Beck. *Computers and Composition*, vol. 30, no. 4, 2013, pp. 349–57.

Hawisher, Gail E., et al. *Computers and the Teaching of Writing in American Higher Education, 1979–1994: A History*. Greenwood Publishing, 1996.

Holdstein, Deborah H. *On Composition and Computers*. Modern Language Association of America, 1987.

Holdstein, Deborah H., and Cynthia L. Selfe, editors. *Computers and Writing: Theory, Research, Practice*. Modern Language Association of America, 1990.

Kaplan, Nancy. "Ideology, Technology, and the Future of Writing Instruction." Hawisher and Selfe, *Evolving Perspectives*, pp. 11–42.

McDaid, John. "Toward an Ecology of Hypermedia." Hawisher and Selfe, *Evolving Perspectives*, pp. 203–23.

McKenzie, Alan T., editor. *A Grin on the Interface: Word Processing for the Academic Humanist*. Modern Language Association of America, 1984.

Moran, Charles. "Computers and the Writing Classroom: A Look to the Future." Hawisher and LeBlanc, pp. 7–23.

Noble, Safiya Umoja. *Algorithms of Oppression: How Search Engines Reinforce Racism*. New York UP, 2018.

Schwartz, Helen J. "Ethical Considerations of Educational Computer Use." Holdstein and Selfe, pp. 18–30.

Selfe, Cynthia L. "Redefining Literacy: The Multilayered Grammars of Computers." Hawisher and Selfe, *Critical Perspectives*, pp. 3–15.

Taylor, Paul. "Social Epistemic Rhetoric and Chaotic Discourse." Hawisher and LeBlanc, pp. 131–48.

Vaidhyanathan, Siva. *Antisocial Media: How Facebook Disconnects Us and Undermines Democracy*. Oxford UP, 2018.

William J. Vande Kopple and Syntactic Subjects

Philip Eubanks

> William J. Vande Kopple, "Sentence Topics, Syntactic Subjects, and Domains in Texts," *Written Communication* (1985)

I first became aware of William Vande Kopple's work in the early 1990s at the University of Illinois, Urbana-Champaign. I was one of an enthusiastic cadre of teaching assistants who, under the direction of Greg Colomb, taught from a set of materials called *The Little Red Schoolhouse*. LRS, as we affectionately called it, emphasized such things as avoiding nominalization, placing old information before new, and managing topics strings. It helped my students (I believe), and it certainly helped me as I wrote and rewrote (and rewrote) my PhD thesis.

But there was still a nagging doubt that *The Little Red Schoolhouse* did not resolve for me. Was my confidence in its wisdom more than just a product of my own intuition? Although I was aware that the materials' foundation, Joseph Williams's *Style: Toward Clarity and Grace*, drew on the work of linguists, rhetoricians, and other language scholars, I nonetheless remained ill at ease with my own intellectual lacunae. Had I been asked, I could not have answered the simple question, How do you know this is right?

That is why I have continued to think back to the work of William Vande Kopple. To put it simply, he wanted to find out whether or not our intuitive judgments can be supported empirically. That inclination may not seem terribly unusual in a field such as writing studies, which trains its collective eye so intently on research and research methods. Yet my writing life began at a time when expert advice rested on nothing more than claims of expertise asserted by the culturally exalted. Vande Kopple was among those who persuaded me that our pedagogical judgments might possibly amount to something more than that.

Vande Kopple's "Sentence Topics, Syntactic Subjects, and Domains in Texts" (1985) investigates one of the most complicated areas for writing advice: the use of metadiscourse. The article would be worth a second look simply because it contributes useful information to a continuing line of inquiry (see, for instance, Hyland). However, for me, its chief value lies not in its conclusions but rather in its inconclusions. In this article, Vande Kopple is at least as intent on questioning the validity of his work as he is on presenting it. Thus, as I view it, he shows us a way of thinking about experimentation that suits writing studies well, despite the field's widespread—though not universal—suspicion of research that seems too closely modeled on hard science.

Indeed, as naturalistic inquiry has grown in the field, an accompanying repudiation of experimentation has emerged (or perhaps the other way around). No doubt that is because the social dimension of writing is difficult to detect in most or all experimental designs. "Sentence Topics" is no exception. The tests on which it reports are far more attuned to the particulars of texts than to the rhetorical situations that might inform them. For many of us, that textual focus calls to mind asocial, ahistorical approaches to reading and writing that have been, more or less, and for sound reasons, pushed aside. I want to note, however, that Vande Kopple makes no assumptions about textual structures in and of themselves. Rather, he is concerned with how readers make use of those structures.

In addition, writing studies' critique of experimentation cannot be separated from a broader philosophical current: in the last century, postmodern theory did a lot to dismantle naive understandings of science in general. Perhaps no one in writing studies prosecuted that case more forcefully or memorably than Carolyn Miller in her 1979 essay, "A Humanistic Rationale for Technical Writing." Miller denounces the idea that science merely uncovers objective facts that require no rhetorical interpretation. She calls scientific positivism a form of "intellectual coercion" (613), indeed "intellectual tyranny" (616). Strong words, but not the words of an outlier. I think it is useful to read Vande Kopple with Miller's words in mind. His science-minded approach to texts seems to me anything but coercive or tyrannical. In fact, what I note most of all about "Sentence Topics, Syntactic Subjects, and Domains in Texts" is its intellectual humility.

Asking the Question and Performing Immediate Recall Tests

In "Sentence Topics," Vande Kopple investigates what might seem to be a straightforward question. I would frame the question this way: What difference does it make to readers when writers begin their sentences with lengthy metadiscourse?

Most often, of course, sentences in plainly written texts have grammatical subjects that align with the sentence's or paragraph's topic—loosely defined, what the sentence or paragraph is about. But sometimes that is not so. Sometimes sentences begin with what Vande Kopple calls a "validity marker." Consider a sentence from one of his test paragraphs: "All high school seniors who plan to go on to college must take the American novels course" (344). Here, the grammatical subject, "all high school seniors," names the people of most interest in the sentence overall—the "seniors" are integral to the topic. However, as Vande Kopple notes, the sentence might just as easily have been composed like this: "*It is the department's position that* all high school seniors who plan to go on to college must take the American novels course" (345). According to Vande Kopple (and I have to agree), "department's position" is not closely related to the main topic of the sentence or of the rest of the paragraph in which it appears. The initial clause exists only to put the rest of the sentence into context. It is metadiscourse.

Writing teachers often advise their students to avoid such metadiscourse. Perhaps it seems to us unnecessary hemming and hawing. Vande Kopple is not inclined to take such speculations as mine at face value though. He wants to know exactly how or how much a lengthy validity marker at the beginning of a sentence might affect readers' ability to recall what they have read. As a general matter, he hypothesizes that such validity markers "will have either negative or no effects on readers' memory for the topical material [because they] do not contribute important information to the gist of the passage" (340). That much seems clear to him.

But this point of clarity leads him to consider three uncertain hypotheses about how readers might process such metadiscourse. In his words:

> It is possible that readers are able to distinguish such nontopical subjects and adjuncts from the topical material as soon as they perceive and comprehend them, that the readers then disregard them, and that all of this happens so quickly that readers' processing of the topical material is not affected in any measurable way. (340–41)

> Another possibility is that readers process sentences with such elements by beginning with the belief that these elements are what the sentence is about. Later they recognize that these elements are not topical; then they decide that they do not have to retain them. Ultimately, though, they have their attention to the topical material delayed and perhaps vitiated in these processes. (341)

> Perhaps readers recognize that certain subjects and their adjuncts are not topical, realize that these modify or qualify the topical material in an important way, hold them in some kind of buffer, and then as, or after, they process the topical material, do the necessary modifying or qualifying. . . . These processes also probably strain or vitiate the attention readers can give to the topical material. (341)

This list of possibilities is intriguing. However, the immediate recall tests conducted by Vande Kopple only shed light on—and could only have shed light on—the first possibility. And doing that required a lot of light.

Vande Kopple says that he put the first hypothesis—that is, that readers quickly forget validity markers and so they have no deleterious effect—to a "severe test" (342). In other words, he presented participants with lengthy validity markers rather than single words and placed those markers in passages where they were given "as much chance as possible to be recalled" (342). It turned out that his readers did recall many validity markers, and validity markers did interfere with his participants' recall of topical material. The possibility that validity markers are quickly forgotten and thus have no effect was not supported.

So what purpose does raising the second two possibilities serve? Are they merely idle conjectures of a curious mind? That could well be. But I think, instead, that they indicate intellectual humility. Vande Kopple's project here is not to reenact the grand narrative of science in which the experimenter heroically vanquishes human ignorance but rather to recognize the vexing difficulty of explaining phenomena when the possibilities are many and they all seem plausible. It is easy to imagine a research report that refuses to engage in such mystifications. Such a report could simply raise the question of whether or not validity markers are cast aside and forgotten and then report its rather suggestive, if not definitive, result. But Vande Kopple offers only to "begin seeking answers to some of these questions" (342)—questions whose answers are bound to be elusive.

Perhaps my reading of this passage is too generous. But it is not the only part of "Sentence Topics" that leads me in this direction, as I will discuss further in a moment.

The immediate recall tests followed a familiar pattern. Just under one hundred high school students were divided into four test groups. They were simply asked to read a paragraph once through and then to write down what they recalled. In the first phase, all paragraphs included several sentences that began with clause-length validity markers. Paragraphs A and B had identical topical content but arranged the information differently, one placing old (or given) information before new, the other placing new information before old. Paragraphs C and D had identical topical content and varied the arrangement of information in the same way as paragraphs A and B (346–47).

The aim was to find out how much, if any, of the metadiscourse the readers remembered and, in turn, to find out how much of the topical material they remembered by comparison. At first, complete paragraphs were analyzed, which showed that readers remembered some of the metadiscourse and somewhat more of the topical material. To make sure that the analysis was fair—that is, to make sure that readers' tendency to recall metadiscourse was not exaggerated—the results were reanalyzed without the first sentence of each paragraph, where the metadiscourse was especially prominent. That analysis showed that the participants tended to remember much less of the metadiscourse relative to topical material, though some (347).

I will not attempt to report all the numbers here. Let me just provide what is most striking to me. When the results were analyzed without the paragraphs' initial sentences, readers consistently remembered more topical material than metadiscourse. For one test paragraph, they remembered 25.2% of the topical material and only 7.43% of the metadiscourse. For another test paragraph, readers only remembered 13.52% of the topical material and just 1.17% of the metadiscourse. For all test paragraphs, readers remembered more topical material than metadiscourse (347–51).

The second phase sought to answer what are to my mind the key questions: Do readers remember significantly more topical material if there is no metadiscourse? In other words, do lengthy initial validity markers actually interfere with readers' ability to recall topical material? Would writers, therefore, be better off leaving them out? To answer these questions, Vande Kopple repeated the immediate recall test with a similar number of students, following the same procedures, the only difference being that the test paragraphs omitted the validity markers. It turned out that participants did, by and large, remember more topical material when not hampered by metadiscourse.

For three out of four paragraphs, readers remembered more topical material in phase 2 than in phase 1. Most dramatically, readers of paragraph C recalled on average 37.42 correct words versus an average of just 21 correct words for the corresponding paragraph in phase 1. However, one paragraph had a very different result. For that paragraph, readers recalled an average of 27 correct words versus an average of 28 correct words for the corresponding paragraph in phase 1—virtually no difference. The paragraph in question placed new information before old (351–52).

Vande Kopple's Discussion (and Mine)

The results of these recall tests may not strike everyone as earth-shattering. They are what might have been expected but were, perhaps, less dramatic. My own belief has been that metadiscourse mars otherwise lucid, forceful writing by distracting readers from what really matters. (Notice, however, that I could not resist using some metadiscourse just now.) "Sentence Topics" supports that belief but not unequivocally.

Thus, Vande Kopple gives us the kind of bite-size results we ought to hope for from a serious piece of empirical research.

I would like to set aside the results per se, though. For me, Vande Kopple's discussion is at least as important as his results are. Against (my) expectations, he works diligently to convince us that we should not place too much weight on his tests because they leave too many important questions unanswered. Indeed, he points out, they are incapable of answering many "disturbing" questions (353).

In the first paragraph of his discussion section, he ticks off four serious shortcomings of his own method and design, noting how they fail even on their own terms. He only conducted one kind of test, the participants were high school students who may not have been skilled readers, the paragraphs were contrived so that only validity markers interrupted the flow of topical material, and the tests were probably not "ecologically valid"—that is, there was no natural context (353). These caveats are important and, as it happens, all but one crossed my mind when I first reread the article.

But Vande Kopple's reservations about his own work go much deeper and, I believe, go to the heart of his research question if not his entire program of research. Even though his readers tended to forget some validity markers but not all, and even though their presence tended to impede readers' memory of topical material, Vande Kopple warns against using those results to inform our teaching practice. He writes:

> [V]alidity markers appear often in the most admired prose and . . . their function of assessing truth or probability seems very important. Must one conclude that readers ignore linguistic elements that indicate such assessments, that seem to encourage refined discernment, that seem essential to critical thinking, honest debate, and ethical words of discourse? Should writing instructors advise students that they might just as well omit any validity markers they are inclined to include in texts—or, at any rate, the validity markers occupying syntactic subject and adjacent slots? (353–54)

It strikes me as both startling and admirable to raise this question—which casts doubt on the very pedagogical practice his tests seem designed to validate.

Vande Kopple then goes on to cast doubt on the very validity of the tests he performed. Of course, he does not question whether or not the tests were honestly and diligently performed. Overall, readers did recall more topical material than metadiscourse, and they did recall more topical material in the absence of metadiscourse. Still, he notes, some readers remembered some validity markers. In fact, a number of participants seemed to take the validity markers rather seriously. That raises a serious concern for him because the tests he performed may not have properly considered the way readers retain and discard information. As he notes, readers may

> keep qualifying or modifying information in a buffer, and then as or after they process the topical material do the necessary modifying or qualifying. If a strategy something like this is employed, an immediate recall test . . . will not record many nontopical validity markers, no matter how extensively the experimental materials are manipulated to facilitate their recall. (354)

This is a worthwhile reservation. Even if the tests genuinely showed what they showed, they may nonetheless have been inadequate to the task at hand.

Even more troubling to Vande Kopple is the possibility that recall has nothing to do with how we ought to evaluate validity markers. He points to Michael Halliday's interpersonal functions of language, which "convey essentially social meanings" (355). Vande Kopple writes:

> The interpersonal set deserves special attention here because validity markers probably belong in it. They represent a writer's personal assessment of truth or probability and are often judged not in the abstract but in terms of the character, perceptions, and past judgments of the person who uses them. . . . This interpersonal domain of experience probably is not tapped by most kinds of tests of various discourse processes currently being used. In the case of the immediate recall test reported here, it is possible that the validity markers worked interpersonally to affect readers' stances on, attitudes toward, or feelings about the topical material without most of the markers being recalled themselves. (355)

This seems a valuable criticism of the tests reported in "Sentence Topics." It is more than just an enriching observation. It has the flavor of authentic curiosity, a kind of curiosity that might well undermine not just the particular study being discussed but, in fact, the very type of study Vande Kopple has undertaken.

This line of reasoning leads Vande Kopple to question even more broadly the discourse models prevalent in his kind of work: "Many of these [models] treat discourse processes as primarily or solely a matter of processing information, of the movement of chunks of information from texts to readers' minds. This view is limited and limiting" (356). Given the limitations of such a discourse model, Vande Kopple goes on to advocate additional tests—new kinds of tests—that do not simplify "the nature of the interactions associated with texts," that illuminate "the complexity of human motivation, actions, and interactions in texts, the reactions to personalities projected in texts, and the sharing of cooperative experiences in texts" (356).

In the end, Vande Kopple does not eschew his interest in texts. Rather, in my estimation, by recognizing the limitations of the tests he conducted, he expands the possibilities for taking a scholarly interest in what texts consist of and how they work. Because he critiques his own efforts so thoughtfully, he shows us that even limited work need not be limiting—so long as we are willing to wonder about what is missing.

Works Cited

Hyland, Ken. *Metadiscourse: Exploring Interaction in Writing*. 2005. Bloomsbury Academic, 2018.

Miller, Carolyn R. "A Humanistic Rationale for Technical Writing." *College English*, vol. 40, no. 6, 1979, pp. 610–17.

Vande Kopple, William J. "Sentence Topics, Syntactic Subjects, and Domains in Texts." *Written Communication*, vol. 2, no. 4, 1985, pp. 339–57.

Possibilities Rather Than Certainties: William Irmscher's "Finding a Comfortable Identity"

Christine Farris

> William F. Irmscher, "Finding a Comfortable Identity," *College Composition and Communication* (1987)

Like many of his generation, William Irmscher (1920–2007) found his way to composition through literature. He earned a PhD from Indiana University in 1950 with a dissertation on the English poet John Donne. While directing the expository writing program at the University of Washington for twenty-three years, Irmscher held a number of key leadership positions in the expanding field of rhetoric and composition studies. He served in 1979 as chair of the Conference on College Composition and Communication (CCCC), in 1983 as president of the National Council of Teachers of English (NCTE), and from 1965 to 1974 as editor of *College Composition and Communication* (*CCC*), as it came into its own as a scholarly journal. On his watch, *CCC* published articles by a range of rhetoric and composition historians, theorists, researchers, and practitioners, including James Kinneavy, Ann Berthoff, Janice Lauer, and Mina Shaughnessy, as well as a special issue devoted to the resolution on language adopted by CCCC in 1974, *Students' Right to Their Own Language*. It was Irmscher who first proposed what became in 1984 the CCCC monograph series Studies in Writing and Rhetoric (Tracey 178).

Irmscher's textbook, *The Holt Guide to English: A Contemporary Handbook of Rhetoric, Language, and Literature*, and his volume on pedagogy for new instructors, *Teaching Expository Writing*, both include adaptations for composition of Kenneth Burke's dramatistic pentad. Introduced by Burke in *A Grammar of Motives*, the pentad is a heuristic procedure for examining relationships among rhetorical elements (action, agent, agency, scene, purpose) in any narrative or situation involving human motives.

Irmscher sought systematic invention strategies that would encourage greater focus and complexity than the prewriting moves characteristic of the process approach that was becoming popular at the time.

As new graduate instructors under Irmscher's direction at the University of Washington, I and others in my cohort didn't immediately grasp the utility of the pentad. Most likely, we didn't yet know how to teach invention without codifying techniques to the point of inefficacy. New instructors I have supervised have similarly struggled at first with concepts in curricula not of their making—for example, the "unexamined warrant" in a course on argument and "representation" in one aligned with cultural studies. Key to Irmscher's supervisory approach was a trust in new instructors to draw from and sharpen intuition derived from their lived experience, language experience, and critical judgment as readers (*Teaching Expository Writing* 34).

Over the years I have come to appreciate the ways in which Irmscher's affinity for Burke's pentad and his trust in intuition were all of a piece with his humanistic approach to writing. At the center is an openness to possibility in student work that would eventually include my own. It is this magnanimity and a belief in both the imaginative and rhetorical power of language as symbolic action that underlies the call in his essay "Finding a Comfortable Identity" for a reassertion of "the humanistic nature of our own discipline" (85). Reacting to several decades of controlled experimental studies of composition, Irmscher calls for methods of inquiry derived from a full understanding of human expression within cultural contexts, methods that are distinct from those drawn from the sciences.

A call for greater alignment with the humanities from a onetime Donne scholar and proponent of Burke—a literary and rhetorical theorist—might have been viewed in 1987 as deference to the literature wing of English and, hence, dismissed by some. Now, however, academics in composition, rhetoric, languages, and literature alike struggle to maintain the humanities in institutions fixated on workforce preparation. Some thirty years later, Irmscher's essay has implications for a field still questioning its identity and its role in higher education. Irmscher offers a note of caution to those who would seek a consensus on core principles of knowledge in the field of writing studies informed by schema from other disciplines.

Citing Maxine Hairston's prickly 1985 CCCC chair's address, which urges compositionists to free themselves from the need for approval from their colleagues in literature, Irmscher argues that if the field of composition feels undervalued, it should look not just outside the field but within it for causes and "examine itself honestly, not take refuge in the ploy that others are to blame" ("Finding" 82). He traces composition's battle for academic respect to its relationship not just to literature but also to the field of education and to a concomitant research methodology fostered by NCTE and its publications. He finds a positivist model with a "zeal for verifiable data" (84) inappropriate to understanding and teaching the nuances and complexities of the composing process.

Irmscher's essay appeared in *CCC* in 1987, the year I defended, under his direction, my doctoral investigation of the theory and practice of new composition instructors, which would later become a book (Farris, *Subject to Change*). I had read the essay months before publication when Irmscher gave me a purple dittoed version, which I recently discovered while emptying my office files. At the time—even still—I wonder if slogging through chapters of my foray into grounded theory and triangulated data played a part in Irmscher's final gesture to a field he epitomized for forty years. In "Finding a Comfortable Identity" he bemoans PhD candidates who think they are "obligated to undertake quantitative projects in order to write acceptable dissertations. In Education, probably; in English, no" (82).

I don't recall feeling "obligated." Inclined in that direction, perhaps. Like many scholars in the 1980s, I wanted to understand how people learn to write. I had taken a number of paths on my journey to Composition with a capital C, employing practices that ran the gamut from expressivist to empirical. A senior practicum in college led to my cofounding and directing an alternative school that aimed to make space for students to grow and learn. My pedagogy was somewhat hastily drawn from James Moffett's integrated approach to reading, speaking, and writing and from the published ideas of the Teachers and Writers Collaborative, a group of writers teaching in New York public schools. Later I would work for the group as both a visiting writer and a research assistant on a project headed by the psychologist Sylvia Scribner of Rockefeller University. Although Scribner would make her name as an ethnographer focused on the role of culture in literacy, our two-year investigation of the syntactic complexity of writing produced in school settings—both with and without the intervention of creative writers—was more quantitative than qualitative in its methodology. My work with Scribner took me and my colleague-cum-research subject Phillip Lopate to a conference on composing at the University at Buffalo, State University of New York, where we heard presentations by Janet Emig, Donald Murray, and James Britton. The proceedings, edited by the conference organizers, Charles Cooper and Lee Odell, became the 1978 NCTE volume *Research on Composing: Points of Departure* (Cooper and Odell).

In "Finding a Comfortable Identity," Irmscher traces the direction of composition research to the 1963 NCTE publication that preceded Cooper and Odell's—that is, *Research in Written Composition*, edited by Richard Braddock, Richard Lloyd-Jones, and Lowell Schoer. He credits Braddock (after whom the *CCC* article award is named) with "shaping prescriptive, positivist standards for research in composition" (82). Braddock, whose degree, Irmscher notes, is in education, became the founding editor of the NCTE journal *Research in the Teaching of English* (*RTE*) in 1967 (82). These two volumes, *Research in Written Composition* and *Research on Composing*, along with the journal *RTE*, reflect the K–16 common ground for empirically based inquiry in the 1960s and 1970s.

Joseph Harris, among others, has pointed to the significance at this time of the 1966 Dartmouth Conference on the Teaching and Learning of English that brought together British and American scholars from education, psychology, literature, and linguistics to address how English might best be taught (2). James Britton, who attended both the 1966 and 1975 conferences, presented findings on the importance of expressive writing in children's language development that helped shape the frameworks composition studies would adopt for theory, research, and pedagogy (Durst 387). In the following decade, researchers and practitioners would continue, as Britton had, to draw from developmental psychology along with rhetoric, linguistics, literature, and creative writing. By the 1980s, investigation of the composing process and the meaning of writing competence was an interdisciplinary, if not eclectic, enterprise.

In spite of that—or because of that—I was drawn to the emerging field of composition studies. Perhaps I would continue with Scribner's sort of literacy research, but her field was psychology. Despite my admiration for Emig's research on the complexities of composing, she was, alas, in education. Committed to English, I thought I might combine the study of literature, creative writing, and composition and rhetoric. As it turned out, I did. Returning to graduate school in the early 1980s, I was relieved to teach writing courses aligned with the scholarship introduced in our seminars. I became reacquainted with Emig, Murray, and Britton. As Irmscher laments in his essay, at this time the results of empirical research in composition commanded center stage in publications, emerging from the field's concerted effort to understand the habits and processes of successful and novice writers. In response to criticism of early research outlined in *Research in Written Composition* (Braddock et al.), investigators such as Sondra Perl and Linda Flower adopted rigorous experimental methods from the sciences and social sciences. Perl published "The Composing Processes of Unskilled College Writers" in *RTE* in 1979 and "Understanding Composing" in *CCC* in 1980. In 1979 Flower published "Writer-Based Prose: A Cognitive Basis for Problems in Writing" in *College English*, a journal typically devoted to literature and theory as well as rhetoric and composition.

The process approach emphasized the relationship of writing to both self-discovery and intellectual development. As compositionists implemented prewriting strategies such as Peter Elbow's freewriting and peer feedback and Murray's student-centered writing conference, they also embraced the schemata of empirical researchers, or at least incorporated their insights into theory and practice. There was general agreement that the writing process is "recursive," as Perl discovered from her composing-aloud case studies ("Composing Processes" 34). Popular for a while was Flower's "problem-solving" approach to instruction, derived from her research with the psychologist John R. Hayes. Flower and Hayes found the composing of successful writers to be "a goal-directed process" of "planning, translating, and reviewing" (255).

In "Finding a Comfortable Identity," Irmscher distinguishes between the borrowing of insights and the borrowing of methodologies from other disciplines (85). He is troubled that "research in composition has become identified with one kind of research—controlled experimental studies producing statistical evidence" (82). He is skeptical of the urge to ground expertise about writing in positivist research practices more typical of the sciences than the humanities, particularly the practice of using decontextualized conditions to control for variables. "We can learn," he says, "from Polanyi, Vygotsky, Piaget, and others, but we cannot fully share the logic of their disciplines—the characteristic way a member of any discipline thinks" (85). The investigative procedures and laboratory-like conditions of much social-science-based inquiry ignore the totality of the complex acts of both writing and the teaching of writing. Too often, he writes, "one discovers that the investigator has complicated the familiar and obfuscated the obvious" (83)—an astute observation and, I have found, when needed, a snappy quotation.

Irmscher favors a less imitative, more humanities-based mode of inquiry appropriate to the nature and values of English studies, a discipline concerned with "language in all its manifestations" and with "the individual as a human being, not a quantity or specimen" ("Finding" 85). Invoking Kenneth Burke to distinguish between a scientific and a dramatistic approach to language, Irmscher reminds us that writing is a symbolic action inseparable from actor, scene, agency, attitude, and purpose and resistant to quantification. He calls for inquiry tasked with presenting "the fullness of experience"—of the project, the subject, and the investigator (87).

The conclusion of "Finding a Comfortable Identity" lays out a thoughtful set of humanities-based criteria and procedures for a model of inquiry that prefigures the ethical and collaborative research practices scholars of the social turn would promote in the 1990s. In my ethnographic study that Irmscher directed, I think I employed many of them. At the very least, I incited a need for them.

Irmscher's list of "Operating Assumptions" considers the total act of composing in a natural environment and demonstrates trust in anecdotal evidence rather than staged performance. Investigators should "seek possibilities rather than absolute certainties" and view doubt as "a springboard for unanticipated directions" ("Finding" 85–86). Under "Methodology," Irmscher advises investigators to encourage introspection on the part of the subjects and to examine written texts in order to hypothesize about subjects' preconceptions, operating assumptions, and thinking processes. Under "Results," he suggests that investigators "describe and narrate in such a way that the subjects are revealed as living beings, not inanimate objects," and that they "employ metaphor and analogy as a means of explanation" (86). Without apology, Irmscher notes that these recommendations "represent the same kinds of inquiry and attitudes that an author might adopt in 'researching' a novel, not less thorough than scholarly inquiry, not less demanding, not less true to experience" (87).

By the 1990s, the struggle to establish an identity for composition studies included Irmscher's sort of skepticism about the role of empirical research in the making of disciplinary knowledge. The growth of the field featured a recuperation of rhetoric and changing relationships with literary and cultural studies. Cognitive frameworks broadened to include more social, cultural, and ideological views of writing, influenced by scholars both in and outside the field.

In the decades that followed, growing acknowledgment that writing expertise is context-specific became cause for both lamentation over lack of a unified theory from which to work and for celebration of inquiry into multiple literacy venues, including workplaces, community centers, and cyberspace. Linda Flower, once criticized for her cognitivist focus on the individual writer, would go on to examine the literacies of social action (*Community Literacy*). Composition scholars would conduct more qualitative studies than quantitative studies, and their studies were often aligned with feminist and social activism. Embracing research issues now particular to composition and rhetoric, a 1996 NCTE volume *Ethics and Representation in Qualitative Studies of Literacy*, edited by Peter Mortenson and Gesa Kirsch, addresses the complexities of the researcher-subject relationship. In the manner of cultural and linguistic anthropologists such as Shirley Brice Heath, ethnographers in composition would engage in more self-reflective humanist practices that included the voices and collaboration of participants.

In 2012 Jacqueline Royster and Kirsch advocated models for inquiry that "direct more explicit attention not just to writing practices as rhetorical acts . . . but also to reading, speaking, and listening practices as rhetorical acts . . . and not just to what is happening in the western world but what is happening around the globe" (151). In 2014 Perl, revisiting her early-1970s research on the composing processes of unskilled writers, would reflect on the set of "contrived" controls she had imposed on her laboratory-like investigation. She had wanted, she says, "to understand the life of the classrooms and the writers as they unfolded, as they were lived and experienced." At the time, however, "none of this fit in the experimental models championed by Braddock, et al." In accordance with

Irmscher's advice, in subsequent research Perl was able to function as a participant-observer, more comfortable with a researcher voice in first-person narrative (Perl, "Research"). Similarly, in my own investigations into writing across the curriculum (WAC), I pivoted from testing WAC's claim that writing enables critical thinking in discipline-specific courses to understanding such courses on their own terms—through immersion in the classroom cultures where students, instructors, ideology, and disciplinary norms intersect (Farris, "Giving" 122; Smith and Farris).

The field of writing studies continues to embrace new cross-disciplinary possibilities for investigation, posing new questions about writing that spring from the intersection of literacy, technology, gender, and ethnicity. At the same time, in the last decade the discipline has had an even bigger identity crisis to manage than it did in 1987. The pressure to legitimize the field's expertise comes partly in response to secondary and postsecondary accountability efforts that de-emphasize the humanities in favor of STEM and workplace preparation. Composition has had to defend its expertise and curricula as courses are increasingly delivered online, outsourced, and exempted to make room in students' schedules for swifter passage through the liberal arts to job training.

In the face of institutional demands to justify writing courses as gateway experiences, composition has had to investigate the presumption that first-year writing habits and skills transfer to other courses and to future workplace settings. Despite scholarship acknowledging that there is no such thing as universal academic discourse (Russell 58) and research that suggests many students have difficulty repurposing prior knowledge from first-year writing in new contexts (Beaufort 149), the field has once again embraced paradigms from education and the social sciences (transfer, metacognition, threshold concepts) to ground inquiry and to design prescriptive curricula that advance grand claims—for example, that student writers can develop a meta-awareness of key rhetorical concepts and their own theory of writing that is transformative and transferable. *Transfer*, a term borrowed from psychology and learning theory, is the acquisition of a skill or concept learned in one situation that is then applied in another situation. David Smit points to the unpredictability of transfer, which depends on a student's ability to perceive the relevance of the skill or concept to the new situation (130). Also unpredictable are the demands and mixed messages of instructors in other disciplines assigning writing that is not well integrated with particular course goals (Farris, "Giving"; Smith and Farris).

What might successfully transfer and enable connections is a meta-awareness of the ways that language, genre, and conventions are contextual. Drawing from principles of educational psychology, rhetoric, and genre theory and from findings from a number of empirical studies of students' repurposing of prior composition knowledge (Beaufort; Yancey et al.), the approaches known as writing about writing and teaching for transfer view the development of that meta-cognitive awareness as the purpose of first-year courses. The emphasis shifts, then, from learning to write to learning about writing (Wardle 783) as students become more mindful of concepts drawn not just from composition textbooks but also from texts within rhetoric and composition scholarship.

To identify those concepts, scholars such as Linda Adler-Kassner and Elizabeth Wardle have turned to what Jan Meyer and Ray Land, two British education researchers, identify as threshold concepts—transformative thinking central to the mastery of a subject. Adler-Kassner and Wardle's book, *Naming What We Know: Threshold Concepts of Writing Studies*, is an attempt to identify a disciplinary core at the center of what the field of composition knows and what it should impart to students in writing courses. I appreciate the usefulness of threshold concepts as a means of framing what composition knows in, say, a graduate seminar or as a tool for negotiating conflicting assumptions about writing across the disciplines, as Chris Anson suggests (214). I wonder, though, to what extent a focus on discourse about writing in an undergraduate course is a conflation of our agenda as knowledge producers with that of our students.

In requisitioning new frameworks for articulating a disciplinary identity, are we perhaps once again, as in decades past, privileging the importance of fields other than our own? Irmscher poses several questions in the conclusion of his essay: "Do we have to abandon the literary and critical values of our discipline in the name of scholarship? By denying these values, whom are we trying to please? Must we continue to be plagued by the scientific nemesis?" ("Finding" 87).

To contend with skepticism about transfer and the expertise of writing studies, we should not overlook what the discipline of English values across the composition and literature divide—textual analysis and the relationship between engaged, critical reading and successful writing.

Are we selling short the practices that attracted most of us to English in the first place: grappling with something puzzling and unpredictable in texts—what we don't know—and negotiating that uncertainty in collaboration with others?

Particularly in thematic first-year courses that are not about writing per se, we have an opportunity to cultivate not just critical skills but also something deeper and more sustained that argues for the importance of English and the humanities in the larger sense. In unpredictable ways, students often make more of what we have them read and write—in our classes, in their papers, and down the road—what the literary critic Rita Felski refers to as an "afterwardness," unique to each learner (119). Similarly, a recent longitudinal study led by Anne Ruggles Gere at the University of Michigan found students making their own multidisciplinary connections between thinking and writing across their four years of coursework (Gere 142). Thirty-six years after Irmscher called for the discipline to reassert its humanistic nature, it is surely still the case that "introspection and imagination can prompt discovery and elicit truths [just] as well as experiment and demonstration" ("Finding" 85).

Works Cited

Adler-Kassner, Linda, and Elizabeth Wardle, editors. *Naming What We Know: Threshold Concepts of Writing Studies*. Utah State UP, 2015.

Anson, Chris M. "Crossing Thresholds: What's to Know about Writing across the Curriculum." Adler-Kassner and Wardle, pp. 203–19.

Beaufort, Anne. *College Writing and Beyond: A New Framework for University Writing Instruction*. Utah State UP, 2007.

Braddock, Richard, et al. *Research in Written Composition*. National Council of Teachers of English, 1963.

Burke, Kenneth. *A Grammar of Motives*. Prentice-Hall, 1945.

Cooper, Charles R., and Lee Odell, editors. *Research on Composing: Points of Departure*. National Council of Teachers of English, 1978.

Durst, Russell K. "British Invasion: James Britton, Composition Studies, and Anti-Disciplinarity." *College Composition and Communication*, vol. 66, no. 3, Feb. 2015, pp. 384–401.

Farris, Christine. "Giving Religion, Taking Gold: Disciplinary Cultures and the Claims of Writing across the Curriculum." *Cultural Studies in the English*

Classroom, edited by James A. Berlin and Michael J. Vivion, Boynton/Cook, 1992, pp. 112–22.

———. *Subject to Change: New Composition Instructors' Theory and Practice*. Hampton Press, 1996.

Felski, Rita. *Uses of Literature*. Wiley-Blackwell, 2008.

Flower, Linda. *Community Literacy and the Rhetoric of Public Engagement*. Southern Illinois UP, 2008.

———. "Writer-Based Prose: A Cognitive Basis for Problems in Writing." *College English*, vol. 41, no. 1, Sept. 1979, pp. 19–37.

Flower, Linda, and John R. Hayes. "A Cognitive Process Theory of Writing." Villanueva, pp. 251–75. Originally published in *College Composition and Communication*, 1981.

Gere, Anne Ruggles. "The Ways Our Students Write Now." *PMLA*, vol. 133, no. 1, 2018, pp. 139–45.

Hairston, Maxine. "Breaking Our Bonds and Reaffirming Our Connections." *College Composition and Communication*, vol. 36, no. 3, Oct. 1985, pp. 272–82.

Harris, Joseph. *A Teaching Subject: Composition since 1966*. Prentice Hall, 1997.

Irmscher, William F. "Finding a Comfortable Identity." *College Composition and Communication*, vol. 18, no. 1, Feb. 1987, pp. 81–87.

———. *The Holt Guide to English: A Contemporary Handbook of Rhetoric, Language, and Literature*. Holt, 1972.

———. *Teaching Expository Writing*. Holt, 1979.

Meyer, Jan, and Ray Land. "Threshold Concepts and Troublesome Knowledge: Linkages to Ways of Thinking and Practising within the Disciplines." ETL Project, Universities of Edinburgh, Coventry and Durham, 2003. Occasional Report 4.

Moffett, James. *A Student-Centered Language Arts Curriculum, Grades K–13: A Handbook for Teachers*. Houghton Mifflin, 1968.

Mortensen, Peter, and Gesa E. Kirsch, editors. *Ethics and Representation in Qualitative Studies of Literacy*. National Council of Teachers of English, 1996.

Perl, Sondra. "The Composing Processes of Unskilled College Writers." Villanueva, pp. 17–42. Originally published in *Research in the Teaching of English*, 1979.

———. "Research as a Recursive Process: Reconsidering 'The Composing Processes of Unskilled College Writers' 35 Years Later." *Composition Forum*, no. 29, spring 2014, compositionforum.com/issue/29/perl-retrospective.php.

———. "Understanding Composing." *College Composition and Communication*, vol. 31, no. 4, Dec. 1980, pp. 363–69.

Royster, Jacqueline Jones, and Gesa E. Kirsch. *Feminist Rhetorical Practices: New Horizons for Rhetoric, Composition, and Literacy Studies*. Southern Illinois UP, 2012.

Russell, David. "Activity Theory and Its Implications for Writing Instruction." *Reconceiving Writing, Rethinking Writing Instruction*, edited by Joseph Petraglia, Erlbaum, 1995, pp. 51–77.

Smit, David W. *The End of Composition Studies*. Southern Illinois UP, 2004.

Smith, Raymond, and Christine Farris. "Adventures in the WAC Assessment Trade: Reconsidering the Link between Research and Consultation." *Assessing Writing across the Curriculum: Diverse Approaches and Practices*, edited by Kathleen Blake Yancey and Brian Huot, Ablex, 1997, pp. 173–84.

Students' Right to Their Own Language. Special issue of *College Composition and Communication*, vol. 25, no. 3, fall 1974.

Tracey, Richard. "He Takes the Teaching of Writing Seriously: A Bibliography of Works by William F. Irmscher." *Balancing Acts: Essays on the Teaching of Writing in Honor of William F. Irmscher*, edited by Virginia Chappell et al., pp. 175–84.

Villanueva, Victor, editor. *Cross-Talk in Comp Theory: A Reader*. 2nd ed., National Council of Teachers of English, 2003.

Wardle, Elizabeth. "'Mutt Genres' and the Goals of FYC: How Can We Help Students Write the Genres of the University?" *College Composition and Communication*, vol. 60, no. 4, June 2009, pp. 765–88.

Yancey, Kathleen Blake, et al. *Writing across Contexts: Transfer, Composition, and Sites of Writing*. Utah State UP, 2014.

New Literacies and New Coherencies: The Relevance of Betty Bamberg's "What Makes a Text Coherent?"

Larry Beason

> Betty Bamberg, "What Makes a Text Coherent?," *College Composition and Communication* (1983)

For roughly a decade starting in the mid-1970s, many compositionists explored the question posed in the title of Betty Bamberg's 1983 article, "What Makes a Text Coherent?" It is a question that was asked before the mid-1970s and one that is still asked today. Yet with the exceptions of technical writing and applied linguistics, published research on coherence in written discourse has been sporadic at best.

Since 2000, composition research has focused more on global coherence than on cohesion, although, like Bamberg, scholars have acknowledged the differences and the interrelationships of cohesion and coherence. For instance, Scott Crossley and Danielle McNamara's essay reveals statistical correlations among cohesion, coherence, and overall writing quality. Research on coherence, given its relationship to the more quantifiable features of cohesion, has been conducive to empiricism, but not always. Peter Moe and Kyle Winkler's essay takes a rhetorical approach, arguing that incoherence and lack of clarity can be powerful strategies for writers.[1] Since the 1980s, the social turn in composition seems to have left the study of coherence in its shadow, although Bamberg and others expanded the notion well beyond word- and sentence-level matters.

Contemporary thinking in composition is not monolithic, especially regarding classroom practice. Even so, the demise of coherence research was and is no doubt part of a larger trend of distrust of anything that might smack of current-traditionalist pedagogies that emphasize formal features of a text. Robert Connors's "The Rise and Fall of the Modes of Discourse" chronicles the limitations of a central current-traditionalist concept and its deteriorating acceptance (i.e., the modes and their structural forms). But almost twenty years later, Connors himself laments the growing "anti-formalism" that suggests any attention whatsoever to form in composition is akin to a "rhetorical atomism" that reduces discourse to only its textual parts ("Erasure" 110). Today, over two decades after Connors expressed those concerns, Bamberg's article still might be incorrectly categorized and dismissed as current-traditionalist thinking.

Bamberg's article is a landmark work that, rather than offering closing remarks on coherence from a discipline, is a generative theory applicable today, though perhaps it needs an update from compositionists—a "Bamberg 2.0" of sorts. Bamberg's 1983 article provides a framework adaptable to vast developments in determining how people write, such as new literacies in classrooms, workplaces, and personal lives. As I explain, her framework remains relevant, if not necessary, because it is highly flexible and amendable to enhancements—largely because her approach reflects contemporary perspectives on rhetoric and composition that do not limit a discourse situation to one text and its immediate context. These extratextual factors can be essential when considering the role and value of coherence in today's world of digital communication. Without a framework for coherence, we might lose the basis for how to fully examine the problems and theoretical complexities of new literacies. After suggesting two lasting contributions of Bamberg's article, this essay explores their relevance in two examples of new literacies: first, social media; and, second, digital records in technical writing, specifically in the medical field.

At the beginning of her article, Bamberg defines coherence in a conventional way, as an indispensable feature that communicates an intended meaning to readers (417). Her article concludes, though, with an unconventional all-encompassing view of coherence as the integration of textual details into an overall meaning (427). The key point is that her model is all-encompassing, acknowledging that almost anything about the text—from grammar to context—can help make a text more coherent. Below I explain what I believe to be most significant about her article while noting limitations that require renewed consideration.

One of the article's major contributions is that it provides a model of coherence that—although disconcerting in some ways—has substantial support from theory and empiricism across diverse disciplines and contexts. *Coherence, cohesion, structure*—these terms and others are interrelated but different, despite a long history of conflation both within and outside academia. As Bamberg explains, Alexander Bain privileged what she understands to be cohesion, not true coherence—the former normally being limited to wording that connects two sentences, such as pronouns that require readers to find an antecedent and thus connect statements (418).

As Bamberg argues, the relationships among cohesion, coherence, and writing quality should not be oversimplified, especially by focusing too much on cohesion alone—a common mistake even now. For example, most forms of educational assessment still focus on quantifying learning—finding something objective to put in charts for administrators, politicians, and taxpayers. Cohesion in a writing sample is easier to quantify than the abstract concept of overall coherence. In fact, one motivation for Bamberg's article involved conclusions of the National Assessment of Educational Progress (NAEP), which emphasized how insufficient coherence contributed greatly to low scores in its 1974 assessment of secondary school writing. Bamberg contends that the results offered little guidance for teachers, for the NAEP did not clearly indicate what "lack of coherence" meant (418).

Drawing on scholarship in assorted disciplines, Bamberg further argues that the NAEP study overestimated the impact of sentence-level cohesion. Her conclusion remains sound: "Research and theory in discourse analysis now view cohesive ties as part of what makes a text coherent; however, these ties are not, by themselves, sufficient to create coherent text" (418). Quoting the linguist Teun A. van Dijk, Bamberg explains how cohesive ties foster "local" coherence but not the "global" coherence that generates a reader's overall interpretation of a text (419). Bamberg provides support from fields of study such as artificial intelligence and reading education along with composition research that remains influential today. She synthesizes findings and theories that illuminate what coherence is and is not. This breadth of research led Bamberg to assert that predictability of a text is crucial. Thus, coherence is essentially a cognitive process—yet one that depends on social constructions of meaning and discourse. To predict how a text might coherently proceed, readers tacitly or explicitly assume it falls into a genre with established conventions for its structure and content. This process can be like a game of hide-and-seek between writer and reader. Such is the case when the writer, intentionally or not, deviates from socially expected schema, compelling the reader to search again for where coherence might be hidden among textual miscues and the reader's misinterpretations. Or perhaps the game is not meant to end decisively, as I illustrate shortly.

Bamberg's syncing of textual, cognitive, and social components is worth remembering particularly because her framework refuses to jettison traditional textual and sentence-level elements. Doing so would reflect a false binary between global and local coherencies, yet some aspects of her approach might appear out of step today. The significance Bamberg gives to predictability and patterns also has likely given compositionists pause for years because she might seem to favor formulaic writing.[2] However, we should notice how Bamberg's article begins and ends by going well beyond local coherence and traditional pedagogy.

A second major contribution of Bamberg's article is its framing of coherence as both a practical and theoretical matter that extends well beyond the immediate text. This might in fact be the article's most far-reaching effect: an adaptable, generative model of what coherence means and how it can be constructed. While Bamberg often associates coherence with sentence-level skills, her answer to her article's title is that everything in the text, along with the text's contextual environment, can create or preclude coherence—even usage errors (421).

Bamberg's approach is applicable today because it is rhetorical—not just in the classical sense but also in terms of contemporary rhetoric's emphasis on social, cultural, and ideological contexts other than the immediate situation of the text. Indeed, we might say that Bamberg offers a rhetoric of coherence just as much as a framework. Bamberg facilitates contemporary rhetorics by conceiving coherence so extensively that it is only natural to consider how larger, nontextual issues affect global meaning. Her model anticipates prevailing rhetorics by being generative: its inclusiveness helped open the door to how far we can go with a definition of something regularly seen as involving mere textual matters or structure. As Bamberg concludes, "When we look at coherence in its broadest sense, almost any feature—whether seen locally or over the whole text—has the potential to affect a reader's ability to integrate details of a text into a coherent whole" (427). In light of current writing theories, we should go further, examining coherence in emerging literacies that involve digital communication that can almost constantly evolve by adding and subtracting an array of audiences, information, purposes, and even authorial personas.

Although Bamberg could not predict technological changes to come, her adaptable approach encourages us to understand not only how her framework remains relevant but also how to enhance it in light of new literacies. Consider Michele Knobel and Colin Lankshear's definition of new literacies: "Specifically, the idea of 'new literacies' focuses on ways in which meaning-making practices are *evolving* under contemporary conditions that include . . . technological changes associated with the rise and proliferation of digital electronics" (97). I focus on such technological changes as exhibited in two distinct examples of coherence involving digital writing. One is from Amber Buck's 2012 study of a student's personal writing on social media. The second is delineated in Danielle Ofri's 2020 book, *When We Do Harm: A Doctor Confronts Medical Error*, which describes digital interfaces in medical professions.

Coherence and Digital Literacy across Social Networks

Buck examines "ecologies of practice" that define the rhetorical work of writers in new literacies (10). Her approach necessitates a consideration of not only static texts but also "medial interfaces"—digital systems for continuous, evolving writing (11). Using this lens, Buck studies one young adult's digital presentations of self on social media. Her ethnographic methods recognize the outside-the-text context that Bamberg encourages, but Buck extends it further.

Buck details how an undergraduate student, Ronnie, integrates social network sites into his daily literacy habits, especially when creating his self-identity both on and off the Internet. Ronnie is very active on social media—*Facebook*, *LinkedIn*, *Twitter*, and eleven other social media sites. His activity results in writing that is neither discrete nor static, producing "continuous literacy activity" not only on a given site but across his social media accounts (Buck 11). Buck finds she must follow, "trace" (12), and find connections between the self-identities Ronnie creates in his writing across the web. His literacy activity is dispersed "across different spaces and over time" (12), and Buck searches for a coherent message about the self-identity Ronnie constructs. But with his scattered and mercurial writing, readers face the indomitable task of synthesizing a single self-representation—finding instead a portrait drawn in churning waters.

Even Bamberg's open-ended approach to global coherence is not sufficiently encompassing for this complicated social web of discourse, but her framework clearly suggests a suitable foundation. We might supplement her model by considering coherence in two ways: what I refer to as "in-coherence" and "out-coherence." In-coherence, which certainly can be coherent, refers to finding meaning and connections within the text and situation, much as Bamberg proposes. Out-coherence demands looking for coherencies well outside one static text or one context, moving the rhetorical situation to a webbed ecology beyond unchanging texts, interlocutors, and settings. Many scholars (in literary and cultural studies, for example) have long argued that to understand a text we must consider its situatedness in extensive contexts of cultural, political, and historical influences. Even so, coherence—having yet to escape the stigma of appearing to be a sentence-level matter—is rarely framed as part of a comprehensive ecology.

In contrast, Buck demonstrates the value of out-coherence by examining Ronnie's self-representations across more than one text, site, or purpose. His construction of self-identity, it turns out, is not singular at all. His writing on *Twitter*, for example, reflects a "stream of consciousness" on various personal matters, such as random musings on the way to class (Buck 15). Writing under a different name on his *Tumblr* blog, Ronnie constructed a "musical alter ego" to highlight his lyrical interests (24). On *Facebook*, he constructed another fictious identity, his supposed friend "Allison," to provide another "contrast to his own perspective" (27). In his postings, then, Ronnie eschewed one coherent self-representation.

My point is not to explain Ronnie's motivations but to underscore why coherence (or lack thereof) across his "chains of activity" in new media cannot be understood by in-coherence alone (Buck 24). The implication of Buck's study is that social media discourse—when out-coherence is explored by moving beyond a fixed text, situation, or goal—breaks with academic expectations for coherence and opens up the possibility of alternatives to coherence. Reconsidering and enhancing Bamberg's approach allows us to examine how coherence within new literacies is best understood across a multiplicity of digital texts on disparate sites. Additionally, we should consider why coherence as it is typically defined both within and outside academia is not optimum for all writers on social media, given the various goals and selfhoods a person might have.

The Perils of Digital Interfaces for Medical Communication

Unlike Ronnie's case, coherent writing can be a matter of life and death when the text is not conducive to one primary meaning. In her recent book, Danielle Ofri—medical practitioner, author, editor, and professor—delineates the medical errors that occur despite (or even because of) advances in technology, especially the Electronic Medical Record (EMR).

After being shuffled to an examination room, you have no doubt seen an EMR device. A medical professional taps information about your health onto a laptop, tablet, or cell phone. The clinician inputs codes, notes, and data into your EMR—the digital equivalent of paper charts and records. Using a medical-software program, the system stores such information and can use it to provide feedback to your doctor and others that have access. Feedback includes potential causes of a symptom, requests to confirm prescriptions, and alerts that require medical staff members to confirm certain decisions made about the patient.

The EMR, including its clinical notes and the codes and data entered, qualifies not only as a new literacy but also as writing. Whether numbers or letters, graphic symbols are used by the clinician to create meaning with each entry—a form of writing. Using the EMR mirrors Knobel and Lankshear's definition of new literacies: the EMR enables communication based on a meaning-making procedure stemming from technological developments. Once, the paper chart made sense of a patient's health; the EMR is the digital replacement.

Ofri devotes a chapter to communication issues involving the EMR while recognizing its remarkable ability to store, access, and correlate information such as demographics and medical history (83–101). But here is where coherence becomes problematic. The human ability to make meaning of so much fragmented information is not so remarkable.

"WHAT MAKES A TEXT COHERENT?"

Feedback and prompting from the EMR can create avalanches of fractured messages and required approvals (e.g., certifying that vitamin D is not a controlled substance). The EMR generates numerous alarms, heard and seen—resulting in so much cognitive overload that health-care professionals often use shortcuts or ignore alerts so that they can focus on patients. Many alerts are false alarms, but not always. Ofri references a *Boston Globe* investigation of "alarm fatigue" that led to 211 deaths nationwide over five years. There were so many alerts that they became "background noise," causing nurses and others to lose "the ability to alarm anyone" (91).

These issues highlight the foundational nature of Bamberg's work, which underscores the importance of the situation of a text. With the EMR, reading and writing call for coherence among myriad texts and goals arising from differing situations. The EMR was originally designed for billing purposes, and it continues to be used for such purposes today. Its design was also intended to help a hospital (and the EMR itself) avoid legal liability. Or as Ofri writes, "The whole warning system feels like a transfer of blame . . . onto the medical staff" (90).

Of course, the EMR is also meant to facilitate health care, yet these mixed purposes arising from dissimilar rhetorical situations hamper the coherence of the EMR because one aim (health care) is not dominant, leading medical staff members to spend less time on patients and more time attending to EMR information provided in no coherent order.

Although going beyond the structure of a text, Bamberg acknowledges the significance—in Ofri's profession, the life-and-death significance—of connecting ideas to foster coherence. The EMR, as Ofri states, is not structured in a way that is favorable to global coherence and meaning. At one time, for instance, the EMR had only two checklist fields. Now it has dozens, resulting in workloads that often induce staff members to check off items perfunctorily, a "survival mechanism" allowing them to allocate more time to patients (Ofri 15). Coherence is threatened, for the EMR compartmentalizes and structures information such as checklists and alerts so that they are convenient for billing or legal purposes perhaps, but the result "fundamentally changed how medical professionals process medical information" by placing information into "fields that are not logically connected" (84, 85). The EMR imposes a rigid thinking structure that compels users to document health matters in the machine's order, not the medical professional's own arc of thinking (84). Previously in her career, Ofri habitually used a schema based on hard-copy charts, a pattern allowing her to "write down my thoughts exactly in the order in which I processed them," starting with the patient's reason for visiting and ending with an explicit, comprehensible plan of action (84). As Bamberg's framework anticipates, Ofri's nondigital chart encourages coherence by maintaining one purpose (i.e., improving a patient's health) and a schema that reflects that intent.

Consider an example Ofri provides of how human error is compounded by the EMR's shortage of such Bamberg-style coherence. Its compartmentalized structure was partially responsible for the first Ebola-related death in the United States during the outbreak of 2014. Thomas Eric Duncan flew from Liberia to Dallas, soon arriving at an ER where a nurse noted in his EMR that Duncan had flown in from an endemic region. His doctor at the ER did not see the note, so Duncan was neither quarantined nor vaccinated, leading to his death and that of others. The EMR field that the nurse completed, because it was a vaccination matter delegated to nurses, was not designed to appear on the physician's screen, so he did not consider Ebola (Ofri 94–95). The doctor, the nurses, and even the patient share responsibility for what happened, but Ofri illustrates how the EMR produces disjointed texts that exacerbate human error, leading to "a fateful fork in the road in this patient's health care" (95). Fragmented texts and unconnected meanings hampered a coherent reading of Duncan's EMR, and the consequences were lethal.

Ofri is not hoping for antediluvian paper charts but for EMRs that "think a bit more like humans, while retaining the encyclopedic, fatigueless abilities humans lack" (91). More significantly, compositionists might use Bamberg's framework and out-coherence perspectives to address wide-ranging contextual factors that contribute to an insufficient coherency for audiences requiring unequivocal clarity and relevant information from interfaces such as the EMR and, no doubt, other writing contexts that have evolved since Bamberg's 1983 article.

Back when doctors relied on paper and when social media meant three-way calling, I first read "What Makes a Text Coherent?" It was during a lively graduate seminar, but I do not recall the discussion—just my reaction. I was intrigued and could not let go of concepts that made better sense with Bamberg's explanations, but something was unreconciled. The article has tensions that remain with me, as perhaps they do with other readers. Bamberg makes a case that cohesion is overrated, yet she frequently identifies it as a type of coherence, albeit local. Her article is also critical of the NAEP's lack of clarity in defining *coherence* in its 1975 report. In one note, Bamberg adds that NAEP scores for coherence depend on a rubric that relies on an "amorphous term" ("Paragraph Used") that, among other problems, manages to conflate indentation with coherence (428n15)—another way in which the NAEP conception of coherence is unclear. However, Bamberg's open-ended definition could be criticized for being so inclusive that it is boundless if not amorphous as well. Her article thus made me wonder, question, and seek an inclusive conception of coherence that stops short of concluding that almost anything in a text can be a matter of coherence. I never succeeded, realizing I had succumbed to the temptation of wanting boundaries for a concept that is continually pertinent only when it remains broad, abstract, and generative.

Bamberg's approach complicates the classroom for students and teachers who want something concrete, such as a quantitative coherence rubric. But writing is indeed messy. Ultimately, Bamberg's model can assist teachers and researchers by reminding us that coherence, whether it involves traditional pedagogy or cutting-edge theories and technology, is too important, too all-encompassing to reduce. For new literacies of tomorrow that we can scarcely imagine, our paradigms for coherence need flexibility—not static parameters that impede clarity and purpose.

Notes

1. Linguists and educationists focusing on language acquisition have long studied coherence; see, for instance, Le, which draws on translation research. Faradhibah and Nur's study of coherence among non-native speakers is one of many that analyzes data based on student writing—a methodology seen more recently in RahmtAllah's analysis of writing by female Saudi students. Research on technical and workplace writing also continues to examine coherence. Especially common are studies that measure how coherence relates to

other aspects of a text. Mackiewicz and Lam, however, take a more qualitative approach by investigating coherence in workplace-related instant messages, finding connections among cohesion, coherence, and power holdings within an organization. Business and technical writing pedagogy is highly common as well. Wolfe et al. concludes that a certain teaching strategy enabled engineering students to write more coherent reports that were also deemed to be of higher quality than those of a control group. Similarly, Gruber measures the effects on coherence of a teaching strategy used for business-related writing assignments.

2. Moe and Winkler make a similar point about the limits of teachers' insistence on maintaining a traditional definition of coherence and clarity in student writing. The authors wonder whether such an insistence might reflect "something of our own deficiencies as teachers, our own unwillingness (or inability) to engage incoherence" (220).

Works Cited

Bamberg, Betty. "What Makes a Text Coherent?" *College Composition and Communication*, vol. 34, no. 4, Dec. 1983, pp. 417–29.

Buck, Amber. "Examining Digital Literacy Practices on Social Network Sites." *Research in the Teaching of English*, vol. 47, no. 1, 2012, pp. 9–36.

Connors, Robert J. "The Erasure of the Sentence." *College Composition and Communication*, vol. 52, no. 1, Sept. 2000, pp. 96–128.

———. "The Rise and Fall of the Modes of Discourse." *College Composition and Communication*, vol. 32, no. 4, Dec. 1981, pp. 444–55.

Crossley, Scott A., and Danielle S. McNamara. "Say More and Be More Coherent: How Text Elaboration and Cohesion Can Increase Writing Quality." *Journal of Writing Research*, vol. 7, no. 3, 2016, pp. 351–70.

Faradhibah, Ratu Nur, and Nur Aliyah Nur. "Analyzing Students' Difficulties in Maintaining Their Coherence and Cohesion in Writing Process." *Eternal (English, Teaching, Learning and Research Journal)*, vol. 3, no. 2, Dec. 2017, pp. 183–94.

Gruber, Helmut. "Rhetorical Structure Theory and Quality Assessment of Students' Texts." *Information Design Journal*, vol. 14, no. 2, May 2006, pp. 114–29.

Knobel, Michele, and Colin Lankshear. "Studying New Literacies." *Journal of Adolescent and Adult Literacy*, vol. 58, no. 2, 2014, pp. 97–101.

Le, Elisabeth. "The Role of Paragraphs in the Construction of Coherence: Text Linguistics and Translation Studies." *International Review of Applied Linguistics in Language Teaching*, vol. 42, no. 3, July 2004, pp. 259–75.

Mackiewicz, Jo, and Christopher Lam. "Coherence in Workplace Instant Messages." *Journal of Technical Writing and Communication*, vol. 39, no. 4, 2009, pp. 417–31.

Moe, Peter Wayne, and Kyle Winkler. "How to Do Things with Incoherence." *Rhetoric Review*, vol. 38, no. 2, 2019, pp. 219–31.

Ofri, Danielle. *When We Do Harm: A Doctor Confronts Medical Error*. Beacon, 2020.

RahmtAllah, Enas Abdelwahab Eltom. "EFL Students' Coherence Skill in Writing: A Case Study of Third Year Students of Bachelors in English Language." *English Language Teaching*, vol. 13, no. 8, Jan. 2020, pp. 120–26.

Wolfe, Joanna, et al. "Teaching the IMRaD Genre: Sentence Combining and Pattern Practice Revisited." *Journal of Business and Technical Communication*, vol. 25, no. 2, 2020, pp. 119–58.

Enduring Value:
The Case for *Beat Not the Poor Desk*

Eric J. Sterling

> Marie Ponsot and Rosemary Deen, *Beat Not the Poor Desk: Writing: What to Teach, How to Teach It, and Why* (Boynton/Cook, 1982)

The insightful and practical composition guide *Beat Not the Poor Desk: Writing: What to Teach, How to Teach It, and Why* means a great deal to me. This book, written by the renowned poet and composition teacher Marie Ponsot and the longtime poetry editor of *Commonweal* magazine and composition teacher Rosemary Deen, helped me learn how to teach writing effectively to my students. During my senior year at Queens College, City University of New York, I was selected to be an assistant to an English professor who specialized in composition. As an assistant (essentially, an intern), I attended every freshman composition class of one section that she taught that semester, met with her twice a week to discuss pedagogy and lesson plans, and worked with her students individually during office hours and in small group sessions during the class meetings. Furthermore, I had to read *Beat Not the Poor Desk* and discuss the individual chapters and writing pedagogy weekly with the other assistants and the director of composition.

When it was published in 1982, *Beat Not the Poor Desk* was revolutionary and unique for supporting the following: inductive writing, limiting teachers' instructions, students focusing on listening to (as opposed to reading) drafts in order to provide feedback, students taking an active role in—and ownership of—their own writing, and the use of "prolific writing." This pedagogical gem focuses on teaching writing inductively; that is, students learn from their articulation of their personal experiences, and they acquire and hone significant writing and critical thinking skills by doing expository writing. I like the book partly because it concentrates on having students compose structured essays, which was important to composition teachers in the 1980s (and earlier), enabling students to articulate their thoughts in a developed and sustainable way. Today, in contrast, composition students are often asked to submit alternative, informal exercises (such as blogs, vlogs, and *Facebook* posts) that don't require the structure and developed thought that Ponsot and Deen encourage.[1] I consider this a loss because students receive much less practice in formal writing and in the development of sustained arguments and clear thinking, all of which serves as a foundation for their subsequent courses over the next four years of college. Unfortunately, Ponsot and Deen's book has fallen out of favor, perhaps because it advocates for decentralizing power in the classroom (with students taking an active role), using literature in the composition classroom, writing without computers, and minimizing teachers' instructions.

Ponsot and Deen argue that students' own essays are the texts from which composition students learn. No expensive textbook or essay collection is necessary. Rather than read scholarly or published essays as models they should emulate, students are encouraged to create their own texts, their own literature. In "The American Scholar," Ralph Waldo Emerson laments the plight of young writers "who start wrong, who set out from accepted dogmas, not from their own sight of principles. Meek young men grow up in libraries, believing it their duty to accept the views, which Cicero, which Locke, which Bacon, have given, forgetful that Cicero, Locke and Bacon were only young men in libraries, when they wrote these books" (57). Ponsot and Deen would concur with Emerson's premise: they don't want their students to borrow another writer's style; rather, students should possess the self-confidence and be given the freedom to forge their own paths and create their own styles. Students write confidently about themselves because "to know about something is to have experienced it particularly" (Ponsot and Deen 11). The topic can be an everyday event because talented writers create interest and excitement from the ordinary.

Ponsot and Deen also show how a composition and rhetoric class can become student-centered. Students learn by exploring from within rather than by modeling their essays on those of other authors or listening passively to lectures and extensive, generic instructions. Ponsot and

Deen want to help students improve individual style rather than conform to and copy their teacher's specific and favored formula, such as a clichéd five-paragraph essay. Ponsot and Deen regret that many composition teachers of their era spend so much time lecturing or leading discussions in class. Unfortunately, many current composition instructors still rely on the formulaic five-paragraph essay, employing the same tired method that they learned years ago. But Ponsot and Deen eliminated drills, exercises, and workbooks from their courses to devote class time to student writing. The authors stopped lecturing, explaining too much, asking questions that led to "paralyzing, right-answer questions" (Ponsot and Deen 50), and making young writers fear that they were doing the assignment incorrectly. The authors observed, furthermore, that verbose students dominate classroom discussion, while shy and introspective students often feel so intimidated that they fail to participate, thereby becoming passive learners.

Consequently, Ponsot and Deen favor limited teacher guidelines on essay writing, which allows students more freedom as writers. Students compose essays in ways that are natural for them. They are not, in other words, required to write in a style their professors want them to model. Teachers employ literature for inspiration and to stimulate ideas in their students, not to encourage students to use another essay as a model for their own. Ponsot and Deen teach "writing as literature because literature is central to writing" (65). I would like new instructors to read Ponsot and Deen's book because the field has moved away from a focus on structured essays and on student writing as literature to a focus on informal assignments (e.g., blogs) that require neither paragraphing nor correct grammar[2] and because the current field privileges technology, not student writing, as a teaching tool.

After the publication of Ponsot and Deen's book, composition actively began to establish itself as a distinct scholarly field. The fact that composition is now an independent discipline is the result of decades of theory-driven research and development. Christine Farris observes that many composition theorists sought to distinguish their field from literary studies by creating a "disciplinary identity grounded in research" (166). Today, composition theorists consider the inclusion of literature in freshman writing courses "an obstacle to the delivery of direct composition instruction, which had shifted emphasis from the features of finished products to the recursive and collaborative process of writing and revision," and they believe that the "[u]se of imaginative literature, as opposed to texts from a variety of disciplines, risks shifting the emphasis in writing courses from students' composing processes to their teacher-centered reception of texts" (166). Erika Lindemann rejects the use of literature in composition classes, arguing that composition must provide "guided practice in reading and writing the discourses of the academy and the professions. This is what our colleagues across the campus want [composition] to do; that is what it should do if we are going to drag every first-year student through the requirement" (312). According to Farris, writing specialists believe that "literature in composition courses may signal the return of literary interpretation at the expense of attention to students' writing processes and production of texts, which are central to what composition does" (165).

However, there are still some scholars who advocate for the use of literature in the freshman writing classroom, as did Ponsot and Deen. John Schilb and John Clifford's *Arguing about Literature* and *Making Literature Matter* use literature to teach writing, for works of literature "make arguments, as do we, when we interpret them. Schilb and Clifford offer students strategies for constructing arguments that often begin with interesting questions they find in a poem or narrative" (Farris 164). *Integrating Literature and Writing Instruction: First-Year English, Humanities Core Courses, Seminars*, edited by Judith H. Anderson and Farris, is an excellent volume on the effective use of literature in the first-year writing classroom. David Bartholomae, Anthony Petrosky, and Stacey Waite's edited collection, *Ways of Reading: An Anthology for Writers*, also uses literature to inspire students; the fact that the text is currently in its twelfth edition is a testament to its effectiveness in the classroom and its popularity with instructors.

In "Who Killed Annabel Lee: Writing about Literature in the Composition Classroom," Mark Richardson demonstrates how once instructors reassure freshmen that they are capable of creating their own meaningful interpretations rather than merely adhering blindly to established ones, "the knowledge that students already have becomes a key to the unlocking of the mystery of a text and the genuine construction of meaning" (291). Richardson establishes that confident students can create meaningful interpretations in the composition classroom when they rely on their environment and personal experience, which is what students also use in expository writing.

The composition theorist Barry Kroll's seminal book *Teaching Hearts and Minds: College Students Reflect on the Vietnam War* is another text that supports the use of literature in the first-year writing classroom. This powerful book relates how Kroll used literature on the Vietnam War to inspire students to learn more about the war, rethink their views on America's murky role in the war, and write outstanding and poignant essays. Kroll's students were so inspired by class discussions that they felt the need to learn more on their own, and they wrote quality essays that reflected their inspiration. The students became so emotionally involved that they eagerly wrote a great deal in their journals and assignments in class and at home about what they learned about the Vietnam War. Ponsot and Deen would agree with Schilb and Clifford, with Richardson, and with Kroll because Ponsot and Deen saw the value of literature as inspiration in the composition classroom.

One effective example of the use of literature in a first-year composition class that Ponsot and Deen mention in *Beat Not the Poor Desk* involves Jonathan Swift. As noted, a vast majority of composition programs throughout the United States currently and explicitly shun the use of literature as a source of knowledge or inspiration, creating a strict demarcation between composition and literature. Although Ponsot and Deen don't have students read literature as examples to model, they employ literature as inspiration. The purpose is not to focus on literary interpretation or to create models but rather to inspire students to employ their experiences as they create their expository essays:

> The structure enlightened is the model we imitate. The model is always within. An experienced writer or a writer of genius derives the model within from masterful works of literature because the superb power of structure shows itself there.... [S]tudents can discover in college that many of the experiences which they had thought private are in fact universal and will make a difference in their relation to their neighbors. (Ponsot and Deen 66–68)

Ponsot and Deen describe how Swift uses lists effectively to emphasize points, and they exemplify how their students can be inspired to shape lists into their own unique essays. For instance, a Latinx student wrote an essay in which every paragraph listed one way in which he had been unfairly stereotyped. The student wrote that when senior citizens saw him, "[t]hey grasp[ed] with strength their pocketbooks and wallets. . . . Do I look like a criminal? Well, every time I go into a store I attract detectives like a crumb attracts ants. They watch every move I make" (qtd. in Ponsot and Deen 86). Like Swift, the student listed items—showing in this instance how he was unfairly stereotyped and treated with suspicion and prejudice because of his gender and race. The student was inspired by the way Swift employed a list to emphasize a point.

To encourage pleasurable writing and inspire students to write more, Ponsot and Deen recommend "prolific writing"—"writing uninterruptedly for five or ten minutes to release thoughts and images into visible language, without pausing first to organize them into rational discourse—[which] is a technique so fruitful and flexible that we find occasions for it in all our work" (35; see 181–91 and 192–201 for more information on "prolific writing"). Ponsot was a prolific writer, but when she started teaching, she initially ignored how she wrote and instead followed the herd: "[L]ike most beginners, I took my first steps backward, and offered a tottering version of composition as it had been taught to me years before. It included conscientiously ingenious assigned subjects; terms and rules of grammar drilled in rule-related exercises; and corrective rule-book abbreviations" (35).

Interestingly, Ponsot and Deen explored the practice of "prolific writing" long before the publication of their book and before Peter Elbow began to employ a similar exercise with his own students, calling it "freewriting." The fact that Ponsot and Deen created the practice or at least made it popular in their day indicates how important their composition book was in its time—and how their innovative work inspired the theories of others. The low stakes of "prolific writing" removes student anxiety over the fear of making mistakes while "keep[ing] language and perceptions flowing past the fidgets, self-distractions, and bogeys that the mind occasionally throws out when it doesn't care to work (Ponsot and Deen 4). The relaxed classroom atmosphere leads to a communal, noncompetitive writing environment.

Ponsot and Deen want students to see their own writing as literature that is "a product of imagination and thought. . . . The center of writing is literature. The power is there" (65). The authors want students to improve their written communication skills when inspired by exploring their own life experiences. Engaging in self-discovery, they believe, creates a powerful and profound experience for students. Indeed, Ponsot and Deen realize that their students write best when they (the students) are the experts because the truth and experience come from within. The act of writing about a situation one has experienced breeds confidence, and self-discovery incites the author's interest and emotional investment. Unfortunately (and based on my own observations), personal essays have often been replaced today with assignments requiring students to write responses to TV series such as *The Vampire Diaries*, *The Walking Dead*, and *90 Day Fiancé*.[3] Formal essays and revision, strategies embraced by Ponsot and Deen, have been replaced by blogs and posts on *Facebook* pages. Students are sometimes assigned to write a restaurant or movie review. Although students might enjoy dining out and then writing about the meal, some might argue that the event lacks the experience or vitality that enters students' minds when they reflect on a turning point in their lives. I would encourage new instructors of writing to read Ponsot and Deen's book and experiment with its theories and practices.

Although Ponsot and Deen indicate that they don't analyze literature in class or want their students to mimic it, they nonetheless want it to inspire them in the same way that visual art does. The authors believe that students are inspired by an image and then make it their own. A classic example of this type of inspiration is the playwright August Wilson's Pulitzer Prize–winning play *The Piano Lesson* (1987), which Wilson wrote after viewing Romare Bearden's painting of the same name. According to Ponsot and Deen, writing involves "internalizing a sense of product, that is, with the image. The presence of the image shows itself in the way a writer takes a form and makes it so much [their] own that [they] can produce [their] own version of it. We can call this imitation, but ought to understand that the model we imitate is not on the page" (66).

Even before the digital age, Ponsot and Deen abandoned the practice of distributing hard copies of student work, claiming that it often fails to lead to productive discussion: "Teacher-selected essays set up the same guessing-game as right-answer questions: class members knew that the essays were either 'right' or 'wrong,' and they had to figure out which" (50). Instead, writers read their own work aloud to the class as the other students listen intently, do not interrupt, and pay attention by taking notes: "We are learning to listen. . . . [L]istening, more than reading silently, is a communal enterprise" (51). After the student reads the essay, the classmates write observations (not criticisms or attacks, which can lead to anxiety or competition) and read them aloud. Ponsot and Deen claim that "listening is intensely active work. . . . When we write, we discover what we hadn't been aware of when we were listening" (52). The student readings and class observations become an integral part of the learning process. As the authors argue, "Reading to others reinforces the act of writing" (50). Students see themselves as writers, and classmates become friends and people with whom students share their experiences. Ponsot and Deen note that "writing has that power, as teachers of literature know, to tell a truth about who the writer is. Even the least personal writing reveals something of the author's cognitive and verbal style" (39). Thus, students learn much about one another by sharing their essays, which creates a collaborative and congenial writing community.

Ponsot and Deen clearly want peer editing to be done in person. Unfortunately, with the advent of technology, many instructors now save class time for their lectures by requiring students to do peer editing on their own time on *Blackboard* or other learning management systems. Technology can help students learn, but in some cases instructors and students become preoccupied with the electronic tools themselves and lose sight of writing and the learning process. As Flower Darby and James M. Lang warn in *Small Teaching Online*, "[A]lways be wary of the shiny" (62). The problem with requiring composition students to perform peer editing online is that they don't interact with one another or listen to one another's writing. The result of this approach to peer editing is not the communal classroom environment that Ponsot and Deen recommend. Students don't have the opportunity to discuss their essays with their classmates because the peer editing is done at home, which can render the task a mechanical and impersonal chore that inhibits the sense of a class community.

Beat Not the Poor Desk is a classic guide to teaching writing that would prove helpful to new writing teachers and to graduate students studying composition pedagogy and rhetoric. The book effectively demonstrates how writing teachers can minimize their role in the classroom, thereby enabling students to take a more active role in the process of creative learning. Ponsot and Deen write *with* their students, thereby diminishing the rigid separation between professor and student, as Paulo Freire recommends in *Pedagogy of the Oppressed*. Freire writes that "through dialogue, the teacher-of-the-student and the student-of-the-teacher cease to exist and a new term emerges: teacher-student with students-teachers" (67). Instead of simply disseminating instructions or assignments, providing prescriptive templates, or giving orders as a privileged authority at the front of the classroom, the instructor writes with the students and functions as part of the class. Everyone learns together. De-emphasizing their power over the class, Ponsot and Deen encourage their student writers to become active participants, not passive vessels, who lead class meetings by writing and sharing their work with peers and then respond to their own writing and that of their classmates. Ponsot and Deen prefigure or inform other scholarship on active student participation in classrooms in which the instructor's role is limited. Perhaps their work has even inspired scholarship by composition theorists such as Kenneth Bruffee, Diana George, and Elbow. Further, the limited role of the instructor and the active role played by students, who teach one another and lead discussions, serves as a precursor to current notions of the flipped classroom.

Beat Not the Poor Desk was supplanted by newer composition books in the twenty-first century, perhaps because it advocates for the decentralization of teachers' authority in the classroom. Many faculty members feel anxious about relinquishing authority to their students, and some adhere instead to a prevalent framework of power in which the teacher possesses the authority while the students lack control. Ponsot and Deen would argue, however, that instructors are simply more experienced and confident writers. And as the authors emphasize, competition and ego are detrimental to learning and don't belong in a writing classroom. While the book's lack of emphasis on technology in the teaching of writing is perhaps another reason why the book has fallen out of favor and into obscurity, Ponsot and Deen emphasize students' personal interactions in the face-to-face classroom community. But perhaps this valuable contribution has also become lost because the use of literature as inspiration in the composition classroom has become unpopular for reasons that many in composition studies challenge.

Ponsot and Deen's book has been supplanted but not superseded by subsequent composition theory books. Although the book is long out of print, composition teachers still use Ponsot and Deen's ideas without knowing where these ideas come from. For instance, the authors emphasize their concept of "prolific writing," of drafting an essay using stream of consciousness, instinct, and extemporaneous writing, without planning and without being distracted by concerns about grammar and style or by fear of negative criticism, judgment, and grading. Ponsot began working with this concept in the early 1960s—a decade before Elbow popularized the concept of freewriting. Although composition teachers today don't use the term "prolific writing," they employ Ponsot and Deen's method when they inspire students to write—particularly shy students who lack confidence or those experiencing writer's block.

Beat Not the Poor Desk is timeless, demonstrating how elemental skills are teachable and suggesting that all students can improve their ability to write, not by receiving detailed, restrictive directions from instructors but rather through practice and by reading their work aloud in a communal classroom. Ponsot and Deen's book was a revolutionary and groundbreaking composition text when it was published. It continued a conversation about literature as inspiration in the classroom while presenting new ideas that would come to be known as freewriting and student-centered learning. In many crucial ways, Ponsot and Deen have been an unacknowledged influence on contemporary composition scholarship and practice. I would encourage new teachers to read this book so that they can try out Ponsot and Deen's theories and practices—and understand that this lost text is where some current practices, now attributed to others, were first developed.

Notes

1. See, for example, Santos and Leahy; Lindgren; Cope and Kalantzis; and Kress.

2. Informal blogs differ from Ponsot and Deen's "prolific writing" in that the latter helps the student initiate the writing process and is not submitted for a grade or as a final product.

3. See, for instance, Adler-Kassner's essay, which argues against the use of popular culture (such as vampires) in first-year composition classes, and Friedman's article in support of it.

Works Cited

Adler-Kassner, Linda. "The Companies We Keep; or, The Companies We Would Like to Keep: Strategies and Tactics in Challenging Times." *WPA: Writing Program Administration*, vol. 36, no. 1, fall-winter 2012, pp. 119–40.

Anderson, Judith H., and Christine R. Farris, editors. *Integrating Literature and Writing Instruction: First-Year English, Humanities Core Courses, Seminars*. Modern Language Association of America, 2007.

Bartholomae, David, et al., editors. *Ways of Reading: An Anthology for Writers*. 12th ed., Bedford / St. Martin's, 2019.

Bruffee, Kenneth A. "Collaborative Learning and the 'Conversation of Mankind.'" *College English*, vol. 46, no. 7, 1984, pp. 635–52.

Cope, Bill, and Mary Kalantzis, editors. *E-Learning Ecologies: Principles for New Learning and Assessment*. Routledge, 2017.

Darby, Flower, and James M. Lang. *Small Teaching Online: Applying Learning Science in Online Classes*. Jossey-Bass, 2019.

Elbow, Peter. *Writing without Teachers*. 2nd ed., Oxford UP, 1998.

Emerson, Ralph Waldo. "The American Scholar." *Emerson: Essays and Lectures*, edited by Joel Porte, Library of America, 1983, pp. 51–71.

Farris, Christine. "Literature and Composition Pedagogy." *A Guide to Composition Pedagogies*, edited by Gary Tate et al., 2nd ed., Oxford UP, 2014, pp. 163–76.

Freire, Paulo. *Pedagogy of the Oppressed*. Translated by Myra Bergman Ramos, Continuum Press, 1970.

Friedman, Sandie. "This Way for Vampires: Teaching First-Year Composition in 'Challenging Times.'" *Currents in Teaching and Learning*, vol. 6, no. 1, fall 2013, pp. 77–84.

George, Diana. "Working with Peer Groups in the Composition Classroom." *College Composition and Communication*, vol. 35, no. 3, 1984, pp. 320–26.

Kress, Gunther. *Multimodality: A Social Semiotic Approach to Contemporary Communication*. Routledge, 2009.

Kroll, Barry. *Teaching Hearts and Minds: College Students Reflect on the Vietnam War*. Southern Illinois UP, 1992.

Lindemann, Erika. "Freshman Composition: No Place for Literature." *College English*, vol. 55, no. 3, 1993, pp. 311–16.

Lindgren, Tim. "Locating Pedagogy in the Whereness of Weblogs." *Kairos: A Journal of Rhetoric, Technology, and Pedagogy*, vol. 10, no. 1, fall 2005, kairos.technorhetoric.net/10.1/coverweb/lindgren/index.htm.

Ponsot, Marie, and Rosemary Deen. *Beat Not the Poor Desk: Writing: What to Teach, How to Teach It, and Why*. Boynton/Cook, 1982.

Richardson, Mark. "Who Killed Annabel Lee: Writing about Literature in the Composition Classroom." *College English*, vol. 66, no. 3, 2004, pp. 278–93.

Santos, Marc C., and Mark H. Leahy. "Postpedagogy and Web Writing." *Computers and Composition*, vol. 32, 2014, pp. 84–95.

Schilb, John, and John Clifford. *Arguing about Literature: A Guide and Reader*. 3rd ed., Bedford / St. Martin's, 2019.

———. *Making Literature Matter: An Anthology for Readers and Writers*. 7th ed., Bedford / St. Martin's, 2017.

How the Twenty-First Century Changed Ira Shor's *Critical Teaching and Everyday Life*

Michael Bernard-Donals

Ira Shor, *Critical Teaching and Everyday Life* (South End Press, 1980)

When I was in graduate school in the late 1980s, Ira Shor's book—*Critical Teaching and Everyday Life*—wasn't read just because it was on the required reading list for preliminary exams in rhetoric and composition (although it was, right alongside Paulo Freire's *Pedagogy of the Oppressed*). Members of my cohort were also relatively new first-year writing teachers, and by the time we got to prelims we were looking for alternatives to the expressivism in which we'd been immersed by our mentors and teachers Peter Elbow and Pat Belanoff, alternatives that would mirror pedagogically the historical materialist theory we'd been reading in our doctoral seminars.

Shor's book seemed just the ticket. In it Shor adapts Freire's problem-posing model of education, learned through trial and error by Freire among semiliterate laborers in Brazil, for the open access students at the colleges of the City University of New York (CUNY). The book aims to create a "pedagogy which empowers students to intervene in the making of history" and to "prepare students to be their own agents for social change, their own creators of democratic culture" (48). To achieve these aims, Shor adapts Freire's term *conscientização* as "critical consciousness" and creates a series of writing and thinking exercises to develop class consciousness in his students. Those exercises gave students a critical awareness of the extent to which the state was interpellating them, in the historical materialist theorist Louis Althusser's terms, as more or less docile subjects. They also worked to show students the extent to which they were able to change their ideological if not their material circumstances by developing what rhetoricians would call a set of invention skills. The book's first few chapters summarize the history of the open access movement at CUNY and the landscape of two-year and technical colleges. (At the time, Shor was teaching as an assistant professor at the College of Staten Island, CUNY; he is now a full professor there with an appointment at the Graduate Center, CUNY.) The remaining parts of the book lay out principles such as teaching through dialogue with one's students, relinquishing the instructor's authority in the classroom to let students determine the content and direction of the class, effectively seeing students as coequal subjects in the classroom, and fostering a critical engagement with the material through interactive, community-based learning, all accompanied by peer-led writing exercises.

Shor's book was prescient in many ways, and it directly or indirectly helped lead a generation of composition and rhetoric scholar-teachers to experiment with student-centered classrooms, to flirt with if not foster a sense of student activism, and to grant authority to students' discursive, cultural, and educational experiences. Some parts of the book have aged well, and others haven't. I won't focus here on the material in the book's second part, which includes the chapters that are still cited today, if the book is cited at all: "Extraordinarily Experiencing the Ordinary" (92–123) and "Monday Morning" (125–54). Instead I'll focus mainly on the book's first part, which presents Shor's analysis of the predicament of public higher education in the last third of the twentieth century. He gets a lot right, but a lot has changed since the book was first published in 1980, most significantly the circumstances of the teachers who work in the colleges and universities whose students Shor tried so hard to make more critical writers.

Shor announces his intention in the book's introduction: to preserve "the larger social history for the rise of mass higher education" (xxiii) by tracing the creation and failure, over less than a decade, of open admissions at City College, CUNY, a history of the struggle for access, affordability, and—eventually—remediation. The latter are all issues that have become highlighted in debates over the crisis of higher education forty years on, debates about whether higher education is a public or private good, about the rights and responsibilities of faculty members, and on the question of whether higher education is a right or a privilege. Shor puts his finger on the crisis of funding, in which the now-massive scale of public higher education leads to a need for more money that states can't afford to spend but presumably students can (or must); the gross mismatch between the doctoral training received by most faculty members, a privilege even if it is an expensive one, and the lack of privilege and cultural capital of many of their students; the cheapening of public discourse surrounding race and class and the naturalization of a sense of class inferiority among students at non-elite colleges, which has become more or less accepted by the students themselves and by the public at large; and the lack of avenues for participation in the democratic public sphere in a postindustrial economy where labor and value have become irrevocably dissociated.

The parts of Shor's book that haven't aged well sound clunky because the diagnosis Shor provided of what ails late industrial capitalism didn't anticipate its rapid transformation to become what it is today: a rapidly moving service economy founded on a radical neoliberal ideological base that has not only exacerbated the precariousness of working-class students' circumstances but also eroded the professoriat and sharpened the sense of precarity among college and university teachers. This precariousness is exemplified by the collapse of the job market in English within a decade of the publication of Shor's book, a collapse that has begun to affect the market in composition and rhetoric in the last few years, and the so-called adjunctification of large swaths of higher education, especially in two-year colleges and non-elite public universities. In an essay in *College English*, James Rushing Daniel has characterized the teaching of writing as a "precariat," exemplified by a "state of insecurity and alienation" (66), "of impermanence and uncertainty that weakens social and economic relations" (66) among individuals in the profession "lacking access to the conditions of their economic positionality and, hence, lacking access to means of collectivity" (67). Shor also could not have anticipated the extent to which postindustrial capitalism has cultivated what Peter Sloterdijk has called "cynical reason," in which we behave counter to our interests even as we recognize the vulnerable circumstances in which we find ourselves. In Slavoj Žižek's formulation, "the cynical subject is quite aware of the distance between the ideological mask and the social reality, but he nonetheless insists on the mask"

(29). Cynical reason makes it much more difficult, if not impossible, to "dissociat[e] from routine consciousness"—to transform the classroom into a space that exists apart from discussions about "the routines of earning money, commuting, raising children or arranging leisure-time" (Shor 99)—because instructors themselves are worried about those very same aspects of their everyday lives. Working against what Shor calls the "arbitrary and regimented time frames for learning" (103) becomes much harder if the adjuncts doing most of the critical teaching are themselves subdividing time to make it from one workplace to another, when they are juggling several gigs, only one or two of which may involve teaching, and when even the teaching gigs don't come with phones, offices in which to work and meet with students, or parking anywhere near where they're teaching (if they can afford to have a car), let alone a living wage.

So how might Shor's analysis of the precarity of higher education in *Critical Teaching and Everyday Life* be configured for the first half of the twenty-first century? Daniel makes a smart point: precarious conditions make it very difficult for academic workers to form relations of solidarity among members of the working class. Precarity by definition "designates a fragmented and disconnected population" that is inconsistent with the formation of a proletarian class though which associations and solidarities might be made (Daniel 67–68). The alternative to Shor's building of class consciousness among students through critical teaching might be the formation of solidarity around the idea of precarity itself by, as Daniel puts it, "promot[ing] nuanced thinking of economic fracture beyond the purview of class stratification and suggest[ing] modes of resistance attuned to reclaiming agency from territorialized positions" (68). Shor writes that the "teacher accepts a variety of roles, at oscillating distances from the action" (101), including "the unresolved problems of everyday living" in the spheres of "school, family, work, health care, housing, mass transit, the two-party system, [and] welfare" (87). The teacher's role is a mobile one, which demands an engagement in the "unsettling and non-routine" aspects of everyday life (101), pulling teachers in multiple directions—ideologically, spatially, materially—at once. I would go even further and suggest that precarity's correlative, vulnerability, can serve as the condition that grounds a critical pedagogy.

Judith Butler defines *vulnerability* as a radical rootlessness and unsettlement, the norms of which are associated with injury and violence: we find that we are "beyond ourselves, implicated in lives that are not our own" (17). This kind of vulnerability involves certain ethical obligations and political responsibilities, one of which is recognition, both of the other with whom one is implicated and of the vulnerable circumstances in which recognition is possible at all. For Butler, the norms associated with vulnerability are injurious and involve a necessary violence. Danielle Petherbridge extends this definition, calling vulnerability a general openness to others (590). For both Butler and Petherbridge, vulnerability requires a recognition of others with whom one is implicated, but Petherbridge makes a distinction between constitutive and situational vulnerability, in which situational vulnerabilities are violations and abuses of power that inevitably arise in constitutive vulnerability. According to Petherbridge, the openness of constitutive vulnerability is threatened by injustices that create scarcity, suffering, and a devaluation of the person in the eyes of the law and in their relations with others. Petherbridge argues that there is a critical dimension inherent in constitutive vulnerability that cultivates an awareness of suffering and injustice; situational vulnerabilities, as "forms of relationality, social practice or institutions in which [the subject] is unable to prevent abuses of vulnerability or that undermine what [the subject] takes to be important for [their] well-being," require forms of cooperation, care, and socialization, an "affirmation between subjects" (596). In Daniel's words, "[D]espite their collective dislocation the precariat are nevertheless a heterogeneous group that must find connection across difference. In the academic context, application of this idea entails the recognition of mutual precarity among students and faculty" (73). This critical impulse leads to an understanding that all faculty members are variously dislocated by their contemporary conditions, promoting a "flattening of our professional hierarchies and the creation of common cause among academic ranks" and, ideally, with our students (76). I've called this critical impulse "mobility," a "capacity to call into question" and "to move those of us who use it and those it affects," which serves as a "capacity or force, if only those of us in higher education were more able to recognize it" (Bernard-Donals 2). It's an aspect of critical teaching that Shor himself recognizes, if implicitly, when describing the teacher's function in the critical classroom as one that is in constant motion.

There's a lot more to say, but my point is that it would be worth returning to Shor's book, for three reasons. First, Shor's analysis of the political economy of American higher education in the late twentieth century points to the conditions that have essentially bifurcated the workforce and created, in the forty years since the book's publication, the vast disparities in wealth that have made a college education of any kind both absolutely necessary and exceptionally difficult to either afford or complete given the economic needs of many who aspire to it. The years between the advent of the Reagan administration and the end of the Trump administration have seen a further widening of that divide, along with a devaluation of difference and an erosion of the structures of democratic participation that would make change possible. The challenge will be to continue to revise the pedagogies that Shor developed in ways that account not just for student precarity but also for the precarity of the instructors who teach them. An essay by Timothy Barouch and Brett Ommen diagnoses the current conditions of postliberalism. According to Barouch and Ommen, in the face of critiques of liberalism offered by scholars of writing studies and calls for a return to a civic culture that may not exist anymore, we might be better off "not only . . . seeing the shortcomings of liberal public culture" but also finding ways to make "a life within it" (161). Michael Walzer characterizes this type of culture as one that is in random motion, where individuals are continually separating from one another (148). Such an orientation would require a rhetorical education that contends with "the manner in which citizens experience life as perpetually unsettled" and in which "being unsettled is not necessarily a bad thing" (Barouch and Ommen 172).

Second, Shor's emphasis is on the development of aptitudes that will provide working-class students the skills necessary to critically examine how they have been interpellated in order to transform the material conditions of their everyday lives. Daniel suggests that—given the constitutive vulnerabilities that are shared by students and intellectual workers—a more reasonable alternative would be the engagement of social responsibility through activism, which makes good on the critical impulse of Petherbridge's constitutive vulnerability by changing the conditions through which that vulnerability is put at risk (82). We would need to acknowledge that rhetoric's mobility undoes its own sense of methodological stability, and of academics' and our students' places in the institution, and recognize the potential force or power that vulnerability offers.

Finally, it's also worth recognizing that Shor's ideas about the inculcation of critical consciousness, or activism, comes with inherent risk. As Daniel puts it, "[I]t's hard to overstate the immense risk to already precarious faculty that such teaching may involve" (81) because the political and social dislocations experienced by students are similarly experienced by their instructors, and with the lack of job security afforded by tenure, long-term contracts, and an institutional home those instructors may experience dislocation in the form of contract nonrenewal or outright firing. Our mutual openness to one another renders us susceptible to relations of power, to the dynamics of methodological orthodoxies, and to the sometimes cruel institutional politics at the departmental level.

Shor's book makes little mention of the precarious circumstances of college faculty members, let alone the risks faculty members take on by experimenting with activist pedagogy. In short, *Critical Teaching and Everyday Life* is a useful analysis of the contradictions in American public higher education at the advent of the open access movement and a bold call for critical consciousness in the first-year writing classroom. Over four decades later, those contradictions have only become sharper, and the conditions of vulnerability more complex. It's time to revisit the book, take it seriously, and—in the spirit of Daniel's essay—take on the risks and vulnerabilities inherent in creating a new critical pedagogy for the twenty-first century.

Works Cited

Barouch, Timothy, and Brett Ommen. "The Constrained Liberty of the Liberal Arts and Rhetorical Education." *Rhetoric Society Quarterly*, vol. 47, no. 4, 2017, pp. 158–79.

Bernard-Donals, Michael. "Rhetorical Movement, Vulnerability, and Higher Education." *Philosophy and Rhetoric*, vol. 52, no. 1, 2019, pp. 1–23.

Butler, Judith. "Violence, Mourning, Politics." *Studies in Gender and Sexuality*, vol. 4, no. 1, 2003, pp. 9–37.

Daniel, James Rushing. "Freshman Composition as a Precariat Enterprise." *College English*, vol. 80, no. 1, Sept. 2017, pp. 63–85.

Petherbridge, Danielle. "What's Critical about Vulnerability? Rethinking Independence, Recognition, and Power." *Hypatia*, vol. 31, no. 3, summer 2016, pp. 589–604.

Shor, Ira. *Critical Teaching and Everyday Life*. South End Press, 1980.

Sloterdijk, Peter. *Critique of Cynical Reason*. U of Minnesota P, 1998.

Walzer, Michael. *Politics and Passion: Toward a More Egalitarian Liberalism*. Yale UP, 2004.

Žižek, Slavoj. *The Sublime Object of Ideology*. Verso Books, 1989.

Lingering Questions from Lynn Quitman Troyka's "Defining Basic Writing in Context"

Lynn Reid

> Lynn Quitman Troyka, "Defining Basic Writing in Context," *A Sourcebook for Basic Writing Teachers*, edited by Theresa Enos (McGraw-Hill, 1987)

Since its 1987 publication in *A Sourcebook for Basic Writing Teachers*, Lynn Quitman Troyka's "Defining Basic Writing in Context" has prompted reflection on the part of teacher-scholars of basic writing. In this oft cited work to which we must pay renewed attention, Troyka asks her readers to reflect on the dangers of overgeneralizing about basic writing and students enrolled in classes that carry that designation while also pointing to a need for the coherent disciplinary identity that Mina Shaughnessy had sought to develop and that the editor of *A Sourcebook* explicitly notes they intend to build on (Enos, Introduction v). "Defining Basic Writing in Context" takes on a critical question that at the time of this writing remains largely unanswered: What exactly *is* basic writing, as a field, as a course, or even as a written product? Today, as basic writing continues to struggle to locate its disciplinary identity in the face of widespread cuts, remediation, and new initiatives that focus on mainstreaming students into credit-bearing courses, this question has grown increasingly urgent as basic writing professionals struggle to define their work for stakeholders representing wide-ranging and often conflicting interests.

Troyka's perspective on basic writing was naturally shaped by her time at the City University of New York (CUNY), where Shaughnessy launched *Journal of Basic Writing* in 1975 and published her groundbreaking *Errors and Expectations* just a few years later. In the editor's introduction to the inaugural issue of *Journal of Basic Writing*, Shaughnessy begins to define the parameters of basic writing, a subfield of composition studies that was born from CUNY's open admissions policy. Shaughnessy writes that open admissions "reaches out beyond traditional sources for its students, bringing in to a college campus young men and women from diverse classes, races, and cultural backgrounds who have attended good, poor, and mediocre schools" (1). These changes, according to Shaughnessy, had significant implications for faculty members, as "the shock and challenge of this diversity is experienced first through the written words and sentences of the new students, for here, spelled out in words, woven into syntax, is the fact of inequity—in our schools and in the society that is served by these schools" (1). This emphasis on equity and providing access to college for students from communities that had previously been excluded from higher education allowed the term *basic writing* to take hold precisely "because of its appeal to our humanistic impulses" (Troyka 4).

Today, the professional work of basic writing is, in some ways, quite different from the work of basic writing as a field that Troyka was investigating in the 1980s. As Andrea Lunsford notes in her essay in *A Sourcebook for Basic Writing Teachers*, basic writing was then often conceptualized by those outside the discipline through a lens of literacy crises and debates about maintaining academic standards as student demographics shifted (246). Basic writing instructors were often caught between the institutional expectation of gatekeeping, their role being to ensure that only students that the institution deemed to be qualified could enter credit-bearing courses, and a professional ethos that prioritized support for students who had previously been denied access to higher education. While these tensions between access and standards remain common today, another popular argument has taken hold—namely that moving students out of remedial courses will lead to increased retention, persistence, and, ultimately, degree completion. In some instances, moving students more quickly into credit-bearing courses has had tangible benefits, as students are able to more quickly progress toward a degree without noncognitive factors interfering (Adams et al. 53), and these appealing prospects have led to statewide shifts in basic writing instruction across the country, many of which aim to reduce students' time in developmental courses (Venezia and Hughes 39). This has led to a reduction of developmental reading and writing courses across the country (Schrynemakers et al.), and nineteen states have legislated the delivery or curriculum of developmental courses in alternative formats (e.g., corequisite course offerings, stretch models, studio or mandatory tutoring, and summer bridge programs) rather than as stand-alone developmental courses (Education Commission). What is seen by some as a "war on remediation" emerged in response to increased pressure to push students toward degree completion as rapidly as possible (Fain; see also Landesman; Flannery).[1] As George Otte and Rebecca Mlynarczyk have noted in their history of basic writing, "A very real question is whether anyone truly expected basic writing to match the rhetoric or impetus of the anti-remediation forces. Those forces had sent a clear, short message to the [basic writing] administrator, if not the [basic writing] teacher/scholar: blend or die" (75).

Many teacher-scholars with expertise in basic writing have argued eloquently that reforms in developmental education are sorely needed. Mlynarczyk has asserted that stand-alone basic writing courses should be eliminated to create more equitable opportunities for students, as placement in developmental courses has been linked to higher rates of attrition. Importantly, however, Mlynarczyk also notes that even in the absence of stand-alone basic writing courses, the pedagogical practices and social justice principles that many have identified as foundational to the work of teaching basic writing must be preserved. While these positions are certainly not mutually exclusive, institutions that eliminate courses that are explicitly labeled as basic writing courses while continuing to support the needs of students who may have enrolled in such a course might benefit from the professional designation of basic writing and its associated knowledge base. Given these tensions, Troyka's warning that "Basic Writing has begun to lose its identity" (13) is perhaps even more true now than it was in 1987, as courses that carry the designations of "basic writing" or "developmental" are increasingly difficult to identify.

Data on Basic Writing

Troyka's "Defining Basic Writing in Context" is one of many publications that has interrogated the status of basic writing as a distinct discipline (Bloom; Smoke). What sets Troyka's essay apart from many other texts that lament the status of the field, however, is its attempt at a data-driven answer to the question of what basic writing—the actual writing of students who enroll in basic writing courses—is on a broad scale. For her study, Troyka collected samples of student writing from colleagues, the goal being to develop a representative sample of the work of students enrolled in basic writing courses across North America. She then trained raters to complete a blind scoring according to unified criteria, with the hope that the results would be a step toward a comprehensive national definition of basic writing. Unfortunately, Troyka's most significant finding was inconsistency; there were no traits that could serve to immediately classify a writing sample as basic writing, and the continuum along which such samples might be measured was fluid, as raters varied in their assessments. In other words, there was no way to define the writing produced by students enrolled in basic writing courses in a way that would allow for a broad generalization of what the term *basic writing* might mean, as different institutions held different standards for what constituted basic writing.

The inconsistency in Troyka's results warrants a return to data that might help characterize the work of basic writing as a discipline or even simply as an undergraduate course. Surprisingly, though, since the publication of "Defining Basic Writing in Context," few scholars have followed Troyka's lead to rely on qualitative or quantitative data rather than publish about locally focused scenarios or syntheses of existing research in order to define the parameters of the field (scenarios and syntheses that are, of course, valuable in their own right but serve a different function). In fact, there have been few successful efforts at collecting nationwide data samples that capture information about the work of basic writing as a whole. More than a decade ago, Sugie Goen-Salter identified the need for a national database for basic writing programs, students, and faculty members ("Creating"). While a national survey was conducted, the results are somewhat difficult to locate. The only published report is an analysis conducted by Karen Uheling's graduate students that was posted on the CompFaqs wiki (Conrad et al.), but the emphasis of the analysis is on programmatic structures. In a similar vein, the 2017 survey of four-year institutions published by the National Census of Writing does emphasize basic writing to a certain degree, but the information gathered in that survey centers primarily on program structures, not on the construction of a coherent disciplinary identity or even a clearly defined object of study ("2017 Four-Year Institution Survey"). More recently, Emily Suh and Darin Jensen have conducted a survey of 143 developmental education professionals to gain insight into how these educators conceptualize their professional identities as part of a larger community of practice. One notable finding of the survey is that developmental educators find resilience to be a defining characteristic of their professional identities. However, the survey focuses on the broader field of developmental education, including math and counseling in addition to basic writing. While all of these reports represent important scholarly contributions, none provide a clear set of characteristics that define the field of basic writing, as Troyka sought to do in 1987.

Challenges of Disciplinary Identity Formation

This lack of wide-scale studies that attempt to define the discipline of basic writing and its associated disciplinary expertise is surprising given that basic writing as a field has long struggled to maintain its status. In "Defining Basic Writing in Context," Troyka points to her own study of program proposals for the Conference on College Composition and Communication (CCCC) from her year as chair of the organization (1980). Troyka's study found that, after rhetorical theory and technical writing, basic writing was the third most popular category for submissions that year, which highlights the fact that basic writing does exist as a distinct area within composition and rhetoric and writing studies (4). Today, however, the distinction between basic writing and other first-year writing courses is becoming increasingly blurred. In 2012 the removal of basic writing as an area cluster on the CCCC proposals prompted members of the Council on Basic Writing to present (at Troyka's suggestion, in fact) a successful sense-of-the-house motion at the CCCC business meeting to demand that basic writing be reinstated as a conference cluster. In 2020 basic writing was again removed from the list of CCCC clusters and was absorbed into the broader category of first-year writing. In 2012 members of the Council on Basic Writing were so outraged about the elimination of basic writing as a CCCC cluster that they quite literally crashed the organization's national Listserv as colleagues emailed to sign on to support the sense-of-the-house motion, and yet the 2020 removal of basic writing slipped under the radar. This is of little surprise: with the national trend toward mainstreamed and corequisite models of basic writing, even other professionals in rhetoric and composition believe that basic writing is no longer a distinct area of professional focus.

Basic Writing Expertise

Despite substantive arguments that suggest that basic writing is a distinct area, Troyka's own study reveals that basic writing resists definition. Troyka acknowledges this challenge as she cautions her readers against painting all students enrolled in basic writing courses with too broad a brush. Instead, Troyka argues, basic writing is best defined in its local context. This stands to reason, as different institutions serve different demographics of students with different needs. Yet anyone who has had the responsibility of staffing a basic writing course knows what Peter Dow Adams has said publicly on many occasions: teaching basic writing requires more expertise on the part of the instructor than does any traditional first-year writing course.

The need for a particular expertise is evident in "Defining Basic Writing in Context," where Troyka identifies her role as a basic writing instructor as one that required the ability to "slip easily into an individualized curriculum that meets students' diverse needs" rather than fall back on assumptions about what an instructor might expect a student in a basic writing course to benefit from (2). Troyka further reminds her readers that "[n]onacademics, as well as some academics, might assert: 'These students deserve no attention because they are not "college material."' But they have been invited, and they are here" (12).

Thus, as Susan Bernstein argues, to be an effective instructor of basic writing, one must consistently occupy the position of student advocate:

> We can invent as many new terms and new course names as we would like, but one basic truth remains: students by virtue of their placement in courses designated as "basic writing" are considered marginal to postsecondary institutions. Our job as teachers and as administrators is to become a forceful presence that creates visibility for our work and for the work of our students.
>
> ("Unconventional Education" 8)

This is perhaps where the real expertise of basic writing professionals lies. Since the publication of Troyka's essay, the depth and breadth of knowledge that a basic writing professional needs has expanded dramatically. Today's basic writing faculty must continue to address the impact of structural inequality that Troyka alludes to in her essay, but today, so much more is known about the myriad of reasons why students might find a seat in a basic writing course, reasons that include, among others, nonacademic literacy sponsorship (Brandt), previous traumatic experiences (Sitler), non-neurotypical styles of learning or communicating (Bernstein, "Limestone Way"), linguistic background (Matsuda), speaking and writing in nonstandard dialects of English (Shaughnessy), familial responsibility and socioeconomic status (Sternglass), mental health (Shankar and Park), and age (Gleason and Nuckles). With that, basic writing professionals must also be keenly aware of the institutional politics that can—and surely will—complicate their efforts to successfully advocate for students (Gleason; Soliday). Additionally, to ensure that students can demonstrate writing proficiency at a level that the institution expects, basic writing professionals must also be adept instructors of reading (Goen-Salter, "Critiquing") and of metacognitive strategies for learning (Cummings).

Though reenvisionings of curricular and programmatic imperatives are a sign of a thriving field of study, the more that the courses that Shaughnessy designated as "basic" are made less visible through efforts to mainstream students or otherwise reform developmental education, the more difficult it will become for basic writing professionals to advocate for the students we have historically supported. If there are no basic writing courses per se, there is no need for a basic writing specialist to advocate for students. Likewise, if there are no basic writing courses, it will be easy for other instructors to erroneously assume that the challenges that a student might experience in a developmental course will no longer be an issue; if the courses vanish, so too does an awareness of the needs that they may have been filling.

So, then, what would a national study of basic writing look like today? If we know that the writing varies, the students vary, and the conditions that create an exigence for basic writing vary by institution, it seems that targeting our efforts to define *expertise* in the field might yield promising results. As Mlynarczyk notes, "[I]t is essential to preserve, even to strengthen, the kind of enlightened pedagogy and responsible research that have characterized the field of [basic writing] since its inception" (269). What is needed, then, is a study of what basic writing experts *do* rather than how programs are structured or how students in our courses write. The latter two are necessarily institution-specific, but as Troyka suggests, the most important work of the field is actually teaching (3). To argue for the validity of basic writing as a distinct area of expertise, it is time to look beyond the course itself and instead consider the knowledge, skills, and techniques that basic writing teacher-scholars have cultivated to support students who have been deemed underprepared for college-level writing. Troyka's study clearly outlines the challenges inherent in providing a generalized definition of basic writing, but her work also calls attention to a significant gap in empirical studies of the field at large. Such work is necessary for the field of basic writing to move beyond the identity crisis that Troyka identified in 1987 and that has plagued the profession ever since.

Note

1. Fain's *Inside Higher Ed* article was originally titled "Complete College America Declares War on Remediation."

Works Cited

Adams, Peter, et al. "The Accelerated Learning Program: Throwing Open the Gates." *Journal of Basic Writing*, vol. 28, no. 2, 2009, pp. 50–69.

Bernstein, Susan Naomi. "Limestone Way of Learning." *The Chronicle of Higher Education*, Oct. 2003, p. B5.

———. "An Unconventional Education: A Letter to Basic Writing Practicum Students." *Journal of Basic Writing*, vol. 37, no. 2, 2018, pp. 6–34.

Bloom, Lynn. "A Name with a View." *Journal of Basic Writing*, vol. 14., no. 1, 1995, pp. 7–14.

Brandt, Deborah. "Sponsors of Literacy." *College Composition and Communication*, vol. 49, no. 2, 1998, pp. 165–85.

Conrad, Rick, et al. "What Are the Trends Shown in the CBW Survey of Writing Programs When Collated by Type of School?" *CompFaqs*, compfaqs.org/CollatedbyTypeofSchool/HomePage. Accessed 1 May 2020.

Cummings, Chris. "Engaging New College Students in Metacognition for Critical Thinking: A Developmental Education Perspective." *Research and Teaching in Developmental Education*, vol. 32, no. 1, 2015, pp. 64–67.

Education Commission of the States. "50 State Comparison: Developmental Education Policies." *Education Commission of the States*, www.ecs.org/50-state-comparison-developmental-education-policies/.

Enos, Theresa. Introduction. Enos, *Sourcebook*, pp. v–vii.

———, editor. *A Sourcebook for Basic Writing Teachers*. McGraw-Hill, 1987.

Fain, Paul. "Overkill on Remediation?" *Inside Higher Ed*, 19 June 2012, www.insidehighered.com/news/2012/06/19/complete-college-america-declares-war-remediation.

Flannery, Mary Ellen. "The Wrong Answer on Remediation." *NEA Higher Education Advocate*, vol. 31, no. 5, 2014, pp. 3–5.

Gleason, Barbara. "Evaluating Writing Programs in Real Time: The Politics of Remediation." *College Composition and Communication*, vol. 51, no. 4, 2000, pp. 560–88.

Gleason, Barbara, and Kimmie Nuckles. *The Bedford Bibliography for Teachers of Adult Learners*. Bedford / St. Martin's, 2015.

Goen-Salter, Sugie. "Creating a National Database about Basic Writing Programs, Students and Faculty." *Basic Writing e-Journal*, vol. 7, no. 1, 2008, bwe.ccny.cuny.edu/7.1%20Creating%20a%20National%20Database.html.

———. "Critiquing the Need to Eliminate Remediation: Lessons from San Francisco State." *Journal of Basic Writing*, vol. 27, no. 2, 2008, pp. 81–105.

Landesman, Charles. "The Remediation War at the City University of New York." *Academic Questions*, vol. 10, no. 4, 1999, pp. 77–86.

Lunsford, Andrea. "Politics and Practices in Basic Writing." Enos, *Sourcebook*, pp. 246–58.

Matsuda, Paul Kei. "Basic Writing and Second Language Writers: Toward an Inclusive Definition." *Journal of Basic Writing*, vol. 22, no. 2, 2003, pp. 67–89.

Mlynarczyk, Rebecca Williams. "Rethinking Basic Writing: Reflections on Language, Education, and Opportunity." *Talking Back: Senior Scholars and Their Colleagues Deliberate the Past, Present, and Future of Writing Studies*, edited by Norbert Elliot and Alice S. Horning, Utah State UP, 2020, pp. 261–70.

Otte, George, and Rebecca Mlynarczyk. *Basic Writing*. Parlor Press, 2010.

Schrynemakers, Ilse, et al. "College Readiness in Post-Remedial Academia: Faculty Observations from Three Urban Community Colleges." *Community College Enterprise*, vol. 25, no. 1, 2019, pp. 10–31.

Shankar, Nilani L., and Crystal L. Park. "Effects of Stress on Students' Physical and Mental Health and Academic Success." *International Journal of School and*

Educational Psychology, vol. 4, no. 1, Jan. 2016, pp. 5–9. *Taylor and Francis Online*, https://doi.org/10.1080/21683603.2016.1130532.

Shaughnessy, Mina P. Introduction. *Journal of Basic Writing*, vol. 1, no. 1, 1975, pp. 1–4.

Sitler, Helen Collins. "Teaching with Awareness: The Hidden Effects of Trauma on Learning." *Clearing House*, vol. 82, no. 3, Jan. 2009, pp. 119–24. *EBSCOhost*, https://doi.org/10.3200/TCHS.82.3.119-124.

Smoke, Trudy. "What Is the Future of Basic Writing?" *Journal of Basic Writing*, vol. 20, no. 2, 2001, pp. 88–96.

Soliday, Mary. *The Politics of Remediation: Student and Institutional Needs in Higher Education*. U of Pittsburgh P, 2002.

Sternglass, Marilyn. *Time to Know Them: A Longitudinal Study of Writing and Learning at the College Level*. Routledge, 1997.

Suh, Emily, and Darin Jensen. "Examining Communities of Practice: Transdisciplinarity, Resilience, and Professional Identity." *Journal of Basic Writing*, vol. 39, no. 2, 2020, pp. 33–59.

Troyka, Lynn Quitman. "Defining Basic Writing in Context." Enos, *Sourcebook*, pp. 2–15.

"2017 Four-Year Institution Survey." *National Census of Writing*, writingcensus.ucsd.edu/survey/4/year/2017.

Venezia, Andrea, and Katherine L. Hughes. "Acceleration Strategies in the New Developmental Education Landscape." *New Directions for Community Colleges*, no. 164, winter 2013, pp. 37–45. *EBSCOhost*, https://doi.org/10.1002/cc.20079.

"Bound to Sound": Reaffirming Walter J. Ong

Clint Bryan

> Walter J. Ong, *Orality and Literacy: The Technologizing of the Word* (Methuen Publishing, 1982)

No matter how literate we as writing teachers become in our pedagogical craft, some of us may remember how insecure we initially felt as beginning writing students stringing together words, only to cringe at the instructor's marginal note "Awk.," for awkward syntax, in jarring red ink. Therefore, we temper our comments aimed at students who are just gaining semantic fluidity. Learning how to read works similarly: instructors may plow through dense texts using close reading practices learned in graduate classes, but we readily recall childhood experiences of sitting on the lap of a parent, guardian, or educator with a stack of books that came alive only when our sage decoded the squiggles into stories. In a real sense, an individual's development from the preliterate, verbal language of toddlerhood (gaining vocabulary by pointing and mimicking voices) to a literate, competent writer resembles the way societies as disparate as ancient China, Arabia, and Greece moved from oral to written cultures. A faint remembrance of the time before literacy sticks with us, as it has with humanity, informing how we approach other communicative areas requiring mastery.

Despite their ubiquity, computers represent another field where users develop literacy over time, as familiarity with hardware and software grows and with the proliferation of new gadgetry. Even if a preschooler knows how to use a tablet, their ability to launch apps or play educational video games does not mean that they are ready for spreadsheets or HTML. Neophyte computer users need repeated exposure over time and to be led by competent guides, many of whom may still retain a faint memory of a time before computers dominated the communicative landscape. The fact that many writing teachers model sophisticated search techniques within library databases—especially when their own undergraduate research started with index cards stuffed in card catalog drawers, call numbers scrawled on scrap paper, and labyrinthine trips to the library's stacks in search of a moldering tome—reimagines the self-deprecatory adage for the present era in writing studies: "Those who can't, teach." My memory of life before *Google* or *Google Scholar* actually helps me prepare my students to peer at screens for the remainder of their researching and composing careers.

True, the advent of the microchip forever altered communication—a shift so dramatic that the only plausible parallel to the digital revolution came 2,500 years prior, when oral cultures shifted to writing. Composition's harnessing of technological advances means that some English instructors assign videos, PowerPoint presentations, and podcasts—modes that bear little resemblance to those of the past. However, we cannot discard the solid principles of drafting an argument that existed long before IBM, Microsoft, and Apple forever changed the way that students complete and submit assignments. Fortunately, we retain a collective memory of writing before computers, word processors, and dot-matrix printers, when the only available font came from our manual typewriters.

The traditional meaning of *literacy* as the capacity to read and write, as something one either possesses or does not possess, misses the gradations of writing genres and features that first-year composition instructors seek to foster. Indeed, literacy exists on a competency continuum. This nuanced definition encompasses the notion of digital literacy too. Despite the fact that many students are now viewed as digital natives, few know how to use all the available features in the Microsoft Office suite in order to produce standard academic work. If Gen Z students enrolled in English courses require training in computer literacy, certainly the general public has not achieved full competence, despite the growing presence of digital content. To meet the demand for digital literacy, many first-year composition classes employ multimodal assignments along with traditional essays, hoping to emphasize conventional discursive literacies while giving students occasions to practice with software or modes in which they are not yet conversant. Technological advances enable compositionists to envision new vistas. At the same time, technology leads to challenges never before encountered in the classroom (e.g., students' having to consider basic design principles to create assignments that emphasize visual rhetoric as well as written genres). The communicative process existing where speech and writing overlap echoes the innovative ideas promulgated by the literacy theorist Walter J. Ong's *Orality and Literacy*, a text that warrants rediscovery in a digital age, to assist writing instructors thrust into this liminality.

Ong's thoughts on oral and written connections to consciousness helps us navigate this latest turn toward multimodality. In a significant understatement, Ong observes that "[w]riting was . . . an invaluable intrusion into the human lifeworld, much as computers are today" ("Writing" 27). When *Orality and Literacy* was published, personal computers were expensive, clunky, and cumbersome. Ong, no matter his correct estimation of the "intrusion" of computers, could never have imagined the smartphone. The pocket-size device that accompanies its operator holds thousands of audio files, connects users globally, enables file sharing that would have dazzled early NASA scientists, and has established itself as an external human organ. While this statement might sound grandiose, the shifts in human consciousness that have been caused by computers are not to be underestimated. While digital discourse appears transitory, every hastily written text is stored for posterity in binary code. Similarly, Ong calls sound "evanescent," whereas writing seems permanent ("Writing" 25). He posits, moreover, that "[s]ound . . . exists only when it is going out of existence" (*Orality* 90). When Ong's groundbreaking ideas are viewed in light of the computerized revolution that followed *Orality and Literacy*, strong connections among discourse, consciousness, and rhetorical principles emerge—with implications for today's compositionists.

To instate Ong as the poster child for multimodality will not be easy, as Ong remains a polarizing figure. Few literacy theorists have been valorized and vilified in such equal measure as Ong has been.[1] For thirty years, critics have dissected the assumptions of the great divide, or great leap, theory.[2] Certain linguists in the 1970s and 1980s advanced the theory that literacy itself enacted a "Great Leap" forward in human cognition, as oral-based societies gave way to analytical thinking with the capacity to store and later retrieve information (Daniell, "Uses" 2). Labeling Ong a proponent of a "Great Divide" vision of history reduces his characterization of literacy to a dichotomous view of what being able to read and write does for a society to an on-and-off duality akin to a light switch: either a culture is literate, or it is not. Because his critics rendered Ong's name nearly synonymous with this controversial theory, his work was discredited long before *cancel culture* became a household term. That he was a Jesuit priest certainly did not help his popularity among some academics. Despite the early dissent, recent critics have returned to the work as a way to inform multimodality with proven rhetorical theories. Of interest to composition scholars today is Ong's notion of "secondary orality," which results anytime a student writer drafts content using electronic media, instantiating "essentially a more deliberate and self-conscious orality, based permanently on the use of writing and print, which are essential for the manufacture and operation of the equipment and for its use as well" (Ong, *Orality* 134). While ostensibly about the differences between cultures that use written communication and those that are reliant on oral communication, Ong's research raises complex challenges within contemporary composition studies, a field led by a new generation of instructors wrestling with technology's limits and affordances.

Instructors who employ multimodal methods must complicate the binary inherent in the contested term "Great Divide," confronting epistemological issues raised as technological advancements overtake human communication and restructure consciousness. John Hartley succinctly notes that "Ong is a theorist of media change" (206), thereby linking him as an acolyte of the media theorist Marshall McLuhan (209). Moreover, Hartley invokes Tom Pettit's "Gutenberg parenthesis," the idea that the advent of the printing press divided history into a primitive, preliterate era and a sophisticated, postliterate epoch, explaining how, "despite its dominance . . . , print-literacy is an exception in a much longer trajectory of human thought which may be in the process of restoring earlier modes of communication based on speech and instantaneity rather than space and time-delay" (207). In other words, today's computers rely on visual and auditory aspects of communication that hearken back to earlier anthropological periods when human beings could not rely solely on writing to convey information. Moreover, the ability to communicate with these digital tools (e.g., smartphones, tablets, and personal computers) develops a fluency within the discourse communities that use them similar to the way ancient peoples spoke to others. Hartley likens Ong's "primary orality" to pre-Gutenberg civilization (stuck in a prewriting stage), whereas "secondary orality" is akin to post-Gutenberg digital literacies. As Hartley explains, "This approach allows the topic of orality and literacy to be pursued in the era of the internet, digital media, mobile devices and social networks without reducing it to an argument about 'primitivism versus civilization'" (207). Hartley observes that human beings "are in a time of unprecedented convergence among oral, written, and print-literate modes, where oral forms like phatic communication are migrating to the web, the turn-taking modes of speech are augmented by links, photos, and file-sharing" (208). The blurring of communicative modes requires first-year composition classrooms to respond accordingly.

The theories developed in *Orality and Literacy* are broadly applicable and nuanced, with far-reaching implications. A salient issue is the traces left behind in writing, the "explicit or even implicit commitment to the formal study and formal practice of rhetoric [that] is an index of the amount of residual primary orality in a given culture" (Ong, *Orality* 109). While he notes the rise of computers, Ong argues that the residue of a primarily oral society is still evident. According to Bruce Gronbeck and Roberta Binkley, "[C]ontemporary culture is usefully seen as a period of 'secondary orality,' a literate culture where characteristics of oral society are reinscribed upon our lives, albeit in the form of electronic rather than face-to-face interactions" (480). Within this digitally wrought (and fraught) arena, astute scholars draw from ancient progenitors of today's composition studies. With regard to orality, Andrea Lunsford and Lisa Ede concede that "[d]espite the work of scholars such as Walter Ong, Kenneth Burke, and Jacques Derrida, many questions about the relationship of speech and writing remain unanswered, and, in some cases, unexplored" (46). They maintain that modern rhetoric lacks the "fully confident epistemology" found in Aristotle (47). *Orality and Literacy*, Ong's swan song, offers a new arrangement of Aristotle's familiar refrain.

One critic writing at the time *Orality and Literacy* was published nearly guaranteed that Ong's tune would never become a hit. Myron Tuman's 1983 review in *College English* recognizes the book's breadth while questioning Ong's "strict dichotomy between orality and technology"; the former is "an expression of the soul . . . innate and natural," while the latter is "a form of technology . . . alienated, artificial, and commercial, especially when transformed by the machinery of printing" (776). Tuman's disdain could stem from Ong's vocation as a Jesuit priest: "There is no Edenic world of speech that has been corrupted by a serpent in the guise of a stylus; there is instead only a single developmental history of our collective efforts to create a world and to understand and control the world we have created" (777). One of Tuman's better quips, however, belies his argument against *Orality and Literacy:* "Ong is wrong" (779). For the clever rhyme to work, this line must be recited aloud, a nod to the oral residue of a preliterate culture. Tuman continues, "For all the sweep of his writing, Ong has very little to say about such matters. Literacy for him remains part of the problem, not the solution; as the inevitable component of technology, its future is both assured and seemingly unrelated to our real concerns" (779). However, Tuman notes the link that Ong establishes between sound and conscious awareness: "For Ong it is sound, as spiritual breath, that unifies experience and makes us whole . . . [,] consciousness that emphasizes difference and distance" (771).

To ground this discussion, it is helpful to read closely a chapter of *Orality and Literacy* alongside Ong's subsequent essay on consciousness, "Writing Is a Technology that Restructures Thought." Caught in the interstitial period between the Athenian oral tradition and the fecund written era, rhetoric flourished, albeit carrying traces that retain "much of the old oral feeling for thought and expression as basically agonistic and formulaic" (Ong, *Orality* 108). A paradigmatic shift occurred when writing overtook oratory as the dominant form of public discourse. Nonetheless, every document retains oral residue because individuals silently speak words in their heads as they compose or read. In "Writing Is a Technology that Restructures Thought," Ong clarifies the aural connection between reading text and the oral roots of human communication:

> For a text to be intelligible, to deliver its message, it must be reconverted into sound, directly or indirectly, either really in the external world or in the auditory imagination. All verbal expression, whether put into writing, print, or the computer, is ineluctably *bound to sound forever.* (31; emphasis added)

This shift from visual, semiotic markings to auditory (albeit interiorized) impulses enables readers to comprehend an author's meaning. When Ong asserts that "we have interiorized the technology of writing so deeply that without tremendous effort we cannot separate it from ourselves or even recognize its presence and influence" ("Writing" 24), he gestures to the recursive tension between speech and writing by predicting the emerging importance of digital composition modes now dominating English courses and to the ways classical rhetoric fills existing gaps between orality and literacy. As he argues, silence (no matter how intrinsic it is to reading and writing processes) is never a lasting option: "Writing distances the word from the sound, reducing oral-aural evanescence to the seeming quiescence of visual space. But this distancing is not total or permanent, for every reading of a text consists of restoring it, directly or indirectly, to sound, vocally or in the imagination" (39). The rhetorical revolution from orality to literacy engendered the abstract thinking that enabled Ong to craft his layered work, a form of thinking "more abstract, which is to say more removed from the sound world into the space world of sight" (42). At its most fundamental level, however, language is inherently phonological because the "alphabet operates more directly on sound as sound than the other scripts, reducing sound directly to spatial equivalents" (Ong, *Orality* 90). Later, Ong calls the alphabet "the ruthlessly efficient reducer of sound to space" since it is initially "memorized orally ... and then used for ... retrieval" and decoding (99–101). No matter how advanced written literacies become, sound is inescapable.[3]

Technology's dizzying development continues to restructure consciousness, inviting the use of proven oral-based modes of meaning-making to interpret new media. By linking newer first-year composition pedagogies with ancient rhetoric—connections traced by Ong between orality, sound, writing, and consciousness—instructors may embrace the benefits of multimodal assignments. Ong credits writing with initiating what print and computers perpetuate for good and ill—"the reduction of dynamic sound to quiescent space, the separation of the word from the living present, where alone spoken words can exist" (*Orality* 81). Multimodal assignments, given their interdisciplinarity, blend the oral and the textual, the aural and the visual, the presentational and the pedagogical; nevertheless, these new assignments are built on the same five canons of rhetoric that Cicero expounded in ancient Rome, canons that have guided the academy ever since. The prescient twentieth-century scholar Edward P. J. Corbett predicts rhetoric's "future in the continuing struggle for freedom," which will require effort; without intentionality, "we will inherit the alternatives of babble or silence" (208). This conflation of rhetoric with aurality is timely for the twenty-first-century composition classroom, as a key essay pointed out on the eve of the new millennium.

Darsie Bowden's 1995 article connects Ong's theories on consciousness with the inescapable sonic element in first-year English classes. In describing sound's prevalence, Bowden notes Jacques Derrida's concept of "'phonocentric orientation' . . . that spoken language, because it consists of sounds we utter (even to ourselves silently), is more 'interior' to consciousness than writing—in fact, that spoken language is inseparable from consciousness" (185). Bowden echoes something of practical concern for teachers: How can we help students find their authentic voices in writing? Bowden's claim might speak well to future editions of *Orality and Literacy*:

> Spoken language is naturally closer than writing to the lifespring, to consciousness, and to presence—all significant attributes of an orientation in which the spoken voice is the privileged term. Speech (conveyed by the human voice) gets closest to what's real, genuine, legitimate, or in other words, the endpoint or final objective of our meaning-making or communicating and does so in the most powerful way, through personal presence. (182)

Good writing, undeniably the goal of composition courses, involves an "intermingling of oral and written modes, with oral becoming the favored term" (Bowden 184). It should not be a "great leap" in pedagogy, therefore, to reintroduce actual human voices into a class that squelches verbal expression outside written lexis. By historicizing the influence of orality on literacy, Bowden demonstrates that the "use of 'voice' reflects the reinstitution of an oral component into the classroom in the form of talk—literal, active, and dramatic . . . , emphasizing not only what the student has to say but how the student says it in efforts to valorize and *author*-ize [their] words" (180). Ensuring that students' voices emanate from their writing is important because speakers are therefore "injected back into the discourse, implying that speech by its nature has more 'life' than writing" (182). Lifeless writing does little to inspire students to excel. Composition teachers should design assignments that employ sound in order to span the interjacent space between orality and literacy that rhetoric fills.

If arguments exist only on paper, untested by voices, students likely cannot support their views. The human voice conveys power, commanding attention. Too frequently, voices are untapped compositional tools, while hands alone are used in the service of writing. Ong's valuable voice deserves a hearing amid the din of contemporary scholars. As an experienced professor, critic, and theorist, Ong drafts concepts that ring with pedagogical language:

> Writing has enabled us to identify the orality . . . antecedent to it and to see how radically it differs from that orality. Writing has the power to liberate us . . . from the chirographic bias and confusion it creates, though complete liberation remains impossible. For all states of the word—oral, chirographic, typographic, electronic—impose their own confusions, which cannot be radically eliminated but only controlled by reflection. ("Writing" 47–48)

Ong's trailblazing *Orality and Literacy* prompts meaningful reflection and renewed attention, even decades after his death. Ironically, Ong writes in his most famous book among his six-hundred-work bibliography that "[m]ost books extant today were written by persons now dead. Spoken utterance comes only from the living" (*Orality* 101). Compositionists should listen to Ong's posthumous voice, which still offers sound advice, in order to meet new technological challenges.

Notes

1. Responses to Ong's magnum opus run the gamut from scathing to laudatory. Compositionists panned Ong's theories—especially after the publication of *Orality and Literacy*. Beth Daniell provides the sharpest critique of Ong's perspective on orality and literacy—namely, summarizing critics' charges of ethnocentrism, denigration of the term *orality* as a "pejorative," and the "essentialism of Ong's association of orality with women" ("Orality" 483). Daniell criticizes Great Leap research as biased by personal values, adopting "an isomorphic relationship between thought and language" (483). These valid

concerns could provide helpful context for reintroducing Ong's ideas to new generations.

2. John Hartley identifies David Olson and Nancy Torrance as the coiners of the moniker "Great Leap Theory" (213), a term that implies that Ong divides Western civilization into two distinct ages—before and after chirographic systems—that thought fundamentally differently, a simplification of his original argument.

3. Ekaterina Haskins recognizes the residual traces that Ong uncovers, yet Haskins also mentions the "surprising survival of the 'oral' tradition within the literary practices of philosophers and rhetoricians," noting that "[s]ome scholars have called into question the deterministic approach of such general theorists of orality as Walter Ong, who argued that the shift from oral to literate modes of communication causes drastic transformation in mentality" (158). It is this "drastic transformation"—of consciousness achieved by moving from orality toward literacy—that reifies Ong's essential notions, reinforcing the idea that his work deserves rereading.

Works Cited

Bowden, Darsie. "The Rise of a Metaphor: 'Voice' in Composition Pedagogy." *Rhetoric Review*, vol. 14, no. 1, 1995, pp. 173–88.
Corbett, Edward P. J. "Rhetoric, the Enabling Discipline." *Selected Essays of Edward P. J. Corbett*, edited by Robert J. Connors, Southern Methodist UP, 1989, pp. 192–208.
Daniell, Beth. "Orality." Enos, pp. 480–84.
———. "The Uses of Literacy Theory: The Great Leap and the Rhetoric of Retreat." Conference on College Composition and Communication, Mar. 1987, Atlanta. *ERIC*, files.eric.ed.gov/fulltext/ED281197.pdf.
Enos, Theresa, editor. *Encyclopedia of Rhetoric and Composition*. Garland, 1996.
Gronbeck, Bruce E., and Roberta Binkley. "Walter J. Ong." Enos, pp. 479–80.
Hartley, John A. E. "After Ongism: The Evolution of Networked Intelligence." Ong, *Orality*, pp. 205–21.
Haskins, Ekaterina. "Rhetoric between Orality and Literacy: Cultural Memory and Performance in Isocrates and Aristotle." *Quarterly Journal of Speech*, vol. 87, no. 2, 2001, pp. 158–78.
Lunsford, Andrea A., and Lisa S. Ede. "On Distinctions between Classical and Modern Rhetoric." *Essays on Classical Rhetoric and Modern Discourse*, edited by Robert J. Connors et al., Southern Illinois UP, 1984, pp. 37–49.

Ong, Walter J. *Orality and Literacy: The Technologizing of the Word*. 30th anniversary ed., Routledge, 2012.

———. "Writing Is a Technology that Restructures Thought." *The Written Word: Literacy in Translation*, edited by Gerd Bauman, Clarendon Press, 1986, pp. 23–50.

Tuman, Myron C. "Words, Tools, and Technology." *College English*, vol. 45, no. 8, 1983, pp. 769–79.

Geneva Smitherman's "Toward a National Public Policy on Language"

Staci M. Perryman-Clark

Geneva Smitherman, "Toward a National Public Policy on Language," *College English* (1987).

Geneva Smitherman, university distinguished professor emerita at Michigan State University and a pioneer in language policy education and African American language studies, has published more than fifteen books and 125 articles and essays ("Dr. Geneva Smitherman"). Her work is widely read across academic disciplines ranging from English studies and education to anthropology and psychology. Despite their broad appeal to diverse scholarship and practices, some of Smitherman's texts have become lost or, at the very least, are less visible when compared with her other work. This seems to be the case particularly in rhetoric and composition, where Smitherman's work focuses on language rights for students.

While scholars in rhetoric and composition are familiar with much of Smitherman's work on language policy, including articles such as "CCCC's Role in the Struggle for Language Rights" and "Students' Right to Their Own Language: A Retrospective," her essay "Toward a National Public Policy on Language" is less frequently included in the canon of scholarship on language rights and language policy. Given present-day policy debates concerning the so-called English-only movement as well as recent immigration proposals from a previous administration that focus on English-language proficiency—and the likelihood that such proposals will resurface in the future—I see the present moment as a highly opportune time to revisit Smitherman's lost text in rhetoric and composition.[1] Given the recent events surrounding the policing of Black bodies, especially in relation to linguistic and racial justice in the wake of the murders of George Floyd and Breonna Taylor; the Conference on College Composition and Communication's "This Ain't Another Statement! This Is a DEMAND for Black Linguistic Justice!"; and the CCCC's call for proposals for its 2022 annual convention, a call that demanded a heighted awareness of the relationships among diversity, equity and justice, and enrollment management in US higher education ("2022 Call"), there couldn't be a more appropriate time to revisit Smitherman's text.

While the numbers or any other analytics one might use to measure scholarly impact might be imprecise and are not my focus here, a simple *Google Scholar* search indicates that "Toward a National Public Policy on Language" is cited by fifty-one sources. In comparison, Smitherman's article "CCCC's Role in the Struggle for Language Rights" is cited by 107 sources, "The Blacker the Berry the Sweeter the Juice" by 137 sources, "Students' Right to Their Own Language: A Retrospective" by 104, and *Talkin and Testifyin: The Language of Black Americans*, one of Smitherman's most popular books, by 2,540, according to *Google Scholar*'s h-index analysis. In fact, the publication under discussion here is not in the top thirty most commonly cited works by Smitherman. This one indicator highlights the contrasts among the number of citations for some of Smitherman's most frequently cited scholarship. While some of Smitherman's texts have fewer citations than "Toward a National Public Policy on Language," this text clearly falls in the second-to-middle tier of referenced sources for a widely cited and influential scholar such as Smitherman. As such, I think it's time that we revisit the impact of this article and its potential contribution to current debates regarding linguistic diversity and the relationship of such diversity to public policy.

Again, I acknowledge that analytics such as those used by *Google Scholar* are not a definitive measure of citation engagement or scholarly worth and therefore should not be overemphasized. Nonetheless, such measures for scholarly engagement can be helpful. For example, John Trimbur's essay "Linguistic Memory and the Politics of U.S. English" is cited fifty-nine times, according to *Google Scholar*. Trimbur's essay begins with the notion that the Founding Fathers were intentional in their refusal to designate English as the official language (575–76), an argument often referenced by opponents of English-only legislation, legislation currently adopted by thirty-one states. Trimbur's nuanced understanding of language policy, however, asserts that just because the Founding Fathers did not designate English as the official language does not mean that the United States did not have a covert national language policy. Furthermore, Trimbur contends, the "suppression of African languages through the slave trade and the formation of a plantation labor force offers the most revealing evidence of how language policy operated covertly, yet systematically, in the colonial and national period" (576). Trimbur's essay concludes by urging rhetoric and composition to "take up the unfinished business" of students' right to their own language (586), a call that Smitherman first made in "Toward a National Public Policy on Language" (31). At that time, Smitherman called for a national public policy on language that "(1) teach[es] standard edited English as the language of wider communication, (2) recognize[s] the legitimacy of nonmainstream languages and dialects and promote[s] mother tongues, along with English, as the medium of instruction, and (3) promote[s] the learning of one or more additional languages, such as Spanish or other relevant languages" (Trimbur 586). In taking up this call, Trimbur asserts that national language policy is not simply an affirmation of students' home languages, but, more importantly, it recognizes the benefits and sophistications associated with the ability of every speaker to be multilingual and to communicate in a global context (579).

In short, here is why we need to revisit "Toward a National Public Policy on Language" as a lost text. First, as Trimbur acknowledges, the business of the CCCC—and perhaps rhetoric and composition more broadly—that would affirm our commitment and promise to affirm students' rights to their own language is unfinished. Second, this work is unfinished in large part because of our inability as scholars in rhetoric and composition to influence effectively public policy against English-only movements. Third, and finally, I think that the Trump administration's stances on English add another layer to this unfinished business, particularly in times when political pundits are so quick to reference the intentions of our Founding Fathers. Let me offer just a few examples that validate my concern that such stances can easily resurface in the future—and still fester.

Let's first consider the English-only campaign during the 2016 and 2020 US presidential election seasons. Despite the fact that the majority of the US Latinx community is English-speaking, it is noteworthy that

Donald Trump refused to campaign in Spanish, a move that contrasted with the campaigns of politicians from both major political parties (Goldmacher). (As of 2020 Spanish was still missing from Trump's campaign website.) Such a move underscored his "Make America Great Again" rhetoric and xenophobic practices, particularly those directed at Mexicans and Mexican Americans. Fast-forward, though. In 2018 three different organizations—U.S. English, ProEnglish, and English First—all met with Trump administration aides (Cremean).[2] In addition, when Trump took office, the White House removed all bilingual content from its web pages (Sonnad). And, finally, let us not forget Trump's previous pitches to require immigrants to demonstrate English-language proficiency in order to immigrate to the United States (Hauslohner).

Much more recently we have seen the CCCC renew its call for linguistic justice with the statement approved by the 2020 executive committee, "This Ain't Another Statement! This is a DEMAND for Black Linguistic Justice!" In the spirit of social justice and activism, the statement demands that

1. teachers stop using academic language and standard English as *the accepted communicative norm*, which reflects White Mainstream English!
2. teachers stop teaching Black students to code-switch! Instead, we must teach Black students about anti-Black linguistic racism and white linguistic supremacy!
3. political discussions and praxis center Black Language as teacher-researcher activism for classrooms and communities!
4. teachers develop and teach Black Linguistic Consciousness that works to decolonize the mind (and/or) language, unlearn white supremacy, and unravel anti-Black linguistic racism!
5. Black dispositions are centered in the research and teaching of Black Language! (emphasis mine)

At a first glance the statement, which contends that "teachers stop using academic language and standard English as the accepted communicative norm, which reflects White Mainstream English," seems in conflict with Smitherman's call for teaching "standard edited English as the language of wider communication" (Trimbur 586); however, on closer examination, one notices that Smitherman does not privilege edited American English as the language of wider communication. The language of wider communication does not suggest that mainstream English is the only acceptable communicative form. It is simply the language that is used most widely and most frequently. Likewise, the 2020 CCCC statement does not suggest that we not teach edited American English. Instead, it states that we should not teach edited American English as the only acceptable mode of communication. Smitherman's article merely asks that it be taught as a wider form of communication, which suggests that edited American English is simply the mode of communication that is most typically understood by speakers in the United States. In short, wider communication suggests wider usage. One should not necessarily conflate wider or most frequent usage with acceptability and suitability.

The CCCC's nuanced understanding of language rights in relation to Black lives and survival is part of the reason why we must not only revisit Smitherman's text but also place it within current contexts and in relation to updated statements such as the 2020 CCCC statement. Given the timeliness of Smitherman's text, especially in conjunction with the 2020 police killings of George Floyd and Breonna Taylor and with the 2020 presidential election, where both major political parties were forced to confront the rhetoric of police brutality and the Black Lives Matter movement, it is paramount that the CCCC as an organization and writing teachers connect linguistic justice with racial justice and Black lives. A rebuttal of English-only discourse, then, requires an acknowledgment that the survival and livelihood of racial minorities hinges in large part on the acceptance of historically oppressed communities and on their freedom to celebrate and use their languages.

Given the recent updates to how we understand race, language, and power in a twenty-first-century context, now is the time to revisit Smitherman's text. In recent years we have witnessed key historical events that have affected the lives of Black bodies. While many might read Smitherman's 1987 text as more palatable in tone than the tone of current discussions of language, Smitherman's article was actually quite revolutionary and controversial for its time, in much the same way that the stark tone of the 2020 CCCC statement has provoked controversy in recent years. Further, "[t]hrough her activism from 1987 to present, as Chair of the Language Policy Committee, she lobbied for the support of the National Council of Teachers of English (NCTE) and the Conference on College Composition and Communication (CCCC) to launch campaigns and policies, such as the National (multilingual) Language Policy, in opposition to oppressive 'English-Only' legislation around the country" ("Dr. Geneva Smitherman"). Her activism overlapped with the English-only movement and with the formation of English-only political organizations including U.S. English, which was established in 1983 ("About U.S. English"), and ProEnglish, founded in 1994 ("About Us"). Put simply, the work and activism of the CCCC, which is reflected in its 2020 statement, is borne on the shoulders of Smitherman's work and her previous political activism, both of which are associated with current material and physical conditions affecting the lives of people of color.

Smitherman has been a pioneer not only for language rights in the United States but also for helping the field understand the benefits of multilingualism and the ways in which composition scholars can articulate these benefits in public discourse in pursuit of civic engagement and political activism. Given that the updated CCCC statement asserts that "political discussions and praxis center Black Language as teacher-researcher activism for classrooms and communities," I conclude with Smitherman's final words in "Toward a National Public Policy on Language," which provide us with a scholarly and intellectual framework for tangibly engaging multilingualism in civic discourse:

> As a third step, speech, language, and composition professionals are the ideal group to conduct the language awareness campaigns needed to accompany the movement for a language policy. These campaigns would be geared toward combating the myths about language use. Campaigns would be conducted through newspapers, television and radio programs, magazines, and in other popular media, in community forums, churches, and throughout the general public domain. The objective would be to combat the myths and misconceptions about both non-mainstream languages and the language of wider communication. (34)

Today we have many more platforms from which to work on messaging. It is time that we use Smitherman's text as an opportunity to finally take care of our unfinished business.

Notes

1. In *Students' Right to Their Own Language: A Critical Sourcebook*, my co-editors, David E. Kirkland and Austin Jackson, and I included three of Geneva Smitherman's articles—"CCCC's Role in the Struggle for Language Rights," "Students' Right to Their Own Language: A Retrospective," and "African American Student Writers in the NAEP, 1969–88/89 and the 'Blacker the Berry, the Sweeter the Juice'"—but we did not include "Toward a National Public Policy on Language" in this canon of sources on language rights and language policy. While it's hard for me to theorize precisely why "Toward a National Public Policy on Language" was not included in this collection, I might surmise that this article has become not only one of the lost texts of rhetoric and composition but also perhaps one of the lost texts of Geneva Smitherman.

2. U.S. English, ProEnglish, and English First are political advocacy organizations dedicated to preserving English as the official language of the United States.

Works Cited

"About Us." *ProEnglish*, 2022, proenglish.org/about-us/.

"About U.S. English." *U.S. English*, 16 Feb. 2018, www.usenglish.org/about-us/.

Cremean, Samantha Yenger. "Inside the Racist Push to Make English the United States' Official Language." *The Establishment*, 17 July 2018, theestablishment.co/inside-the-racist-push-to-make-english-the-united-states-official-language/index.html.

"Dr. Geneva Smitherman, Distinguished Professor of English and Director of the African American Language and Literacy Program at Michigan State University." *Association for Black Culture Centers*, www.abcc.net/geneva-smitherman.

Goldmacher, Shane. "Trump's English-Only Campaign." *Politico*, 23 Sept. 2016, www.politico.com/story/2016/09/donald-trumps-english-only-campaign-228559.

Hauslohner, Abigail. "Trump Wants a Different Kind of Immigrant: Highly Skilled Workers Who Speak English and Have Job Offers." *The Washington Post*, 15 May 2019, www.washingtonpost.com/.

Perryman-Clark, Staci, et al., editors. *Students' Right to Their Own Language: A Critical Sourcebook*. Bedford / St. Martin's, 2014.

Smitherman, Geneva. "CCCC's Role in the Struggle for Language Rights." *College Composition and Communication*, vol. 50, no. 3, 1999, pp. 349–76.

———. "Students' Right to Their Own Language: A Retrospective." *The English Journal*, vol. 84, no. 1, 1995, pp. 21–27.

———. *Talkin and Testifyin: The Language of Black America*. 1977. Wayne State UP, 1986.

———. "Toward a National Public Policy on Language." *College English*, vol. 49, no. 1, 1987, pp. 29–36.

Sonnad, Nikhil. "The White House Is Ignoring 41 Million US Spanish Speakers." *Quartz*, 12 Feb. 2018, qz.com/1204953/the-white-houses-spanish-language-site-is-still-missing/.

"This Ain't Another Statement! This Is a DEMAND for Black Linguistic Justice!" *Conference on College Composition and Communication*, July 2020, cccc.ncte.org/cccc/demand-for-black-linguistic-justice.

Trimbur, John. "Linguistic Memory and the Politics of U.S. English." *College English*, vol. 68, no. 6, 2006, pp. 575–88.

"2022 Call for Proposals." *Conference on College Composition and Communication*, cccc.ncte.org/cccc/call-2022. Accessed 16 May 2022.

Part Five

After 1992

The Importance of Being Readers Reading in Robert P. Yagelski's *Writing as a Way of Being*

Asao B. Inoue

> Robert P. Yagelski, *Writing as a Way of Being: Writing Instruction, Nonduality, and the Crisis of Sustainability* (Hampton Press, 2011)

In her review of Robert Yagelski's *Writing as a Way of Being: Writing Instruction, Nonduality, and the Crisis of Sustainability*, Paula Mathieu calls the book "revolutionary," saying, "This is a radical book" (177). I agree. While I'd already been practicing labor-based grading contracts before the book was published, this book provides a good argument for why labor-based grading in a writing classroom makes sense, even beyond my own arguments for it being a practice that opposes racism and white language supremacy.[1] And it's this potential for the field and its teachers that I think we risk losing by ignoring Yagelski's text.

Now, Yagelski isn't arguing for grading contracts, or explicitly antiracist pedagogies. He's thinking about the ontological aspects of the act of writing next to the ways everyone is connected to the earth, and how we might cultivate more sustainable lives. But it is this ecological, interconnected argument that I find makes much of his discussion agreeable to antiracist writing assessment in classrooms. If part of being an antiracist teacher is orienting ourselves against harmful systems and disciplinary structures that created inequality, and if that orientation is to be one that is ecologically sustainable, helping us all see our humanities (plural), then Yagelski may very well offer us valuable ways to understand this practice as being, that is, writing as an ontological act that also can be an antiracist orientation.

It would seem that the environmental aspect to his discussion could limit his book's scope or reach in writing classrooms. For instance, it may seem to offer less to many classrooms that don't discuss explicitly the environment or sustainable living. However, there are lessons that are critical for all teachers in this book that do not focus on the environmental aspects of his discussion. Focusing our attentions in classrooms with students on the act of writing itself, on what it offers us in the moment beyond a future product or writing goal, is a mindful act that can bring people joy or relieve stress, or provide ways to understand ourselves through the act of writing. Writing to write and noticing as you write can be a kind of liberatory act that is compassionate to ourselves. Understanding Yagelski's critique of the Cartesian paradigm of writing instruction that is typically used in schools is also vital for any teacher to understand. These kinds of experiences and insights can be deeply meaningful to teachers and students, no matter their political orientations or goals for their courses.

In the book, Yagelski argues that writing might be taught as an ontological practice. This is opposed to conventional process pedagogies that teach writing as purely transactional, an act based on the Cartesian duality of mind versus body. In the "Cartesian view of writing," students are habituated in school to act as if they are autonomous beings, separated from their environments, and separated from their peers (Yagelski 47). That Cartesian way of teaching writing assumes that we are not all interconnected, that we learn and act in the world purely from individual motive and goals without a need to consider too carefully the needs and motives of others, the things around us, our environment, our histories, what happened to who in this place where we learn, write, and do things. Yagelski explains how typical schooling works against our interrelatedness to the world:

> The basic lesson of conventional schooling, then, is less a matter of learning what is outside us than learning that there is something outside us that we can see, describe, and understand, a something that is fundamentally separate from our selves. To put it in simpler terms, in school we teach separateness rather than interconnectedness; we see a world defined by duality rather than unity. As a result we promote an idea of community as a collection of discrete, autonomous individuals rather than a complex network of beings who are

inherently interconnected and inextricably part of the ecosystems on which all life depends. (17)

A complex network of interconnected beings who are also interconnected to the ecosystems around them, the idea of community as a complex network of beings who are inextricably a part of their lived ecosystems, these ideas made into daily practices—not just classroom practices (Yagelski is thinking far wider than just what happens in writing classrooms)—seem like good writing lessons for all of us.

Pausing to Read My Students

I often ask my students to pause for a minute or two as they read texts outside of our class sessions and post something to the class on our private messaging technology, for instance, *Slack*. This post is usually something that tells us how they are feeling in that moment of reading, what they are thinking about, or what's troubling them. It might also be just a picture of their reading environment, showing us where they are doing that labor for our class. We get these messages and pictures on our phones and computers in real time.

The practice of pausing and posting to each other something about our feelings or thoughts in the act of reading offers a way to be connected as we are going about our daily lives and labors for the class. It helps us know each other a little bit more through our daily routines and work rhythms that make up each of our lives. It values and makes present the doing of reading as we do it. It perhaps resists thinking of our readings as just texts to finish and process in order to do something else more important, like talk about them or use the ideas we take from them. It helps us see the embodied human ways we struggle or find joy in our reading practices. It keeps our emotional states and environments connected to the reading labors asked of everyone in the class. As a teacher, it's really enlightening—and encouraging—to see where and how students do the work we ask of ourselves. It makes me feel more connected to my students. I get to see just a little glimpse of them doing the work of the class, and that's humanizing for me. I'm guessing many of my students feel the same way, at least several each semester tell me so.

Yagelski's discussion helps me think more deeply about this practice. The pausing and posting allows my students and me to make visible our interconnectedness and our humanness. It helps us experience in a small way the experience of another's reading of a shared text, while also helping that person pause and notice their experience of reading in the act of reading. It asks us to use writing, even if just a few words, to make ourselves and our reading, to express the latent meaning we are trying to conjure from and in words. It shows our learning as we learn with each other, or maybe for each other. We are not just learning or reading separately. We are trying to do it together, to be in our separate readings together, just as our learning and selves are already interconnected in other ways.

In a recent graduate course on judgment and bias in US narratives, we read Eduardo Bonilla-Silva's *Racism without Racists*. I asked the students to pause a few times during their reading sessions and post a picture and tell us what was on their minds or how they were feeling in that moment. Mike, a fortyish, white male student posted: "Lots to chew on here—I recognize pretty much all of these arguments and frames and also the ways in which folks made them without seeing the effects of their rhetoric. It's nice to have everything laid out in one place!" This came with a picture of his dog next to him in his reading place at home, maybe a chair in a quiet room, a kitchen? His dog shows up a lot in his pictures to us. I think of his dog always next to him when I think of Mike doing the labors for our class at home. He works for the university full-time, and is thoughtful about pedagogy. He reads carefully always, but he often keeps the ideas at arm's distance from him in order to see and think about them better. And he appears to get much joy and ease from his dog.

Kendall, an early-twenties, Black female student, posts: "Grateful for the mindfulness break because this book. . . . Had to listen to my favorite, Earth, Wind, and Fire, and relish in my love of being black." She takes a screen capture of her phone. It's the cover of the album *The Eternal Dance*. Bonilla-Silva's book discusses the ways white people talk about race, how they perpetuate racism while proclaiming to not be racist. I believe it's likely a bit stressful for her. So relishing and proclaiming her Blackness is important at this moment. I'm glad she gets this opportunity to do so. It makes her in a wonderful way. From the picture, it appears she's listening to a good song too, "That's the Way of the World." I imagine Kendall taking a walk outside in the warm Arizona air, the sun almost ready to set. Her post is at 5:09 p.m. As the easy rhythms of the song surround her, they sing about recollecting "sorrowful days" and about the future "pass[ing]" and "disappear[ing]." They sing in Kendall's ear about finding "peace of mind" and remaining young, "'cause you're never, never old."

Delena, an early-twenties, white-passing Latina, offers more words in her post, but she thinks through her acts of writing a lot—that is, writing is her act of thinking often. Like the other students, this is a typical kind of post from her. She uses the pausing to think through her emotional and intellectual responses to the text, blending them together. She starts with a reference to her picture, a selfie:

> My face while reading this book. The deeper I get, the more I want to scream. How can these quotes be real? This has got to be a joke, right?
>
> BUT ITS NOT. Seeing the ways in which whites justify their racist takes on life makes me cringe, while also inspiring shame around my own perceptions on race. Do I employ these strategies, and if I do, who have I hurt? Even though I am a Hispanic woman, I do not claim to be a POC. I'm white, and seeing these "arguments" for justifying deeply entrenched racism is a hard one to swallow.
>
> I love it.

Delana's post is like her in class. She's vocal, expressive, thoughtful. She seamlessly mixes her emotional response to the text with an interrogation of herself, her own habits of language. She keeps her own complex racial identity complicated. I see her talking to herself as she reads, screaming, like I would, maybe reading something to her partner. In this post, she feels like her words to me. And I think about her human and compassionate response that comes into being here: "Do I employ these strategies ... who have I hurt?"

All these posts come in one channel in the *Slack* application. I see them together as they accumulate over four days. In a way, it feels like us reading together, with each other, for each other. We all inter-are reading Bonilla-Silva.

Returning to Yagelski

Ultimately, I wonder how much teachers and students in writing classrooms today explore writing as an ontological practice, as a way of being? I think most of us (writing teachers) want to. I think Yagelski is prompting us to consider this in the book. When I ask writing teachers what they want from their students, they often tell me things like, "I want my students to feel confident in their writing"; "I want them to love writing as I do"; "I want them to experience writing's power to liberate, to engage, to know, and to question." These are good things, I believe, things I know firsthand that writing can offer anyone. I wonder if they equate to another kind of purpose for students and their writing in our classrooms, one I hear Yagelski asking us to consider: wanting our students to feel confidence, love, and liberation *because they are writing* in this moment, not because they wrote about something already. Writing isn't an accomplishment, rather an accomplishing. It's the difference between a trophy in one's hand and running the race.

But as Yagelski explains in his preface, these things are not how writing is typically taught in schools and colleges (xv). When reflecting on a writing experience with other National Writing Project teachers, he says that the power of the experience of writing that he felt with all those other teachers "was missing from the experience of writing that students tend to have in school, where the focus is on the production of a narrow range of texts constrained by rigid conventions, where the purpose of writing is almost always to demonstrate mastery and to be judged" (xiv). He goes on, "We teach students that writing is a procedure rather than a way of experiencing themselves as beings in an inherently interconnected world" (xv). Writing as experiencing oneself in an interconnected world. I wonder: If we help students do that kind of writing, then would we be getting them to write compassionately—that is, can our language acts be ontological acts of compassion?

These ideas sound very philosophical and abstract, something likely not for an introductory writing classroom, but maybe they are, maybe they are more accessible than one might initially think. What Yagelski is talking about is centering the writing classroom on the experience of writing, on the act of languaging itself, not on what gets produced from that experience, even though those products are still circulated and discussed, judged. Many of us may think we focus on the act of writing already. We assign and scaffold a lot of writing. We write every week. We do writing in class. We reflect on what we wrote and how we wrote it. We don't grade all the writing we assign, and we assign a lot of different kinds of writing. But that's not exactly what Yagelski is saying, at least not how I read him.

He's not saying that we can just assign writing. I hear him asking us to teach writing by teaching students how to be *in that writing*, to stop thinking primarily about what that writing is supposed to do after you're done with it. Yagelski is arguing that if writing is an ontological act then writing as *means* is more important than the *ends* of our writing processes or the products we give to others. As a teacher, the book makes me continually ask: How do I teach students to notice what happens to them during the experience of languaging? How do I help them feel language as a practice toward being in the world, a practice that affords you some kind of awareness of yourself in an interconnected world? This isn't simply writing process theory recast in ecological terms. He's not asking us to teach process. He's saying the process itself is ontological, if we pay attention to it, and that is the goal.

Yagelski makes a distinction between an experience we might have in the world and the experience of writing about that experience. He calls the latter, the one we often ask students to do in our classrooms, a "rendering into language" (73). And while he admits that our languaging may very well influence any given experience in the world we may have, our language and the experience of rendering into language something else is not that something else. So we have two kinds of experiences, he says, that matter in writing classrooms: one, experiences in our life, and two, experiences of writing about those other experiences. But, Yagelski explains, and here's the difference I'm trying to understand better for my own teaching and writing life, "In the end, the moment [the worldly experience] simply was, and I was at that moment" (73). What does this mean? How do I enact it meaningfully in my classroom? A bit later, Yagelski thinks more carefully about the second kind of experience:

> As I write, I *am*—but not *because* of the writing; rather the writing intensifies my awareness of myself, my sense of being, which is prior to but, right now, coterminous with this act of writing. . . . I *am* as I

am writing. The *writing* does not create me, but in the *act* of writing I *am*; by writing I reaffirm and proclaim my being in the here and now. The act of writing, in this sense, is a way of being; it is an ontological act. (104)

Ultimately, I think Yagelski's book asks us to shift our classroom practices, to "shift our theoretical gaze from the written text to the self writing—from the writer's writing to the *writer writing*" (107). I think my pause and post reading activity mentioned above enacts this kind of language as ontological pedagogy. It helps my students and me focus on readers reading, not simply the readings we read. It keeps us human, interconnected, and maybe helps us toward compassion. I think the practice of learning literacy, of languaging in classrooms and schools and colleges, needs to center more of ourselves in our practices of reading and writing. We might find some social justice movements, some antiracist awareness and action, in our writing as one way of being among others who are writing alongside us.

If as teachers of writing we do this shift with students, our classrooms might be radical, revolutionary, maybe even revelatory for our students and ourselves. It's not easy to do when our programs, departments, and schools demand that we hold to their standards and rubrics, or teach to a set of predefined outcomes, but it's not impossible. Teaching using outcomes, or even a prescriptive rubric, doesn't mean that your students will do that kind of writing better. It does mean they'll be judged against it though. And that may be the main lesson they learn.

And if this is true, then there is little if any actual pedagogical value in unified rubrics, standards, and outcomes, beyond weeding through lots of different students, creating groups of haves and have-nots. There's lots of political and institutional value to predefined, universal standards, rubrics, and outcomes. But those values don't teach students how to be writers writing, or readers reading, compassionate *languagelings being* in and through language. They don't teach how to mindfully, ethically, and sustainably exist in an ever-changing world with ever-changing language practices. They don't help us in our interconnectedness become antiracist, orienting ourselves together against harmful white supremacist systems and histories.

But when I think of what might be most meaningful to my students in my writing classes, I wonder, could it be ontological in nature? Could it be their own experiencing of their interconnectedness, of their own human *beingness* among other humans *being*?

Note

1. I have argued in several places for the use of labor-based grading contracts for writing classrooms, which focus only on effort or labor completed as a way to calculate course grades (Inoue, "Grade-less Writing Course," *Labor-Based Grading Contracts*, and *Antiracist Writing Assessment Ecologies*). This focus on the labor of reading and writing as a way to determine what is expected of students in writing classrooms is similar to writing as an ontological act. Yagelski's view of teaching writing as ontological is similar to the ecological metaphor for writing assessment I offer in *Antiracist Writing Assessment Ecologies*. In fact, I discuss his ideas in that book, which helps explain the ways that the various elements of assessment ecologies "inter-are" or are interrelated to each other (93–95).

Works Cited

Inoue, Asao B. *Antiracist Writing Assessment Ecologies: Teaching and Assessing Writing for a Socially Just Future*. WAC Clearinghouse / Parlor Press, 2015.

———. "A Grade-less Writing Course That Focuses on Labor and Assessing." *First-Year Composition: From Theory to Practice*, edited by Deborah Teague and Ronald Lunsford, Parlor Press, 2014, pp. 71–110.

———. *Labor-Based Grading Contracts: Building Equity and Inclusion in the Compassionate Writing Classroom*. UP of Colorado / WAC Clearinghouse, 2019.

Mathieu, Paula. Review of *Writing as a Way of Being: Writing Instruction, Nonduality, and the Crisis of Sustainability*, by Robert P. Yagelski. *Composition Studies*, vol. 42, no. 2, 2014, pp. 175–78.

Yagelski, Robert P. *Writing as a Way of Being: Writing Instruction, Nonduality, and the Crisis of Sustainability*. Hampton Press, 2011.

Becoming Which Composition? James Thomas Zebroski's "Toward a Theory of Theory for Composition Studies"

Julie Jung

> James Thomas Zebroski, "Toward a Theory of Theory for Composition Studies," *Under Construction: Working at the Intersections of Composition Theory, Research, and Practice*, edited by Christine Farris and Chris M. Anson (Utah State UP, 1998)

During my twenty-plus years as a faculty member, I have been asked on occasion by colleagues, usually those specializing in literary and cultural studies, to recommend an article they might assign as a way to introduce graduate students to the field of composition studies. Such requests carry for me the weight of heavy responsibility. I know the article I suggest might be for some students the only text in composition studies they will ever closely read and, further, that whatever article I suggest will inevitably exclude other ways of understanding the field, thereby minimizing the field's complexity. I've changed my suggestions over the years, depending on the rhetorical situation, but my selections are always guided by my sense that the recommended article constitutes a "hot potato," which is how one of my graduate school mentors, Tilly Warnock, used to describe readings that make you want to write. Hot potatoes, as I understand Tilly to mean, energize us not so much because they inspire argument through controversy but because they make apparent complexities deserving of further inquiry. For me, hot potatoes are texts that excavate the layers of a purportedly sedimented research subject, thereby exposing how that subject emerges and exists in relation to others.

When invited to select a lost text for this project, I felt that same weight of responsibility. There are so many. So, I returned to the hot-potato criterion to make my selection while remembering, too, the texts

I've recommended to colleagues in the past. In the end, I landed on James Thomas Zebroski's "Toward a Theory of Theory for Composition Studies," an essay that makes apparent the complexity of composition for those who might otherwise reduce and underestimate it (and us). Because it examines composition theory in historical, relational, and material terms, Zebroski's essay can be taken up and extended in many ways (hence its status as hot potato). In the spirit of this volume, I argue that Zebroski's essay warrants our renewed attention because it offers a framework for investigating how some histories of composition come to be written to the exclusion of others; in so doing, it calls on us to engage in practices that reconfigure social relations in order to create a more ethical and inclusive discipline.

Published in the edited collection *Under Construction: Working at the Intersections of Composition Theory, Research, and Practice*, Zebroski's essay has not garnered the attention it might have otherwise received had it been published in an academic journal. The ease with which scholars can access journal articles digitally, coupled with the fact that subscriptions to journals in writing studies (such as *College Composition and Communication*) are a benefit of membership in professional associations, collectively ensure that scholars are less likely to be exposed to scholarship published in edited collections—a reality that underscores the importance of this volume, which not only draws attention to some of these texts but also reminds readers of the unique affordance of the edited collection as a genre: its ability to demonstrate how a unifying thematic can sustain its complexity through interactions across difference.

Published in 1998, *Under Construction* came out during an era of disciplinary self-reflection, one that sought to legitimize the field, historicize its origins, and chart its future trajectories (Berlin; Bloom et al.; Brereton; Connors; Crowley; Rosner et al.). In his contribution to the collection, Zebroski draws on composition's historical relationship with literature to argue for a different way of engaging with theory. Rather than mimic the theoretical pursuits of literary scholars, Zebroski argues that we must pursue theory that "arises from the grassroots of composition," theory that makes use of key concepts from literary theory but that "still preserve[s] a space for us to learn about and teach writing" (32). His origin story for composition theory, which he situates in the late 1960s and early 1970s (mentioning in particular a 1966 conference at Dartmouth

College that informed James Moffett's groundbreaking *Teaching the Universe of Discourse*), suggests that we should build theory as he describes and that it was this way of theorizing that gave rise to the field in the first place (31).[1]

Zebroski builds his theory of theory by drawing on Bertell Ollman's philosophy of internal relations in order to explain how a seemingly stable and distinct concept (such as theory) emerges from a web of situated and dynamic relations, including the social formation that gave rise to and assigns value to that concept. Thus, the concept of a tree, Zebroski explains, can best be understood as tree-ing practices, which are enabled by the processes that constitute a given tree, including not only photosynthesis, reproduction, and climate but also capitalism, tourism, and insect infestation (35). Importantly, each of these processes also constitutes other trees, making every tree related to every other such that changes in one will affect them all.

Extending this ecological perspective to the scene of composition studies, Zebroski casts theory as theorizing practices that exist in dynamic relation to, affect, and are affected by other practices, such as teaching, curricular, administrative, and professional practices. It's here that we can get a sense of the exigency for Zebroski's project: in 1998 the field had become robust enough to invite internal conflict, but the manner of conflict (reductive categorizing and easy dismissals [e.g., expressivists] and calls to jettison an entire portion of our work [first-year composition]) threatened a solidarity necessary to combat the hegemony of literature. Zebroski's theory cuts across this divisiveness by "creat[ing] a place for nearly every sort of practice in our field" (44). But which practices find a place—and which don't—matters, since the inclusion or exclusion of any one practice will affect everything else.

In terms of its import for the field today, Zebroski's theorizing of theory as discursive-material practices that emerge from an ecology of relations parallels more recent scholarship in posthumanist rhetorics and writing studies (Edbauer; Gries; Mays; Rivers and Weber; Yood). But more than simply an earlier echo of rhetorical ecology—indeed, his essay's final section is titled "Implications of Understanding Composition as an Ecology of Practices" (43)—Zebroski's theory of theory can extend this scholarship through its conceptualization of relational time.

To explain how, I turn now to Zebroski's discussion of what he terms "temporalities of change" (45), a conceptual framework for tracking flows of connections between relational practices at different historical moments for purposes of generating new questions that can guide future research. Studying temporalities of change, or how change is experienced at differing historical moments, can prompt us to investigate the rate of flow between relational pairings and possible reasons for it. As an example, Zebroski argues that in the 1970s "the flow from teaching to theory" seemed faster and stronger than the flow from disciplinary practices of knowledge production to professional practices—most notably book publishing, which, according to Zebroski, "was nearly nonexistent in the 1970s and was slow and weak in the 1980s" (46). "What might account for this?" he asks (46). By way of answer, he observes that despite the outpouring of composition scholarship during this time there were very few presses willing to publish single-authored monographs in composition. The social formation of publishing plugged the flow. How the flow got unplugged—and the relations that made this possible—is a history worth writing. Indeed, as Zebroski writes, "There is a whole history that needs to be written about the publishers [e.g., Boynton/Cook] who were willing to take the chance" on composition (46).

Zebroski's concept of "temporalities of change" aligns with posthumanist frameworks that talk in terms of experientially emergent temporalities rather than universal time. As the historian Matthew S. Champion explains, "Temporalities are to time what materialities are to matter: a blurring of what might seem determined" (248). Such an understanding pushes back against a modern Western capitalist notion of clock time, which Laurie Gries explains

> is perceived as durational and linear—a succession of instant moments in which events unfurl into an irreversible future. Time is also decontextualized from matter, as well as from the rhythms and seasons of the earth, and divisible into uniform, quantifiable units. . . . [It] is conceived of as neutral, something that objects and persons move through, and abstract, without the capacity to affect actual change in the world. (30)

In contrast, posthumanist temporalities consider the "ongoing simultaneity of times, an ongoing *now*" (Omry 124)—with "now" itself understood "not as a static moment in time" but rather as an event "always undergoing a process of transformation" (Gries 54n9). In such a view, the world consists of multiple relational temporal systems in a constant state of becoming, each "opening up . . . into an unknown future" (Gries 37; see also Connolly 27).

To understand the idea of multiple temporal systems, consider Karen Barad's description of the temporalities of nuclear warfare:

> [H]ow can anything like a fixed, singular, and external notion of time retain its relevance or even its meaning? In a flash, bodies near Ground Zero become particulate, vaporized—while hibakushas, in the immediate vicinity and downwind, ingest radioactive isotopes that indefinitely rework body molecules all the while manufacturing future cancers, like little time bombs waiting to go off. What would constitute an event when an atomic bomb that exploded at one moment in time continues to go off? The temporality of radiation exposure is not one of immediacy; or rather, it reworks this notion, which must then rework calculations of how to understand what comes before and after, while thinking generationally. . . . Radioactive decay elongates, disperses, and exponentially frays time's coherence. Time is unstable, continually leaking away from itself. (63)

Given posthumanism's tendency to herald the potentialities of futures yet to come, Zebroski's historical approach makes an important contribution to the conversation: his concept of "temporalities of change" focuses our attention on past relational practices that are inextricably connected to the field's continuously emerging now. His theory of theory thus calls on us to consider how *composition history*—now defined as composition's historicizing practices, including the tendency to mark certain moments as worth noticing to the exclusion of others, such as that 1966 conference at Dartmouth—affects what composition becomes. Understood as such, *composition history* makes apparent multiple histories, each pushing toward a particular version of the field, and *becoming* becomes an opening up to an uncertain future that is disclosed by a particular version of the past.

One exemplary model of such a project—indeed, the project that reminded me to return to Zebroski's essay precisely because of the way it enacts a history-theory relationship—is Carmen Kynard's *Vernacular Insurrections: Race, Black Protest, and the New Century in Composition-Literacies*

Studies, which offers a layered historical approach to composition studies that I won't sufficiently address here. Truth be told, I originally wanted to select Kynard's hot potato as the focus of this essay, but since it was published in 2013, won the 2015 ELATE James A. Britton Award, and has been reviewed in *College Composition and Communication*, *Composition Studies*, and *Radical Teacher*, I thought maybe it wasn't lost enough to be described as such. Still, I suspect the book hasn't gotten the readership it deserves, so I sneak it in here as a second lost text—lost (*for whom?*) because not sufficiently read, contended with, and cited.[2]

"History is important," Jacqueline Royster and Jean Williams explain, "not just in terms of who writes it and what gets included or excluded, but also because history, by the very nature of its inscription as history, has consequences—social, political, cultural" (563). In brief, Kynard historizes and studies the literacies of Black freedom movements, demonstrating how these movements have both contributed to composition studies and gone largely unnoticed. This elision then authorizes the field to disregard how it has been shaped by Black intellectual, political, and artistic movements and traditions; Black college students' exercises of rhetorical agency; and Black writing teachers' pedagogical practices—all of which enact revolutionary possibilities that the field itself has yet to realize. Using as an example the impact of the Black Arts movement (BAM) of the mid-1960s—a different temporality than that of the 1966 Dartmouth conference—Kynard argues, "[M]ovements in our field that have been related to social justice, radical multiculturalism, black and brown solidarity, multimodal communication, and visual rhetoric have ideological and intellectual origins in BAM" (122). BAM's celebration of Black Language as well as Geneva Smitherman's early work and her seminal *Talkin and Testifyin* are cited by Kynard as evidence that multilingualism, linguistic border crossing, and transcultural rhetorics are not "'privileges' only afforded by our current 'historical moment,' as some compositionists have argued" (131). "The continual dislocation and erasure of BAM as a historiographic locus for composition studies," she concludes, "means that we have left its impact and ongoing importance unread and unreadable" (131). Including BAM, however, as Kynard argues and demonstrates, demands a radical rethinking not only of composition's origin story but also of contemporary stories, including, to name just one example, a tenacious White liberal narrative—and the web of relational practices constituting it—that posits "disadvantaged" students' mastery of "standard" written English as a universal ticket to economic equality and liberation (Kynard 93, 98, 104, 285–86n166).

Taken together, Zebroski's theory of theory for composition studies and Kynard's historiography of composition demand that we recognize a now in which practices of normative Whiteness infiltrate every relation constitutive of the field—including posthumanist theorizing practices that fail to recognize how possibilities for becoming are unevenly distributed, how, as decolonial and critical race theorists have long argued, "[t]heories of time are not only spatial, they are racial" (Solomon 87; see also Adeyemi; Glasbeek et al.).[3] They make apparent that how we tell the story of our field's emergence affects what we do in our classrooms, how we design and implement curricula, what we write about, and which scholarship gets published—and which doesn't. And, too, flowing back the other way, they suggest that how we teach, what we write about, which scholarship gets published, and which scholarship we choose to read can disclose alternative pasts capable of remaking the field otherwise.

Notes

1. In his analysis of how the term *native speaker* functioned rhetorically to construct English as a US and British export and to reproduce the myth of linguistic and cultural homogeneity in a postwar era, John Trimbur notes that the official title for the Dartmouth conference was "The Anglo-American Seminar on the Teaching of English" (143).

2. As empirically unsophisticated but nevertheless persuasive evidence in support of my suspicion, consider that as of today (29 May 2022) *Google Scholar* reports Kynard's book has been cited 150 times, whereas another award-winning book that was also published in 2013 and is informed by Greek and Western object-oriented philosophies has been cited 732 times. Comparing apples to oranges? Maybe, but you get my drift.

3. As Glasbeek and colleagues explain, "[C]olonial subjects occupy a place of 'belated-ness' in Western thought, such that their human agency is always considered to have evolved after, and in the shadow of, Western theories of subjectivity that focus on sovereignty, enlightenment, and rationality. . . . By definition, . . . colonial subjects are always 'belated' modern subjects" (744).

Works Cited

Adeyemi, Kemi. "The Practice of Slowness: Black Queer Women and the Right to the City." *GLQ: A Journal of Lesbian and Gay Studies*, vol. 25, no. 4, 2019, pp. 545–67.

Barad, Karen. "Troubling Time/s and Ecologies of Nothingness: Re-turning, Re-membering, and Facing the Incalculable." *New Formations*, vol. 92, 2017, pp. 56–86.

Berlin, James A. *Rhetorics, Poetics, and Cultures: Refiguring College English Studies*. National Council of Teachers of English, 1996.

Bloom, Lynn Z., et al., editors. *Composition in the Twenty-First Century: Crisis and Change*. Southern Illinois UP, 1996.

Brereton, John C. *The Origins of Composition Studies in the American College, 1875–1925: A Documentary History*. U of Pittsburgh P, 1996.

Champion, Matthew S. "The History of Temporalities: An Introduction." *Past and Present*, vol. 243, no. 1, 2019, pp. 247–54.

Connolly, William E. *A World of Becoming*. Duke UP, 2011.

Connors, Robert J. *Composition-Rhetoric: Backgrounds, Theory, and Pedagogy*. U of Pittsburgh P, 1997.

Crowley, Sharon. *Composition in the University: Historical and Polemical Essays*. U of Pittsburgh P, 1998.

Edbauer, Jenny. "Unframing Models of Public Distribution: From Rhetorical Situation to Rhetorical Ecologies." *Rhetoric Society Quarterly*, vol. 35, no. 4, 2005, pp. 5–24.

Glasbeek, Amanda, et al. "Postcolonialism, Time, and Body-Worn Cameras." *Surveillance and Society*, vol. 17, no. 5, 2019, pp. 743–46.

Gries, Laurie E. *Still Life with Rhetoric: A New Materialist Approach for Visual Rhetorics*. U of Colorado P, 2015.

Kynard, Carmen. *Vernacular Insurrections: Race, Black Protest, and the New Century in Composition-Literacies Studies*. State U of New York P, 2013.

Mays, Chris. "Writing Complexity, One Stability at a Time: Teaching Writing as a Complex System." *College Composition and Communication*, vol. 68, no. 3, 2017, pp. 559–85.

Omry, Keren. "Ozeki's Mirror Rooms: Posthumanism and *A Tale for the Time Being*." *New Centennial Review*, vol. 19, no. 2, 2019, pp. 117–38.

Rivers, Nathaniel A., and Ryan P. Weber. "Ecological, Pedagogical, Public Rhetoric." *College Composition and Communication*, vol. 63, no. 2, 2011, pp. 187–218.

Rosner, Mary, et al., editors. *History, Reflection, and Narrative: The Professionalization of Composition, 1963–1983*. Ablex, 1999.

Royster, Jacqueline Jones, and Jean C. Williams. "History in the Spaces Left: African American Presence and Narratives of Composition Studies." *College Composition and Communication*, vol. 50, no. 4, 1999, pp. 563–84.

Solomon, Marisa. "'The Ghetto Is a Gold Mine': The Racialized Temporality of Betterment." *International Labor and Working-Class History*, vol. 95, 2019, pp. 76–94.

Trimbur, John. "The Dartmouth Conference and the Geohistory of the Native Speaker." *College English*, vol. 71, no. 2, 2008, pp. 142–69.

Yood, Jessica. "A History of Pedagogy in Complexity: Reality Checks for Writing Studies." *Enculturation*, no. 16, 2013, enculturation.net/history-of-pedagogy.

Zebroski, James Thomas. "Toward a Theory of Theory for Composition Studies." *Under Construction: Working at the Intersections of Composition Theory, Research, and Practice*, edited Christine Farris and Chris M. Anson, Utah State UP, 1998, pp. 30–48.

Me, Myself, and All of Us: Revisiting Linda Brodkey's "Writing on the Bias"

Jonathan Alexander

Linda Brodkey, "Writing on the Bias," *College English* (1994)

The first thing I notice on rereading after a couple of decades Linda Brodkey's narrative essay, "Writing on the Bias," first published in *College English* in 1994, is how funny it is. The essay opens with a story of a very young, preschool Linda conducting survey research. Inspired by a recent visit from a census taker, Linda goes door to door in her neighborhood, asking folks when they think they are going to die and "recording their answers—one to a page—in a Big Chief tablet" (527). This opening anecdote was easy for me to forget, first reading this essay as a young scholar new to the field and the profession. Like Brodkey, I came from the working class, was a first-generation college student, and experienced formal education at times as stultifying and lacking creativity, even as I, also like Brodkey, assiduously learned all of the rules so that I could make it, be successful, and rise above my roots. A young man, the first in my family not just to get a PhD but also to graduate from college, I too felt increasingly alienated from my family, just as Brodkey, in "Writing on the Bias," describes the distance she felt from her working-class midwestern upbringing and family as she steadily moved into the middle class. My memory of this piece was of the particularity of that pain, of feeling myself a class traitor of sorts, and Brodkey's essay gave me my first way to articulate that feeling to myself.

Brodkey's essay remains significant, like Mike Rose's *Lives on the Boundary*, as a crucial reminder of the challenges facing many young writers in a society that has had difficulty recognizing its unmarked classist structures. "Writing on the Bias" has a particularly interesting contemporary relevance as more individuals grapple with classism and the persistence of class structures and class-based values; the essay shows us one writer's experience as they adeptly navigate class constructs and the strong affects generated by class positioning—some of which manifest as expectations for how to write and what kind of writing to like and emulate. As Brodkey puts it soon after relating her early attempt at survey research, "I would like to think that the story of my pre-school experience sustained me through what I now remember as many lean years of writing in school"—years in which she comes to experience how "school writing is to writing as catsup to tomatoes: as junk food to food" (528). Before that realization, however, Brodkey describes a kind of addiction to the rules learned in her classes and how "[a]t school I learned to trade my words for grades and degrees, in what might be seen as the academic equivalent of dealing in futures—speculations based on remarkably little information about my prospects as an academic commodity" (529). Accuracy of grammar trumped creativity and discovery, an approach that spilled over into her study of dance. She kept lists of what she felt she was supposed to read, retrospectively identifying herself as wanting to be "someone who liked literature" (534).

What were the stakes of such wanting? Brodkey the adult, the writing scholar, reads critically and ideologically the experiences of her younger self: making checklists of the great books she had read constituted "early tokens of my longing to replace the working-class fictions of my childhood with a middle-class fiction in which art transcends class" (534). Brodkey intuited how her class roots needed to be shaken off if she was to succeed in school, one of the most important and early encounters with the regulating systems of a culture. As she puts it, "There are times when I see each great book I filed as also recording an inoculation against the imputed ills of the working-class childhood that infected me and that in turn threatened the middle-class children with whom I studied" (535). I can certainly relate. I, too, filed away lists of the great books I'd read as I advanced through the canon. I believed these books would save me from the backwardness I began to see in my parents, my relatives, and my neighborhood.

In her younger years Brodkey worked hard at learning the rules, but as a scholar she looks back and wonders what was lost. She realizes that she had forgotten that story of young Linda, going door-to-door, collecting stories from her bewildered neighbors. And, in remembering it later in life, she writes about how "uneasy I became about having forgotten that I had learned to read and write at home before I started school" (527). Only with age and experience, degrees and success, can Brodkey reflect on her upbringing and schooling and realize the extent to which, on the one hand, "reading had . . . been part and parcel of the social fabric of home" (537), while, on the other, she had steadily been "taught to unlearn how I already read by a well-meaning and dedicated teacher" (537). The canon replaced drifting through library stacks; approved lists of fiction, often about elites, trumped the wandering eye of a young girl picking up books at random, drawn more by her interest than by anything else. Indeed, in class Linda was "reading about people, places, and lives utterly unlike mine" (537). At the same time, however, "[t]he educational opportunities that thrilled me contradicted most of what was expected of me at home" (543).

"Writing on the Bias" tracks the consequences of such a contradiction through its primary metaphor, the figure of sewing on the bias. *On the bias* refers to sewing "a line at a 45° angle" to the edge of the fabric, which "produc[es] a cut with some stretchability" ("Bias"). Brodkey learned about sewing on the bias from her mother, often while sitting by her mother's side, reading while her mother chatted about her life. Brodkey's description of such scenes are among the most moving in her essay:

> I suppose what I remember is seeing her thoroughly at ease, for the woman who sewed was entirely different from the one who cooked, cleaned, shopped, talked, and cared for her children. That woman was preoccupied, often weary and worried, and awkward in the presence of strangers. The woman who sewed was none of these. This woman would discuss ideas that animated her long before she ever spread out the newspapers she saved for her patterns, bought the fabric, laid out the pieces on the bias, cut the cloth, hand-basted and machine-stitched the darts and seams of a garment. (544)

For Brodkey, these early memories, now recovered, speak to a vibrant home life, the sharing of pleasures, the delight in talk, the care of craft—all of which Brodkey at school was invited to set aside, to forget, to exchange for the knowledge of books, of a canon, of the formal rules of reading and writing that could themselves be exchanged in the marketplace of professional education for increasing success and entrance into the middle class. But as Brodkey admits, however successful she may have become, "[f]luency has not ... made me a native speaker" (542). She can code-switch, making her way as a former working-class girl in the halls of the academy, but questions emerge, doubts surface, loss lingers at the edges. She poignantly considers how the idea that "the ostensible autonomy of middle-class professionals depends on children internalizing the rules that regulate reading (and writing) seems obvious to me. Less obvious, however, is what part reading and writing practices learned at home, and at variance with those learned at school, continue to play in my intellectual life" (537).

Making clearer that which is "less obvious" is the goal of "Writing on the Bias." In recovering this memory of sitting with her mother, Brodkey—the educated, well-read, astutely critical scholar of writing—can read that early scene of learning about sewing on the bias as a hidden metaphor for working against the grain, for the desire to give what is stable a bit more stretch and flow, for making things a bit less predictable. What was hidden from Brodkey was the memory of these early pleasures, of how she learned the joy of reading and writing—and more broadly the joy of exchanging ideas—before she began her formal education. Brodkey can now articulate, in the form of an accusation, what was taken from her as a child: "It seems to me that middle-class culture and schooling gratuitously and foolishly rob children of the pleasure of the physical and intellectual work of learning generally and writing in particular" (547). She learned the rules, yes, but forgot the joy.

This sentence, this claim, resonates powerfully with me—a former working-class student who now, as a scholar and writer of some modest success, is discovering what I, too, lost in the pursuit of my own class aspirations. Like Brodkey, I now look back in "sorrow" (her word [546]) at the child I was, bullied by homophobia and wanting out—out of the southern working-class community that I couldn't imagine understanding me. School was at times a refuge and a way out. In retrospect, though, I see how long I forgot my own mother and what she had taught me. Brodkey articulates her struggle to understand the legacy of her mother's impact on her this way: "I meet my sorrow by sorting the details of [my mother's] longing to be middle class from those of her struggle against the indiscriminate eradication of the intellectuality of her family at school" (546). In my own life, as my husband and I have invited my elderly mother, our last remaining parent, to live with us, I have been learning from and appreciating anew, on a daily basis, her fierce intelligence, her hardbought wisdom of experience, her ongoing desire to know and learn and explore and discover. I couldn't appreciate as a young man what I am fortunate enough—like Brodkey—to have the chance to appreciate now.

I realize, too, like Brodkey, how a little bit of what was once suppressed has stayed with me, animating my approach to the academy and to writing. I see things at an angle, I sometimes work against the grain, I delight in a bit of unpredictability. For me, such an approach has manifested as a kind of queerness, what Harriet Malinowitz once called a "queering of the brew" (251), arising not only from my queerness as a gay man but also, importantly, from the contrarian streak I inherited from my mother and from my sense of working-class outsiderness as I sit in my ivory-towered office. My pleasure in writing comes in part not just from the execution of rules well learned but also, even more, from writing on the bias. I have learned to appreciate my unique perspective, just as Brodkey learned to appreciate hers. And I have come to agree with her when she asserts, "I wish everyone were taught to write on the bias, for finding and following a bias is as critical to writing as sewing.... To write is to find words that explain what can be seen from an angle of vision, the limitations of which determine a wide or narrow bias, but not the lack of one" (546).

Finding that "angle of vision" rooted in one's experience—and not just finding it but also valuing it, asserting its simultaneously creative and critical value within the academy—had been emerging as an important line of thought for Brodkey for some time before she wrote "Writing on the Bias." As early as 1987, in an article in *Written Communication* entitled "Writing Ethnographic Narratives," Brodkey waded into contemporary debates between cognitivist and social epistemic approaches to writing pedagogy and unequivocally claimed that any mutual and just "social understanding . . . seeks to redress inequity by asking individuals to describe and analyze ways in which social circumstances systematically impinge on their lives" (37). Asking people to describe their lives is, for Brodkey, always political, even if the tellers themselves do not understand their stories as such. Having read deeply the work of the anthropologist Clifford Geertz, she passionately defends ethnography as an ideal approach to elicit such narratives, even as she recognizes that her advocacy for an ethnographically oriented pedagogy and scholarship faces an uphill battle; personal narrative, after all, has often been undervalued in the academy, as it is considered neither empirical enough (for the social scientists) nor literary enough (for the humanists) but mired rather in the "hopelessly subjective" (Brodkey, "Writing Ethnographic Narratives" 46). But Brodkey persists, claiming that "[e]thnography attempts to bring stories not yet heard to the attention of the academy. Stories introduce inconsistencies of one kind or another into the attempt to represent experience as wholly accounted for by our respective ideologies" (48).

A contemporaneous article, "Writing Critical Ethnographic Narratives," published in the same year in *Anthropology and Education Quarterly*, picks up on this assertion. This time Brodkey makes an even bolder claim: "I am arguing that critical narratives be written and read as yet another kind of academic discourse, as narratives that can be understood and evaluated in terms of critical theory" (70). In other words, the personal narrative can itself become an act of not just critical thinking but also critical theorizing. Decades later we have come to call such work "autotheory," a form of writing that actively theorizes through the personal, foregrounding personal narrative in what Jane Gallop has called "anecdotal theory." Such work is currently flourishing in many scholarly venues, but when Brodkey was writing in the late 1980s, she could justly point out that "theory, including critical theory, without research on practice is dangerously abstract" ("Writing Critical Ethnographic Narratives" 74). For Brodkey, the way to counter such abstraction was through telling different kinds of stories, which includes retelling and questioning the stories (both personal and theoretical) that we have become accustomed to tell; as she puts it, "*critical* ethnographic narrators would interrupt their own stories" (73; emphasis added).

Such work continued—and intensified—in articles such as "Transvaluing Difference," published in *College English* in 1989, in which Brodkey asserted that she is "obligated to instruct and support [students] in a critique of received wisdom, which in their case, as in mine, means a sustained interrogation of the doxa out of which claims about reality arise and to which their claims and mine contribute" (600). Interrogating such doxa means not just recognizing differences in opinion or view but also actively valuing such differences. What Brodkey wrote over thirty years ago is worth quoting in full because it is just as true today as it was then:

> It's not tolerance or diversity that feminist, African American, Third World, and progressive scholars are talking about. We're talking about the limits of universality, about the need to recognize that the negative valuing of difference—*not* white, *not* male, *not* heterosexual, *not* middle class—is socially constructed and can therefore be socially reconstructed and positively revalued.   (598)

And again, in a well-cited (and controversial) article also from 1989, "On the Subjects of Class and Gender in 'The Literacy Letters,'" Brodkey mobilizes a series of case studies of personal writing to chastise teachers for failing to pay sufficient attention to the terms, issues, and critiques of the social order and status quo offered in their students' literacy narratives, and instead essentially writing over such organic intelligences with their own educational discourses.[1] She is increasingly pointed in her critique: "The salient factor here is that educational discourse empowers teachers to determine what is worthwhile in a student's contributions, presumably even if that judgement has little or no linguistic basis" (135).

For Brodkey, the personal narrative was no longer a de rigueur modal assignment in the first-year composition classroom in which instructors could have students practice the art of narration; it was now the entry point to a critical theory and a critical pedagogy in which contact could be made with different views, standpoints, and positions. It was an invitation to recognize and then value alternative epistemologies.

The theoretical groundwork, bolstered by Brodkey's own emerging pedagogical practice, was being laid for the "Writing about Difference" curriculum, a set of curricular innovations that Brodkey made at the University of Texas, Austin, in the early 1990s that centered multiculturalism and asked students to become aware of and grapple with a variety of social differences in US society. The curriculum created a firestorm that forced Brodkey to leave her position as Texas legislators denounced what they took to be the politicization of the writing classroom in particular and the academy in general.[2] Of course, Brodkey, in insisting that received wisdom, or doxa, be held up for analysis and critique, was holding true to her post-structuralist belief that the classroom is always already politicized; one is never just teaching writing but always already participating in indoctrinating students into received values and norms, even if one is not aware that one is engaging in such indoctrination.

In the context of the trauma of Brodkey's experience at the University of Texas, Austin, "Writing on the Bias"— which cites only the content of Brodkey's own experience—seems like both an assertion and a negation: the text is both an affirmation of the critical value of one's story, one's perspective, one's history and a poignant, even painful critique of the systems of schooling that had still, despite her successes, failed her. Indeed, sorrow permeates much of "Writing on the Bias"—the sorrow over what Brodkey lost as a child as she moved from the working class through schooling and into the academy, and another sorrow, not explicitly articulated but still palpable, of then being misunderstood by that academy.

What a surprise, then, to revisit this narrative and encounter—to discover—a funny story, one in which little Linda asks her neighbors when they think they might die while she jots down their likely perplexed answers in her Big Chief tablet. For all the sorrow, we as readers can also feel the joy in writing, the pleasure of the well-told story, and the desire to know and articulate the critical knowledge of experience. In the prologue to "Writing on the Bias," Brodkey refers to the essay as an "experiment," one in which "no textual authority was summoned to underwrite the telling of the narrative" (527). I imagine her writing these lines and feeling a bit naughty, as though she is knowingly and purposefully breaking the rules, transgressing one of the primary requirements of scholarly genres in nearly every academic discipline, namely the requirement of situating one's thinking within ongoing academic conversations. I like to think that Brodkey remembered and relished her early joy in writing and that in composing "Writing on the Bias" she might have experienced a renewed pleasure in breaking the rules of academic writing. A small joy at a great cost—but a joy nonetheless.

Notes

1. Space doesn't allow for an explication of the controversies surrounding this article's publication. But responses to the article should be readily searchable.

2. This "firestorm," as I put it, is well described and documented from Brodkey's perspective in her book *Writing Permitted in Designated Areas Only*, which collects and revises some of the articles described in this essay.

Works Cited

"Bias, N. (2)." *Merriam-Webster Unabridged Dictionary*, 2023, unabridged.merriam-webster.com/unabridged/bias.

Brodkey, Linda. "On the Subjects of Class and Gender in 'The Literacy Letters.'" *College English*, vol. 51, no. 2, Feb. 1989, pp. 125–41.

——. "Transvaluing Difference." *College English*, vol. 51, no. 6, Oct. 1989, pp. 597–601.

——. "Writing Critical Ethnographic Narratives." *Anthropology and Education Quarterly*, vol. 18, no. 2, June 1987, pp. 67–76.

——. "Writing Ethnographic Narratives." *Written Communication*, vol. 4, no. 1, Jan. 1987, pp. 25–50.

——. "Writing on the Bias." *College English*, vol. 56, no. 5, Sept. 1994, pp. 527–47.

——. *Writing Permitted in Designated Areas Only*. U of Minnesota P, 1996.

Gallop, Jane. *Anecdotal Theory*. Duke UP, 2002.

Malinowitz, Harriet. *Textual Orientations: Lesbian and Gay Students and the Making of Discourse Communities*. Boyton/Cook/Heinemann, 1995.

Vernacular Scholarship and Craig S. Womack's *Red on Red:* Native American Literary Separatism

Stephen Donatelli

> Craig S. Womack, *Red on Red: Native American Literary Separatism* (U of Minnesota P, 1999)

Craig S. Womack's *Red on Red* is an experiment in vernacular scholarship. Though attentive to the narrative predilections of Native American storytelling, especially in the Creek tradition, Womack's innovative book goes beyond commentary. It employs Indigenous speechways mimetically to assess Native American literary storytelling over the last two centuries. Moreover, even though the book does not speak directly to rhetoric and composition studies, it lays down a challenge to critical discourse in our field and in adjacent fields such as literary criticism, literary theory, Native American studies, and anthropology. By counterpointing chapters of impeccable literary scholarship with experimental interchapters written in a lively English-Creek vernacular—comic vignettes populated by the author himself, his friends, and the actual writers and characters selected for study—Womack poses a question about the relationship between academic writing and the narrative stratagems that often concern rhetorical scholars. Womack asks to what extent scholarly writers may take mimetic license when speaking of vernacular topics and—as I would suggest—about any other subject.

Can Indigenous epistemologies and ways of speaking be properly known through normative academic discourse? Or—for some reason—must the separation of professional and vernacular registers be maintained, as Jacques Derrida says, in one of several iterations in "The Law of Genre": "Genres are not to be mixed. I will not mix them" (55).[1] As a Creek national, Womack has a strong interest in this question of mixture. It is a question of identity for him. But even for scholars who have no particular Indigenous affiliation, the problem of vernacular contamination may still obtain. Womack's book allows us to ask to what extent the critical act ought to remain unmixed with its vernacular ("home-born") matter ("Vernacular").

Appreciations of *Red on Red* by literary historians have noted Womack's commitment to Native American issues, such as the improvisational agility of Indigenous conversation, the storyteller's genetic recapitulation of origin myths, topographical memory as a kind of homing device for oral performance, as in Bruce Chatwin's *The Songlines*, and the political rationale behind the call to literary separatism (Hollenberg; Krupat 3–10). In a timely review of *Red on Red*, Patricia Penn Hilden was quick to notice how the irreverent manner of Womack's critical experiment, counterpointing chapters of impeccable archival scholarship with Creek-voiced responses to those chapters, exposes the insufficiencies of conventional critical practice for capturing meaning in the Native American context. The present essay may be regarded as a continuation of Womack and Hilden's concern with how to square the incommensurability of narrative art with the rule of critical etiquette. In both a narrower and a broader sense, can critical practice in composition and rhetoric question this relation? If it can, *Red on Red* may be seen both as a lost text in rhetorical studies and as a lost epistemological position actually expressed in Womack's own Native American critical practice.

The potentials of vernacular speech for critical utterance, especially in communication studies and in composition and rhetoric, where the subject of language as an object is routinely taken up, may always begin prudently with the first great statement about the literary and the vernacular in the West: Dante Alighieri's *De vulgari eloquentia* (*On Vernacular Eloquence*), written circa 1304 (Zompetti). The critical polemic that had preoccupied Dante's coevals—the *questione della lingua*, or the debate over the permissibility of vernacular speech in learned circles—concerned him both as a literary scholar and as a poet. He wanted to know the extent to which a living, regional speech could tenably interact, if at all, with the classical Latin model. Might some synthesis at least be theorized? Dante's own critical stance is both affirmative and conservative on this question of the *formal norm*: he elected to write his treatise on the vernacular in best classical Latin—the courtly speech of scholarship. Womack displays similar professional deference in those chapters of *Red on Red* written up to the expectations of scholastic standards, frequently raising those standards, since Womack's prose is marked by an archness reminiscent of the writings of Desiderius Erasmus and Lorenzo Valla. On the question of joining normative and vernacular discourses, Dante's previous *Vita nuova* (1293; *The New Life*) treats the problem by means of counterpoint. In this work, forty-two of Dante's own lyric poems are alternated with brief explanations of how each poem works. (The genre is known as the *prosimetron*.)

I would postulate that Dante's experiment in the *Vita nuova* resembles the counterpoint solution adopted by Womack in *Red on Red*, not so much to claim a direct lineage as to identify a generic crossover space—a "kindness," as the Renaissance scholar Rosalie Colie has put it (128). Dante's own development carried him forward to the landmark rapprochement of high and low in the *Commedia* (c. 1308–21). If we take that text as a poetic response to the *questione della lingua*—that is, as an event that did actually happen in literary history—might we now not also consider a nonstatic future for the interaction of vernacular speech and scholarly practice? In his own context, Dante's name for such a hypothetical resolution—articulated speculatively before he wrote his masterwork—was something we render in English as "the illustrious vernacular," an artful kind of speech transcending the tension between learned speech and regional dialect. Such a speech was a theory for Dante before it became manifest in the classic poem of his maturity. Womack's critical handling of the Native American speech world may also be viewed as a threshold for the development of academic discourse.

Among writers, readers, and critics, vernacular sensitivity is related to the search for freedom. Why, then, should critical practice not at least question its own comportment in this regard? When James Baldwin wrote "If Black English Isn't a Language, Then Tell Me, What Is?," he was declaring his stake in this question, his diction ranging freely across vocal registers, from prophecy to pranking (see also Young). Voiced critique, though suspect, is always significant in professional critical behavior, whenever it is permitted to occur, and when critics feel drawn to it. Geneva Smitherman's *Talkin and Testifyin* is an early and now effectively ignored appeal in this line. In *Ghostly Matters: Haunting and the Sociological Imagination*, Avery Gordon addresses a common cultural uncanniness inaccessible to conventional sociological method. She devises a customized, critical method for handling her elusive material, affording her unusual critical access to it, by allowing her, as it were, to speak spookily. In *To Nietzsche: Dionysus, I Love You! Ariadne*, the philosopher Claudia Crawford addresses the Dionysian spirit of Friedrich Nietzsche's work by means of a mythical persona capable of singing and dancing with the beloved subject. Crawford says that this radical mimetic freedom allows her to speak in a register more sympathetic to Nietzsche's own critique of Apollonian thinking, which favors "science, doxa, reality [and] reason" (xv). Crawford's performative strategy will not be found in any existing catalog of traditional genres. She simply calls her book "a wedding" (3). Such experiments, outside the field of rhetoric and composition proper, may nonetheless be admired for their resistance to normative best behavior in a bid to preserve the genius of their material. The influential case of W. E. B. Du Bois's "double consciousness"—a prescient concept elaborated throughout *The Souls of Black Folk*—may initially seem to bear some comparison with modalities of mind and speech that move in a helical way. In Du Bois's words, "[O]ne ever feels this two-ness" (38). But Womack's project takes a different tack. Instead of nursing the conflicted sensation that the master's language must be well-imitated while speakers remain inwardly loyal to their own dialect, Womack regards the presumably disadvantaged position—vernacular ingenuity—as fully capable of achieving a comic and critical advantage over the relatively stilted conventions of dominant, academic discourse: "Making the letter sound like talk instead of writing" (184).

Critical theory in composition and rhetoric has occasionally engaged with the idea of a learned discourse more receptive to vernacular influences, if only through the wistful recognition that something soulful is missing in professional discourse: lexical range, modal variety, narrative artistry, beautiful statement, wit. In *The Methodical Memory: Invention in Current-Traditional Rhetoric*, Sharon Crowley rightly inveighs against our lack of progress in rhetorical education, both in the way that we write about it and in the way that we teach prim writing to others. Theory and pedagogy during this *longue durée*, says Crowley, have been "pretty much moribund" for decades (179), possibly for six or seven generations, owing to corporate insensitivity to the classical value of eloquence, which is always actually and already available to everyone, even to children, as the painter Mark Rothko understood when he taught art in a Depression-era synagogue school in Brooklyn (Ashton 19). Over thirty years ago, in *Killing the Spirit: Higher Education in America*, Page Smith was similarly urging humanities education to question its inertial default to the script-bound lecturing model, a one-way kind of speech more literary than oral (199–222). To underscore this idea that oral and vernacular modes may have something invigorating to offer to critical writing and to student writing, Womack invokes Walter Ong's 1975 essay, "The Writer's Audience Is Always a Fiction," where the superior dividend afforded to listeners of being able to talk back is compared with "literate cultures [that] do not address an immediately present audience" (Womack 166).

By adapting the ways of myth and story for rhetorical education—surprisingly by exploiting existing opportunities offered by new electronic technologies in combination with a return to classical texts—Gregory Ulmer has for some time been devising lively collaborative experiments in uncertainty, aporia, and improvisation as antidotes to the flatlined pedagogy that has long dominated composition instruction at all levels in the United States. With our uncritical emphasis on structure, planning, outlining, style, and precept (at the expense of logic and invention, intellectual astuteness, and meaning), current-traditional rhetorical pedagogy for Crowley has been "a bizarre parody of serious discourse and the process by which it is produced" ("Evolution" 159). As if in logical response to Crowley's call, Ulmer has pushed for the development of "a new poetics" and "a new genre or mode of production" (*Heuretics* xiii), what he elsewhere calls "the genre of theoretical art" (*Electracy* 14).

The particular, deliberate mischievousness of Native American oral-storytelling strategies poses wonderful difficulties for professional discourse. Our predicament may plausibly be laid at the feet of insufficient respect for vernacular ways of speaking, a kind of fear of freedom. Humorous recognitions of this fear may be found in the work of enlightened Western and Native American ethnographers (e.g., Nabokov 29–57; Nequatewa). The anecdotes they tell effectively reveal how the Native perspective itself apprehends the classic literacy-orality contact scene through the activation of shared myth-memories, accessible even to uninitiated outsiders. In what follows I propose to run through a series of loosely affiliated topical specimens for the purpose of asking whether a sort of vernacular intelligence can be captured in normative scholarly discourse. The samples are drawn from works by or about Native peoples.

We may seize on the core problem of *Red on Red* by examining how the book asks us to move between its main critical chapters and the Creek-voiced conversations that follow each chapter. We begin therefore with ourselves as readers pinned into this singular hybrid text, caught within crossover space that Womack is discussing. In one of his chapters, "In the Storyway" (75–101), he records five different versions of how the traditional figure of Turtle got his shell. The story itself is characterized by Turtle's wily ways and by the misfortunes that befall him, notably the fracturing of his shell by a pestle thrown at him by an irate Creek woman. Disoriented, his shell now broken into many pieces, Turtle "now began to sing in a faint voice" (93). In the way of the story, Turtle "sings himself back together" (100), and through this captivating image we find a clue to a better way of understanding the critical/vernacular divide: it is a way, as Womack puts it, "to break down the oppositional thinking that separates orality and literacy" (15). Here Womack acknowledges Ong's argument for the "primacy of orality" (with repetition being an incantatory feature of oral telling, as I have done just now with *singing back together*), even to the extent that "oral tradition [may] generate vital approaches to examining Native literatures" (qtd. in Womack 166; 66–67).

In a vernacular Creek-English riposte to his own critical introduction to *Red on Red*, Womack has his speaker, Rabbit, explain how Native storytelling can circumscribe the divide between orality and literacy, or between low and high speech, on a wholly new plane. Rabbit says of Womack's own scholarly book, "I think Red stays Red, most ever time, even throwed in with white. Especially around White. It stands out more" (24). Rabbit's "more" is nothing less than a kind of critical quantum leap made possible by Native storytelling behaviors. "More" is the trickster's trademark manner of undercutting oppositions, including the trickster's own bipolar wavering between self-aggrandizement and despondency. By descending deeply into the Turtle story, Womack is also able to make his listeners remember Oklahoma Creek myth and history, summoning the weight of cultural memory within this single image. The Turtle story bears intergenerational wisdom about how the Muscogee Creek people were able to survive their forced removal to Oklahoma during the 1830s. Their brokenness is made whole at each retelling of Turtle's story, as the people's survival can be seen again in the distinctive, mended lozenge pattern visible on Turtle's shell today. This reconstituted shell is the sign of how Turtle's "busted-up self starts pulling back together" (91). Might this manner of apprehending have a place in the historical development of professional rhetorical discourse? A fragmented response may be appropriate.

In a recent Supreme Court decision favorable to the Muscogee Creek people (*McGirt v. Oklahoma*), Justice Neil Gorsuch, writing for the six-to-three majority and apparently enchanted by his reading of tribal histories, found himself affirming the legal sovereignty of the five eastern Oklahoma nations with a lyric touch that owes something to the tribes' understanding of themselves: "On the far end of the Trail of Tears was a promise" (United States). Nine days later, speaking to this landmark judgment, Joy Harjo (Creek) identified certain tribal values that she says encompass difference: *eyasketv* ("humbleness") and *vnoketkv* ("love"). This notion—that a congenial reciprocity already active within vernacular-speech communities may carry lessons for "the formation of shared judgments" across the oral/literary divide (Harjo)—seems congruent with Gerard Hauser's "publics theory," as expressed in his *Vernacular Voices* (11).

In an essay about narrative wisdom, "Philosophy, Argument, and Narration," the preeminent American scholar of Giambattista Vico, Donald P. Verene, has said, "Arguments must be mediated within some context that is *not itself argued, but there*" (143; emphasis added). To understand how Indigenous storytelling may operate through imaginative insignia such as Turtle's mended shell, Womack expresses skepticism that formalist, postmodernist, or deconstructive strategies can be of much use: "It is way too soon for Native scholars to deconstruct history when we haven't yet constructed it" (3).

In his magisterial novel about Hopi life, *The Place in Flowers Where Pollen Rests*, Paul West provides grounds for exploring the benefit to rhetorical studies and literary art and criticism of vernaculars beyond the literal lands of Indigenous peoples. The vernacular liberation that so captivates West is instantly apparent in Womack's own performance of Native American English speech:

> Stijaati he was had say, "Hey, I read that book over at the Oklahoma Historical Society, how bout it? I reckon I gotta throw in with [Alice Callahan's] Wynema. I remember when I was reading thinking some-

thing ain't right here; they's a white man in the sofky pot. Let me expoundulate on my methodism. I found ever single little place in the book where an Indian got to say anything and counted their words. . . . My calculator says there are 34,840 words in the novel . . . [and] 5,528 belong to Indians. . . . What happened to Creek viewpoint?" (125–26)

Taking place on what might be called—anagrammatically—the same mesa, West's novel imagines a Hopi speech conditioned by conversations the author actually heard during his visits to Arizona. Two examples from *The Place in Flowers* are given here, the first spoken by a pair of inseparable itinerant twins, BertandAnna, and the second from a repatriated Vietnam veteran, Oswald Beautiful Badger Going Over The Hill:

We got time and the willingness. It don't matter how little, it worth telling somebody hello. Even those who stare don't hello you back, maybe because we smell or burp a bit, maybe because we don't walk quite straight withouting our sticks, wobbly on the ice, a bit stoopy in the July sunshine, you can't be right all the time, but you got to look a better happy, among all these folks who say, Where *these* from? (321)

Unhandy names, these, but they bring something to life on the mesa: a touch of color, which is the obvious thing to say, but also, to the very act of naming, something narrative, as if all of nature had been in motion at the moment of your birth. It was. They are names for when there is lots of time, not so much to kill as to tread down, reverent as can be. (81)

Womack tells us that, as a university professor and as a tribal insider, he came to "a crisis of faith regarding ethnographic work" (75). The crisis brought him, in *Red on Red,* to wonder how "ethnography could be accomplished under any circumstances without objectifying people—that is, turning them into objects of study instead of representing the depth of their humanity" through their own speech (75). It goes without saying that West's characters haven't the verifiability of actual Hopi nationals. His narrative artistry simply sets into motion an illustrious language that transcends the opposition of orality and literacy, operating according to a more conciliatory set of aesthetic laws. One may thus ask—offensively—on what grounds critical commentary should be denied the freedom to make use of such discourses. In *Red on Red*, Womack's mixture of criticism and storytelling may or may not signal some kind of mending taking place in the historical development of scholarly writing.

Notes

I am grateful to Shannon Butts for valuable suggestions in the development of these ideas.

    1. The quoted statement represents Derrida's third sounding of this idea in "The Law of Genre." This statement—setting mixture against non-mixture—takes many shifting shapes in this text. Derrida opens by saying, in a one-sentence paragraph, "Genres are not to be mixed" (55). He then makes a new paragraph and offers, again in one sentence, the second part of his "law": "I will not mix genres" (55). A new tension—*to mix or not to mix*—now intensifies the prior tension of *what the law says I can say, and what I dare say before the law*. In his third paragraph, again in a single sentence, Derrida writes, "I repeat: genres are not to be mixed. I will not mix them" (55). The two parts of this new statement now abut each other in a single paragraph. Shortly thereafter, in paragraph 6, Derrida writes, "I merely said, and then repeated, genres are not to be mixed; I will not mix them" (55), signaling, through the winking semicolon, that some sort of forbidden rapprochement may be underway. Derrida will not mix genres, and he declares that he will not mix them, but he will exercise his freedom to act otherwise through signs.

Works Cited

Alighieri, Dante. *De vulgari eloquentia*. Edited and translated by Stephen Botterill, Cambridge UP, 1996.

———. *Vita nuova e rime*. Edited by Guido Davico Bonino, Arnoldo Mondadori Editore, 1985.

Ashton, Dore. *About Rothko*. Da Capo Press, 1983.

Baldwin, James, "If Black English Isn't a Language, Then Tell Me, What Is?" *New York Times*, 29 July 1979, archive.nytimes.com/www.nytimes.com/books/98/03/29/specials/baldwin-english.html.

Colie, Rosalie Littel. *The Resources of Kind: Genre-Theory in the Renaissance.* U of California P, 1973.

Crawford, Claudia. *To Nietzsche: Dionysus, I Love You! Ariadne.* State U of New York P, 1995.

Crowley, Sharon. "The Evolution of Invention in Current-Traditional Rhetoric, 1850–1970." *Rhetoric Review*, vol. 3, no. 2, 1985, pp. 146–62.

———. *The Methodical Memory: Invention in Current-Traditional Rhetoric.* 1990. 20th anniversary reissue ed., Southern Illinois UP, 2010.

Derrida, Jacques. "The Law of Genre." Translated by Avital Ronell. *Critical Inquiry*, vol. 7, no. 1, autumn 1980, pp. 55–81.

Du Bois, W. E. B. *The Souls of Black Folk.* 1903. Edited by David W. Blight and Robert Gooding-Williams, Bedford Books, 1997.

Gordon, Avery. *Ghostly Matters: Haunting and the Sociological Imagination.* Introduction and foreword by Janice Radway, U of Minnesota P, 1997.

Harjo, Joy. "After a Trail of Tears, Justice for 'Indian Country.'" *Santa Fe New Mexican*, 18 July 2020, www.santafenewmexican.com/opinion/commentary/after-a-trail-of-tears-justice-for-indian-country/article_0ef8713a-c7bc-11ea-83c2-4366ee70048e.html.

Hauser, Gerard A. *Vernacular Voices: The Rhetoric of Publics and Public Spheres.* U of South Carolina P, 1999.

Hilden, Patricia Penn. Review of *Red on Red: Native American Literary Separatism*, by Craig S. Womack. *American Literature*, vol. 17, no. 4, 2001, pp. 88–89.

Hollenberg, Alexander. "Speaking with the Separatists: Craig Womack and the Relevance of Literary History." *Studies in American Indian Literatures*, vol. 21, no. 1, 2009, pp. 1–17.

Krupat, Arnold. *Red Matters: Native American Studies.* U of Pennsylvania P, 2002.

Nabokov, Peter. *A Forest of Time: American Indian Ways of History.* Cambridge UP, 2002.

Nequatewa, Edmund. "Dr. Fewkes and Masauwu." 1935. *Truth of a Hopi: Stories Relating to the Origins, Myths and Clan Histories of the Hopi*, by Nequatewa, A and D Publishing, 1985, pp. 123–25.

Ong, Walter J. "The Writer's Audience Is Always a Fiction." *PMLA*, vol. 90, no. 1, Jan. 1975, pp. 9–21.

Smith, Page. *Killing the Spirit: Higher Education in America.* Viking Penguin, 1990.

Smitherman, Geneva. *Talkin and Testifyin: The Language of Black America.* Wayne State UP, 1977.

Ulmer, Gregory L. *Electracy: Gregory L. Ulmer's Textshop Experiments.* Edited by Craig J. Saper et al., Davies Group, 2015.

———. *Heuretics: The Logic of Invention.* Johns Hopkins UP, 1994.

United States, Supreme Court. *McGirt v. Oklahoma.* 9 July 2020. *Supreme Court of the United States*, www.supremecourt.gov/opinions/19pdf/18-9526_9okb.pdf.

Verene, Donald P. "Philosophy, Argument, and Narration." *Philosophy and Rhetoric*, vol. 22, no. 2, 1989, pp. 141–44.

"Vernacular, *Adj.*" *Oxford English Dictionary: Complete Text Reproduced Micrographically.* Vol. 2, Oxford UP, 1971, p. 3614.

West, Paul. *The Place in Flowers Where Pollen Rests.* Doubleday, 1988.

Womack, Craig S. *Red on Red: Native American Literary Separatism.* U of Minnesota P, 1999.

Young, Vershawn Ashanti. "Should Writers Use They Own English?" *Iowa Journal of Cultural Studies*, vol. 12, no. 1, 2010, pp. 110–17.

Zompetti, Joseph P. "A Theory of Vernacular Rhetoric: Reading Dante's *De vulgari eloquentia.*" *Inquiries Journal*, vol. 9, no. 4, 2017, www.inquiriesjournal.com/articles/1617/a-theory-of-vernacular-rhetoric-reading-dantes-de-vulgari-eloquentia.

Rediscovering Deborah Cameron's *Verbal Hygiene*

Pegeen Reichert Powell

Deborah Cameron, *Verbal Hygiene* (Routledge, 1995)

Twenty years ago, on the last day of a first-year writing course, my students presented me with a T-shirt on which they had printed "Ask me about verbal hygiene!" That T-shirt, a nod to Deborah Cameron's *Verbal Hygiene*, which we had read together that semester and which this essay is about, wasn't the best part of the gift, though. The best part was that they had printed enough shirts for each of them and their friends to wear, too, so that occasionally on campus in the following semesters, I would see kids I didn't even know honoring a relatively obscure book about language that I had taught.

A book that inspires a brief sartorial fad among college students is clearly a lost text worth recovering. Originally published in 1995 (and reissued in 2012 in the series Routledge Linguistics Classics), *Verbal Hygiene* offers a framework for studying practices that are motivated by "an urge to improve or 'clean up' language" (Cameron 1). Cameron is interested in practices as petty as swear jars, as esoteric as the development of a wholly constructed language such as Esperanto, as politically charged as English-only movements, and as widespread as grammar instruction. This last example indicates the relevance of this book to composition and rhetoric scholars and teachers. I argue that our entire profession might be considered an exercise in verbal hygiene. Certainly, any time writing instructors scribble "awkward" or "unclear" in the margins of a student's essay, they are practicing verbal hygiene, according to Cameron's definition. More broadly, though, our most enduring and important scholarly debates—first-year writing and the problem of access, students' rights to their own language, our approaches to assessment—are all motivated by questions surrounding what makes some forms of language use better than others.

Despite its relevance to our work, *Verbal Hygiene* has not garnered the attention it deserves. This is not too surprising, given Cameron's disciplinary affiliation with sociolinguistics. Research in sociolinguistics has not been embraced in composition and rhetoric as much as it should have been, although our fields share some theoretical foundations and an interest in the relationship between one's identity and one's communication practices. While the easiest explanation for this disconnect is that sociolinguistics focuses on spoken language use, while composition and rhetoric tends to focus on written language use, it is perhaps less the focus of our scholarship and more the scope that distinguishes our two fields. Sociolinguists study language difference in a wide variety of contexts, whereas, historically, mainstream composition and rhetoric scholars have limited their area of study to postsecondary education. One point I want to make by recovering *Verbal Hygiene* is to illustrate what we may be missing when we overlook scholars like Cameron: specifically, models for studying everyday language use outside of educational settings and an attention to varied and specific sociohistorical contexts.

Although Cameron identifies as a linguist and addresses debates within that discipline, her framework offers a very useful way in to thinking about composition and rhetoric. She provides an accessible and thorough introduction to the theories and concepts surrounding language use that dominate current approaches to writing pedagogy. As such, the book is well suited to both undergraduate courses (I've taught the book in first-year and upper-level writing courses) and in graduate-level introductions to the field. For example, in chapter 1, in just a few pages, Cameron covers the range of arguments about the relationship between language and identity—drawing on Judith Butler, among others, to do so—and concludes that "the norms that regulate linguistic performance are not simply reflections of an existing structure but elements in the creation and recreation of that structure. It therefore becomes necessary to ask where the norms 'come from' and how—that is, through what actual practices—they are apprehended and internalized, negotiated or resisted" (17). For our students, Cameron's book can open up the conversation to the role that college writing classes play in reinforcing the "norms that regulate linguistic performance," a worthwhile conversation for undergraduates as the objects of that regulation and for graduate students as the future agents of that regulation.

Verbal Hygiene also poses a useful challenge to experienced scholars and instructors. As much as the field's scholarship and stated principles might embrace assumptions about language varieties and the racism inherent in teaching and enforcing Standard American English and traditional academic prose, our practices don't often align with what we know.[1] As a sociolinguist, Cameron deftly and gently explains why we might cling to the authority of the grammar and prose styles we are familiar with; the mirror she holds up to readers like me reflects an ugliness, but she does so with such affection and sympathy that I am willing to take a hard look. She admits that part of what we're dealing with is simply the "respect people have for custom and practice, for traditional ways of doing things" (13). However, it is more than that. Language use is different than the kind of authority that other social norms like dress codes or dinner manners might impose, in part because of how we acquire the rules. Cameron states that our investment in the authority of linguistic conventions manifests "an attachment to values and practices that were impressed on people in the formative stages of their personal and linguistic histories." Moreover, "by the end of my apprenticeship [into specific linguistic conventions] I will probably have internalized certain norms to such an extent that I am no longer capable of experiencing them as arbitrary. . . . [L]inguistic conventions are routinely felt to be of a different order than many other social rules and norms. Their authority is not just an external imposition, but is experienced as coming from deep inside" (14).[2] Cameron challenges us to consider the origins of our norms and standards, which dictate everything we do from marking misplaced commas to teaching citation practices to reading student work against our ingrained fluency with Standard American English. She says that "there is nothing wrong with idiosyncratic preferences which have no rational justification, so long as we acknowledge that this is what they are" (225); however, we need to be reminded that our "idiosyncratic preferences" have real consequences for our students.

Beyond just a theoretical foundation for thinking about our field's most significant assumptions, Cameron provides a methodology that we might consider seriously in our scholarship. She asserts that "verbal hygiene is not a unified and coherent discourse" and that "verbal hygiene practices are interesting and significant in their complex particularity, their fine detail" (30). Therefore, the majority of the book is devoted to a careful study of specific practices: the house style guides used by publishers; a national debate about curriculum and the teaching of grammar in elementary schools in England; a debate about political correctness (perhaps the one chapter that feels dated, but no less relevant); and self-help literature on how to communicate effectively. Cameron presents close analyses of the texts that codify the verbal hygiene practices and situates these texts within the context of the arguments surrounding them, the practices' histories, and interviews with participants.

Cameron's focus on specific practices and the specific texts that produce these practices is a useful counterpoint to two dominant threads in the current field. The first is the turn toward empirical research on writing studies. Richard Haswell's 2005 article, "NCTE/CCCC's Recent War on Scholarship," introduced RAD—replicable, aggregable, and data-driven—as the goal for research methods in composition studies. Haswell's call for such research has been heard, in large part because it aligns with discourses of accountability and the corresponding accounting practices that have arisen in higher education more generally. This is the kind of research that people measuring retention rates and ROI can understand. The second dominant thread in our scholarship is the initiative to codify general principles in composition and rhetoric as threshold concepts. This initiative, most prominent in Linda Adler-Kassner and Elizabeth Wardle's 2015 *Naming What We Know: Threshold Concepts of Writing Studies*, is also a response to pressures exerted by forces outside the field. Threshold concepts are "gateways" or "portals" into a discipline's key concepts (Meyer and Land 373). In her introduction to *Naming*, Kathleen Blake Yancey argues that threshold concepts "articulate the substance of the field as a mechanism for mapping the field itself" and that "the assumption underlying *Naming*, of course, is that the field is now established" (xxix). Threshold concepts are an attempt to claim the disciplinary foothold necessary for continued institutional recognition—in the form of tenure-track lines and graduate programs, for example.

Both of these strains in our scholarship are trying to exert a centripetal force on what can feel like an undisciplined field. It is not surprising that these threads have grown alongside a greater attention to multimodality, which introduces more and more technologies and genres to our classrooms. However, while these threads attempt to give some shape to the body of knowledge in composition studies, both do so, ironically and unproductively, by pointing to further abstractions, such as data sets and lists of concepts. While the work that follows from Haswell's and Adler-Kassner and Wardle's appeals may be useful, Cameron challenges us to complement these tendencies with a focus on specific practices in which real people are engaged.[3]

As a counterpoint to these current trends in rhetoric and composition, we can follow Cameron's lead and study specific practices and the personal, historical, and political contexts in which such practices exist. One of the students in my course on verbal hygiene studied Klingon dictionaries—this kind of work can be fun! Another studied debates surrounding the language portion of SATs—this kind of work can have serious consequences for real people. Cameron accumulates a series of such studies and is able to draw some (contingent) conclusions about them that can inform further studies. I imagine a series of case studies of writing practices and debates, historical and contemporary, that could yield a greater appreciation for and understanding of nondominant varieties of English, emerging genres, and texts that challenge what we know.

Rooted in specific places and times, these kinds of studies may not be replicable and aggregable, nor will they necessarily yield universal principles. One thing these studies can do, though, is inform our teaching. In *After Pedagogy: The Experience of Teaching*, Paul Lynch addresses the impasse posed by post-process theory.[4] He notes that to advance or adopt a single pedagogy (such as writing as process or any other pedagogical approach) is to deny the very nature of writing and teaching as context-specific, and yet to thoroughly embrace the contingent nature of writing and teaching means proceeding with no plan, no predetermined set of principles (Lynch 34–35). While we typically understand pedagogy as taking theoretical principles and applying them to the classroom, Lynch argues that pedagogy is more productively understood as a reflection on the experiences of the classroom, in the context of previous classroom experiences and in light of the principles and theories that have arisen from those experiences (128). Understood in this way, pedagogy can account for the surprising moments and student writing that don't quite fit with what we thought we knew and can help us teach "the student whom the law does not serve, the student whose work—at least at that particular moment—seems to make us choose between being attentive to her specific needs on the one hand and supporting the curriculum we have designed on the other" (115). *Verbal Hygiene* models the approach of studying the politics, tactics, arguments, and values that surround specific instances of people using and talking about language, and from this derives a framework for thinking about future instances. More of these kinds of studies would productively complement, and perhaps at times challenge, the data-driven research and threshold concepts that circulate in our scholarship now.

Cameron brings her training as a sociolinguist to her analysis of particular examples, but she is not merely describing phenomena. In chapter 1, she dismantles the descriptive/prescriptive binary on which sociolinguistics rests and argues that "'description' and 'prescription' turn out to be aspects of a single (and normative) activity: a struggle to control language by defining its nature" (8). As scholars and teachers of writing, we should never aspire to neutral, unbiased conclusions and principles. We, too, "struggle to control language by defining its nature." Cameron takes clear stances in the debates she analyzes, but only after carefully delineating the values at stake in the various positions. She argues that "one *can* legitimately make value judgements on the use of language," but that "it needs to be recognized that not all judgements are equally valid" (224). While we might take her assertions here for granted, especially in our classrooms, we tend to posit much of what we teach as value-neutral: students need to know *this* in order to be prepared for future classes or the workplace; the best way to format or organize or punctuate an assignment is *this*; teaching *this* genre or technology in our courses is not relevant. As Cameron asserts, we "*can* legitimately make value judgements" like these, but we must be prepared to articulate the values underlying these judgements both to our students and to our colleagues. We must be prepared to address the probability that students will make different judgements, often more conservative ones than ours. (For instance, whenever I've taught the debates surrounding Standard American English in first-year writing, the majority of my students argue that they need to know traditional grammar.)

Arguments with colleagues about learning objectives, statements that frequently ossify into objective facts, should surface assertions of value as well.

Finally, if we recognize what writing scholars and teachers do, first and foremost, as engaging with practices of verbal hygiene, as I argue here, then we should be the experts on debating language use. We should be working to craft an accessible discourse that makes it easier for others to talk about language in an informed manner, and we should be modelling for our students and other constituencies how to articulate our own values so that they can articulate theirs. To this end, *Verbal Hygiene* is an excellent model. The T-shirts that my students made invited these debates—"Ask me about verbal hygiene!"—in part because students responded so enthusiastically to Cameron's writing. As we worked our way through the book, they raised more and more questions about the author, what she would think of this or that thesis, how she might respond to their own writing. In one of those risky but magical teaching moments, I scrapped the last project I had planned for the semester and reached out to Cameron herself, described the course, and asked if she'd be willing to receive a portfolio of my students' writing. My students organized their portfolio, worked in groups to write prefaces to the three sections of it, and drafted a longer introduction to their portfolio. After receiving the portfolio, Cameron wrote back, answering students' questions and responding to the specific pieces in the portfolio.

What that experience taught me is the potential value of our work to reach not just our students but also wider audiences. *Verbal Hygiene* is absolutely an academic text: it was published by Routledge not once but twice and includes in-text citations, footnotes, and all the trappings of a scholarly book. Cameron does write in a way that is accessible and, at times, funny, but, more than that, she is writing about something that is fundamentally interesting to people: she writes that "we are constantly intervening in language, whether in support of what we perceive as the *status quo* or in pursuit of something different" (215). Both our teaching and our scholarship can speak to these interventions and help shape the debates, debates that are almost always not just about language but also about something else: they provide "a symbolic way of addressing conflicts about race, class, culture, and gender" (216). Sometimes this is rather obvious—as in the case of debates about the singular *they* and preferred pronouns—and those may be the cases when our expertise is most important. It may take a generation for our country to recover from the discourse of so-called fake news and the debate about how to call lies "lies"; we are mired in conspiracy theories that circulate in online written forums and attempts to debunk them. These are debates about language use, and the very future of democracy is at stake in these debates. *Verbal Hygiene* is not necessarily about winning the arguments. Rather, it is about generating the vocabulary and the framework for others to engage in the arguments more ethically and more productively, a task our field is primed to undertake.

Notes

1. See, for example, the continuing influence in our scholarly discourse of the statement on language published by the Conference on College Composition and Communication in 1975, "Students' Right to Their Own Language" (Committee), despite the fact that, as Keith Rhodes wrote recently, the right "has in practice proven to be a hollow claim" (256). See also Inoue; Canagarajah.

2. Cameron's use of the first person here might explain, in part, why this critique is palatable; there are some moments of real humor when she implicates herself in arbitrary verbal hygiene practices.

3. In addition, the 2018 Conference on College Composition and Communication featured a session entitled "Questioning the Rush to Discipline; or, Daring to Teach What We Don't Know," which challenged the push for and posited alternatives to models such as teaching for transfer, writing about writing, and threshold concepts. The panelists on this round table included Mary Boland, Christine Farris, Anne Gere, Deborah Holdstein, John Schilb, and Victor Villanueva.

4. Post-process (or, sometimes, post-pedagogy) theory, for example in the work of Thomas Kent, is a reaction to the way that teaching writing as process codifies the way writing works in unproductive and unrealistic ways. According to Kent, post-process proponents foreground "the unpredictable, elusive, and tenuous decisions or strategies we employ" when we use language (qtd. in Lynch 33). The implication is that there is no one way to teach writing, and in fact, some would argue, no way at all.

Works Cited

Adler-Kassner, Linda, and Elizabeth Wardle, editors. *Naming What We Know: Threshold Concepts of Writing Studies*. UP of Colorado, 2015.

Cameron, Deborah. *Verbal Hygiene*. Routledge, 1995.

Canagarajah, A. Suresh. "The Place of World Englishes in Composition: Pluralization Continued." *College Composition and Communication*, vol. 57, no. 4, 2006, pp. 586–619.

Committee on CCCC Language Statement. "Students' Right to Their Own Language." *College English*, vol. 36, no. 6, 1975, pp. 709–26.

Haswell, Richard. "NCTE/CCCC's Recent War on Scholarship." *Written Communication*, vol. 22, no. 2, 2005, pp. 198–223.

Inoue, Asao B. *Antiracist Writing Assessment Ecologies: Teaching and Assessing Writing for a Socially Just Future*. Parlor Press, 2015.

Lynch, Paul. *After Pedagogy: The Experience of Teaching*. Conference on College Composition and Communication / National Council of Teachers of English, 2013.

Meyer, Jan H. F., and Ray Land. "Threshold Concepts and Troublesome Knowledge (2): Epistemological Considerations and a Conceptual Framework for Teaching and Learning." *Higher Education*, vol. 49, no. 3, 2005, pp. 373–88.

Rhodes, Keith. "Feeling It: Toward Style as Culturally Structured Intuition." *College Composition and Communication*, vol. 71, no. 2, 2019, pp. 241–67.

Yancey, Kathleen Blake. "Coming to Terms: Composition/Rhetoric, Threshold Concepts, and a Disciplinary Core." Adler-Kassner and Wardle, pp. xvii–xxxi.

The Intellectual Work of Composition: James F. Slevin's *Introducing English*

Bruce Horner

> James F. Slevin, *Introducing English: Essays in the Intellectual Work of Composition* (U of Pittsburgh P, 2001)

James F. Slevin's name is not unknown in composition studies. Those of us of a certain age and disposition, at least, may well know and think of Slevin as an important voice in pertinent debates on the relationship between composition studies and literary studies, on "the profession" (of either), on labor in composition, and on writing across the curriculum and writing in the disciplines—debates that have since been displaced, or perhaps eclipsed, by other debates. But with Slevin's untimely death (in 2006) at the age of sixty came the silencing of his voice and, I believe, a neglect of his work.[1] This neglect, I argue, is unfortunate in that Slevin offers a powerful alternative to both conventional and seemingly oppositional movements in composition work past and present, such as the move, affiliated with work by Elizabeth Wardle, Linda Adler-Kassner, and Doug Downs, to transform composition into a conventional discipline with its distinctive "threshold concepts," and recent calls for composition to become anti-racist in its programs and pedagogy.[2]

I won't speculate about how well Slevin's scholarly publications might have fared had he lived longer and been able to continue speaking, writing, teaching, and publishing. But I can establish that his work has suffered neglect. In this essay I focus on his book *Introducing English: Essays in the Intellectual Work of Composition*, published in 2001, which has been described by the composition luminary David Bartholomae as "the most important book to address writing, student writing, teaching and the profession since Mina Shaughnessy's *Errors and Expectations*" (17). Notwithstanding Bartholomae's claim, at the time of this writing, at least one source of citations to scholarly work, *Google Scholar* (while certainly not the sole arbiter of any text as a must-read), indicates that Slevin's book has been cited a mere seventy-three times, in sharp contrast to the number of citations that same source indicates for two other books offering comparably sweeping accounts of composition. For *Google Scholar* indicates that David W. Smit's book *The End of Composition Studies*, published three years after Slevin's (2004), has been cited no less than 310 times and that Sidney Dobrin's book *Postcomposition*, published in 2011, has been cited no less than 159 times, or twice as many times as has Slevin's book, despite being published ten years after Slevin's book.

Of course, one might dismiss the disjunctions in these citation numbers by considering the possibility that many of the publications on which Sleven drew in preparing chapters for *Introducing English*—Slevin acknowledges that seven of the twelve chapters do so—may themselves have enjoyed significant numbers of citations. But, again, at least to go by *Google Scholar*, this does not seem to be the case. *Google Scholar* reports that Slevin's 2001 *College English* essay, "Engaging the Intellectual Work of Assessment," on which chapter 11 of *Introducing English* draws, has been cited independently no more than thirty-three times, and the other essays on which chapters in that book draw have been cited even less frequently, despite appearing earlier (1983, 1988, 1992, 1994, 1997, 2000) and thus having had more time to draw citations. It appears, then, that despite Bartholomae's claim for the value of Slevin's book, it has largely been ignored.

Given that the book's publication predates Slevin's death by at least five years, I suggest that the neglect of his work results not from the silencing of his voice but from his work's refusal to adhere in its arguments to beliefs so dominant in composition about composition as to be unrecognized as beliefs at all—beliefs that contribute to a prevailing ideology that, at least in one sense of ideology, do not announce themselves as an ideology but, rather, as simply the way things are. More specifically, I argue that Slevin's book challenges what dominant US academic culture generally and composition specifically believe about composition, including those imagining themselves as resisting it: an ideology of functionalism to which both those aligning with and attempting to resist what composition seems to be appear to subscribe.[3]

Functionalism, Anthony Giddens has explained, redefines specific historical effects of particular institutions and institutional arrangements, such as disciplines, as, instead, those institutions' function, thereby removing those effects from history and granting those institutions autonomy to work on history from a location outside it.[4] Functionalism aligns with a view of hegemony as uniform and total in its reach. By contrast, Slevin insists on and brings out the resistant and alternative already, as well as potentially, operating at the ostensible site of such hegemony: here, the academy. He does this in part by identifying alternative traditions within which to identify and locate academic culture, and in part by bringing out the historical—hence changeable and variable—character of that academic culture that dominant ideology denies.[5] That character is encapsulated in Slevin's book, as elsewhere in his writings, by the phrase "intellectual work," a phrase that, like the subject of a fugue, Slevin repeatedly returns to.

Bartholomae provides a useful description of the book worth repeating in full:

> It is unpredictable and urgently necessary; there is no available program of study, no line of research or school of thought, no field or discipline or PhD program that would prepare one to read this book or to write it. It brings together Claude McKay, Miguel de Cervantes, and E. B. White; John Brinsley's *A Consolation for Our Grammar Schools* (1622), Ralph Hamor's *A True Discourse for the Present State of Virginia* (1612), and the *New Yorker*; Pocohantos, Don Quixote, Fredric Jameson, Mary Louise Pratt, and Ann Berthoff; the work of students and teachers in the Writing Program at Cornell and the work of a junior, Andrew, in a DC public high school. It brings the writing together as equivalent texts, all necessarily connected, all worth the same care and attention. It assembles the work across time and across venues to give depth and range and critical attention to a national project for promoting, managing, and valuing writing in America, a project with an impressive range, history, and urgency. Jim calls this project "composition." (17)

Of course, Bartholomae's description can be read as an unwittingly backhanded excuse, or at least explanation, for the neglect the book has suffered: after all, what else should we expect of a book that "no field or discipline or PhD program" would prepare one to read? But it also suggests that to read Slevin's book requires that we unlearn assumptions about composition learned from such programs of study in order to learn new ways to think composition. For rather than imagining composition as the site for improving student writing or, more ominously, sifting out undesirables, Slevin asks us to think of composition, including what composition students as well as their teachers do, as, in Slevin's insistent phrase, "intellectual work."

What Slevin means by that phrase, and what his book advances, runs counter to two common responses of those of us who think of ourselves as working "in" composition to the difficulties we face in that work. On the one hand, there are those who accept the official institutional charge to composition programs to improve, usually by somehow fixing or addressing, the perceived deficits in student writing (and in the students themselves), but complain that this work gets neither the respect it deserves nor the support it needs to carry out that charge. Composition is here defined as a purely remedial enterprise directed at safeguarding the quality of writing students produce, with little questioning of what constitutes "good" writing or what it might be good for. Against this response, Slevin cheerfully insists that we should give up on any attempt at such improvement and cautions that such enterprises are part of the legacy of imperialism aimed at "improving" those subjected to it. The other response appears to be more closely aligned with Slevin's in rejecting this official charge. However, in rejecting that charge, this response simultaneously rejects the real and potential value of the academic site itself. Assuming that site to be irredeemably bankrupt, this response turns for redemption instead to nonacademic sites—for example, by valorizing vernacular language and knowledge and ways of knowing that the academic site typically distinguishes and distances itself from, at least officially.

While sympathetic to the limitations imposed on composition that prompt both types of response, Slevin sees those limitations as belonging not to composition per se, nor to the academy per se, but, instead, to dominant "representations" of composition and the academy (*Introducing* 3), representations that, he insists, correspond minimally to what composition is and might become. For in response to rejections of both composition specifically and the academy generally, Slevin defends both—not in terms of what they are commonly represented as being and doing but instead in terms of what he sees them actually doing and being for—occasions for intellectual work, defined as "the critical examination of the truthfulness of knowledge created, received, and exchanged" (235).

Of course, many might accept the value of such work and identify the academy as an official site for undertaking that work. Commonly, however, that is imagined to be the province of professional academic scholarship, performed by professional scholars. Slevin, however, identifies it as work in which students, from the first moment of their admission to college, participate, proposing that

> the moment a student walks into our classroom, the first day of class, the student would be seen—and see himself or herself—as a full participant in the work of the discipline. *Just for showing up.* She would not have to *negotiate* entry; she would not have to *earn* the right to speak and participate. She has already entered and by definition has that right. The discipline includes her as a *given*, and the intellectual work of the discipline includes her work and our work with her.
> (*Introducing* 44–45)

Likewise, whereas many have argued for broadening the range of students admitted to postsecondary education as a matter of honoring the right to access to knowledge, Slevin, by contrast, argues for the vital role those students have played in a writing "movement" that "questioned the hegemony of received ways of reading and writing" (*Introducing* 2). Thus, for Slevin, broadening the range of students admitted to postsecondary education is a matter not of granting students access rights and addressing student needs but, rather, of meeting the needs of the *academy* by drawing on students' intellectual energy—*student* questioning of "the hegemony of received ways of reading and writing." As Slevin put it, "A discipline . . . has essentially to do with the work of transmission and transformation, and its representation [of knowledge] therefore incorporates all the agents, students as well as teachers, teachers as well as scholars, who engage in this activity" (41).

Thus, on the one hand, Slevin insists on a definition of the charge of the academy that many professional academics might well subscribe to—the "critical examination of the truthfulness of knowledge created, received, and exchanged" (*Introducing* 235). But he breaks with common understandings of academic work by including students—and, pointedly, first-year students enrolled in composition courses—among those responsible for carrying out that charge. He thus confounds both those who would reject the legitimacy of academic work in response to hegemonic views of the academy as a site for merely preserving knowledge from the threats of barbarians from without and also those who, on the flip side, would want to preserve students from the academy in light of the dangers of "assimilation" to its putatively corrupt ways. For example, in chapter 9, Slevin notes that critical examination of the forms of academic discourse "does not entail a particular (that is, an 'antiestablishment') judgment about these forms" (194). Critical work, for Slevin, is not synonymous with condemnation. Instead, as he points out, such critical examination is a crucial element of all intellectual work, including that which confirms the value of particular forms. As he reminds us:

> [W]e engage in this critical examination simply because we *must* if we really want to understand these forms. Students might conclude that apprenticing themselves to these forms, accepting them, and using them, is an entirely desirable choice, but it will be a different kind of choice if they are fully aware, through their own active investigation and analysis of why they decide to do that. (194)

Key to Slevin's confounding of received ways of understanding composition and its work is his treatment of academic discipline as not "a field one works 'in' but rather as a set of activities and practices one works 'with'" (*Introducing* 3). Such a reconceptualization, he suggests, "refines the meaning of disciplinary work to include teaching and learning and broadens the meaning of workers to create alliances of literacy teachers and learners across conventional educational boundaries and even beyond educational institutions as ordinarily conceived" (3), a redefinition that he argues is in fact not new but, rather, a recuperation of its earlier, long-standing meaning (41–43). In Slevin's reconceptualization of discipline, composition can abandon the effort to meet students' ostensible needs and focus instead on making "other needs imaginable and their realization possible" (239). In this way, for Slevin, composition is, or can become, a "movement for institutional change within and among all levels of education and many different fields of study and learning," one "concerned not with remediating lack but with examining and understanding differences as they enrich education" (52).

Slevin's argument for what does, or should, count as composition, and his reconceptualization of academic disciplinary work and workers, stands in sharp contrast to dominant critiques and current projects for composition and thereby points the way for working past the impasses these constitute. In his defense of the academic site and its charge to produce and test the truthfulness of knowledge, he rejects arguments that dismiss the academic site as hopelessly compromised and bankrupt and that turn toward uncritical valorizations of recognizably nonacademic sites, writers, and epistemologies merely for being nonacademic. Conversely, in his insistence on students, and (to boot) first-year undergraduate students, as participants in the work of academic disciplines and on their participation as indeed necessary to that work, Slevin rejects traditional definitions and defenses of the academy as means of preserving knowledge and of composition as transmitting knowledge (including skills). So, for example, if we were to adopt Slevin's perspective, continuing education could be defended not as a means of reskilling students but, instead, as a means of drawing on their intellectual labor to test (and presumably revise) the truthfulness of what is represented as knowledge—necessary not so much as a way of meeting students' needs but, instead, as a way of enabling the academy to meet its charge to test the truthfulness of what it represents as knowledge. And recognizing the contributions of students' labor would in turn justify compensating them for that labor rather than burdening them with the cost incurred for doing that work—which from this perspective is a perverse requirement that workers pay for the opportunity to do work.[6] Slevin's argument thus advances, and can enlighten, the move toward free college tuition.

Slevin's argument for an "interpretive" pedagogy (and curriculum) of inquiry based on his identification of the charge to all in the academic community, including students as well as teachers, of testing the truthfulness of knowledge also poses a significant alternative to recent arguments in composition for composition to assert itself as representing a body of knowledge. Those arguments are represented most forcefully in

Adler-Kassner and Wardle's *Naming What We Know: Threshold Concepts of Writing Studies* and Downs and Wardle's call for a "Writing about Writing" curriculum for composition. *Naming What We Know* seems to adopt a pedagogy of transmission in positing a body of knowledge to be named and grasped—"what we know"—at odds with Slevin's interpretive pedagogy of inquiry, which assumes instead that anything we might think we know is and should be subject to challenge.

Current calls for anti-racist composition pedagogy seem to adopt a similar model of enlightening the benighted.[7] Slevin expresses uneasiness about comparable calls, questioning universities' calls to "educate for justice" by "inculcating the habit of justice in students and then releasing them into adult society to behave justly and to require of others ... that they also behave justly" ("Educating" 2). Without rejecting the value of just behavior, Slevin, in keeping with his argument for an interpretive pedagogy, suggests that education for justice should instead direct its efforts at "clarifying systems of injustice and imagining alternative systems" (5) and exploring the following questions: "What works for justice do universities perform as universities? How are students able to participate in that work [for social justice] *as students*?" (3). Thus, instead of assuming a fixed definition of justice whose habits are to be inculcated, Slevin argues for justice as the focus for intellectual work, asking us to imagine a university in which

> a number of faculty and administrators, including the president, decide that their university will devote itself to *producing knowledge* that analyzes the causes and conditions of oppression and inequality, and in doing so support the achievement of social justice for all citizens. *The goal would be to create through rigorous inquiry an understanding* of the intersecting historical realities of colonialism, racism, sexism, and other forms of oppression. Imagine that these faculty and administrators consider this purpose not as *a* (as in *just one*) desirable effect, but as the single, organizing goal of the institution. That is, this purpose would govern the work of the university and shape the projects of faculty and students so that all research and teaching would be geared toward the study of culture and society with the aim of advancing social justice. The knowledge sought would be the

understanding of systemic political, cultural, economic, and social injustice, the structural causes of it, the ways in which its nature and causes are distorted, and the possibilities for genuine, structural social change. (5–6; emphasis added)

So, while anti-racist pedagogy is defined in terms of its stance, anti-racism, which presupposes agreement about what constitutes racism, Slevin (writing long before the current anti-racist movement) calls for a pedagogy of "rigorous inquiry" and sees any resulting effect of justice as dependent on that inquiry: the work of students *as students*," understood by Slevin as fellow participants in intellectual inquiry. For Slevin, to do otherwise is to abandon the proper role of the academy, albeit a role the academy always only partially fulfills: education as "the intellectual work of engaged interrogation [of practices, meanings, and states of affairs]" ("Educating" 3).

Slevin's call characteristically confounds how many of us have come to think, believe, and behave about matters of justice and the academy. Against those insisting on activism, Slevin argues for interpretation; against those arguing for the academy as the site for the preservation of hard-won knowledge, he argues for the value of students who will question that knowledge; against composition's pursuit of the conventional trappings of disciplinarity, he argues for the value of its basement status in freeing it from the traps these bring. *Introducing English* confounds dominant ways compositionists (to invoke an increasingly archaic term) think about the nature and value and participants of those doing composition work. But precisely for that reason, Slevin's articulation of this seemingly confounding vision of and for composition merits our renewed attention. It both introduces and models what Slevin calls "the intellectual work of composition."

Notes

1. This is not to say that Slevin the person has not earned recognition. For example, he was a recipient of the ADE Francis Andrew March Award, which is intended "to recognize and honor distinguished service to the profession of English at the postsecondary level" ("ADE Francis Andrew March Award"), and has fellowships and awards named after him.

2. See Adler-Kassner and Wardle; Downs and Wardle; Condon and Young; Inoue; WPA-GO Anti-Racist Assessment Task Force.

3. I've argued elsewhere that an ideology of functionalism dominates academic culture generally and composition specifically (Horner, "James Slevin").

4. See Giddens's critique of functionalism in *Central Problems*.

5. See, for example, Slevin's discussion of academic genres as historical (*Introducing* 195). I am of course drawing here on Raymond Williams's distinction between hegemony and the hegemonic (112–13).

6. For a more extended version of this argument, see Horner, "Writing Language."

7. See, for example, Condon and Young's provision of a glossary of "Working Definitions and Key Concepts" and "Manifestations" in the introduction to their collection, *Performing Antiracist Pedagogy* (13–15).

Works Cited

"The ADE Francis Andrew March Award." *MAPS: MLA Academic Program Services*, www.maps.mla.org/About-MAPS/ADE/The-ADE-Francis-Andrew-March-Award.

Adler-Kassner, Linda, and Elizabeth Wardle, editors. *Naming What We Know: Threshold Concepts of Writing Studies*. UP of Colorado / Utah State UP, 2015.

Bartholomae, David. "Remarks in Honor of James F. Slevin." *ADE Bulletin*, no. 140, fall 2006, pp. 17–21.

Condon, Frances, and Vershawn Ashanti Young, editors. *Performing Antiracist Pedagogy in Rhetoric, Writing, and Communication*. WAC Clearinghouse / UP of Colorado, 2016. Across the Disciplines Books.

Downs, Douglas, and Elizabeth Wardle. "Teaching about Writing, Righting Misconceptions: (Re)Envisioning 'First-Year Composition' as 'Introduction to English Studies.'" *College Composition and Communication*, vol. 58, no. 4, 2007, pp. 552–84.

Giddens, Anthony. *Central Problems in Social Theory: Action, Structure and Contradiction in Social Analysis*. U of California P, 1979.

Horner, Bruce. "James Slevin and the Identifying Practices of Composition." *ADE Bulletin*, no. 143, fall 2007, pp. 14–17.

———. "Writing Language: Composition, the Academy, and Work." *Humanities*, vol. 6, no. 2, 2017, https://doi.org/10.3390/h6020011.

Inoue, Asao B. *Antiracist Writing Assessment Ecologies: Teaching and Assessing Writing for a Socially Just Future*. WAC Clearinghouse / Parlor Press, 2015.

Slevin, James F. "Educating for Justice." *Conversation on the Liberal Arts*, 1 Feb. 2003, Westmont College, westmont.egnyte.com/dl/fCleg0mVNU.

———. *Introducing English: Essays in the Intellectual Work of Composition*. U of Pittsburgh P, 2001.

Williams, Raymond. *Marxism and Literature*. Oxford UP, 1977.

WPA-GO Anti-Racist Assessment Task Force. "WPA-GO Statement on Anti-Racist Assessment." *Council of Writing Program Adminstrators*, 17 July 2020, wpacouncil.org/aws/CWPA/pt/sd/news_article/313021/_PARENT/layout_details/false.

The Radicalism of Marilyn Sternglass

Joseph Harris

> Marilyn S. Sternglass, *Time to Know Them: A Longitudinal Study of Writing and Learning at the College Level* (Lawrence Erlbaum Associates, 1997)

"Marilyn Sternglass used to get especially short with me," wrote James Traub, "when I wondered whether students like Tammy would be truly educated even if they managed to get their degree" (129). The passage comes from Traub's *City on a Hill: Testing the American Dream at City College*, a book that questions the value of the open admissions experiment at City College, City University of New York (CUNY), from the 1970s through the 1990s. A graduate himself of Harvard University, Traub worries that someone may not be *truly* educated unless they can show evidence of "intellectual discrimination"—by which he means an easy familiarity with "philosophy and history" (132).

Marilyn Sternglass was not that kind of snob. "What does that *mean*?" Traub tells us she answered him, "How are you measuring education?" (129). Sternglass's career as a teacher and writer was animated by a deep respect for the students she worked with. She was not one to confuse intelligence with an Ivy League glibness or the ability to write an impromptu essay about nothing in particular in the idiom of the academy. Tammy, the student she was discussing with Traub, was a young African American woman from the Bronx, visually disabled, living in a public housing community with her ailing mother, who over a span of six years put herself through City College, earning a BS in psychology while also working several jobs. She had trouble passing proficiency tests in math and writing (although she eventually did), and she never developed the kind of intellectual "discrimination" that might impress the likes of

James Traub. But after having read almost every piece of writing that Tammy had produced over those six years, Sternglass became convinced that Tammy was someone who had learned how to learn and, in particular, had learned how to use writing to apply "principles and theories not only to cases presented in her psychology classes, but also to literary works she was being asked to interpret" (Sternglass 264). Sternglass watched in admiration as, with remarkable tenacity, Tammy overcame one obstacle after another, earning her degree and becoming a full-time counselor in a methadone clinic.

Tammy was one of nine students whose progress Sternglass documents in her landmark study, *Time to Know Them: A Longitudinal Study of Writing and Learning at the College Level*. Eight of the students were persons of color, several spoke a language other than English at home, and most came from lower-income families. Sternglass draws their portraits with passion and care. She interviewed each of them twice a semester, and she collected and read nearly all the writing they did for their courses. She began her research by tracking some fifty-three students but ended up centering her book on the nine who were able both to continue to meet with her and to earn their degrees in six years. In a way, that feat of endurance is the main point of her research. Sternglass argues that what students, especially those on the margins, need most in order to succeed is time to practice and grow, much like we, as their teachers, need time to get to know and help them. Her work celebrates stamina, patience, and compassion.

But it is not sentimental. Sternglass was annoyed by the callow elitism of critics of open admissions like Traub and infuriated by proficiency exams, like CUNY's notorious writing assessment test, that mistook the struggles of some students to write polished academic prose for an inability to do college-level work. That anger pulses through *Time to Know Them*. But Sternglass was also frank in describing the blind spots and stumbles of the students she followed. She faults one student for playing it safe intellectually, notes the willingness of another to let stereotypes about his Latin American heritage pass without challenge, and calls the story of an immigrant student who allows his family to push him into a practical major "a sad one" (xxi). Her analysis of student writing is always evenhanded, as she notes how sentence-level mistakes persist in the work of many students even as their reasoning and use of evidence grow more sophisticated. She conceptualizes learning not as transformation but as growth—and even then she shows how such growth is often fragile and unsteady, in need of ongoing support. The critics of open admissions grumbled that City College was no longer producing Nobel laureates. Sternglass saw how schools like City College could do something else, something perhaps more crucial, how they could be engines of democracy, of a broad public literacy. She spoke for that tradition of work in composition that is concerned less with building an academic discipline than with improving how we teach undergraduates to write.

In this sense *Time to Know Them* continues the project of the other great book to come out of the open admissions era at City College, Mina Shaughnessy's 1977 *Errors and Expectations*. Shaughnessy is rightly celebrated for the elegance of her prose and the immense sympathy and intelligence she brought to her reading of student texts. She inspired generations of writing teachers. But it is also worth noting that no student is ever named or described as a person in the pages of *Errors and Expectations*. All we know about the actual people who produced the writing Shaughnessy analyzes is what we can glean from their texts—usually handwritten, impromptu placement essays composed with little time to spare and under considerable stress. For all its brilliance, then, *Errors and Expectations* is rooted in the study of discrete, isolated moments of writing, quick snapshots of literacy made by unknown students.

Sternglass took a deeper approach in *Time to Know Them*. She was interested in tracing what she called the "effect of complex social histories" on the writing of each of the students she studied (60). And so, while never reducing individuals to social categories, she paid close attention in each of her case studies to the ways gender, race, sexuality, class, family, neighborhood, and place of origin were intertwined and helped shape the approach of a particular writer. In contrast, Shaughnessy had simply noted that the student papers in her book had been, for the most part, composed by writers from the "racial and ethnic enclaves" of New York City (3)—and pretty much left her analysis of social context at that.

Even more important, Sternglass took her time as a researcher. The main point of *Time to Know Them* is to argue against a quick sorting of students, to resist judging their potential based on their early performances on placement tests and in skills-based courses. Instead, Sternglass showed that, given enough time and support, most college students can learn to do high-level intellectual work. She never argued for lowering academic standards. Rather, she argued for a recognition and relaxing of the constraints—including the need to work outside jobs, to commute long distances, to find childcare, and to fulfill skills requirements in a fixed number of semesters—that cause so many lower-income students to drop out of college. It thus seems fitting that Sternglass allowed herself a similarly long stretch of time—six years of research, two of writing—to complete her own project.

That commitment was rewarded. *Time to Know Them* was the crowning achievement of Sternglass's long career. In 1999 it won the Conference on College Composition and Communication Best Book Award, and in 1997 it aptly won the MLA Mina P. Shaughnessy Prize. The book also earned glowing reviews in *College Composition and Communication*, *TESOL Quarterly*, the *Journal of Basic Writing*, and the *Journal of Adolescent and Adult Literacy* (Haswell; Zamel; Liese; Pekosh). And so, in that sense, *Time to Know Them* has not been lost to us. But I worry that Sternglass's values as a teacher and researcher have gone out of fashion. I think she had a different view of our field than the one now offered by proponents of writing studies. *Time to Know Them* is grounded in her scrupulous work as an ethnographer and her wide reading of other research in composition. It is intellectual work of the highest caliber. But it does not aim to provide us with knowledge about writing or rhetoric or literacy in the abstract. It is meant instead to make an argument about how to support undergraduate students and writers. *Time to Know Them* offers empirical evidence for the democratic promise of the first-year writing course. It shows how, if we invest the time to know and support them, we can help working-class and minority students acquire the languages of the university. It is through this quietly activist side of her work that I would most like to see Sternglass continue to influence our field.

Marilyn Sternglass died in 2004, in Pittsburgh, her hometown. Her husband, Ernest Sternglass, was a distinguished nuclear physicist who became an ardent activist against nuclear war. He died in 2015. I can only imagine that they were well suited as a couple, since both saw themselves as working in the service of democracy.

Works Cited

Haswell, Richard H. "Grades, Time, and the Curse of Course." *College Composition and Communication*, vol. 51, no. 2, 1999, pp. 284–95.

Liese, Daniela. "Marilyn Sternglass's *Time to Know Them*: A Review Essay." *Journal of Basic Writing*, vol. 18, no. 1, 1999, pp. 21–26.

Pekosh, David G. Review of *Time to Know Them: A Longitudinal Study of Writing and Learning at the College Level*, by Marilyn S. Sternglass. *Journal of Adolescent and Adult Literacy*, vol. 42, no. 3, 1998, pp. 237–38.

Shaughnessy, Mina P. *Errors and Expectations: A Guide for the Teacher of Basic Writing*. Oxford UP, 1977.

Sternglass, Marilyn S. *Time to Know Them: A Longitudinal Study of Writing and Learning at the College Level*. Lawrence Erlbaum Associates, 1997.

Traub, James. *City on a Hill: Testing the American Dream at City College*. Addison-Wesley, 1994.

Zamel, Vivian. Review of *Time to Know Them: A Longitudinal Study of Writing and Learning at the College Level*, by Marilyn S. Sternglass. *TESOL Quarterly*, vol. 34, no. 1, 2000, pp. 186–87.

Notes on Contributors

Jonathan Alexander is Chancellor's Professor of English at the University of California, Irvine. He is the author, coauthor, or coeditor of twenty-two books and focuses his scholarly energies on life writing, lifespan writing, and the rhetorics of popular culture.

Paige Davis Arrington is a Marion L. Brittain Postdoctoral Fellow in the School of Literature, Media, and Communication at the Georgia Institute of Technology. She received her PhD in rhetoric and composition from Georgia State University. Her teaching philosophy and scholarship, which draw on her experience as a Montessori teacher and a teacher trainer, focus on understanding and optimizing the role of digital and physical materials in the learning and composing practices of young adults.

Rebecca Day Babcock is William and Ordelle Watts Professor at the University of Texas of the Permian Basin, where she teaches writing and linguistics and serves as the freshman English coordinator and director of undergraduate research. She has authored, coauthored, or edited several books on tutoring, writing centers, disability, and metaresearch. Her latest book is *Boom or Bust: Narrative, Life, and Culture from the West Texas Oil Patch*, coedited with Sheena Stief and Kristen Figgins. Her book *Theories and Methods of Writing Center Research*, coedited with Jo Mackiewicz, recently won the award for best edited collection from the Association for Writing across the Curriculum. She has also won best article awards from both the International Writing Centers Association and the Council of Writing Program Administrators.

David Bartholomae is professor of English and Charles Crow Chair of Expository Writing, emeritus, at the University of Pittsburgh. He served as chair of the Conference on College Composition and Communication (CCCC), as president of the ADE, and on the Executive Council of the MLA. His honors include a Chancellor's Distinguished Teaching Award, the ADE Francis Andrew March Award, the CCCC Exemplar Award, the CCCC Richard B. Braddock Award (for "The Study of Error"), and the MLA Mina P. Shaughnessy Prize (for *Writing on the Margins*). He has published widely on composition and teaching. With Jean Ferguson Carr, he edits the University of Pittsburgh Press book series Composition, Literacy, and Culture. His most recent book is *Like What We Imagine: Writing and the University* (2021).

Larry Beason is professor of English at the University of South Alabama, where he teaches assorted courses in rhetoric, writing, and literature. He has published in journals such as *College Composition and Communication* and *Research in the Teaching of English* on topics including the linguistic development of ethos, a sense of place in academia, and the impact of grammar policing in social media. He recently published a third edition of his coauthored book *The McGraw-Hill Handbook of English Grammar and Usage*. Currently he is examining the distinctive roles of discourse and rhetoric in postapocalyptic narratives found in popular culture. He is working on a book tentatively entitled "Language at the End of the World: Subversion and Discourse in Post-apocalyptic Narratives."

Michael Bernard-Donals is Chaim Perelman Professor of Rhetoric and Culture and Nancy Hoefs Professor of English at the University of Wisconsin, Madison. He is the author of *Figures of Memory: The Rhetoric of Displacement at the United States Holocaust Memorial Museum* (2016) and coeditor, with Kyle Jensen, of *Responding to the Sacred: An Inquiry into the Limits of Rhetoric* (2021).

Clint Bryan is associate professor of English at Northwest University, where he primarily teaches writing courses and has been named the dean of the College of Arts and Sciences. An ordained Protestant minister, Bryan served as a local church pastor for decades prior to entering academia midcareer. He studies and publishes work at the confluence of popular religious expression, sociolinguistics, and genre studies.

NOTES ON CONTRIBUTORS

Mary C. Carruth is associate professor of English at Southern University and A&M College. She edited the critical collection *Feminist Interventions in Early American Studies* (2006). She has published essays on Mary Rowlandson, Anne Bradstreet, and Charlotte Perkins Gilman. More recently, she has published and given presentations on the contemporary writers Natasha Trethewey, Frank X Walker, and Suzan-Lori Parks. Her current interest is the intertextuality between early and contemporary American writings.

Tiane K. Donahue is professor of linguistics, director of the DartWrite Digital Portfolio Project, and former director of the Institute for Writing and Rhetoric at Dartmouth College. She teaches writing, and her research focuses on writing, translingualism, cross-cultural comparisons, and research methods. She earned a PhD in linguistics in France. Her work with the French research laboratory Théodile-CIREL (Théories et didactique de la lecture-écriture) at Université de Lille and her participation in multiple European research projects, networks, conferences, and collaborations inform her understanding of writing instruction, research, and program development in European and US contexts.

Stephen Donatelli has taught writing and rhetoric at Harvard University, Cornell University, Princeton University, and New York University.

Philip Eubanks retired as professor and chair from the Department of English at Northern Illinois University, where he taught courses in rhetoric and writing. He is the author of *A War of Words in the Discourse of Trade: The Rhetorical Constitution of Metaphor* (2000), *Metaphor and Writing: Figurative Thought in the Discourse of Written Communication* (2011), *The Troubled Rhetoric and Communication of Climate Change: The Argumentative Situation* (2015), and, with John D. Schaeffer, "A Kind Word for Bullshit: The Problem of Academic Writing" (2008).

Douglas Eyman is senior editor of *Kairos: A Journal of Rhetoric, Technology, and Pedagogy*, an online journal that has been publishing peer-reviewed scholarship on computers and writing since 1996. He is the author of *Digital Rhetoric: Theory, Method, Practice* (2015), and his scholarly work has appeared in *Pedagogy, Technical Communication, Computers and Composition*, and several edited collections. His current research interests include digital rhetoric, new media, electronic publication, information design, digital pedagogy, and massively multiplayer online role-playing games as sites for digital rhetoric research.

Christine Farris is professor emeritus of English at Indiana University, Bloomington, where she directed the composition program and taught writing, rhetoric and composition theory, and literature. Her publications include *Subject to Change: New Composition Instructors' Theory and Practice* and the coedited collections *Under Construction: Working at the Intersection of Composition Theory, Research, and Practice* and *Integrating Literature and Writing Instruction*. Her coedited collection *College Credit for Writing in High School: The "Taking Care of" Business* won the Council of Writing Program Administrators Best Book Award in 2012.

Sergio C. Figueiredo is associate professor in the Department of English at Kennesaw State University. He is the editor and translator of *Inventing Comics: A New Translation of Rodolphe Töpffer's Reflections on Graphic Storytelling, Media Rhetorics, and Aesthetic Practice* (2017) and coeditor of *Immigrant Scholars in Rhetoric, Composition, and Communication* (2019).

Anne Ruggles Gere is Arthur F. Thurnau Professor of English and Gertrude Buck Collegiate Professor of Education at the University of Michigan, Ann Arbor, where she serves as chair of the joint PhD program in English and education. From 2008 to 2019 she directed the University of Michigan Sweetland Center for Writing. In 2018 she served as president of the Modern Language Association. Her scholarly interests include composition and rhetoric, literacy studies, pedagogy, and gender. Gere has published a dozen books and over a hundred articles and is currently writing a book about Indigenous women who taught in boarding schools.

Rachel B. Griffis is assistant professor of English at Texas A&M International University, where she teaches American literature courses. Her writing has appeared in *The Cormac McCarthy Journal, Nathaniel Hawthorne Review, Studies in American Indian Literatures, Christianity and Literature, Women's Studies: An Interdisciplinary Journal*, and elsewhere.

NOTES ON CONTRIBUTORS

Joseph Harris is professor of English at the University of Delaware, where he teaches composition and creative nonfiction. He was the founding director of the Thompson Writing Program at Duke University, an independent, multidisciplinary program noted for its approach to teaching writing as a form of intellectual inquiry. His books include *The Work of Teaching Writing: Learning from Fiction, Film, and Drama* (2020), *Rewriting: How to Do Things with Texts* (2017), and *A Teaching Subject: Composition since 1966* (2012). He served as the editor of *College Composition and Communication* from 1994 to 1999.

Douglas Hesse is professor of writing, university distinguished scholar, and the former founding executive director of writing at the University of Denver. He has been president of the National Council of Teachers of English, chair of the Conference on College Composition and Communication, president of the Council of Writing Program Administrators, and chair of the MLA division Teaching as a Profession, and he became chair of the Association for Writing across the Curriculum in 2022. His four coauthored books and more than eighty articles, chapters, and essays focus on creative nonfiction, writing pedagogy, program administration, and the nature and prospects of English studies.

Deborah H. Holdstein is professor of English in the Department of English and Creative Writing at Columbia College Chicago. From 2007 to 2014 Holdstein served as dean of the School of Liberal Arts and Sciences at Columbia. She is a past editor of *College Composition and Communication* (2005–09) and a past director of the consultant-evaluator service of the Council of Writing Program Administrators and continues to serve as a consultant to colleges and universities. She has published widely, and her work includes books, textbooks, book chapters, and articles. Her first book, *On Composition and Computers*, was published in 1987. Holdstein's most recent, coedited textbook is *The Oxford Reader* (2022). Her current research involves Hebraic sources of Jesuit rhetoric and a book project on the 1953 film *The Bandwagon*.

Bruce Horner teaches composition at the University of Louisville. His recent books include *Rewriting Composition: Terms of Exchange* and the coedited collections *Economies of Writing: Revaluations in Rhetoric and*

351

Composition (with Brice Nordquist and Susan Ryan), *Crossing Divides: Exploring Translingual Writing Pedagogies and Programs* (with Laura Tetreault), *Mobility Work in Composition* (with Megan Favers Hartline, Ashanka Kumari, and Laura Sceniak Matravers), and *Teaching and Studying Transnational Composition* (with Christiane Donahue).

Asao B. Inoue is professor of rhetoric and composition in the College of Integrative Sciences and Arts at Arizona State University. In 2019 he served as chair of the Conference on College Composition and Communication (CCCC). He is a recipient of the Council of Writing Program Administrators Outstanding Scholarship Award (2014) and Outstanding Book Award (2015), and in 2014 and 2017 he won the CCCC Outstanding Book Award. He has published many articles and chapters on race, racism, and antiracist writing assessment. His latest book is *Above the Well: An Antiracist Argument from a Boy of Color* (2021).

Julie Jung is professor of English at Illinois State University, where she teaches graduate and undergraduate courses in rhetoric and writing. Her current research interrogates normative Whiteness in rhetorics of quantification.

Peter Wayne Moe is associate professor of English at Seattle Pacific University. For six years he served as director of campus writing. He has published, among other places, in *College Composition and Communication*, *Rhetoric Society Quarterly*, *Longreads*, and *Fourth Genre: Explorations in Nonfiction*. He is the author of *Touching This Leviathan* (2021).

Staci M. Perryman-Clark is professor of English and African American studies and the director of the Institute for Intercultural and Anthropological Studies at Western Michigan University. Perryman-Clark currently serves as the associate chair of the Conference on College Composition and Communication. She is a 2008 recipient of the CCCC Scholars for the Dream Travel Award and a 2020 recipient of the Council of Writing Program Administrators Best Book Award.

Pegeen Reichert Powell is professor of English at Aurora University. Previously, she was professor of English and chair of the English and creative writing department at Columbia College Chicago. Reichert Powell is the author of *Retention and Resistance: Writing Instruction and Students Who Leave* (2014), a study of the role of writing instruction in institutional retention efforts, and the editor of *Writing Changes: Alphabetic Text and Multimodal Composition* (2020). Her work on pedagogy, writing program administration, and critical discourse analysis has been published in several journals and edited collections.

Lynn Reid is assistant professor of rhetoric and composition and director of basic writing at Fairleigh Dickinson University. She holds a PhD in composition and TESOL from Indiana University of Pennsylvania, where she received the Patrick Hartwell Memorial Award for Promising Research in Composition. Her work has appeared in *WPA: Writing Program Administration*, *Journal of Basic Writing*, and several edited collections, including *The TESOL Encyclopedia of English Language Teaching*. Reid serves as cochair of the Council on Basic Writing, a standing group of the Conference on College Composition and Communication, and as associate editor for the *Basic Writing e-Journal*.

Jim Ridolfo is professor of writing, rhetoric, and digital studies and director of composition at the University of Kentucky. He holds a PhD in rhetoric and writing from Michigan State University, and his research focuses on the intersection of rhetorical theory and technology. He most recently coedited, with William Hart-Davidson, *Rhet Ops: Rhetoric and Information Warfare* (2019).

John Schilb is Culbertson Chair and professor of English emeritus at Indiana University, Bloomington. From 2005 to 2012 he was editor of the journal *College English*. He is the author of *Between the Lines: Relating Composition Theory and Literary Theory*. His book *Rhetorical Refusals: Defying Audiences' Expectations* won the Modern Language Association Mina P. Shaughnessy Prize.

Kurt Spellmeyer is professor of English at Rutgers University, New Brunswick, where he directed the writing program from 1985 to 2021. His books include *Common Ground: Dialogue, Understanding, and the Teaching of Composition* and *Arts of Living: Reinventing the Humanities for the*

Twenty-First Century. He has also published articles on the politics of academic institutions, the sociology of written knowledge, and the rhetoric of religion.

Eric J. Sterling is professor of English, Ida Belle Young Endowed Professor, and distinguished teaching professor at Auburn University, Montgomery, where he has taught for the past twenty-eight years. Sterling earned his PhD in English from Indiana University in 1992. He has published four books and ninety refereed articles.

Howard Tinberg, professor emeritus of English at Bristol Community College and former editor of the journal *Teaching English in the Two-Year College*, is the author of *Border Talk: Writing and Knowing in the Two-Year College* and *Writing with Consequence: What Writing Does in the Disciplines*. He has published articles in *College English, College Composition and Communication, Teaching English in the Two-Year College*, and *Change*. In 2004 he was recognized as US Community Colleges Professor of the Year by the Carnegie Foundation and the American Council on Education.

Jessica Yood is associate professor of English at Lehman College and Graduate Center, City University of New York. She recently completed a book entitled *The Composition Commons: Writing a New Idea of the University*.

Morris Young is Charles Q. Anderson Professor of English at the University of Wisconsin, Madison. His work focuses on writing and identity, the intersections of literacy and rhetorical studies, and Asian American culture. His current project considers the generation and function of rhetorical space as a response to exigencies of exclusion, marginalization, and containment. His book, *Minor Re/Visions: Asian American Literacy Narratives as a Rhetoric of Citizenship* (2004), received the 2004 W. Ross Winterowd Award and the 2006 Conference on College Composition and Communication Outstanding Book Award. His coedited collection, with LuMing Mao, *Representations: Doing Asian American Rhetoric* (2008), received honorable mention for the 2008 MLA Mina P. Shaughnessy Prize.